MARION MAIL MEMORIAL AWARD

_____NOV 6 '56_____19____

With Sincere Good Wishes
and praying that God will make this
book a Blessing to you.

Mrs. A. G. Mail
Edmonton

The
Parables and Metaphors
of Our Lord

by

G. CAMPBELL MORGAN, D.D.

Fleming H. Revell Company
NEW YORK AND LONDON

Printed in the United States of America

New York : 158 Fifth Avenue
London : 99 Anerley Road

Foreword

These lectures were delivered to the Westminster Bible School, stenographically reported, and are printed without material alteration.

The method is that of taking each Gospel in sequence and considering the parables and parabolic illustrations therein, but not repeating the consideration, when these are repeated in other Gospels. Following the rule, Mark has only one.

G. C. M.

London, Eng.

Contents

PART I

1. The Parabolic Method 13
2. Parabolic Illustrations in the Manifesto (1) 17
3. Parabolic Illustrations in the Manifesto (2) 22
4. Parabolic Illustrations in the Manifesto (3) 26
5. Parabolic Illustrations. Matthew ix and x 31
6. Parabolic Illustrations. Matthew xi and xii 35
7. The General Scheme. Matthew xiii 41
8. The Sower. Matthew xiii: 3-9, 18-23 45
9. The Darnel. Matthew xiii: 24-30, 36-43 49
10. The Mustard Seed. Matthew xiii: 31, 32 54
11. The Leavened Meal. Matthew xiii: 33 59
12. The Treasure Hidden. Matthew xiii: 44 66
13. The Pearl. Matthew xiii: 45, 46 72
14. The Drag-Net. Matthew xiii: 47-50 77
15. The Householder. Matthew xiii: 51, 52 83
16. Parabolic Illustrations. Matthew xv 89
17. Parabolic Illustrations. Matthew xvi 95
18. Parabolic Illustrations. Matthew xvii, xviii 101
19. Parabolic Illustrations. Matthew xix 106
20. Labourers in the Vineyard. Matthew xx: 1-16 112
21. The Cursing of the Fig-tree. Matthew xxi: 18-22 . . . 116
22. Two Sons and Husbandmen. Matthew xxi: 28-44 . . . 122
23. The Marriage Feast. Matthew xxii: 1-14 127
24. Parabolic Illustrations. Matthew xxiii 134
25. Parabolic Illustrations. Matthew xxiv 140
26. The Ten Virgins. Matthew xxv: 1-13 147
27. The Talents. Matthew xxv: 14-30 152
28. Sheep and Goats. Matthew xxv: 31-46 157
29. The Growth of the Seed. Mark iv: 26-29 163

Part II

30. The Two Debtors. Luke vii: 41-43 171
31. The Good Samaritan. Luke x: 25-37 176
32. Parabolic Illustrations. Luke xi 181
33. The Rich Fool. Luke xii: 13-21 187
34. The Watchful Servants. Luke xii: 41-48 191
35. The Barren Fig-tree. Luke xiii: 6-9 196
36. The Great Supper. Luke xiv: 15-24 201
37. Parabolic Illustrations. Luke xiv: 25-35 206
38. The Lost Things. Luke xv 211
39. The Unrighteous Steward. Luke xvi: 1-13 216
40. The Rich Man and Lazarus. Luke xvi: 19-31 222
41. The Unprofitable Servants. Luke xvii: 5-10 227
42. The Unrighteous Judge. Luke xviii: 1-8 232
43. The Pharisee and the Publican. Luke xviii: 9-14 . . . 238
44. The Pounds. Luke xix: 11-28 243
45. Rock Personality. John i: 40-42 249
46. Angels and Ladder. John i: 47-51 254
47. The Temple of His Body. John ii: 13-22 260
48. The Wind and the Spirit. John iii: 8 266
49. The Lifted Serpent. John iii: 14 272
50. Living Water. John iv: 1-15 278
51. The Lamp of Prophecy. John v: 35 284
52. The Bread of Life. John vi: 35-58 289
53. Flesh and Blood. John vi: 53-58 294
54. Rivers. John vii: 37-39 298
55. Light. John viii: 12 303
56. The Door of the Sheep. John x: 1-9 309
57. The Good Shepherd. John x: 11-18 314
58. Death as Sleep. John xi: 11-15 319
59. A Grain of Wheat. John xii: 20-26 324
60. The Washing of Feet. John xiii: 1-11 330
61. The Father's House and Many Mansions. John xiv: 2-6 . 335
62. The Vine. John xv 341
63. A Woman in Travail. John xvi: 21, 22 347

Part I

1. *The Parabolic Method*

Mark iv: 1, 2a, 10-12, 21-25, 33, 34.

A CONSIDERATION of the metaphorical or parabolic method of our Lord is necessary as a preliminary study, for there has been some misinterpretation of our Lord's reason for His use of such method. There are two self-evident facts: first, that our Lord did use the parabolic method; and secondly, that at a certain stage in His ministry He employed it in a new way.

The fourth chapter of Mark's Gospel opens with the statement that on that day Jesus went out of the house, and went into a boat, and He spoke "many things in parables." The thirty-third and thirty-fourth verses declare, "With many such parables spake He the word unto them . . . and without a parable spake He not unto them." This means that He used parables constantly in what He said to the multitudes. In the course of these thirty-four verses there are two sections dealing with the reason of His parabolic method. The first is found in verses ten to twelve. There He answered a question, and told the disciples the reason of His method. The second section is in verses twenty-one to twenty-five, again an explanation of His method.

In the first paragraph we have not a full explanation from our Lord, and that section demands the second paragraph. In the first explanatory paragraph we are faced with a difficulty, which we will state and consider, and make certain deductions therefrom.

At this hour in the ministry of Jesus He specially adopted the parabolic method for addressing the crowds. He had used parabolic illustrations before this time, notably to the woman of Samaria, when He spoke of the water of life; to the disciples, when He told them fields were white to harvest; in Nazareth, when He spoke of the physician and his healing work; to the disciples again, of fishers of men; and in His Manifesto, of salt and light and building. But the Sower was the first full parable, uttered at this time.

Tracing the course of our Lord's ministry we shall find that there had come a moment when definite and positive hostility had hardened in a peculiar manner. In the home at Capernaum He had been challenged, because He had claimed to forgive sins. In the house of Levi

He had been challenged because He permitted His disciples to omit fasting, and because He consorted with sinners. In the cornfields He had been criticized for allowing His disciples to pluck the ears of corn on the Sabbath. In a synagogue on a later Sabbath, He was challenged, and they counselled to destroy Him. Again, in the house in Capernaum He was charged with being in complicity with the devil. All this had its definite effect upon the minds of the people. In the third chapter we find it said, "He looked round about on them with anger, being grieved at the hardening of their heart." That was the mental condition of the hour, of the rulers, which affected the crowds. This hardening of heart meant callousness, blindness, determination not to listen, nor to obey; or if to listen, then only critically, and destructively.

At that time Jesus adopted this parabolic method when speaking to the multitudes. When their hardness of heart made Him angry, then in a very definite and enlarged form He began to use parables; His anger being the result of His grace, in the presence of their attitude.

The difficulty here is found in the tenth to twelfth verses. Much has been said about it, and there have been differing interpretations. The apparent meaning of the passage is that Jesus adopted the method of the parable to prevent these people understanding, and to be forgiven. That is the first impression made upon the mind as the verses are read.

There have been two methods of dealing with that difficulty. The first is that this is a truth which must be accepted though not understood. Some Bible teachers and expositors take the view that our Lord deliberately adopted the parabolic method here that the people should not see, or understand, or be forgiven. The second method of dealing with this passage is that the statement is not true, that He never said it, and therefore the passage is untrustworthy. That second method is impossible of belief by those who hold that the record is true.

But is the difficulty due to what the passage really says, or to long-continued interpretation, or misinterpretation of it? Was the reason of the parabolic method that men should be prevented from understanding, and so be excluded from the mercy of God? That would surely be blasphemy, and would contradict the whole purpose of God in Christ, and of Christ in the world. Consequently we must look at this a little more particularly.

There is one important fact to bear in mind, that the narrative of Mark is condensed; and that of Luke is even more so at this point. Matthew's account is much fuller. In the thirteenth chapter of that Gospel, after the parable of the sower, "The disciples came, and said unto Him, Why speakest Thou unto them in parables?" And He answered, "Unto you it is given to know the mysteries of the Kingdom of heaven, but to them it is not given. For whosoever hath, to him shall be given, and he shall have abundance; but whosoever hath not, from him shall be taken away even that which he hath. Therefore speak I to them in parables; because seeing they see not, and hearing they hear not, neither do they understand." Carefully notice the change. "Seeing they see not," not that they may not see. "Hearing they hear not, neither do they understand." They are seeing, but they do not see. They are hearing, but they do not understand. Therefore He spoke to them in parables.

Our Lord then quoted Isaiah, and Matthew writes, "And unto them is fulfilled the prophecy of Isaiah, which saith, By hearing ye shall hear, and shall in no wise understand; and seeing ye shall see, and shall in no wise perceive." Why?

"For this people's heart is waxed gross, and their ears are dull of hearing and their eyes have they closed; lest haply . . ." Matthew and Mark both use the word "lest," but the word needs a context larger than Mark quoted. The "lest" is the "lest" of their attitude, their hardness, of their persistence in unbelief. He was grieved with their hardness of heart, and that was the reason why He adopted the parabolic method. They had hardened their hearts until they had become gross; until they with seeing eyes were nevertheless blind. That was their attitude. They had done this lest they should be drawn back to God, and halted, and be forgiven. They were not aware of that ultimate, but that was their condition.

Carry the thought a little further. According to Matthew, the disciples had enquired the reason for speaking in parables. The Lord's answer was that it was given to them to know the mysteries. He told His disciples that the difference in method was due to a difference in relationship. To those of His disciples who were obedient, who submitted to Him, the mysteries could be made known. To those without, those not yielded, and not obedient, those refusing and hardening the heart, the parabolic was the necessary method.

Go on to verses twenty-one to twenty-five in this fourth chapter of Mark. He used the lamp as His illustration. This lamp is not put under the bushel, which would extinguish it. It is put on a stand. The parables therefore constituted a lamp, a lamp shining. It was not in order to hide things, but that the hidden things might be brought to light. These people could not, because of the attitude they had assumed, receive the mysteries, the profound things of the Kingdom of God. His disciples could receive those mysteries; but to those without, the parable was a lamp. There is nothing hidden except that it may be manifested. There is nothing secret but that it may be revealed. He gave them parabolic pictures, so that they might enquire. The purpose of the story, the picture, was to lure them to think, in order that they might find their way into the higher mystery.

Therefore it is important that the passage in Mark should be interpreted by the fuller passage in Matthew. Take that matchless triptych of stories constituting one great parable, recorded in the fifteenth chapter of Luke, the lost sheep, the lost silver, and the lost son. That was spoken to men who were blundering, and protesting against Him. There is nothing in that story of the mysteries of the Kingdom; but it is there. Can we suppose Jesus told those men that story of lost things sought, and found, in order to prevent their coming to God, and finding mercy? If they had heard that story, enquired concerning it, sought its deep significance, they would have found themselves in the presence of all the height and depth and length and breadth of the mystery of the Kingdom of God.

In other words, the parable is ever the open door to the mystery. If men will consider the picture, and enquire, He will always answer. The parables therefore do but illustrate the whole fact of His approach to the human heart.

There is a remarkable statement in the Proverbs.

"It is the glory of God to conceal a thing;
But the glory of kings is to search out a matter."

That is true in Nature. God conceals behind that which is sacramental that which is supreme, so that men may take the thing that is manifest, and so following and enquiring, may find the deep secret. It is the glory of God to conceal a thing, but it is the glory of kings to search out a matter. The writer did not mean merely kings on the earthly level, but the kingly nature, which is always seeking for the secret thing.

The same philosophy is in the great word of Moses, uttered long ago, "The secret things belong unto the Lord our God; but the things that are revealed belong unto us and to our children for ever." The secret things are there that we may discover them. Nature is a great parable. Think of the earth, and of research, the things man has been finding out. They were all there from the beginning, but were hidden.

With reverence let it be said that the Lord Himself and the whole fact of the Incarnation is a parable. "No man hath seen God at any time, but the only begotten Son Which is in the bosom of the Father, He hath declared Him." The secret hidden, mysterious, of the Being of Godhead. No man has seen that; but as the old philosopher talking to Job, said,

"Canst thou by searching find out God?
Canst thou find out the Almighty unto perfection?"

That is perfectly true, but God has revealed Himself, and supremely, in His Son. The Son therefore becomes the picture, the parable, which being known and investigated, God Himself is found.

Our Lord did not intend then in the use of the parable to prevent men seeing, but to help them to see. He did not want to prevent them hearing, but to quicken their power of hearing. He did not keep men away from the forgiveness and the mercy of God, but He lured them towards it. As we come to these wonderful illustrations, and the more definite parables, we shall see He is not hiding, but veiling

"The light that were else too bright,
For the feebleness of a sinner's sight."

If the truth can be suggested by the story, in the presence of that story men may presently find the depth and wonder of the mystery.

2. *Parabolic Illustrations in the Manifesto*

Matthew v and vi. (1)

THE FIRST parabolic illustration is found in the fourth chapter of this Gospel of Matthew, when Jesus spoke of His disciples as "fishers of men." This is postponed now, to be returned to at a later chapter, where again the figure is more particularly used.

The Manifesto is radiant in its wealth of parabolic illustrations. Salt, light, a city on a hill, lamp, bushel, lampstand, house, Gehenna, adversary, judge, officer, prison, throne, footstool, feet, inner chamber, door, moth, rust, thieves, eye, darkness, birds, lilies, oven, mote, beam, dogs, pearls, swine, loaf, stone, fish, serpent, gate, way, sheep, wolves, fruits, grapes, thorns, figs, thistles, tree, fire, rock, floods, winds, sand. There are forty-nine, and these are not all. They are all common things, and familiar to everybody.

Here we shall look at those illustrations of definite statement, rather than those of incidental reference. These illustrations moreover are all within the moral realm, ethical. The Manifesto is the ultimate code of laws for the Kingdom of God, established upon earth. We shall endeavour in each case to find the subject our Lord was intending to illustrate when He used the particular parabolic illustration, or parable.

In these first two chapters we shall look first at the parabolic illustration of salt and light; secondly, those of moth, rust, and thieves; and, thirdly, the illustration of the eye.

Salt and light. What was the subject with which our Lord was dealing, and which He intended to illustrate? The influence that was to be exerted by the subjects of His Kingdom. He had begun with those wonderful beatitudes; and then had enunciated certain laws, and showed that in His Kingdom character was supreme. He had proceeded to show that the reason of such character is not so much of personal value, but of the influence such character exerts. Oh, the marvel of these illustrations, their choosing, the brilliance of them, the finality of them. Whenever He spoke He did so with authority, the authority not of dogmatism, but of inherent, necessary, and inevitable truth.

The influence then is twofold, salt and light. There is a distinction and a difference, and yet the figures merge into one thought, "salt of the earth," "light of the world."

"Salt of the earth." What is the value of salt? It is not antiseptic, but aseptic. Antiseptic is something which is against poison, and which tends to its cure. Aseptic is something which is devoid of poison in itself. Salt never cures corruption. It prevents the spread of corruption. If meat is tainted and corrupt, salt will not make it untainted and pure. But salt in its neighbourhood will prevent the spread of corruption to that which otherwise would become tainted. The figure is that of a moral quality operating on the earth level, amongst men living in the midst of material things, preventing the spread of corruption. The impurity of an evil man cannot be cured by a good man, working at his side in an office; but the things the good man will not do, and the things he will not say will give the boy in the same office a chance, because it will check the evil man. Salt is aseptic.

The function of the subjects of His Kingdom is to live in the midst of humanity in the terrible condition of sin, and by living there according to the ethic of the Kingdom of God, to prevent the spread of evil.

It is the Lord's work to cure it, thank God. However impure and corrupt the heart may be, He can cleanse it, and make it purer than the driven snow. The subjects of His Kingdom are so to live that they give goodness its opportunity, and hold in check the forces of corruption. Our Lord emphasized this with those words of satire, gentle, but clear and sharp as the lightning. "If the salt have lost its savour, wherewith shall it be salted?" I like the Scotch rendering of that, "If the salt has lost its tang." That is a great word, tang, the pungent power of salt. Jesus says His people are to exercise that influence in the world. That is our responsibility, though men may not be pleased.

But again, not only the salt of the earth, referring to a moral quality of things; but, "Ye are the light of the world." That refers to a spiritual revelation which is to radiate from these subjects of the Kingdom. We are the light of the cosmos, of all the order, not merely of the earth, but of the universe. We remember another occasion when the Master said, "I am the Light of the world." Linking this up with that great full word concerning Himself, we understand when we are yielded to Him, subjects of His Kingdom, obeying Him, then we too become the light of the world. The quality of light is not that it desires to be looked at! Light enables other things to be seen by its shining. The sun is in the heaven, not to be looked at, but the sunshine enables us to see other things clearly. "Ye are the light of the world." Let your light so shine that men may glorify your Father. The light of the Christian shining in the world illuminates all the worldly order, so that men see the true way.

In this connection two figures are employed by our Lord, "a city set on a hill," and "a lamp . . . on the stand." The city set on a hill is for the illumination of vast distances. No Christian can fulfil that ideal alone. That demands fellowship, a corporate relationship. That demands the whole Church. Every church should be a city set on a hill, illuminating the far expanses of life.

Then He came from the figure of the city on a hill into a house, and there took the figure of a lampstand, illuminating the home, and the near. Inevitably the mind goes back to a word of the psalmist in the Old Testament,

"Thy word is a lamp unto my feet,
And light unto my path."

Keep the figures separate. The light shines from some eminence, indicating the road, the pathway. The light shines on the way to be trodden, so that the way may be found along the illuminated path by the lamp. Thy word, says the psalmist, is a lamp. Each Christian man and woman has to fulfil a double function in the world. The whole Church in its corporate relationship, in the bonds of love, friendship, and service, is to illuminate the distances; and then in the home, with the shut door, the lamp is to illuminate everything there. Christ said here the lamp is not put under a bushel but on a stand. Many years ago I heard that prince of expositors, Dr. Maclaren say this illuminative thing: "No man lights a lamp and puts it under a bushel. If he did, what would happen? Either the bushel would put out the light, or the light would set the bushel on fire!" We can apply that. That is exactly what our Lord was teaching here.

He then used three illustrations, moth, rust, and thieves. The subject that He was illustrating here was that of the futility of earth-centred life. He was showing the folly of living such a life. He showed what the attitude of His subjects should be toward necessary things, and the superlative things. He was talking to them about amassing treasure, and He used finely sarcastic language about the treasures of earth "moth and rust corrupt," and "thieves break through and steal." These are Eastern figures. At the time the wealth of the East consisted in fine fabrics, fine twined linen, and purple; and of metal, in coinage, or in precious things that rust spoiled. Treasure was kept underground, and there was the possibility of thieves digging and so treasure would be lost. The moth, the rust, make things worthless. Thieves steal, and everything is gone. Remember that thieves steal only things that are moth-eatable, and rust-consumable. There are things of possession, treasures in heaven, "where neither moth nor rust consume, and where thieves do not break through nor steal." These things moths cannot touch, rust cannot corrode, thieves cannot find. Oh, the foolishness, the stupidity of men and women who think riches consist in treasures on the earth. All the time the swift, silent messengers of destruction are breaking in upon it, and the equally silent corrosive fire of Nature is biting into the metal and destroying it. Presently we hear of burglary—thieves! To repeat the word, mark the fine satire of our Lord on the men who are not rich toward God, and who are proud of their accumulations.

Once again, He took the illustration of the eye. The subject He was illustrating was the necessity for singleness of motive in life, having one aim, purpose, passion. He ended this section by saying, "Ye cannot serve God and mammon." He says the eye is the lamp of the body, not the light of the body. Think of the human eye, and of its value. If there be no light the eye is quite useless. The light is not in the eye, but the eye is the means of interpreting the light and applying the light. The eye is that which regulates the motions of the body. It is wonderful how those denied the great blessing of sight have other senses sharpened. But those blind would be the first to admit that the natural order is that the eye is the lamp, in which the light shines, and through which things are seen because light is shining.

Then with marvellous scientific accuracy, Jesus used two words as to the condition of the eye, the "single" eye, and the "evil" eye. The contrast is the more remarkable, in that it is not an exact contrast, which would have been single and double, or good and evil.

The word "single" is *aplous,* which means single-folded, without a fold. If thine eye has no complications within itself. Anyone who has visited an oculist has probably heard him use the word astigmatism. I give the definition of an authority. "An astigmatism is a structural defect of the eye so that rays of light do not converge to a point in the retina." That means there is some fold there, something out of place, something complicated. The eye is not single. The single eye is the opposite of the eye suffering from astigmatism. Jesus said, If the eye is single, not folded over, nothing out of place, what then? Things are seen clearly, in right perspective, and the whole body is illumined, it is full of light. The eye is the lamp, and the light shines through it into the whole body, and there is nothing complicated.

Then He gave the contrast. "If thine eye be evil," and the word is *poneros,* evil in influence. Now, He did not deal with the structure of the eye. That had been indicated in what had already been said. The single eye is never evil, *poneros.* The word now indicates not merely an obliquity of vision, but that there is a squint. Everything is seen double. That eye is evil in its influence upon the one possessing it, and upon others. The eye regulates the body, and if the eye is wrong, then all the light of God leaves such an one in darkness.

What is meant by the single eye? "No man can serve two masters. . . . Ye cannot serve God and mammon." The teaching is the necessity for the unification of life at a centre, from which everything is viewed. So these first parabolic illustrations in the Manifesto all move in the realm of the ethical, and are concerned with the Kingdom, and the Kingship of God; and the responsibility of those who are in that Kingdom for the earth and for the world.

3. *Parabolic Illustrations in the Manifesto*

Matthew vi and vii. (2)

AGAIN we take three groupings of illustrations, on three subjects or themes: the first, the birds and the lilies; the second, that of the mote and beam, and dogs and swine; the third, the loaf and stone, the fish and serpent, or scorpion. Our Lord used all these as illustrations in His ethical teaching.

The birds and lilies are very familiar. What then was the subject the Master was illustrating? That of the futility of anxiety about necessary things. In the former illustration of true wealth, the folly of laying up treasure destroyed by moth, rust, and stolen by thieves He was not looking at necessary things. If His subjects are not to be careful about laying up treasure on earth, there are things that are essential and necessary.

What are the necessary things? They are revealed in His teaching; food, drink, raiment. Here He reduced everything to the last necessity. The word raiment here covers more than the covering of the body. Paul writing to Timothy says, "Having food and covering we shall be therewith content." Covering means not merely the covering of the body, but covering of our personality, shelter, home. That also was surely in the mind of our Lord. Things can be accumulated, without any home. However, keep to the simple ideas, food, drink, and raiment. These are necessities to those in His Kingdom, until the consummation. He insisted upon the futility of being anxious about these necessities in a threefold repetition of a phrase, "Be not anxious." The Authorised Version renders here, "Take no thought" for food and drink and raiment, which is a little misleading. We are to take thought, but we are not to be anxious. That is the important word, the anxiety which is carking care, and that is unfruitful, feverish and worrying. How constantly His subjects, submitted to His rule, face these problems of food, clothing and covering, necessary things, until the anxiety reacts upon them, and they become hot and restless, fretful and worried.

There is a threefold movement in the teaching. He shows first that anxiety is unnecessary. The necessity is known to God. "Your Father knoweth that ye have need." Secondly, it is unworthy. We are frittering away great forces that inspire life, on unworthy objects. Direct that driving energy and urge of personality into its true line of action.

By seeking the Kingdom and His righteousness, we shall be taking our powers, and spending them in that way. Lastly, with a fine touch of satire, He says it is not only unnecessary and unworthy, it is quite unfruitful. Worry does not get us anywhere, nor bring us anything. By taking thought we cannot add one cubit to our stature.

The marginal reading for the word "stature" is "age" in the Revised Version. Either word carries the meaning. By worrying one cannot add a cubit to his stature, or live longer. See the playful irony of the word. Remember the teaching that has preceded this word; the supremacy of character, revealed in the beatitudes, that character as influence, salt and light, followed by binding laws. We are still in the world, and must have food, drink, and raiment, necessary things. We are not to be anxious about these things.

How shall we avoid anxiety? Jesus looked out upon the common, everyday things, the birds and the lilies, the Huleh lily of Palestine, varying from brilliant scarlet to a fine deep purple, one of the most gorgeous of the flowers, blooming there amid the fields where He was talking. Look at the birds as they nestle there in these trees, and as they fly. They have no intelligence that enables them to make provision. They have no gathering power. They do not lay up in barns; but they are fed, and the Father feedeth them.

These are illustrations by contrast rather than similarity. If our heavenly Father feeds those whom He has not endowed with a capacity for thinking and planning and arranging and laying by in store, how much more likely He will feed those whom He has created with the capacity to lay up, and arrange, and plan. Man is intelligent, is made for forecasting, to arrange. He is created with the intellectual capacity that enables him to do what the birds cannot do. Our Father feeds the birds, notwithstanding their lack. He will feed us on the basis of our possessions. Man will use the faculties, but the greatness of his humanity, and all his cleverness will not feed him, unless God does so. The Lord was driving His listeners back to a recognition of the futility of worry and anxiety, teaching that the beings He has thus endowed and endued, using those powers so given, to such God always responds in supplying need.

Then He looked at the flowers. He said, Look at them. God has garbed them, and all the glory of Solomon's fine twined linen and purple and flashing beauty do not compare with the beauty of those flowers. Is anyone inclined to think that here Jesus used rhetoric? No, it is cold, scientific fact. Some day take a piece of the finest material ever employed in the making of garments of kings, the most beautiful and costly, and most delicately woven in the looms of humanity, and put it under the microscope. Then put under that same microscope a rose, a lily, any flower, a daisy plucked from the common sod. The material will be like sackcloth, its edges frayed. The flower will be wonderful with all the efflorescent beauty of accuracy. God clothes the lilies, and Solomon in all his glory was not arrayed like one of these. To us He has given power both to toil and to spin. How much more may we expect to be clothed by that God Who clothes the lilies in that manner. Today they are in the field. Tomorrow they are for burning, they are gone. We are for the eternities, and He has given us power to toil, and to spin.

In these illustrations our Lord was not telling us not to think, for He did not say, Take no thought. We were made to think, to gather, to put by in barns, to learn how to toil and spin. Use those powers, knowing that they are given by God, and that He will co-operate with us in all our gathering, in our toil, and spinning. It is quite unnecessary therefore that we should have any anxiety about the things of necessity, for the supreme thing here, that flames with beauty, is that "your heavenly Father knoweth that ye have need of all these things."

The second group of illustrations concerns one subject again. The mote and the beam, and dogs and swine. It is a curious conjunction, but they are together, and are kept together. The mote and the beam illustrated one realm, and dogs and swine another, but they are in the same possibility of action and activity in life. The subject which our Lord was illustrating was that of the principles that are to actuate us in the exercise of judgment. The word "judge" here has many meanings and applications. The Greek word is translated in ten or eleven different ways, every one having some essential thought, but with varied applications. When our Lord said here, "Judge not that ye be not judged," the sense in which judgment is forbidden is the judgment that condemns. Discrimination however is necessary, and is enjoined. His use of the mote and the beam shows us that we may use judgment wrongfully; and He charges us not to do that thing. His use of the dogs and swine shows how judgment must be exercised, and is somewhat terrible in application. Judgment is necessary. As John records in another connection, He said once, "Judge not according to appearance, but judge righteous judgment." That was distinct instruction to exercise the power of distinction and discrimination. That is part of our human nature. But there is a censorious attitude of soul, in which judgment deteriorates into the judgment of unfairness and condemnation, and that is what He forbids. In that connection He used these startling figures of the mote and the beam. The beam is something big, and the mote a tiny thing. The word used for beam means a great massive piece of timber. The beam in the eye becomes almost grotesque by its bigness; and the mote, the little chip off the beam, cannot be seen, although it causes suffering. A man sees the mote in his brother's eye. Jesus does not deny he may see it. He does see it. It is something wrong, that ought not to be there. But Christ says there is a beam in that man's eye who is looking at his brother's mote. The beam is not a vulgar sin. The man guilty of a great sin is never critical of a man who has committed a little sin.

Then what is the beam? That very spirit of censoriousness which is watching for something in his brother, that blinds him to all the facts of the case. Sins of the spirit are always worse than the sins of the flesh; and there is no sin so blasting, so blighting, so damning, as the spirit of censorious judgment of another man. Cast out that beam, said Jesus, get rid of that; then one will see how to take the mote out of the brother's eye. Censoriousness dwells upon the mote, and criticizes the brother. That censoriousness is a beam that is blinding the man. Remove it, and approach that same man in love, with the very spirit of Christ, and the brother will be helped to get rid of his mote in his eye. Judge, not in the spirit of censorious condemnation; for we shall be judged in the way we judge; that is the measure of our judgment.

Then sharply, almost suddenly, He insisted upon the necessity for discrimination. "Give not that which is holy unto the dogs, neither cast your pearls before the swine." That is a tremendous saying, and a terrible one. If there is to be no hindering beam that prevents us from removing the mote, there is to be no blindness that prevents us from seeing corruption that is hopeless and helpless. We are not to take precious things, and give them to dogs, to cast our pearls before the swine. Peter doubtless heard that word, and at the end of his letter he spoke of people like dogs, returning to their vomit, and sows wallowing in the mire. There are such people, and Christ says we have no right to give such our treasure, our pearls.

A tremendous application can be made of that, the necessity that the Church should guard her most holy things. In past history the Church gave over her sacred deposit to dogs, and cast her pearls before swine when she admitted government within her borders by pagan nations. She does it today whenever she compromises with the sacred things of her faith.

The final illustrations here, the loaf, the stone; the fish, the serpent. The subject illustrated here was that of prayer, the way in which God gives as compared with the way of men, and men at their highest level, as fathers give. He had just uttered the tremendous word about freedom from censoriousness, and yet the importance of the power of discrimination that prevents handing over of sacred things to dogs and swine. Immediately there He said, "Ask, and it shall be given you; seek, and ye shall find; knock, and it shall be opened unto you." That has a wide and general application, but notice its placing in this ethical Manifesto. As one faces the difficulty of judging, and the fear to form any judgment, He says, The power-house is there, the light is there. "Ask, seek, knock." This is an ethical Manifesto. These are the laws of the Kingdom, and here prayer is enjoined as a necessity. Has any other code of laws included prayer as a necessity? I think none; and that is why they all break down. Jesus here introduced prayer, and shows how God gives. He will give. If they ask, they will receive. If they will seek, they shall find. If they knock, the door will be opened.

Having said that, he went on, "Which of you, being evil . . . ?" The immediate application is that God is not evil, and we are. Evil there means more than sinful. It includes everything of narrowness. All we are, God is not. We, being evil, have the high capacity for giving good things to our children. Then our Lord illuminated it all. Will a father for a loaf give a stone; for a fish, a serpent? How much more shall your Father God give good things to them that ask Him. God gives the best, always the best, as they would give. He will never offer us a stone, even if we ask for a stone. He will give us bread. He will never offer us a serpent or a scorpion, if in foolishness we ask for a serpent. He will give good things. "Ask, seek, knock." That is the dynamic centre of all ethics, because God is at the centre. Entering into this we can find the infinite machinery, with its wheels turning, revolving; but at the centre of that wheel there is an axle, that of the heart of our Father. Oh, do not be anxious. Use judgment in accordance with the principles of God, and if we find it difficult, go into the power-house, and ask, and seek, and knock.

4. *Parabolic Illustrations in the Manifesto*

Matthew vi. and vii. (3)

AGAIN we take illustrations used by our Lord on three subjects; first, that of two gates and two ways; secondly, that of wolves in sheep's clothing, and fruits; and thirdly, that of rock and sand.

In these final words of application, it would seem as though our Lord employed a crescendo, and reached a climax of illustration. Taking the first, the figure of two gates and two ways, He was speaking generally of life, and life as a pilgrimage. The distinct ethical teaching now being finished, He had reached the realm of application. There are two gates through which we may enter upon an experience of life. He was bringing His hearers back to the starting point, to the beginning of life. In order to travel upon these ways, men must pass through these gates, the narrow or the wide. The narrow gate "leadeth unto life." The wide gate "leadeth to destruction." We have a plan of pilgrimage in these figures of speech.

There is a way of life into which man can pass through a wide gate. It is easy of entrance, and there is a broad way stretching out before us. But there is another gateway, leading to another way; a narrow gateway, and a straitened way.

The wide gate "leadeth to destruction," and the word literally and simply means narrowing limitation, confinement, imprisonment; until everything is brought to an end under crushing pressure.

On the other hand is the narrow gate. As we pass through it we begin to walk a straitened way, but it "leadeth unto life," in all its fulness. There are many things which have to be left outside if we pass through this gate. It is a narrow gate and a straitened way; none of the breadth of license, but the straitness of law. But go on, and walk along it, and we find all the way it is widening, broadening, expanding with new breadth and glory and view, until at last it reaches unto life. When Jesus said "life" He did not mean mere existence. He meant eternal life, deep life, high life, broad life, full life.

Two ways of life are thus presented. Any man reading that Sermon on the Mount has to hide himself as he stands in the light of His appalling measurements. A man can live by high devotion of his own life to the awful law of purity, and reach the glorious clear shining of health and holiness; but he must begin at the narrow gate. Thus the two ways of life's pilgrimage are illustrated by the use of the gates and ways, to be interpreted in that way, and none other.

Our Lord did not say that the way of evil is broad and easy and natural, and that it would work out rightly. "Destruction" is the last word. He did not say the narrow way would mean narrowness constantly, the cutting out of everything worth while. No, it is the finding of everything worth while; and at last it is life in all its breadth and length and beauty. The narrow and straitened way leads to breadth, to life. The wide and broad way leads to narrowness, and issues in destruction.

In close connection He used the next figure of speech. If in the first He took His hearers to the point of beginning, the narrow and wide gates, and foretold the issue, He now brought them face to face with one of the gravest perils that would threaten them. "Beware of false prophets." In order to beware of them they must be tested. The subject illustrated was the testing of the prophets. This particular subject has its supreme application to those who are called of God to prophetic work, though our Lord's first application was not for them, but for those who wait upon their ministry and teaching.

What a description of the false prophets. They come in sheep's clothing, but inwardly are ravening wolves. Our Lord was dealing here with life, not with what we call orthodoxy or heterodoxy. These men are not those teaching a false doctrine. They may be teaching a perfectly correct doctrine, but if in their own lives they are wrong, beware of them. This is orthodoxy, dressed in sheep's clothing, proceeding from one who in life is a ravening wolf. It is a perilous thing to follow such. He is now following those who have passed through the narrow gate along the road of progress, when they will need teachers, and guidance. He warns such to be careful to whom they give attention and allegiance. The prophets who destroy men's lives are those who may be dressed in sheep's clothing, but if they are evil, their influence is destructive.

In the next saying of Jesus the figures seem to mix, but they do not; they merge. "By their fruits ye shall know them." That is twice repeated, and in between He emphasized the statement with a question, "Do men gather grapes of thorns, or figs of thistles? Even so every good tree bringeth forth good fruit; but the corrupt tree bringeth forth evil fruit. A good tree cannot bring forth evil fruit, neither can a corrupt tree bring forth good fruit. Every tree that bringeth not forth good fruit is hewn down, and cast into the fire." Mark the drastic note of His declaration, "A good tree cannot bring forth evil fruit, neither can a corrupt tree bring forth good fruit." The prophet may be in sheep's clothing. There may be the outward appearance, but He warned those who have entered upon the highway, through the gateway that is narrow, to take heed how they hear. They are to be careful lest they be beguiled, all unknowingly, by those who are false prophets.

Our Lord then antedated the ultimate. He looked on to the day when all life should come to consummation and manifestation and judgment. He put Himself as Judge at the close. "In that day many will say to Me, Lord, Lord, did we not prophesy by Thy Name?" They had done many wonderful works in the Name, but He will have to say, "I never knew you." The peril of this halts us, and drives us not to discussion, but to heart-searching. I may prophesy in the Name. I may cast out demons in His Name. I may do many things in His Name; but if I do not know Him, and He does not know me personally, the last word is, "I never knew you."

The final word is, "He that doeth the will of My Father." That is the final test of everything. He antedates in this figure of speech the hour when He shall appraise the life of those who are presented to Him. There will be those who have done everything except the one thing, the will of God. As He said on another occasion, Who is My mother, who are My brethren and sisters? They that do the will of My Father Who is in heaven. So He warns us to beware of false leaders, false prophets; who are to be tested by the fruit they bear.

The last of these illustrations in the Manifesto is characterized by the same attitude of majesty. He took two figures, rock and sand, and the subject He was illustrating was the importance of foundation in building life. It has reference to the whole Manifesto and to all the teaching that had preceded it. "Every one therefore which heareth these words of Mine." He had uttered the whole scheme of law in the Kingdom of God to those disciples. Others had heard Him. Now He declared that men who built on His words were building on rock foundation.

Look at this carefully. Every man is building something. He is building something into which he can go and live, that will create for him a refuge, a place of rest, a home for his soul. The materials of the building may be correct, and as two houses go up, one cannot see any difference between them. Everything seems correct in both cases. Summer suns are shining, and they look beautiful, and no difference can be detected. But summer suns do not shine for ever. There come days of storm and stress, of sweeping winds, and whistling howling rains, days of tempest. Look at those two houses, what is happening? One of them, under the pressure of the storm, is crumbling, falling, and the man is rendered homeless. The other is standing erect, firm, and strong. What makes the difference? Foundations. One man built on the sand; the other upon rock.

The figure of speech is so simple that a child can understand it. Christ says there are two foundations upon which we can build. If we want to build more stately mansions for the soul, watch the foundations. Notice carefully the words of august majesty. He that heareth and doeth, builds on rock. He that heareth and doeth not, builds on sand. It is not a comparison between a man who hears, and another who has never heard. Those who have heard and have not obeyed, have gone on with their building, neglecting the teaching; when the storms strike, the building is destroyed. Those who have heard, and have obeyed, and kept it, no storm that blows can destroy the house of such as have built on the teachings of Jesus. August in majesty, and final to His Manifesto is that figure of building on sand or on rock.

All these illustrations were employed to emphasize ethical teaching, and illustrate moral standards in the Kingdom of God. According to these illustrations, it is immoral to live in this world, and not exert the influence of salt and light. We are not moral Christians if we are living without influencing others. It is immoral to live an earth-centred life, with supreme care for things that moth and rust destroy and thieves steal. We are searched by this teaching of Jesus. It is immoral to attempt to live a double-governed life. The eye which is the lamp of the body must be single. It is immoral to worry over necessary things. What an immoral crowd we are! So wrote Fay Inchfawn in a little poem, which has a touch of humour, but it has searching power:

"Well, I am done, my nerves were on the rack;
    I've laid them down today.
It was the last straw broke the camel's back;
    I've laid that down today.
And I'll not fume, nor fret, nor fuss, nor fight;
    I'll walk by faith a bit, and not by sight;
I think the Universe will work all right;
    I've laid it down today:

"So, here and now, the overweight—the worry!
    I'll lay it down today.
The all-too-anxious heart, the tearing hurry;
    I'll lay these down today.
O eager hands! O feet, so prone to run!
    I think that He, Who made the stars and sun,
Can mind the things you've had to leave undone;
    Do lay them down today!"

In the illustration Jesus gave of the birds and lilies, we see that worrying is a form of immorality. It is immoral to exercise judgment wrongly, to cast out the mote in my brother's eye, when the beam is in my own eye; or to take the precious things and cast them to dogs and swine. It is immoral to neglect prayer. Our Father gives the best. If we do not ask, seek, knock, our life is immoral. Of course it is immoral to travel on the wrong road, to take the wide gate and the broad way. It is immoral to listen to false prophets. It is immoral to build a dwelling for the soul on sand, when the rock of His teaching is at our disposal. These things all wonderfully illustrate the great ethical standards of Jesus.

5. *Parabolic Illustrations*

Matthew ix. and x.

THE ILLUSTRATIONS in these chapters are found in a section of the Gospel dealing with the servants of our Lord, and of His sending them forth. In the charge which He laid upon them, we find these parabolic illustrations: a marriage, the mending of a garment, and wine skins; the harvest; sheep and wolves, serpents and doves; sparrows; and the sword. The background here is not of ethical teaching, but of His working of wonders in the midst of human dereliction, and of His commanding and calling and commissioning some to go out upon His great business.

The first illustration was of a marriage feast (ix:15). What was the subject He was illustrating? The joy of His disciples and the reason for the joy. He used this illustration to account for the absence of an ascetic attitude towards life on the part of those round about Him. Here the disciples of John had come to Him and asked why His disciples did not fast as those of John and the Pharisees. I believe it was a sincere question. They had watched the disciples of Jesus, and had noticed an entire absence of ascetic practices, which they thought were of the essence of religion. Our Lord in reply, used this figure of the marriage, an Oriental figure. The ceremonies lasted for seven days of merriment and festivity.

His application was simple. The sons of the bride chamber never fast, or lack joy during these festivities. While the bridegroom is there, they do not fast. Applying the illustration directly to Himself, He said that was the reason why His disciples were a happy crowd. These men could not understand why, and Jesus gave them the reason, the Bridegroom was still with them. He then told them that presently He would be taken away, and then they would mourn. He there used a remarkable verb. The Bridegroom will be taken and caught up, a word that marks exaltation. He was looking on to the end when He would be lifted up.

The first part of His illustration has its application to us, but not the second. How can the children of the bride chamber mourn while the Bridegroom is with them? It cancels for ever anything in the nature of ascetic practices, in order to demonstrate loyalty. The absence of the Bridegroom is the reason for mourning, but He is not absent, and never has been since His victory, His resurrection, and ascension, and return in power by the Spirit to take up His abode with His own people. He was talking to His group of disciples later on in those intimate discourses, and said to them, "And ye therefore have sorrow, but I will see you again, and your heart shall rejoice, and your joy no one taketh away from you." The application here is that the true evidence of our relationship to Christ is our constant joy and rejoicing.

> "O happy day that fixed my choice,
> On Thee, my Saviour, and my God."

That is the keynote of Christian experience. As we are in fellowship with Christ, we know what it is to rejoice always, and again to rejoice.

In the same connection, and to the same men, He used the figure of the mended garment and wine skins, in order to make His meaning plainer. He was illustrating the nature of His Kingdom. Briefly this is what He meant: He could not crowd into an outworn formula the new things He was teaching men. He had come, not to mend an old garment, but to make a new one. Therefore new methods were necessary; and among them were these that they could not understand, the very happiness, which was the demonstration of the new method.

If we put a piece of a new garment on an old, the rent is made greater. The garment cannot be mended in that way. The illustration of the wine skins illuminates and enforces the same truth. The new demands the new. "Wine skins" is a correct translation, skins used as bottles. Wine, when fermentation is complete, can be put into any bottles, whether new or old, without harming bottles or wine skins, and without harm to it. Wine, intended to ferment, would burst any bottles, whether new or old. Those two statements being understood, then unfermented wine must be put into new bottles. To put it into old bottles would produce fermentation, which is always a sign of breakdown.

Thus our Lord was teaching that to put His enterprise into the old formulae would bring about decomposition and ruin. When we have taken the claim and teaching and power and work of Jesus, and have tried to press them into some other form than His, it has deteriorated, as fermented wine. To those who objected to the merriment of His disciples He replied that the very merriment was inevitable while He was with them; and the whole system He was creating, was not something crowded into the old, but was something new.

We come next to that marvellous figure of the harvest (ix:37, 38). Notice the subject illustrated. He used the figure to His disciples when He was preparing them, appointing them, and charging them. It reveals His own outlook on His work. The figure in itself is suggestive, and needs no elaboration. Harvest is always the result of previous activity, is the victory of that activity, and is also a call to activity. Can there be anything more disastrous than an ungathered harvest? Wherever He clothes the smiling fields with corn, they are asking men to garner them, to bring in the corn.

We have here a remarkable background. Matthew says that He went about all the cities and villages, teaching, preaching, and healing; and when He saw the multitudes He was moved with compassion for them, for they were distressed and scattered, as sheep having no shepherd. Why had He compassion on these multitudes? Because He saw them as others did not see them. His vision of the crowd was of a multitude distressed and scattered, without a shepherd, a flock of sheep harried by the wolves, and fleeced; fainting, wounded, bleeding, dying. It was our Lord's picture of the condition of the multitudes, in spite of their professions, and supposed orthodoxies to religion.

With that background in mind, He said harvest. Could two more apparently contradictory figures be put together? A flock of sheep, fainting, wounded, dying, and harvest. Here is the deep truth concerning His mission. Human need, distress, and dereliction constitutes harvest for Him and for His workers. Wherever the day is darkest, wherever the need is sorest, wherever human government is at its worst, there the fields are white to harvest for the Christ of God. So He said to His disciples before He called and commissioned them. He knew the distressed and awful condition of humanity, but He did not say it was a hopeless case; but that it was harvest, and was plenteous.

In the next illustration He spoke of sheep and wolves (x:16). Again to His disciples He said, "Behold, I send you forth as sheep in the midst of wolves." Take another figure with that, "Be ye therefore wise as serpents, and harmless as doves." He was illustrating now the work that lay immediately ahead of His disciples. This tenth chapter needs careful reading. In His commission to the twelve He saw three periods of service ahead, the immediate, then that which should follow His departure; and then beyond. In this first period we see what was before them. "I send you forth as sheep in the midst of wolves." The wolves were those preying upon the people, and were producing that state of weariness and weakness, wounding and fleecing. Mark the "therefore." "Be ye therefore wise as serpents, harmless as doves." Wise as serpents. Note, it is the wisdom of the serpent, not its poisonous capacity. It is the harmlessness of the dove, not its helplessness. Our Lord chose His words carefully to show what He meant. His disciples were going out to serve the needs of the sheep, into the midst of wolves. His workers are harmless only as they are wise, and wise when they are harmless. Any man going out upon the Master's business who lacks wisdom, is not harmless. Any man going out is not wise unless he is harmless. These are the two great qualifications for going out into a hostile world, facing the wolves that have destroyed the sheep. There are times too when His business demands our fighting with the wolves, as well as shepherding the sheep.

He then used that exquisite figure of the sparrows (x:29-31). Talking to the same men, He was illustrating God's tender care of His messengers. "Not a sparrow falleth on the ground without your Father." Do not spoil that in quoting it, without your Father's knowledge! If the sparrow sickens and dies in winter frost, or summer heat, and it falls to the ground, and with a tremor in its feathers we say it is dead, yes, but God was there. It died upon the bosom of God. "Ye are of more value than many sparrows." As His messengers go out to fight the wolves they may be killed; they go out as sheep in the midst of wolves. They need the wisdom of the serpent, combined with the harmlessness of the dove. As they go, however, the Father Who cares, is with them. He Who is with the dying sparrow will be with them, even if their service leads them to the place of death.

"Think not that I came to send peace on the earth. I came not to send peace, but a sword" (x:34). At that point our Lord was illustrating the effect produced by His enterprise and work. His work, and theirs through Him, would be divisive. It would mean the break-up of households. The sword here means that His work would be divisive; but loyalty to Him and to His enterprises must be the supreme thing, calling for complete devotion.

Our Lord's references to a sword are very interesting. Of course the ultimate meaning of His mission is peace. But here He was speaking of the importance of the effect of the process of His work. "I came not to send peace, but a sword." He used the figure again when predicting the coming judgment of Jerusalem (Luke xxi:24). Again at the end He used it a remarkable way (Luke xxii:36). When His disciples said, "Lord, behold, here are two swords," He said, "It is enough," so dismissing the subject. They had failed to understand that He was emphasizing that which He had already said, that they would go out on their mission, a divisive mission. When they now said, "Here are two swords," He was not telling them that two were enough, but He was dismissing the subject. Again in the Garden Peter was sternly rebuked, Put up thy sword into its sheath, that material sword of thine, for they that take the sword shall perish with the sword. He came to send a sword in that sense, of the breaking up of households; yet He came also to make households, and to gather them together. But because His teaching would be contrary to all the impulses of the human soul, inevitably there would be division. That has gone on ever since. All His workers have found the sword, dividing and setting into different camps.

All these illustrations have moved in the realm of humanity's need, and of His conception of what that work really means; and of His call to those who follow Him, to follow according to His own purpose.

6. Parabolic Illustrations

Matthew xi. and xii.

IN THESE two chapters we have the story of happenings in the ministry of Jesus during the period when the twelve were away from Him on their first mission. The eleventh chapter opens, "And it came to pass, when Jesus had made an end of commanding His disciples, He departed thence to teach and preach in their cities"; that is, in the cities of the twelve apostles. While they were sent on a wider mission and over a wider area, He went to the cities from which these twelve had come.

Taking the section from chapter twelve to the middle of chapter sixteen, we are in that period of His ministry when He was enforcing His claims against the opposition of the rulers, which by this time was growing. In these two chapters, eleven and twelve, we have six parabolic illustrations: of the reed and the man in soft raiment; children playing in the market-places; a sheep in a pit on a Sabbath day; a tree and the fruit it grows; Jonah, a historic illustration; and, finally, that weird and wonderful illustration of an empty house, and the dispossessed spirit.

Beginning first with the subject illustrated, and our Lord's use of it, take those of the reed and a man in soft raiment. Simply and naturally He was illustrating the greatness of His forerunner, John, and that by contrast. John was now imprisoned, and he had sent to Jesus that enquiry through his disciples. This showed how alert and keen he was, and yet also how strangely perplexed.

"Art Thou He that cometh, or look we for another?"

Jesus answered, and answered wonderfully, and when the messengers had been sent back, He used these illustrations in the presence of the crowds, two illustrations, and a direct word about the prophet.

Look at the illustrations. In that listening crowd there were un-doubtedly those who would be impressed when they heard John's enquiry, and might be inclined to think of John as wavering. Some today say this was so, and that it was produced by his depression in the prison. I do not think so. John's enquiry meant rather that he did not understand the method of Jesus. However the crowd might be inclined to think that John, the great forerunner, whose message and mission had led up to the work of Jesus, was hesitating, was halting, was weakening, Christ, with that strange and yet wonderful nobility that characterized all His dealings, saved John from misapprehension. Said He, What did you go out to the wilderness to see? Did you think you would find in the wilderness a reed, shaken by the wind? Perhaps they were thinking at that moment that John was vacillating, was being blown about by the winds sweeping over his life. A reed is always the emblem of weakness. There in the Jordan valley it was a beautiful thing to look at, often growing twenty feet in height, but it was always slender and weak, and as the winds swept across the valley the reeds were agitated, because they were unstable. Jesus said, Is that what you went out to see? He did not answer His own enquiry, nor add any-thing to it.

Again He said, Did you go out to see a man in soft raiment? Soft raiment was the emblem of enervation. Writing to the Corinthians Paul used that word which here is rendered "soft raiment," "effemi-nate," and that undoubtedly was its meaning. Did you go out to see a man in soft raiment? Here Jesus used two Greek words, in which the letters are exactly the same, differently arranged. A reed, *kalamos;* a man in soft raiment, *malakos.* Had they gone out to see a *kalamos,* or a *malakos;* a reed blown about with every breeze, or an enervated man, a man in soft raiment? To that second suggestion He did add a most illuminative word.

"Behold, they that wear soft raiment are in kings' houses," kings' palaces. John was in a king's prison. If he had been a man in soft raiment he would not have been in prison, he would have been in a palace. Mark the satire of it. Did you go out to see a man capable of being shaken with the wind? Did you go out to see a man in whose life there was a prostitution of virility for personal pleasure? Those familiar with John would know no reed was he, no effeminate dilet-tante, hanging on at the courts of kings for the gratification of their lusts. The very suggestion was enough. They went out to see a prophet, but he was far more than a prophet. So with great dignity our Lord defended John from the possibility of misunderstanding.

We gather therefore that there are two characteristics that dis-

qualify any man for prophetic work. What are they? Weakness that
yields to every passing wind that blows, or such self-indulgence as can
be expressed only when they wear soft raiment.

When Jesus had defended John, He talked about the generation in
the midst of which He was doing His work. In this figure of the children playing in the market-place, the subject He was illustrating was
that of the unreasonableness of that age. It was a homely and beautiful figure. There He was in the cities of the twelve, while they were on
their mission, preaching; and He suddenly illustrated the fact that
His preaching, and the preaching of John, whom He had just defended, was preaching to an age that was characterized by its unreasonableness. I think this might also be applied to this age in which
we are living.

What is the figure? Children playing at marriages and funerals.
Children were playing in the streets, in the market-place, probably at
setting sun, when market was over, and the day was waning, and the
bairns were getting tired. Some of them wanted to play at a wedding,
and the others would not. Then they changed, and they said, Let us
play then at a funeral. No, they would not do that. You will not
mourn to John's wailing, and you will not dance to My piping. John
came with the stern, hard, ascetic and profoundly necessary message,
calling men to repentance, and you say he has a demon, and you will
not listen. I have come with such humanness that men say of Me, I
am a gluttonous Man, and a winebibber, a friend of publicans and
sinners. It was the age that would not mourn to John's wailing, and
would not dance to Jesus' piping. Or we could turn that round, and
say this, John would not dance to their piping, and Jesus would not
mourn to their wailing. It was an unreasonable age. The harder,
sterner, severer note was denounced as being the utterance of a man
who was demon-possessed. The tender, human, and happy note of
Jesus was refused because it lacked the ascetic note. John lacked the
human touch, and they said he had a demon. Jesus seemed to lack
the harder and the ascetic outlook on life, and they said, Do not listen
to Him, He is a gluttonous Man and a winebibber. Christ ended all
by saying, "Wisdom is justified by her works," as in the Revised;
and some MSS render it, "justified by her children." The principle
is the same. Wisdom knows the necessity for the real reason of mourning, and the true inspiration of dancing, and she is justified in her
methods as they are presented to men.

Again in this twelfth chapter, verses eleven and twelve, we have
that simple figure of speech of a sheep fallen into a pit on the Sabbath
day. What was the subject our Lord was illustrating? Many applica-

tions can be made of it, but here He was showing the dishonesty of traditionalism, the dishonesty of these men of His own time who were traditionalists. In that same chapter when passing through the cornfields, the question was raised, and now again when He healed a man on the Sabbath, Luke shows that it was on another Sabbath, but Matthew puts the two incidents close together. It was the Sabbath, and the traditionalists' attitude toward the Sabbath was marked by their question about the disciples, and the question of what Jesus would do on the Sabbath. What He did to that cripple gave rise to the figure of speech.

We know how constantly our Lord flung Himself against the bondage of traditionalism because it overlay the law of God. What a distinction He drew. They taught for commandments of God the traditions of men, and neglected the greater matters of the law. Go back to that age. They had the law of God as it had come to them through Moses, the written law in their Scriptures. To that they had added the oral law. Now the oral law consisted of interpretations of the written law by the Great Synagogue, that was called Abhoth, which means Fathers. The opinions of the Fathers constituted tradition laid upon them, and were attempts to interpret the actual law. Again, from these traditions which they called Abhoth, they had another section called Toldoth, and Toldoth meant descendants. These were rules deduced from the interpretations of the Fathers, supposedly resulting from the law itself. The result was tradition heaped upon tradition, which had bound upon the people intolerable burdens.

Take this matter of the Sabbath, in illustration. The law said that on the Sabbath there should be no manner of work. The Abhoth, or the Fathers, in this application said, Reaping and threshing are both work; therefore reaping and threshing must not take place on the Sabbath. Then going down to Toldoth, they said, Plucking the ears of corn with the hand is reaping, and rubbing them is threshing. That is why the Pharisees objected to what the disciples were doing. Their secondary interpretation of the law was that if the disciples plucked ears of corn and rubbed them, they were breaking the law, they were reaping and threshing. It is very natural, and quite possible. People even today are mastered by tradition in stupid matters, and in religion; something the fathers said, which was said sincerely, and the sons have come along and taken what the fathers said, and they have added something to it, and the result has been all manner of futile, stupid, ridiculous laws governing men.

These Pharisees were criticizing Jesus, and wondering what He would do on the Sabbath with the crippled man; and He said, Which of you, having a sheep fallen into a pit on the Sabbath day, would not draw it out. Many of them, if they had seen a sheep that had fallen into a pit, would not have drawn it out on the Sabbath; but if the sheep had been their own, they would! That is the whole point. Which of *you*, having one of your own sheep fallen into a pit, would you not pull it out on the Sabbath? How much more is a man better than a sheep! This man is God's property. The sheep is yours. You have one law which you observe for your own personal property, and another that you observe for God's property. A sheep, if it is yours, you would deliver. A man, if he is God's man afflicted, you say the Sabbath is broken if he is delivered. The final application was that He took the man and He healed him. The man because the property of God was sacred, and was restored to sanctity as Jesus healed him. Traditionalism is dishonesty.

Then in verses 33-35 we have the illustration He had already used in the ethical Manifesto, of the tree and fruit. The subject illustrated was the dishonesty of His enemies. Here we are in the realm of controversy. He was enforcing His claims against opposition. These men were dishonest. They were attributing good fruit to an evil source. They were going so far as to suggest He was casting out the demons by the prince of the demons. His victory over Satan was declared to be complicity with Satan. In effect Christ said to them, Be honest. Judge Me honestly, as though He had said, by the fruits.

Then He immediately applied His illustration to them, and declared that they were incapable of honesty, for that is the meaning of the explanation, "How can ye, being evil . . . ?" He called them to consider this illustration of the tree and its fruit in application to Himself and His work. He appealed to these men to test Him, and to find out the secret of His ability, by the things at which they were looking, the things done, by the fruit produced.

At the 40th and 41st verses, again, these men were asking for a sign from heaven. It is an amazing thing to read, considering all He had done in healing the man. Yet they said they would like a sign from heaven. He used the historic sign of Jonah. What was the subject He was illustrating there? He was showing the valuelessness of a sign as a credential; but there was the ultimate value of one inevitable and overwhelming sign. Notice in this connection He declined to give them any sign except one that they had in their own literature, that they could read, and interpret only as He used it in application to Himself. There shall no sign be given but the sign of the prophet Jonah. As He addressed them He revealed the secret of their seeking a sign. "An evil and adulterous generation seeketh after a sign." Evil, *poneros*, harmful; and adulterous, faithless; marking their relationship to God, appearing in the figures of the Old Testament of the betrothal of God's people to Himself. Jesus told these rulers, asking Him for a sign, calling Him Teacher, while not obeying what He had to say, asking in mockery for some spectacular sign from heaven, I know the meaning of your question. You are evil, and you are adulterous. The effect of your life upon others is harmful, because you are out of harmony with God, and are infidel. There is no sign that shall be given to you except the sign of the prophet Jonah, for as Jonah was three days and three nights in the belly of the fish, so shall the Son of man be three days and nights in the heart of the earth. The Scriptures never say whale, but a "great fish." Some men are so busy with the tape measure trying to find out whether a man could get inside a fish, they never plumb the depths of Deity. The book of Jonah says that "God prepared a great fish." Jonah was a sign to Nineveh. There is no meaning in that sign if the story was not true. It demands the historicity of the story of Jonah. How was Jonah a sign to Nineveh? The crew of the vessel had flung him overboard reluctantly. Undoubtedly they were a fine body of men. They did not want to do so, but he was insistent. To them he was dead, and gone. Then they reached the land, and the man they had flung to death appeared in Nineveh, preaching. That strange and mystic sign of a man coming back from the dead to preach to Nineveh produced a repentance in Nineveh, that spared it for a hundred years. Jesus took these men back in their history, and predicted the future concerning Himself.

Once before in the earlier days of ministry, as John records, they asked Him for a sign. The answer He gave those rulers was, "Destroy this temple, and in three days I will raise it up." That is exactly the same thing. The only sign of the divinity of His mission, and of the interpretation of His personality will be found through His death and His resurrection. This was a great word He uttered. Whether anyone caught the significance of it at the time we do not know; but there remains the record for us, and for all time, to show that the spectacular thing these men wanted He never granted; and indeed, so evident is it, that during His ministry, repeatedly when some miracle had been wrought, out of His compassion of heart, He charged people not to talk about it.

The last illustration is in verses 43-45. It is important to notice that whatever the illustration was, the application was to that generation. That does not exclude an application of it to personal and individual lives. He was however speaking to that generation, in the midst of which He had been conducting His ministry, following upon that of John. The whole of John's ministry, and that of Jesus, had had the effect of casting out of evil spirits. It was a cleansing, purifying, exorcising ministry. That was what our Lord was illustrating. He took this story of a house which had become tenantless. The whole emphasis in His description of that house was His account of how the returning demon found it. "He findeth it empty, swept and garnished." Yes, but empty. He was speaking of His generation, an evil generation, swept and garnished by the teaching of His predecessor and His own teaching, but not possessed, empty. He was emphasizing the fact that if that or any other generation is left like that, it may become the home of demons sevenfold. The illustration is that of the danger of a tenantless house.

The application was to that generation. The house was freed from evil mastery for a while, but it was empty. It lacked a new possessor. It lacked a master in place of the one exorcised and the empty house was the opportunity for the re-entry of the demon, reinforced sevenfold. We must take it, and make application of it to ourselves, or to an age. Reformation without regeneration is no use. Oh, we may sweep the house, and garnish it, and improve certain conditions by creating a new environment but unless there is a new possessor, a new Lord, a new Master, instead of the old demon, the demons will return with sevenfold force. Reformation is ultimately of no value alone. It is only preparation for worse desolation. The only possible cure for a man or an age is reformation, followed by regeneration and the incoming of the new Lord and Master. That is so with the individual.

7. The General Scheme

Matthew xiii.

THIS chapter contains at some length our Lord's explanation of His reason for using the parabolic method, and it is of vital importance and interest. Chronologically in the ministry of Jesus the record in this chapter marks a stage in that ministry when our Lord turned largely to the parabolic method when dealing with the multitudes, employing it also with His own disciples. This chapter contains eight parables, all delivered on the same occasion, though not as one set discourse. That fact is proven by the fifty-third verse. This study then is of the nature of a general survey, important to a more detailed consideration.

At the seaside Jesus gave the first complete parable, that of the sower and He gave an explanation of that parable in answer to the request of His disciples, doubtless also given in the hearing of the multitudes. Following that explanation, He uttered three other parables, still by the seaside, sitting in the boat, while the multitudes thronged the shore. At the 36th verse we see that He left the multitudes, and went into the house. The first thing that happened in the house was that again, in answer to the request of His disciples, He explained one of the parables, the second that He had uttered in public. Then He gave to them, in the house, four other parables.

To take a general survey. We find in these parables the King's own view of His Kingdom as to its history in the age which He had then initiated. These parables, pictures, stories reveal His view of the Kingdom, not in its eternal and abiding sense, but in its history in the age which He had initiated by His coming into the world.

The first of these parables simply reveals the nature of His mission. It is the parable of the sower. The second parable begins with the words, "The Kingdom of heaven is likened unto." The first parable has no such reference, and He never again used this particular phrase in this chapter, but said, "The Kingdom of heaven is like." Here in the second parable the phrase might be rendered, The Kingdom of heaven has become like. In that introduction the phrase shows our Lord was thinking of the Kingdom of heaven as an abiding fact, but one that changed in its conditions and in its expression. The Kingdom of heaven has become like; there was a change through His own coming, and He shows the nature of the change.

Then the next five parables, two uttered in public, and three in private all begin, "The Kingdom of heaven is like." Here is the general character of the change, and the result thereof. These are the pictures of a definite period. The limit is found in two verses 39 and 49, when our Lord spoke of the end of the age, not of the world, an unhappy translation. When some people talk of the end of the world they mean a cataclysm, an annihilation, and a ceasing to be. That is not what our Lord meant. He spoke of "the consummation of the age." A period of time was in His view.

Our Lord spoke here to illumine, not to becloud, to illustrate, and to lure men toward the mystery through the symbol. Therefore these parables should be considered on the simplest level. Taking the symbols, and mastering them, we touch the sublime.

The second canon is that the application should be restricted to the period of time which was in view. To fail to do that is to fail to understand what our Lord was intending to teach. They are pictures of one age, beginning with His first advent, and ending with His second advent, of the period in which we are living today. This restriction of application will save us from stupid blunders being made today about the work of the Church, and of the condition of the world.

Again in studying the figurative teaching of Jesus, we find His consistent use of such figurative terms. They are never mixed. I would go further and say that applies to the whole Bible. The figurative language of the Bible is always consistent with basic principles.

In our general survey of these parables in this chapter, the Kingdom is viewed in its progress in this age among men. Those spoken to the multitude present the Kingdom process from the human viewpoint. In the second group of parables spoken to the disciples, the same age is in view, but the Kingdom is seen from the Divine aspect.

In the first four parables, those presenting the human viewpoint, our Lord described two antagonistic forces at work in human history. He not only referred to these forces, but He made it perfectly clear that there would be long and continuous conflict btween them. Taking those four parables, the apparent issue is the victory of evil, on the earth level, and the human standpoint. Remember, He was looking at the processes of the Kingdom as He saw them, and portraying God's vision of that period.

In the parable of the sower and the seed, the work of the King is seen, scattering men of the Word in order to produce Kingdom results. Sons of the Kingdom are scattered, in whom the Word is incarnate, so as to produce Kingdom results; and the results of victory seem to be very small; for there is the work of the enemy, the injury of the seed through the soil, to prevent the fruit of the Kingdom.

In the next parable there are two sowings. Again the King is the Sower, sowing His field with the sons of the Kingdom. At the same time the work of the enemy is that of sowing the field with sons of the evil one. Wheat and darnel, that weed of the East so alike in its growth to wheat that experts can hardly detect the difference in its early stage.

In the third parable the Kingdom is presented as a mustard tree, an unnatural growth, a manifestation of earthly greatness which is not in harmony with the intention of the King, in the false values that will be manifested.

Once more, the leaven in the meal, the introduction of a principle of decomposition and disintegration, with the result of external corruption and paralysis. Those are our Lord's four pictures of Kingdom processes, spoken to the crowds; and that view harmonizes with the history of nineteen hundred years, and all the newspapers of tomorrow morning.

When we turn to the second group of parables, after He had gone into the house, we find Him talking to the men immediately round Him, who were to be responsible for His enterprise in the world, and He was showing them the Kingdom as viewed from the Divine standpoint. Here the one activity running through them all, and in every case the complete success of that activity, both in the ending of the age which He was initiating, and in the processes of the Kingdom which He was describing. Then that which in evil had seemed to be victorious is destroyed; and that which has been the purpose of the King is brought to a glorious finality and realization.

The parable of the treasure in the field, the latent possibilities of the field. The field is the world. There is the purchase of the whole field at cost. That is the Divine attitude. The pearl in the field, with its latent possibilities, and amid the treasure, one supreme treasure; and there is a personal sacrifice in order to secure possession of that treasure. Again that is the Divine outlook. Some of us have sung in old days, with much enjoyment,

> "I've found the Pearl of greatest price!
> My heart doth sing for joy;
> And sing I must, for Christ is mine!
> Christ shall my song employ."

That is beautiful and very true, but that is not what this means. Christ here is not the pearl. His Church is the pearl. Remember, this man, this merchant sold everything in order to possess the treasure. What have we to sell that is worth anything? Nothing! Again, the parable of the drag-net. No hand is spoken of as flinging out that drag-net. It swings in the tide. That is the Divine action, and He is flinging out that drag-net. That is the method of the age, and all conditions of people are included therein, all sorts of fishes; but there is a final discrimination. In each case when referring to the consummation, or final discrimination, our Lord shows the finality will be supernatural. It will not be in men's hands at all, but in the hands of angels. Angels are the reapers. Angels pull in the net and sort the fishes. At Cæsarea Philippi when Jesus first told His disciples about His Cross and His Church and His coming, He said that the Son of man should come in the clouds with all the holy angels. There is a supernatural ending for the age, in which angels actually take part under His direction, in the affairs of men.

When He had finished His seven parables, He looked at that little group of men and said, Have you understood these things? They said,

Yes. They evidently understood in such a measure as to make it possible for Christ to utter one more parable, showing their responsibilities
about all these things, as scribes, instructed to the Kingdom of heaven.

It was a great day when He began uttering parables: four to the
crowds, and four to His own. The first four revealed the processes of
the Kingdom through an age, on the human level. Three revealed the
processes of the Kingdom from the Divine viewpoint, of the Divine
purpose and standard; and the final one showed the responsibility of
His own in view of that view of the Kingdom.

If any should believe that the whole world is to be converted and
changed, and presently be transformed as the result of their work,
they are blind. Christ is against such a belief, History is against it.
The activities in the world today are against it. When we see this
movement through this age from the Divine standpoint, then the heart
is at rest as to the issue. The final parable here reveals the importance
of the fact that we are scribes, instructed in the Kingdom of heaven.
We must have the Master's conception if we are to serve the Kingdom
without fret, without fever, without failing in quiet calm strength.

8. The Sower

Matthew xiii:3-9 and 18-23.

THE FIRST parable of the Sower is one of two which our Lord
Himself explained. Herein lies the great value of the two parables.
We are not left to any speculation as to what our Lord meant, because
of the record of His explanation of them to His own disciples.

First let us see the picture which He presented, that of a sower;
then consider His explanation of that story, as He told it to the
crowds, and from these two careful considerations finally deduce the
instruction which they convey for us.

The picture of the sower is perfectly natural, but with Eastern
rather than Western colour. There are senses in which those born and
brought up in the country are familiar with a sower going forth to
sow, at least as it used to be done. We know the picture of the sower
in our own land. Yet we come to clear apprehension of the story only
as we remember that this was in the East. In Thomson's *Land and the
Book* he therein described the sower in the Eastern lands very clearly,
as he wrote:—

" 'Behold, a sower went forth to sow.' There is a nice and close adherence to actual life in this form of expression. These people have actually *come forth* all the way from June to this place. The expression implies that the sower, in the days of our Saviour, lived in a hamlet, or village, as all these farmers now do; that he did not sow near his own house, or in a garden fenced or walled, for such a field does not furnish all the basis of the parable. There are neither *roads,* nor thorns, nor stony places in such lots. He must go forth into the open country as these have done, where there are no fences; where the path passes through cultivated land; where thorns grow in clumps all around; where the rocks peep out in places through the scanty soil; and where also, hard by, are patches extremely fertile. Now here we have the whole four within a dozen rods of us. Our horses are actually trampling down some seeds which have fallen by this wayside, and larks and sparrows are busy picking them up. That man, with his mattock, is digging about places where the rock is too near to the surface for the plough; and much that is fallen there will wither away, because it has no deepness of earth. And not a few seeds have fallen among this *bellan,* and will be effectually choked by this most tangled of thorn bushes. But a large portion, after all, falls into really good ground, and four months hence will exhibit every variety of crop."

Keeping that Eastern picture in mind, look at the picture first generally. There are four things in the story as Jesus told it that arrest attention; first, the sower; secondly, the seed; thirdly, the soil; and, lastly, the sequence.

Then we are concerned with our Lord's explanation of the picture. Notice that the sower is not named. He began bluntly, "Behold, a sower went forth to sow." It was an actual fact, but so far as the teaching is concerned, He did not name the sower, neither did He do so in His explanation. He did not say who the sower was who sowed the seed. However, going to the 37th verse we read this. When the disciples asked Him to explain the parable of the tares, He said, "He that soweth the good seed is the Son of man." That applies equally to this parable of the sower.

Notice in the next place that the chief value of the picture is the seed and its relation to the soil. These things are foundation principles, to be borne in mind as we approach the detailed study of these wonderful parables. The sower is not referred to, but unquestionably the Lord was referring to Himself as He said, "He that soweth the good seed is the Son of man."

Then again, bear in mind there is one Sower, and one soil. The Sower is the Son of man. What is the soil? He does not name it. The hard highway, the thorns, the rock, do not constitute soil. The ground does. If we would know what the soil is once again we trespass upon the next parable. Following the statement in verse 37, "He that soweth good seed is the Son of man," He says, "and the field is the world." Let us keep that carefully in mind.

We are next impressed by the fact that there are various conditions of the seed, and various responses of the soil. As our Lord explained His parable, when He referred to the seed, He did so by speaking of persons. These words of explanation are found, beginning at the nineteenth verse,

"When anyone heareth the word of the Kingdom, and understandeth it not, then cometh the evil one, and snatcheth away that which hath been sown in his heart. This is he that was sown by the wayside." Verse 20: "He that was sown upon the rocky places." Verse 22: "And he that was sown among the thorns." Verse 23: "He that was sown upon the good ground."

Our Lord is interpreting the Kingdom, and His work in the Kingdom, and He speaks of seed. He employs the masculine pronoun which covers all human souls. The seed then, as viewed at this point, must be considered in that way. There are varid responses made by the soil, and those responses depend upon the condition of the seed that is sown in the soil. That will become plainer as we proceed.

Take the first. *"He* that was sown by the wayside." Mark the emphasis. What about him? Birds came and devoured them. "Any one heareth the word of the Kingdom, and understandeth it not, then cometh the evil one, and snatcheth away that which hath been sown in his heart." We see a personality, and something more, a person as a seed, the seed of the Kingdom, falling upon the wayside but the birds of the air have devoured that which was sown in his heart, that which made him a seed of the Kingdom. To such the soil is unresponsive. It fell by the wayside. It could not be received and the emphasis— strange as these things seem to merge and mix—is not upon the soil that is an adaptation, it is upon the seed. If the seed has lost its vital power because the birds have devoured it, then the soil is unresponsive.

Again, *"He* that was sown upon the rocky places." When this man was sown, the sun is "risen," and the seed is "scorched." Who is he? Mark the emphasis, "He that heareth the word, and straightway with joy receiveth it, yet hath he not root in himself." He endures only for a little while. "When tribulation or persecution ariseth because of the Word, straightway he stumbleth." Therefore he also is a seed of no value in the sowing of the world, and to such an one the soil is cruel and non-productive. So the rocky places.

Take the next, "He that was sown among the thorns." Again, Who is he? He is the one who has heard the Word, but has allowed the care of the present age, and the deceitfulness of riches to choke the Word, and so he, as a seed, with a Kingdom value, becomes unfruitful. The thorns grow up and choke them. The soil in that case is destructive.

Once more, "He that was sown upon the good ground." Who is this? "He that heareth the Word, and understandeth it," who bears fruit, and brings forth fruit. To such the soil is good ground, is responsive, productive, and constructive.

In this narrative, taken as our Lord explained it, there may seem to be a difference, a disparity. Some may be inclined to say there is a contradiction between the incidence of the teaching in the story and that of the explanation. As a matter of fact, there is no difference or disparity. In the former, emphasis is laid upon the soil. In the latter, the emphasis is laid upon the nature of the seed that falls upon the soil. The seed sown, as we have seen, are men and women. But behind that sowing of human life in the world, with Kingdom intention, there is another sowing, that of the Word in the heart. Turning to Luke's account, there it is seen clearly that the sowing of the Word in the heart of the individuals is the first thing. That being so, these individuals, men and women are sent out into the world, the very seed of the Kingdom. The ultimate seed is the Word itself. The world is the field, to which we come again; and the planting of that field is of men and women in whom the Word of God has been planted. Men and women fructified by the implanted Word, become seeds of the Kingdom in world affairs.

The soil is always the same. The figures employed by our Lord simply describe the response made to it. To men who hear the Word, but do not understand, the soil is unreceptive. To men who hear, and rejoice, but fail to obey, the soil is non-productive. To men who hear, but who respond to the age about them, the soil is destructive. The men who hear and understand in the full sense, to such the soil is receptive, productive, and constructive. Here in this first parable we have an interpretation of the Lord's own work in relation to the Kingdom principles.

9. *The Darnel*

Matthew xiii: 24-30, 36-43.

THIS parable is necessarily closely connected with that of the Sower. That was uttered in public, as well as this one, and the two following; after which our Lord went into the house. He had given His explanation of the parable of the Sower to the listening crowds. However, when they were alone in the house, the disciples came to Him, and asked Him to explain the parable of the darnel. This second of the parables is the second and last one which the Lord Himself explained.

We are at once arrested by the form in which the disciples preferred that request. They asked Him to explain to them "the parable of the tares of the field." That shows that as they listened, they had been impressed supremely by that element of the story that Jesus had told them. They did not ask Him to explain the parable of the two sowings, though that must have surprised them. Evidently the Lord intended to lay stress upon the fact of the darnel, or tares. Darnel was the word used, and the Lord had spoken of darnel being sown.

Again there are three things to do; first to take the picture as our Lord gave it to them simply as a picture in its Eastern setting and surroundings; secondly to pay attention to our Lord's explanation; finally gathering up the instruction for ourselves.

The picture is of a field in which there were two sowings. It is the picture also of the method of the owner of the field in face of the fact of the two sowings. This picture is Eastern. Notice that the field was the property of the man sowing good seed, and not of the enemy who sowed darnel. Whatever was intended by the field, we are looking at an Eastern picture of a field which was the property of one man. It was his field.

Then there were the two sowings. The first was perfectly simple and natural, in the true order of things. The owner of the field sowed his field with harvest in view, that what he sowed should bring forth harvest was natural and proper. It was a picture of something going on year after year; a man owned a field, and in the field that was his, he cast seed, intending thereby to produce a definite kind of harvest.

Then came the amazing part of the story that Jesus told. An enemy came, an anemy of the man and of the purpose of the owner

of the field, and of his intention for the harvest upon which his mind
was set when he sowed the seed. An enemy sowed with the distinct
intention of spoiling the harvest. There is no need to argue that this
was unnatural; it was improper, it was dastardly.

What was it he sowed? Darnel, that is, something which in its
first springing from the ground even experts cannot detect from wheat.
Darnel is sown, and the wheat is sown, and presently when the showers
come, and they begin to sprout, the difference between them could not
be detected. Darnel is like wheat, but it is actually entirely different
from wheat. It is of a different nature. Looking like wheat when it
first springs, as it develops and grows the difference becomes increas-
ingly manifest, until when it has come to full growth, no one could
make any mistake, or fail to distinguish between the wheat and the
darnel. An enemy sowed the field already sown with wheat, with something that imitated it. Evidently the enemy then was a trespasser,
who had no right on that field at all. He was full of subtlety, and came
"while men slept." He was an enemy, animated by malice.

Then the servants of the owner came to him, and told him what
had been going on. Evidently when the manifestation was beginning to
be clear as to the difference, they had found out that what they
thought was wheat only was wheat and darnel. They came perturbed
to the master to tell him someone had sown darnel in his wheat field.
"An enemy hath done this," he replied. What shall we do then, master?
Shall we go through this wheat field and gather out all the tares, this
darnel? No, leave them alone until the harvest. Then no one will make
any mistake as to the difference between them. Do not try to uproot
the tares, because you may not be sure, and may uproot wheat, when
you think you are gathering tares. At the consummation of the age,
at the harvest time the whole field will be dealt with. Then there
will be discrimination according to manifestation. That is the story.

Presently, after Jesus had uttered two other brief but pregnant
parables, they went into the house, and the disciples said to Him,
"Explain unto us the parable of the tares of the field. And He
answered, and said, He that soweth the good seed is the Son of man;
and the field is the world."

Take that last phrase, "The field is the world." The picture drawn
necessitated the recognition of the fact that the field was the property
of the one who sowed good seed. Thus inferentially our Lord was
claiming definitely that the whole world belonged to Him. That is a
philosophy of all life and service that we should remember. Many
years ago now I was in the Isle of Man, and was listening to a sermon
by a local preacher in a Wesleyan Chapel. He said something so full

of simplicity that it fastened itself upon my memory. I have never lost the power of it. He said, "The devil is a squatter." That arrested attention. He did not leave his congregation in the dark. He knew something of life in America, and he went on and said, "A squatter is a man who settles on land he has no right to, and works it for his own advantage." Can the theologians give a better definition of the devil than that? That lies behind this word of Jesus, "The field is the world." It is the property, not of the one who is sowing evil seeds in it, but the property of the One Who according to this aspect of the Kingdom, is sowing good seed in the whole world. In Mark's account of the missionary commission, Jesus said, "Go ye into all the cosmos, and preach the Gospel to every creature." That is the same word, cosmos, the whole world, the world in itself, in its order of life, its peopling, "all the world." When Paul wrote his letter to the Romans, he said, "The whole creation groaneth and travaileth in pain together until now," waiting "for the revealing of the sons of God." When he wrote that stupendous thing he was surely thinking of this parable: the world, the field, groaning, waiting for the manifestation of the sons of God. Undoubtly he was referring to the second Advent, and that is the ultimate fulfilment. But it is also true today. What this world everywhere in its sighing and sobbing and sorrow is needing is the manifestation of the sons of God.

The inferential claim of our Lord must be recognized. He claims proprietorship. "The earth is the Lord's, and the fulness thereof." "The field is the world." Said Jesus, Two sowings are going on. He had introduced this parable by saying, "The Kingdom of heaven has become like . . ." We read "is likened unto," but literally it is, It has become like. He was indicating a change that had resulted in world affairs as the result of His coming. Who is He? He is the Sower, and because that Sower is sowing, the Kingdom has become like this. The Sower is sowing His good seed in His own field. He is "the Son of man."

What seed is He sowing in the midst of the world and all its affairs? "The sons of the Kingdom." The Kingdom is the subject from beginning to end, the Kingdom of God, the Kingship of God. The way to its realization in the midst of a derelict world, and of a blasted and broken race, is that He as the Sower is flinging out into the world, in its order and conditions, in its lack of order and chaos, seed. What is the seed? The seed is the sons of the Kingdom, in His own field.

But He said, Another sowing is going on at the same time. Who is the sower? Here our Lord used the word for Satan, *diabolos*, the traducer, the liar. He named him as the one who is against every thing that is true, and high and noble. Said Jesus, He is busy in My field, sowing his seed. What seed? "Sons of the evil," men and women who are devoted, not to God, but to evil; evil men and women flung into the world order. But there is a peculiar quality about his sowing. He is sowing his seed among the wheat, and the two prepositions are close together, emphasising one another, *ana meson*, showing that the idea is of a sowing so near to something else, so much like it, as to create widespread deception. That is what the enemy is doing.

What shall we do? If we are the sons and servants of the King and the Kingdom, shall we go out, and root up these evil seeds? Let them alone, said Jesus. Let both alone; let the wheat alone; let the darnel alone. Till when? Till the harvest, till the consummation, till that hour which must inevitably come when the true deep meaning of every human life comes into clear manifestation. He was looking on to a consummation, and He said, Harvest will be the consummation of the age, when the difference will be patent, and when, knowing that hour of fulness has come, He will deal with the world situation by supernatural agency. Angels will be introduced into national affairs, and there will be two harvests. The angels will gather out of His Kingdom everything that is harmful, everything that is wrong, and cast it out to the destruction of fire. They will gather out all those who have been truly the sons of the Kingdom, and all those that have resulted from their sowing in the world, and the righteous shall shine forth in the glory of the Father.

That consummation is not yet. It is still postponed. There are moments when in our loyalty to our Lord, and in our impatience we cry out, Lord, how long? Can we not begin to deal with these evil things, and uproot them? His voice is still saying, Let them alone. Let them both grow to the harvest.

It is an old question, often talked about and debated in meetings and in conversations, Is the world getting better, or is it getting worse? There is only one answer, if this parable is true. The world is getting better every day, and worse every day. There are two sowings, two growths, two increasing manifestations. Evil today is more deadly, more damnable, more dastardly than it has ever been in the history of the world. Good today is more pronounced, more definite. There are more signs everywhere of it than there have ever been. Both are growing, growing, growing, and presently the harvest will come. We do not know when.

Mark what this parable teaches quite clearly. The method of

the foe in this age is principally that of imitation. Those who are definitely hostile, and blatantly declare so, are not in view in this parable. I am not saying the devil has nothing to do with them, but that is not his method. It is not his most subtle method. It is not the method most productive of harm in the world. It is imitation. Go back to Acts. Ananias and Sapphira were both members of the outward and visible Church. Simon Magus was also active in the work of the Church. See the writings, and the same thing is evident. What the apostle combated was not the harm of definite opposition, or the massed opposition of godlessness in the pagan world, but that principle, so much like Christianity, darnel, which at the beginning looked like wheat. That has gone on all down the ages. The elements of imitation have been found, so that the Church came to rejoice in a false power, which was entirely antagonistic to her very genius and life, and even to indulge in a false form of supposed purity, which consisted in abstention from trivial things, while the weightier matters were neglected in the depth of her life.

Today we are seeing it in the realm of doctrine, accommodation to supposed modern thought, in which some men are using the phrasing of Christianity, devitalised, and devoid of the fundamental things—imitation. That is the supreme peril today; it is doctrinal.

What are we to do about it? Nothing. Let it alone, resting assured that the hour of actual manifestation is coming. If we begin trying to root up the darnel we are in danger of rooting up wheat, and the process of development can do no harm to the good, and the process of development means always moving towards final judgment for the evil.

Here for the first time our Lord pointed to the consummation of the age. "The Kingdom of heaven has become like . . ." The field in which the Son of man is sowing the seed will come to harvest, the full realisation of the Kingdom of God. The enemy is sowing darnel, imitation; the purpose of which is the hindering of the arrival of the Kingdom of God. But there is a consummation, an hour of harvest, and then the dawning of a new age, when all things that offend shall be cast out, and then the shining of the righteous in the Kingdom of the Son.

No parable must ever be carried beyond the intention of our Lord. In this consideration we may well remind ourselves that there are things implicit here, but not explicit. There are other things to be said about the age than was said in this parable. A man who is a son of evil, and is planted in this field of the world, darnel, can do what no darnel can do in the realm of Nature. He can have his

nature changed and become a son of the Kingdom. That is where
the Gospel comes in. The Gospel is implicit here, and it is well to
remember it. A man who but yesterday, planted by Satan in the
midst of commerce, of society, or recreation, exerting an evil influence,
and hindering the Kingdom of God; blessed be God, can be changed,
and become a son of the Kingdom, and begin to exert the influence
with others, toward the coming of the Kingdom of God.

Our business then is to grow, to develop, and so to fulfil the purpose of our Lord in our own lives, and thus to hasten the coming of
His Kingdom; and never to attempt to pull up darnel.

10. The Mustard Seed

Matthew xiii: 31, 32.

This is the first of the octave of parables contained in this thirteenth
chapter of Matthew, of which the Lord gave no explanation.
The explanation of the Sower was given in public. That of the sowing of the darnel, was given in private to His disciples.

When approaching such a parable, there are two perils to be
avoided, in interpretation. One is that of popularity, and the other is
that of misinterpretation of history, in an attempt to understand the
parable. We have no right to come to this, or any parable, influenced
by the general consensus of expository opinion. Here I would lay
down a principle for all Bible study. Whatever the popular interpretation may be, it is not therefore necessarily the correct one. It may
be correct, but popularity is not any guarantee of accuracy. That needs
no arguing. The acceptation of popular interpretation of Scripture led
to the crucifixion of Jesus.

Then there is a danger of considering history from the standpoint
of observation, and interpreting these parables of Jesus by the facts
of history as we know them. That too may be a perilous procedure
against which we need to guard.

There are general principles of interpretation which must be observed. The first is that of the harmony of the teaching of Jesus
throughout these parables. Referring now only to those parables
contained in this thirteenth chapter of Matthew, we must bear in
mind that there is perfect harmony in the general conception and
teaching of Jesus throughout.

In the second place we must bear in mind the consistency of our Lord's figures of speech. He never used one in two different senses. They are all used consistently in the same way.

To apply these canons of interpretation, the popular conception of this particular parable is that our Lord predicted the great success of the Kingdom. Almost invariably the parable of the mustard seed that became a tree is treated as though our Lord was showing the complete and ultimate success of the Kingdom in this age. We must not forget that all these parables have to do with one age.

That view however has been distinctly disproved by history. There has been growth, but it has been unsatisfactory. We talk today of the Kingdom of God, and of Christian nations. There are no Christian nations. There are nations that profess to be founded upon Christian principles, but there are no Christian nations. We are not a Christian nation. The principles of a Christian nation have never yet been put to the test, and proven, and revealed to the world in national life. There has been a growth in Kingdom understanding, and the application of Kingdom principles, but nothing approaching complete success. On the contrary, there is very much that denies success.

Another principle to be observed is that of the harmony of teaching. Throughout all these parables these things of difficulty, limitation, opposition, and admixture were evidently foretold by our Lord. There is not one parable that moves to a consummation of the age resulting from the activities in the age. The idea that the Gospel is to be preached until all the world is converted, is a mistaken one, if we believe in Jesus, and in what He said. There is nothing that suggests such a result in any of these parables.

To take the figures recurring in all those parables at which we have been looking: the sowing of the seed, and the seed, the Word of God incarnate in human lives, the sons of the Kingdom. The Sower Who sowed the seed is the Son of man. The soil, the field in which the seed is sown, is the world. The birds are symbolic of evil, that come and snatch away the seed. These figures are consistent.

Let us then look at this parable with unprejudiced, and open mind. So we will examine the picture, and apply the teaching.

The picture Jesus drew was of a seed, the smallest of all seeds, which seed grew until it became a tree. Normally the mustard seed never becomes a tree. The mustard is a herb, not a tree. As a tree it has been described as "a garden shrub outdoing itself." That is abnormality. All attempts to make the tree square with popular interpretation is of the nature of special pleading. I have referred to Dr. Thomson's *Land and the Book*, invaluable to every Bible student. But even Dr. Thomson evades this, or tries to account for it. Writing from Palestine, and from his own observation, he plainly says that the mustard there was not a tree, and did not grow to a tree. He then says possibly in our Lord's time there was another variety of mustard that grew to be a tree. I have quoted the spirit of what he says. Others have tried in other ways to account for it. Dr. Carr, in the *Cambridge Bible* has this sentence. "The mustard plant does not grow to a very great height, so that Luke's expression, 'waxed a great tree' must not be pressed."

To deal with the Scriptures in that way is to get nowhere. Our Lord said "A great tree"; and He also said that this particular mustard seed grew greater than all the herbs, of which it is one. Dr. Royle, another writer, suggests that the reference was to Khardal, or *Salvadora Persica*. But Dr. Morrison has declared there is no proof of the growth of either of these specimens in that neighborhood. Our Lord was surely teaching that in this age there would be an abnormal and unnatural growth of the mustard seed, so that it would afford as a tree, a lodging for the birds of the air. The word means a camping in it, and living in it. The parable was never intended to teach the progress and growth of the Kingdom to finality in this age. It does mark development, but it is abnormal development.

To turn from the picture that Jesus drew to mark the unnatural development of the Christian principle and ideal, as taught by Him. What is its natural development? Lowliness, meekness, service. These are the things that mark the true Christian spirit, emanating from those in whom the Word of God is incarnate, and who are flung out into the age as the seed of the Kingdom. The marks of true Christianity are always those of likeness to Him Who said, "I am meek and lowly in heart"; likeness to Him Who said, "The Son of man came not to be ministered unto but to minister, and to give His life a ransom for many."

What are the unnatural notes? Exactly the opposite of the natural, loftiness, pride, dominance. Wherever in the history of Christianity these things have manifested themselves, loftiness, pride, seeking for dominion and mastery, they have proved not a normal development, but an abnormal and false one.

Some years ago in the Isle of Man I had a conversation with Sir Hall Caine. He had just issued his novel, *The Christian*, with John Storm as his hero. It had troubled me, and I said to him, "Do you mean to suggest that John Storm is the normal type of Christianity?" Quickly and sharply he answered me, "By no means. I am only suggesting that John Storm is what Christian people were, or aimed to be; and that it is not Christian." Then he said this remarkable thing, which I am not defending or attacking. "I can put the whole of the works and ethic of Jesus into two brief quotations." I said, "What are they?" He replied, " 'He that is greatest in the Kingdom of heaven, let him be servant of all.' " "And what is the other?" " 'Lay not up for yourselves treasures on earth where moth and rust corrupt.' Now" he said, "test England by those, test the common life of the Christian Church by this, and you will see how little practical vital Christianity is understood."

I have quoted that conversation, and leave it but take a look down history. Yes, the Church has grown in loftiness. It has often become so powerful that it has become proud, and has sought dominion over others. All these things are the outcome not of normal, but of abnormal growth. As we look down the history of the age, so far we shall see the truth illustrated. It began when those first disciples when Jesus was with them, said, "Who is greatest in the Kingdom of heaven?" There was the passion for prominence, position, and power. We know how He answered that. He told them that only those who were prepared to drink His cup, and be baptized with His baptism were great in the Kingdom of heaven. The early Church had illustrations of it. Peter, in his letter, charged them not to lord it over God's heritage.

The supreme illustration of this abnormal growth was in the espousal of Christianity by Constantine, the Roman emperor. That was the darkest day that dawned in all the history of the Church. His espousal of Christianity was an astute and clever political move, and he grafted upon Christianity much of paganism, and elevated it to a position of wordly power; and in that hour the whole Church passed under the blight from which it has never completely escaped. That is the whole sin and wrong of the Papacy, domination won in the name of Christ, the claiming of power to rule over kings, emperors, and rulers and dictate terms to them; a great tree, spreading its branches. That spirit remains in every attempt even today, to realize the Divine purpose by high organization, vested power. It is not a good thing. It is an abnormal growth.

It has gone on, and is still going on. Christ said it would, and the unintended issue has been the false greatness of external position and power, a great tree. The tree is always the symbol of greatness and authority. Nebuchadnezzar was likened to a tree. Pharaoh with all his power was likened to a tree; and the Kingdom of heaven has become like that, a great wordly power, principality occupied with its loftiness, the expressing of itself in pride, seeking dominion, or domination in the affairs of the world; and consequently it has become the refuge of unclean things. Such the parable, and its teaching.

Again we must remember that in these parables our Lord was not dealing with the true nature of the Kingdom. "The Kingdom of heaven is like . . ." He spoke, even in these parables, in the abiding terms, and the abiding tense. He was surveying the age, and He looked on twice to the end of the age, its consummation. It was the age initiated by His first advent, and which is bounded and will be consummated by His second advent. Not in one of these parables was He revealing the inward nature of the Kingdom, except at the beginning, when He showed that the Kingdom principles are found in the Word of God, as it is embodied in the lives of Christian men and women. That of course includes everything, but there is no detailed reference to it in interpretation. The ethics of the Kingdom are not found here in detail. They are found in the Sermon on the Mount.

This is of great importance, for our Lord was not revealing the nature of the ultimate issue. Twice He referred to that issue in this chapter clearly and distinctly; but there is no detailed description. He was depicting Kingdom processes during one age of Divine procedure. This is not the only age. It will come to consummation; but the work of God will not end with its consummation. There are other methods of God predicted in the Word of God, following the ending of this age are other ages, the Kingdom of the Son, and beyond that the hour when Paul says, "Then cometh the end, when He shall deliver up the Kingdom to God . . . that God may be all and in all." What lies beyond that who shall tell? Paul wrote of the great procession of the ages in those descriptive words of infinite poetry, "the generation of the age of the ages." God is not exhausted in this age He has others to come, the details of which are not revealed, but the fact is declared.

Christ was in no doubt about the happenings of this age. There should be the sowing of the seed, its scattering far and wide.

> "Sow in the morn thy seed,
> At eve hold not thy hand."

Said Christ, That seed will be sown by the Sower, but only a portion will be fruitful. There will be the scattering of seed that bears no fruit. He suffered no delusion. He did not say that the seed being planted, a complete and perfect harvest would result. He saw an enemy scattering amid the seed, darnel. He saw that the age must run on with the development of wheat and darnel, until the consummation of the age. So here He saw the growth, out of life, but abnormal. A herb becomes a great tree, and the fowls of the air lodge in its branches.

What is the bearing of this parable on us? It calls us to a recognition of the facts of the age in which we live. That will save us from the delusion that so often fills the minds of honest souls with despair. We thought it would have been so different, that the Kingdom principles were winning. We thought that was so, with a certain measure of arrogance, at the close of the nineteenth century and on into the twentieth. Then like the crack of doom we found the Kingdom ideal rejected by the philosophers of earth, and the earth bathed in blood, and muck, and war. With reverence again I say, Christ had no such delusions.

Finally if this parable corrects our thinking about this age, and tells us of its true nature, it should have its effect on our individual lives, and on our Church life today. We should see to it that there is nothing in our lives contrary to the genius and spirit of our Lord and Master, and of the Kingdom of God; no loftiness or pride, or seeking for mastery, all contrary to the genius of the Kingdom of God and of the Spirit of Jesus Christ. These false things create a false greatness which He disowns. So surely as that false greatness is there, the unclean birds come in, and lodge in the Church, and in our lives; and the Kingdom is thwarted and hindered. We are not to help in the development of a great tree out of a mustard seed, which is the least of all seeds. We are called upon to have faith as that smallest of seeds, as Jesus elsewhere said. If we have that, then by the power of that faith, which is life, we can help to remove the mountains, and to fling up a highway for the coming of the King into His own Kingdom.

11. The Leavened Meal

Matthew xiii: 33.

THIS is a much disputed parable. Again we have no explanation of it given by the Lord Himself. However, in this case, especially to those who first heard it, there was no need of explanation, listening as they did from the Hebrew standpoint, and with their knowledge of the Hebrew writings, and of the symbolism of Hebrew figures of speech. They understood, undoubtedly, what was intended.

Why then has this become a disputed parable as to its true teaching? While not insisting upon it, I think it has been through medieval misinterpretation of it, in which the interpreters attempted to square the parable with what they thought was the fact concerning the enterprise in the world of the Kingdom of God.

There are two interpretations. The first is that the leaven alone is a type of the Kingdom. When our Lord said, "The Kingdom of heaven is like unto leaven," some stop there in their thinking. If that is done, then we are almost driven to the conclusion that the figure of leaven was used as the type of something good, and therefore that the idea of the parable is that the Kingdom will be completely victorious in this age. That is the view which is almost universally accepted as the interpretation of the parable.

The other interpretation is that not the leaven alone illustrates the Kingdom, but that the whole picture is required, that of leaven hidden by a woman in three measures of meal. If that be the true interpretation, then leaven is the type of evil; a principle which, in the working, harms the Kingdom rather than helps it in this age. Those are the two views.

Although the first is popular, we should guard ourselves against accepting the popular interpretation as being correct. I am deliberately convinced that the latter is the true interpretation; first because the former one contradicts the whole symbolic use of leaven in the Bible. If in this case leaven stands for good, it is the only case in the Bible which any expositor claims that it does so. Again, the former interpretation contradicts the teaching of all the other parables so far considered, in every one of which Jesus, referring to the process of the age, always marked limitation. No parable shows all the facts. Our Lord was illustrating the working of the Kingdom principle in the age which is to be consummated by His own advent, as He Himself did show.

Seeing that all the other parables speak of mixture, if this of the leaven is taken as being good, the whole leavened, then there is no mixture at all. This would then contradict the teaching of all the other parables.

Again, I reject the earlier view, because it is disproved by the history of the centuries; and finally because the method is not in harmony with the method of the other parables. In every parable of Jesus the whole picture is needed to understand His teaching.

If we read this parable, "The Kingdom of heaven is like unto leaven," and stay there, we are violating a principle. Jesus did not stop there. He said, "The Kingdom of heaven is like unto leaven, which a woman took, and hid in three measures of meal, till it was all leavened." It is not so that the Kingdom of heaven is like leaven. It is not the leaven alone that is the illustration of the Kingdom of heaven.

Having then cleared the ground a little, let us turn to an examination of the parable, taking our usual method of looking at the picture suggested, and then deducing the teaching.

As we look at the picture, we must carefully examine the symbolism. There is the essential fact of the picture, and the facts which affect the central fact. What is the central fact? Leaven? No, three measures of meal. What are the facts affecting it? Two, a woman, and leaven.

"Three measures of meal." When Jesus said that, He was not using occasional language, but employing a phrase that had a definite meaning and value to those who heard it. It is often very valuable to find where the phrase first occurs in the Bible, and then to trace it through. To do that in the case of these words, we shall find it used in Genesis, before the time of Moses, before the law was given. It occurs in the eighteenth chapter of Genesis, in a wonderful picture. It was used of the home, which was a tent erected under the oaks at Mamre. Abraham lived there. He had left Ur of Chaldea, and had pitched his tent under the oak trees, or the terebinths as it should be rendered. He was living there. One day there came visitors to him, all of them evidently supernatural. He recognized One of them as supreme, and the other two subservient. I imagine Abraham did not know at the beginning Who this supreme Visitor was. He recognized that He was a supernatural Visitor, and immediately they prepared and offered hospitality. In that connection we are told that Sarah prepared "three measures of meal." What was it? It was a meal of fellowship, of hospitality; a meal in which the supernatural Visitor, Whom Abraham soon found to be God Himself, having angelic form, and human language to communicate with him was to take part; and Abraham spread a meal for Him, "three measures of meal." So the phrase went back to that early time, indicating the preparation of a meal.

Come now to the time of Moses, and see the instructions for the meal offering, one of the offerings of a religious rite. Then later, Gideon, on a memorable occasion, brought to God three measures of meal. Hannah, when worshipping, brought as an offering, three measures of meal. Pass on into the prophetic literature, and Ezekiel at one time, when describing the hour of ritual and worship, used the phrase seven times over to mark a certain fact, "three measures of meal."

Coming back for a moment to the ritual of these Hebrew people, the phrase became well known, "three tenth parts of an ephah," which is the same thing as "three measures of meal," in the meal offering. In the ritual of the Hebrew people, the meal offering followed the burnt offering. The burnt offering was symbolic of the dedication of the lives of these people to God. The meal offering following, always symbolized the dedication of the service of the people, whose lives were dedicated to God. The meal offering was first the result of cultivation, and then manufacture; of careful preparation, and so of their service. Always three measures of meal. So that which we first see in the home yet had upon it that great eternal fact of man's communion with God. As Abraham talked with Jehovah, as Jehovah was represented in the angel Presence, that which commenced there we see was embodied in the sacred ritual of the Hebrew people, as an offering marking dedication to God, also marking fellowship with God.

Remembering the institution of the meal offering, every worshipper retained part, while part was devoted to God. Consequently in that division of the three measures of meal there was indicated the hospitality of the soul to God, and the hospitality of God to the soul. Therefore this phrase that we may read so easily and never really understand, these men as they listened to Jesus, understood that figure in their literature as an interpretation of life. When our Lord spoke of three measures of meal, inevitably their minds would go to the meal offering. The essential thing here is that the Kingdom of heaven is like unto leaven which a woman took and hid in three measures of meal, until the whole was leavened.

Two things are here in the picture of Jesus, first fellowship with God, hospitality between the soul and God; and offering and dedication to God. Go on to the apocalyptic literature, and in those wonderful letters written to the seven Churches, the Head of the Church is standing outside the door of the last of the Churches. He had knocked, seeking admission, and He says, "If any man hear My voice, and open the door, I will come in to him, and will sup with him, and he with Me." I will come in, and be his Guest and at the same time he shall be My guest. That is perfect fellowship. In the symbolism of the Hebrew people all that lies behind the meal offering.

Jesus said, "The Kingdom of heaven is like unto leaven, which a woman took, and hid in three measures of meal, till it was all leavened." A woman, and leaven. The woman represented authority and management in the hospitality of a home. Sarah was doing that work on that first occasion, when Abraham held communion with Jehovah about His Kingship over Sodom; and Sarah had her part in that communion. Without criticising her, she broke down, for she laughed at certain things that were said. Oh, it is better to laugh at God than never to talk to Him; and He will be patient with us, if in our blindness we laugh. I think I have often done it in utter foolishness. Here then a woman represented that communion and that authority. We speak of the Church as a mother. The great Roman system ever speaks of Mother Church. I am not objecting to it. Authority within the realm of hospitality and fellowship is provided in the figure of a woman.

What did the woman do? She hid leaven in the three measures of meal. Now leaven is always symbolic of that which disintegrates, breaks up, corrupts. There was no leaven in Sarah's bread when she prepared three measures of meal. Leaven was strictly forbidden in the meal offering. It was to be excluded therefrom. To turn from those ancient suggestions and symbols to the New Testament, Paul, writing to a Corinthian Church that had become leavened indeed, in that bad sense of the word, and had lost its power of witness because it had been harbouring those corrupting, said this:

"Know ye not that a little leaven leaveneth the whole lump? Purge out the old leaven, that ye may be a new lump, even as ye are unleavened. For our passover also hath been sacrificed, even Christ; wherefore let us keep the feast, not with old leaven, neither with the leaven of malice and wickedness, but with the unleavened bread of sincerity and truth."

Or again, in the Galatian letter, he said the same thing in another connection. "A little leaveneth the whole lump." Leaven is always disintegrating. To interpret the parable of Jesus by the common practices of the day, yeast, however used, is a disintegrating force, and in the end it always separates and destroys. That is of its very essence and nature. Leaven always disintegrates.

Jesus said, "The Kingdom of heaven is like unto leaven, which a woman took, and hid in three measures of meal, till it was all leavened." The Kingdom of heaven is likened to that which happens when something is introduced which makes fellowship on the highest level impossible, because it has a corrupting influence: leaven swells, and puffs up. The Bible is a wonderful literature. So many things that seem to be miles apart belong to each other. What was it that stilled the complaint of the soul of the prophet Habakkuk, and made him sing his great song at last, after all his trouble? The announcement by God of a principle of life. Speaking of Cyrus the enemy, and the proud oncoming armies that God was using, under His control, He said, "Behold, his soul is puffed up," that is, swollen; "it is not upright in him but the just shall live by his faith." Take that picture of evil, of pride and crookedness, acting like leaven, until men of a nation become puffed up, swollen. Jesus said that would happen to the working of His Kingdom in this age, that there should be the hiding of leaven in the three measures of meal, until the whole was leavened.

Turning from that attempt to understand the figures of speech, and to gather up its teaching, take the three measures of meal, representing the feast of hospitality and fellowship between God and men. If the Kingdom testimony in the world is to be powerful, it must be based upon the fellowship of the people of God with Him in incorruptness. That needs no argument. We all agree to it. The measure in which our fellowship with God fails to be maintained in incorruptness, freedom from disintegrating forces that destroy it, is the measure in which we fail to bear a Kingdom testimony, or are of value in the world.

Go back once more to Abraham and Lot. Look at the difference between them. Lot was a good man. The New Testament tells us that he was "a righteous man." But he first pitched his tent towards Sodom. Then he went to live in Sodom. Finally he became so identified with Sodom that he lost all his influence. When the crisis came there were not five men in the city whom he had influenced towards righteousness and God. Abraham stood under the terebinths in fellowship with God, and he was able to exert that influence that nearly saved Sodom. So come on down the ages, and see the influence working for the incoming of the Kingdom of God.

We learn then that testimony to the Kingdom is weakened in the measure in which the Church in her management has ever permitted the intrusion of the things which disintegrate, and so mar her testimony to the Kingdom of God. Listen to the Lord Himself upon other occasions. "Beware of the leaven of the Pharisees and Sadducees." Or as Mark records it, "Beware of the leaven of the Pharisees and Herod." Or as Luke has it, "Beware of the leaven of the Pharisees which is hypocrisy." Pass on to Paul, and remember the context in Corinthians. He was dealing with the fact that the Church was tolerating within her own borders an incestuous person, guilty of immorality. The Church was unable to deal with that person. Purge yourself from the leaven, said Paul. Or in the word quoted from Galatians, the context shows that Judaizing teachers were attempting to graft on to the Christian movement a ritual that had no force and value; and so were placing a burden upon believers that they never ought to bear, the leaven of legalism within the Church. Take that little group of Scriptures, and read them, and think the matter out.

What is the leaven intermixed, which has weakened the testimony of the Church to the Kingdom of God? The leaven of hypocrisy, the leaven of rationalism, that showed in the Sadducean questioning of the supernatural, for they did not believe in angel, spirit, or resurrection. The leaven of materialism, was embodied in Herod, who sought for power and greatness upon the basis of material things; "the leaven of Herod." The leaven of the toleration of evil, the failure to exercise a high discipline to keep the Church clean and pure; and the terrible leaven of mere formalism, content with rite and ceremonial, devoid of power. Jesus said, The whole will be leavened. It does not mean that the whole will become leaven, but the influence of leaven hidden in the measures of meal, that illustrate fellowship, will permeate the whole movement.

Here then in the four first parables of Jesus, He saw the Kingdom influence in the age. First the seed, the fact of the giving of opportunity. Secondly, the good seed planted in the world's field, similar in intention to the first. Thirdly the mustard seed that grew abnormally until it became a great tree. Finally the meal into which is introduced the principle of disintegration, breaking in upon the fellowship of man with God. Take these four and notice how in every case He marked the fact of comparative failure in the age, the failure of the seed, only one quarter of it fruitful, three parts of it scattered, and not fruitful at all. Side by side with the work of the Son of man sowing in His field, the world, with His wheat, He saw an enemy sowing the imitation, the darnel. False development into a great tree, magnificent in appearance, a lodging place for the fowls of the air. Then the degeneration in power, breaking in upon fellowship, and so marring the witness of men and women to the Kingdom of God.

To use a phrase employed in our previous study. Whatever we may think of the process of affairs in this age, Christ was under no delusion. He looked on, and saw exactly what has happened. Everything has happened, and is happening according to His teaching. There are other aspects which succeeding parables will unfold. Those to which we come next were spoken to the disciples alone. To cover the whole ground of the two groups of four, the first four were spoken to men of sight, to the disciples and to the crowd; the second four were spoken to men of faith, and were spoken to the disciples only.

12. The Treasure Hidden

Matthew xiii. 44.

THE PARABLE contained in this verse is the first of those spoken to the disciples alone. In verse 36 we read, "Then He left the multitudes, and went into the house." Then the disciples asked Him to explain the parable of the darnel. He did so, and then uttered four more parables to them privately.

These four also deal with the Kingdom in this age. Our Lord was surveying an age which began with His own coming and ministry, and will conclude, as He taught in two of the parables, with the consummation of the age. These parables then have to do with this age in which we are living. In the economy of God other ages stretch out beyond.

It should be borne in mind that the viewpoint is changed in the four parables now to be considered. Having spoken to men of sight, Jesus now spoke to men of faith. That necessarily creates a difference in outlook. He had spoken to men of sight, and therefore had dwelt upon aspects of the Kingdom which would be patent to such and self-evident as the age unfolded. He had foreshadowed that there would be the sowing of seed, with different results, dependent upon the quality of the seed. In the next He had shown how during this age, side by side with the sowing of the good seed, there would be the work of an enemy sowing darnel, imitations of the good seed. He had shown then how during this period there would be unnatural development of a mustard seed to a great tree. Finally He had shown how during the age there would be a process of degeneration in the Kingdom under the figure of the leavened meal. Look back over the age from the word of our Lord while here until this time, and it will be seen how all the things that He foretold have been manifest. The seed has been sown with differing results. The enemy has been sowing the darnel, perplexing even the elect. The Church has been cursed by organisations that have been harboured in her very life, and there has been a breaking down of her testimony, making her fellowship ineffective, and her testimony to men equally ineffective.

Now the Lord spoke to His disciples, to those men of faith who already believed in Him, who would go out to live on the principle of faith, even though everything appeared to be against them. He now gave them four parables, and these have to do with the age, revealing the Divine thought and method, and purpose in it. These are not patent to sight. They constitute the secrets of God, but they are revealed to men of faith, knowing which, and understanding which, they will be strengthened and heartened and equipped for all their service. That is the character of the four parables to which we now come, the first of which we survey in this chapter.

To summarize briefly on the four. In the first He showed the purpose of God for the whole world, "He buyeth the field." In the second, in many ways the most wonderful of them all, He showed the relation to other ages and other spheres of what is now being done, as the pearl is being purchased. The third declared the method of the age in the economy of God, a great drag-net flung out into the sea, enclosing all manner of fish. The last showed the responsibility of those who are His scribes in the new Kingdom.

Turn now to the first. We follow our custom of attempting to see the picture, and then deduce the teaching.

There are parts of this picture with which we are familiar. Our Lord had already used two figures in the earlier parables, which He explained. So there is no difficulty about them. First, "the field," "The Kingdom of heaven is like unto treasure hidden in the field." We have seen that "the field is the world."

Then, again, a man buys the field. We have seen that the man is the Son of man, so named in the earlier parables. Here then is a picture of the world, and the relation of Christ to it. Those two facts of the general picture are quite clear, because of previous explanation.

Then two new ideas are introduced here, treasure, and purchase at cost. The man is seen discovering treasure in the field, as selling all that he had in order to buy that field, and secure that treasure. The treasure is there, but it is hidden. Someone finds it, knows it is there, and realises it. Others do not know it is there. Then in order to possess that treasure this man sells everything that he has to buy that field.

That brief statement of what the picture presents will enable us to begin our study, as it relieves us from speculation on two points, the field, and the Man; and leaves us free to discuss the two new figures in relation to the other two.

What is the relation of this treasure to the whole world? "The field is the world." He sees that treasure in that field, He has discovered it. What was the treasure that He saw, as He looked out upon the world? Unquestionably it was the Kingdom of God hidden in the world, the Divine government, in its principles, its order, and its exceeding beauty. It is a remarkable thing that we are told that this was hidden in the field. He saw the world as made for the display of the glory of God. He saw the vicegerent of the world in rebellion against God, and therefore unable to realise the possibilities of the cosmos. He saw the whole territory waste and void, as the result of misgovernment; but the potentialities were there, and He saw in the world what has well been described as "imprisoned splendour."

I am using the word "world" in the fullest sense, as when our Lord used it, according to Mark and said we were to go out into all the cosmos, the whole order of the material, mental, and spiritual; the cosmic order which had been broken in upon and destroyed. But our Lord saw the possibilities of this world; and His work in life was that of exhibiting those hidden splendours and glories in strange and unexpected ways, and declaring all the time the glory of the Kingdom of God. How the glory of the world is constantly revealed to us. Flowers? Yes, He said God clothed them. Birds? Yes, God takes care of them, and feeds them, and is with them when they die. Children? Their angels do always behold the face of the Father. Men? The highest thing man can do is to seek the Kingdom of God. "Imprisoned splendour," He saw it everywhere. He looked and saw the treasure hidden in a ruined world.

What did He do? He purchased it, and when He purchased it, He hid it. That is the point of mystery, the point at which we must halt. We wonder what it means. It was hidden. He brought it into visibility, and hid it. In the world order we have a revelation of the ultimate, the Kingdom ministry of Jesus while here in the world; not the ultimate limit of it, but the ultimate of it during His own mission. He came to discover and to reveal it. The eyes that could see this splendour that was imprisoned, He made it flash and flame forth. There were those who saw, and gathered round about it. But it was rejected, and He rejected the nation that had been the depository of the Kingdom of God in the solemn words recorded by Matthew, "The Kingdom of God shall be taken away from you, and shall be given to a nation bringing forth the fruits thereof." He postponed the full manifestation to a future age when the Son of man should come in His glory, and the holy angels with Him.

He then turned His face to a larger work, apart from which the splendours hidden could never come to full and final realization. All that is expressed in that simple sentence, "He sold all that He hath, and buyeth that field." Everything is there. It is a complete revelation of the ultimate in the work of Jesus in the world, and for the world. Notice how it begins. "In His joy, He goeth and selleth all that He hath." We interpret that as imprisoned splendour, hidden glories that are not manifest. He revealed them in measure, and yet they were not seen by the vast masses. They were hidden, and yet in His joy He was going to do something that should make possible the realisation of the ultimate meaning of that great cosmic order in the Kingdom of God. "In His joy."

Tarry there for a moment. What He did we will also look at. What was the joy of Jesus? In the great prophetic word uttered concerning Him long before He came, and perfectly fulfilled in all the story of His life, it was written:

> "Lo, . . . in the volume of the book it is written of Me;
> I delight to do Thy will, O My God."

"I delight." The joy of His heart was the will of God. He knew its goodness. He knew its acceptability. He knew its perfection. He knew that within that will of God the wilderness would blossom as the rose, and the desert become as pools of glorious, fertilizing water. He knew, and the joy that filled Him was the contemplation of the realization of the will of God in the world. That was the joy that was set before Him. To quote once more from the Hebrew letter, "Who for the joy that was set before Him, endured the Cross, despising the shame." What was the joy set before Him? God forgive us, we have often been so narrow in interpreting it. Was it the joy of going back to God, and to love and rest and peace with God that filled Him? The joy was the joy of the certainty that at last, as Browning has it,

> "Though a wide compass round be fetched;
> That what began best, can't end worst,
> Nor what God blessed once, prove accurst."

The joy of the Lord was His strength. The joy of the Lord was the delight of His will. The joy of the Lord was the secret power that enabled Him to endure the Cross.

In the parable He has told us what He did. "He selleth all that He hath." Where shall we find an adequate commentary on that? "He emptied Himself," sold all that He had. Silence is the best commentary possible in pondering that. Fill the gap with thinking; "all that He hath." And mark, that was His estimate of the worth of the treasure that He saw hidden in the field of the world. That includes everything in the cosmos, everything in the earthly order, all life as it is, and as it passes, and as it will be; but supremely man, and the infinite and glorious possibilities of humanity, in which He saw this imprisoned splendour. His estimate of its worth, who shall put on it a measure? Think of all that He had, and all that "He selleth." What for? To buy the field, the world, the whole creation. He redeemed it that it might be held waiting for the time of perfect realization of His ultimate purpose, and that it might be claimed ultimately, and filled with the glory of God. The whole earth is filled with the Divine glory. The prophet said there should come a time when all flesh should see it together. In order that that might be so, He purchased the world.

It is important to remember that the word "buyeth" must not be interpreted here commercially. That word "buyeth" may be used in other senses, where there is no commercial transaction. There has been a good deal of expository controversy over this. There are not wanting old and devout expositors who say that He bought the world back from Satan. Never! He never recognized the right of Satan to this world at all. That is what Satan wanted Him to do, and he offered it to Him at a very cheap price comparatively, when he said, Give me a moment's homage, and the kingdoms shall all be Thine. But He never recognized the right of Satan anywhere. He was not buying it from Satan.

Then equally devout expositors say He was purchasing it from God. But that is to divide God, and God is not divided. He was God, He was God in Christ reconciling the world to Himself. It was God in Christ Who purchased. Often the word is used in another way. A man says he will sell his life dearly. It does not mean he is going to offer it at a price. He is going to suffer in order to hold it. A mother will purchase the health of her child by long vigils. She is not paying the price to anyone. He purchased the field, which simply emphasizes the giving up of all things in the richest sense of that word.

Stand back then from this picture, given to the disciples. It was not given to the men of the world. The outside crowd did not understand it any more than some today can understand. It can be understood only by men of living faith, faith in the unseen, believing in the reality of the unseen, and seeing things from that viewpoint. The man of faith in this age will be conscious of all that the man of sight sees, of everything that is named in those first four parables. Men of faith see all the facts of the case as Jesus saw them, with such clarity as those saw when He uttered these parables. Jesus was not deceived. He suffered from no delusion. He knew the delusion that so often has fallen upon the Christian Church, and holds many of those dear and loved members in thrall today in the view that we are to go on preaching the Gospel until all the world is converted. That will not be. He saw the facts, and nineteen hundred years bear witness to the accuracy of His outlook. The men of faith can see that which is not seen by the men of sight; but what the man of faith sees will never make him hopeless, because he also has this parable, and the one following.

Once more, this parable is not final. Nothing here is said of future ages and methods of God in the history of the world. But it does say enough to steady the heart, and strengthen endeavour in the midst of our service.

This parable then first reveals Christ's estimate of the possibility of the world, treasure hidden, but treasure still. The glory of everything in the government of God, in the Kingdom of heaven, the Kingdom of the rule of God, He saw it, the possibility. If we do not see that possibility, what wonder that we lose heart, that our hands hang down, and our knees become feeble, and we cease our efforts. He saw that possibility.

But He saw more, that there was only one way of possessing that treasure, of bringing at last into full and final manifestation and glory; and that was the way of complete self-denial. "He selleth all that He hath." He held back nothing. As a good friend of mine said one Christmas morning, speaking of the love of God, that we do not distinguish between the love of God and the love of Christ, and that in order to rescue the race, "He pauperized heaven for a season." That may be a superlative way of putting it, but it pays for close investigation, having an element of truth. He pauperized Himself.

Yet is there not behind it the warrant of inspired writing? "Who though He was rich, yet for our sakes He became poor." Never forget that whatever the price, true it is that,

> "None of the ransomed ever knew,
>   How deep were the waters crossed,
> Nor how dark was the night that the Lord passed through
>   Ere He found the sheep that was lost."

The price was beyond all our computation. "Not with silver and gold" —that is commercialism—"but with the precious blood of Christ, as a Lamb, without spot." That is the mystery of the Deity in agony. Do not forget, although the price was paid, although it was as great as that, He procured the world. He bought the field. It became His property. It is His property now.

The parable does not end all the story. It does not tell of other processes through which the world will pass but it does tell the Hand that holds the fee simple to the world, and it is the pierced Hand of Jesus. He bought the whole world, and that in itself is a guarantee of the ultimate realization of all the glory hidden and imprisoned.

·The human heart may be inclined to say, Why hide it? Why hinder

it? The necessary Why to the making of any such enquiry be the fact
He did so proves it was necessary, and proves it was right. It takes
ages to grow an oak tree. A ladder can be made in a day. God's way
appears the slow way, but He is growing the ultimate harvest of the
world. May we get His vision, so we shall be prepared to render our
service.

13. The Pearl

Matthew xiii: 45, 46.

SOME figures of this parable have appeared, those of treasure, and of
treasure sought and bought but there are certain new emphases.
The man here presented is a merchantman, who is seeking for the
possession of something by purchase. The treasure referred to by our
Lord is of a peculiar kind—a pearl. The merchantman was seeking
pearls, and he found one pearl of great price. The new emphases then
are the merchantman seeking for the possession of something by
purchase, that something being a pearl, and that of great price.

To understand this parable we need to examine carefully these
emphases, the merchantman and the pearl. That which is central is the
pearl itself. We must be set free from the bondage of popular and
traditional views in interpretation. It does not follow that what is
popular is wrong, or that what is traditional is false. However it may
be so in both cases.

The general interpretation of this parable is that our Lord was
teaching that He is the pearl of great price, and that the sinner is the
one who seeks, and purchases, and possesses his Lord. Indeed, that
interpretation has found expression in a hymn, not often heard now.

> "I've found the Pearl of greatest price,
>   My heart doth sing for joy;
>   And sing I must, for Christ I have—
>   Oh, what a Christ have I!"

It was very beautiful, but quite untrue to the teaching of this parable.
To put it bluntly at the beginning, this is not a picture of the sinner
seeking Christ. It is Christ seeking His Church. That covers the
ground, and may carry at first little conviction perhaps.

To begin then with this figure of the pearl. It is arresting to
remember that the pearl was not counted precious by the Hebrews.

They set no particular value upon it. The pearl is never mentioned in the Old Testament. Other stones are named and described by that marvellous phrase "stones of fire," but the pearl is not referred to. In the book of Job there is an interesting and wonderful passage in which he asked what was the price of wisdom, and named certain things by which wisdom cannot be bought. He named precious stones, and in the margin of the Revised Version we find, when Job referred to "crystal," the revisers have inserted in the margin, "or pearl." Even marginal readings are not inspired. The Hebrew word there is figurative, and means something frozen, and the word "crystal" far better interprets it than "pearl." Thus the pearl had no significance to the Hebrews, and there was no reference to it.

When these Hebrew disciples listened to Jesus when He uttered this parable, I think they opened their eyes in surprise. A pearl! A merchantman seeking pearls! Nobody was particularly seeking pearls. Moreover, He made reference to the pearl as of "great price." Let it be admitted that among other peoples than the Hebrews there was a recognition of the value of pearls, and it is an interesting subject to trace. There was a growing sense of their value. Recent investigations have shown that in the regalia of kings which consisted largely of gold, inset with gems, actually pearls were found. In Nineveh pearls were very highly valued, more so than in other countries.

Today the pearl has become associated with the most precious things, and is of real value. In this parable then of the pearl, as the King revealed secret things to men of faith, whatever His intention was, He turned to something which these people did not consider of value, and He laid tremendous emphasis upon its value.

What are the facts about real pearls? They are the products of a living organism. That is not true of any other precious stone, either of the sapphire, or the diamond, the ruby, the emerald, or any other.

How is it produced? The pearl is the result of an injury done to a living organism. A grain of sand gets within the shell of the oyster, and injury is done to it. That which it injures covers it over with the nacre, layer over layer, until the pearl is formed. Ethel Thorneycroft Fowler wrote these lines some years ago:

> "A pearl is found beneath the flowing tide,
>   And there is held a worse than worthless thing,
>   Spoiling the shell-built home where it doth cling—
>   Marring the life near which it must abide."

That is the history of the pearl. A living organism, injured by contact with a grain of sand, or something equally minute and the living organism answers the injury done with a pearl. So comes the precious thing.

Again, it is a thing of priceless value and of great beauty, and is peculiarly an adornment. There is no real value in the pearl except embellishment, the adding of something to the one who possesses it, or the one who wears it. The very word translated "pearl" is derived from a Sanscrit word which means pure. Every woman who bears the name of Margaret or Margarita, that is the meaning of the name. The pearl stands today in our thinking suggestive of purity. If that be so, the pearl is a symbol of purity resulting from wounding, which has been enclosed in that which has made it a thing of beauty, and a symbol of purity.

Our Lord never used an illustration without complete understanding of all its height and length and breadth and depth; and when He said "a pearl," He knew whence the pearl came, and how the pearl was formed. He knew its real value. That is the first emphasis which arrests us. There is something different here from anything we have seen, nothing that contradicts, but something different.

Then again, in the merchantman we see a man seeking goodly pearls. It is unthinkable that the man seeking pearls is seeking them merely for himself. Pearls in so far as their value was known then, were specifically and particularly for the adornment of kings. The man who was seeking them was seeking in order to provide that embellishment, that symbol of glory, for other than himself. The merchantman was seeking for pearls, not to hoard them, or to possess them, but for some other. Whether this man was purchasing and selling them does not come within our purview. Jesus said he sought for goodly pearls, and he found one of priceless worth. It was a most wonderful victory. A pearl of resplendent beauty is referred to, and in order to possess it, he went and sold everything he had.

Turning from that attempt to look at the picture in itself, we ask its interpretation. Here it is possible that some may be introduced to a line of thought and consideration which is new. We need not argue who the man is. He is the One Who has been named in other places as the Son of man but here He is seen as a merchantman.

What is He doing? He is seeking pearls, and He finds one. Finding means here, He perceives, He discovers, and He obtains. Our Lord is showing what was His mission in the world. This is a parable viewed from the standpoint of heaven's outlook and interpretation. Nothing here contradicts what we have seen of the application to the Kingdom principle, illustrated in the other parables. We are looking from the heavenly height, and we see this merchantman seeking, and seeing what He finds, and seeing how to obtain what He finds. Notice our Lord says, "Having found one pearl of great price, he went and sold all that he had." Went where? Went from the place where He was. Where was that? Heaven. That does not mean He left earth, and went away to purchase it, but He came to earth. The parable is viewing things from the heavenly standard. He has seen the pearl. He knows it, and desires to possess it, and He went to earth, and sold all that He had. It is a picture of the purchase of the Church of God, the whole Church.

All kinds of questions arise, distinguishing between the Church and the Kingdom of God. There is a clear distinction, and in the ages that lie ahead there will be many who are ransomed who are not members of the great, mystical Church of Christ. But the view here is that of the Church. He went and found a pearl. With great reverence we may say He went, and by His action created the pearl. The pearl fastened upon Him, injured Him, harmed Him; and by His action He surrendered all that which wrought Him wrong, and harmed Him, until it, by transmutation, became the very costly pearl for which He was seeking. "He sold all that he had."

With reverence take the picture of the pearl, and the process of its making, that action of a living organism that surrounds the tormented and unperceived thing with mother-of-pearl, with nacre, until presently the pearl is formed. When Peter wrote his letter he said, "Unto Whom coming, a living stone, rejected indeed of men, but with God elect, precious." After that he said this, "For you therefore which believe is the preciousness." In the Authorised Version it reads, "Unto you that believe He is precious." That is a beautiful statement and thought, one of absolute truth. Is He not precious to us? But that is not what the apostle meant. It is not what he wrote. "Unto you . . . is the preciousness." The Stone which the builders rejected, the same was made the Head of the corner and all that constitutes the good pleasure of God in Christ, "My Son, in Whom I am well pleased." The things in Christ that were precious to God, they are all made over to us. "Unto you that believe is the preciousness." But who am I, who are you? We are the people who put Him on His Cross, who wronged Him, the glorious One, who caused His suffering and His pain; and in an infinite mystery of power and grace, greater than the mystery and the wonder of the creating of the pearl in the oyster shell, He covered us over, and changed the thing of injury to the wanted thing, into a pearl of great price.

So the whole Church is seen as the most wonderful and precious thing, resulting from the mission of the Son of man. The Kingdom is here, but also a gathered-out company constituting at last His Church.

The parable does not tell us anything about the purpose. The picture is of what is going on in this age, the finding and the purchasing of this sacred thing. We are warranted however in deducing from it something more. What was the purpose of this purchase? Roughly and commercially, what was the value of that pearl, to obtain which He sold all that He had in order to buy it? We cannot answer that fully in the terms of time, or in the terms of individual and personal experience. We cannot answer that fully in the terms of any one Church, or the Church at any given period in this age. We can answer it fully only when there is given to us to see the ultimate glory of the Church, and her ultimate vocation.

We have never seen the Church of God. Churches, yes we have a conception of the universal Church, the holy, catholic Church as we call it; but we have never yet seen it. It is a sorry thing that Christian men, leaders quarrel among themselves. The day will come when we shall see that our quarrels have been concerned with scaffolding, but behind the scaffolding the Church is growing to a holy temple in the Lord. If we would find the final interpretation in the New Testament of the value of the pearl He bought, of the value of the Church to God, we shall have to turn to one great letter, that to the Ephesians. In that Paul reached the culminating glory of his great theological system. That system began with the Roman letter, of which the one theme is salvation. Then there came to him the mystery of the Church, and by stages he interpreted it. The ultimate glory is found in the twin epistles of Ephesians and Colossians. Colossians is concerned with the glories of Christ. Ephesians is concerned with the glories of the Church as she embodies and reveals the glories of Christ.

Glance at two passages in the Ephesian letter. In the first chapter Paul made use of a remarkable phrase. He prayed that these Ephesian Christians and all others, might know Him, have full knowledge, *epignosis*, "What are the riches of the glory of His inheritance in the saints." It is a daring thought, a tremendous thing. It lifts all our thinking about our holy religion from the commonplace of today and the littleness of our activities here, however true they may be, when we see that God gains something in His Church; that when Jesus sold all that He had to buy that pearl to flash in splendour upon the bosom of Deity, God was enriched. He is enriched not in essential glory, but by finding a medium through which that essential glory can be revealed.

Go on in the Ephesian letter to the fifth chapter. "Christ also loved the Church, and gave Himself up for it, that He might sanctify it, having cleansed it by the washing of water with the Word, that He might present the Church to Himself, a glorious Church, not having spot or wrinkle or any such thing; but that it should be holy and without blemish." The intrusive wounding sand is transmuted into the beauty of a pearl, and that for the honour of God.

In the Ephesian letter there are two statements in which Paul tells what is the ultimate vocation of the Church. It is not earthly at all. She has her vocation here, and her responsibility in the world, which in our measure we are all attempting to fulfil. But the ultimate meaning of the Church is not for time, it is for eternity. It is not for earth, but for heaven, the place where all the company of the ransomed and redeemed will fulfil a sacred mission. Paul has told us two things about that mission. In the ages to come we shall teach angels; and through us there will be manifested the grace and the glory of God. The Church's vocation is that she will be the revealer of the infinite grace of God to all the ages, and to all the unfallen intelligences, the pearl of great price.

> "He found the pearl of greatest price,
>   My heart doth sing for joy;
> And sing I must, for I am His,
>   And He is mine for aye",

It is our business to look for the Kingdom here, to pray for it, to toil for it, to hope and expect its coming in fulness but do not forget that beyond the little spell of earth's limited history there lie the ages, and in those ages the ransomed Church of God will be the pearl through which His grace and His glory are to be manifested.

14. The Drag-Net

Matthew xiii: 47-50.

THE PARABLE of the drag-net is the last concerning the process of the Kingdom in this age. These systematic parables of our Lord found in the thirteenth chapter of Matthew have to do with one age that began with His first advent and ministry, and which will end with His second advent. The dealings of God are not exhausted in any one age in which man is living. These parables however all concern this age, and illustrate the process of the Kingdom.

This particular parable is still an illustration for men of faith.

Retiring from the crowd, and the public, He gave certain parables that illustrated for these men of faith the Kingdom processes, no longer on the level of earthly observation or understanding, but from the level of heavenly purpose and intention. Such was the parable of the treasure in the field, and that of the pearl. Such is this parable of the drag-net.

In our study of this parable of Jesus we are greatly aided by our Lord's partial explanation. That begins with the word "so" (verse 49), "So shall it be in the consummation of the age." Let it be understood at once that our Lord's explanation of this parable is only partial, having to do with the final fact in the picture used, not with the casting of the net, nor even with the swaying of that net in the tides; but with the drawing of it in at the close. "The consummation of the age" is the key to what our Lord emphasized concerning this parable.

This is in itself significant, and enables us to place the emphasis of the parable in the right place. The net and its swaying to the moving tides are simply illustrations of the fact not here and now interpreted. But that which is interpreted, and therefore that upon which we must fix our attention, is our Lord's description of what will happen presently, in what He speaks of as "the consummation of the age." It is the parable therefore of all these which supremely shows the method of the completion of this age, in which the Sower sows the Word.

The main value here is that of the fact of separation which follows the drawing in of the net at the end of the age. Recognition of that fact will save us from wrong conceptions concerning this teaching. "The Kingdom of heaven is like unto a drag-net." In the Revised Version the word is "a net," but the marginal reading gives the literal translation of the Greek word, which explains its meaning, "a drag-net."

Again, those fishermen listening to Him understood perfectly what He was talking about. That was one method of fishing. It had nothing to do with individual fishing. Here is no picture, such as Ezekiel gave, of fishermen standing on the banks of the river from Engedi to Eneglaim. That is individual gathering in. This was not the idea in the mind of our blessed Lord when He said to His disciples, "I will make you to become fishers of men"; and on another occasion, You shall catch men alive. That marks individual life. This is something other.

The fact is so simple that we need not dwell upon it. It is the picture of a great net that is let down into the sea, and is left, and it swings to the moving of the waters, and there are gathered into it fishes of all sorts, all kinds. Then towards the close of day, or early morning more often, the fishermen draw the net in, and as it comes in it enclosed a vast multitude of fishes. Some of them are of no use. Others are valuable. The fishermen are seen settled down on the shore, and their first business is to sort and sift, to take out the valueless, the worthless, and leave in the good, gathering them together, after the worthless have been cast aside.

Said our Lord, The Kingdom of heaven is like that in its consummation. The Kingdom of heaven is like a net let down into the sea; and at the end of the age, the consummation of the age, there will come the drawing in of the net, and separation.

The net here unquestionably stands for the Kingdom influence which is abroad in the world; and those enclosed are such as have come within the sphere of the Kingdom influence. There are parts of the world where there are multitudes who have never come within that sphere. The parable does not apply to such. Wherever the net has been spread, and wherever men and women have come under its influence, there the net is seen in the sea, that sea which is for evermore the type in Holy Scripture of restless, moving humanity. Something is let down into it. It is the message of the Kingdom, the fact of the Kingdom, the vision of the Kingdom, the ideals of the Kingdom, the teaching of the Kingdom. Remember, the Church is only in view here, in so far as its responsibility is concerned. It is not a question of finding a pearl, whose sacred function lies not in time, but in eternity. That was our previous subject. The Church in the world reveals the Kingdom, in herself, and is the instrument in the world of the influence of that Kingdom.

Think of the age in the broadest way, and of the fact that the Church has been in existence for 1900 years and more. Wherever she has been, men have seen something of the glory, beauty, and holiness, and strength and majesty, and mercy and tenderness of the Kinship of God. Do not forget that has been so. Wherever that has been so the Kingdom influence has been felt. All sorts of reforms in human life, in affairs political, and affairs economic, are the result of the exercise of this Kingdom influence; and the Kingdom influence has been exerted by the Church of God. So the Church is here, but it is not the picture of the gathering out of the Church. It is the picture of something else. The race is not all here, only those parts of it where this Kingdom influence has reached, and only those are seen who by its influence have been in some measure, enclosed within the net.

The process is then described, the process at the end, for that is the emphasis; what will happen as the result of the net being flung into the sea, left, enclosing all the while men, women—fishes. Jesus says, when it is filled, it is drawn in, and men gather the good into vessels, and the bad they cast away. So shall it be at the consummation of the age. "The angels shall come forth and sever the wicked from among the righteous; and shall cast them into the furnace of fire; there shall be the weeping and gnashing of teeth." In the 41st verse we get a similar picture of the consummation of the age, "The Son of man shall send forth His angels." "Angels shall come forth." That is what He now said. In the sixteenth chapter, on that memorable occasion at Cæsarea Philippi, our Lord said, "The Son of man shall come in the glory of His Father with His angels; and then shall He render to every man according to his deeds." So the process will be that of separation.

Notice in this parable our Lord did not speak of the taking out of the world the good, but the taking away of the bad. The picture is wholly of this world. Heaven is not in view. The ultimate and eternal state is not referred to. It is an earthly situation at which we are particularly looking. The picture is wholly of this world, and the Kingdom, and its influence here.

What happens? The severance of the wicked that they may be destroyed from all human affairs. The words of our Lord are full of terrible solemnity. We have no more right to forget or neglect this word of Jesus than we have to forget or neglect that He said to humanity, "Come unto Me, and I will give you rest." There was the infinite wooing tenderness of Christ, but He never failed to see the ultimate issue of sin and of evil. His words are characterized by terrible solemnity. There shall be weeping, lamentation, and gnashing of teeth, a figure at once of pain or rage, or both. Persistent rebellion to the end of the age, a separation between good and bad, drawn all into that Kingdom net, all having come within its meshes, and felt its influence; and yet some utterly worthless, utterly bad; and the consummation of the age has this as its outcome with regard to Kingdom influence in the world, a separation.

Notice that angels are to be the agents. We are living in a strange age. It is terrible how even godly people have become Sadducean about angels, and try to escape the clear declaration that at the end of the age angels will once more intervene in human affairs. They have interfered in human history and affairs in the past. This is not the age of the angels. It is the age of the Son. It is the age of the Holy Spirit. But Jesus said when this age is drawing to a close, angels will again actually, positively intervene in human affairs. Angels are serving today, but unseen and unknown very largely, but none the less definitely. We nave our Bibles, and believe it. "Are they not all worship-

ping spirits sent forth to minister to the heirs of salvation?" It is
rendered, "Are they not all ministering spirits?" but the word "ministering" is different in the two places, "sent forth to minister." They
are liturgical spirits, worshipping spirits. That is the function of the
angels, worshipping in the presence of the Most High; but they are
sent forth, their worship in the high places ceasing, to serve, to wait
upon, to minister to the heirs of salvation.

Go back into the Old Testament, and study the sixth chapter of
Isaiah, where the prophet saw the glory of God, and the thresholds
shook, and the house was filled with smoke. He saw the seraphim
veiling their faces as they continually celebrated the holiness of God.
"Holy, holy, holy is the Lord of hosts." Liturgical spirits.

> "He maketh His angels spirits,
>   And His ministers a flame of fire,"

and there they exercise the highest function of their being, worshipping. When the prophet saw that he cried, "Woe is me! for I am
undone; because I am a man of unclean lips, and I dwell in the midst
of a people of unclean lips; for mine eyes have seen the King, the
Lord of hosts. Then flew one of the seraphim unto me, having a live
coal in his hand, which he had taken with the tongs from off the
altar; and he touched my mouth with it, and said, Lo, this hath touched
thy lips, and thine iniquity is taken away, and thy sin purged." Liturgical spirits, their high function, the worship of God; but if, peradventure, some soul cries out in the agony of conscious sin, they become
ministers of God.

We used to sing in old days, "There are angels hovering round."
We do not often sing it now, but it is true. They are not seen. They
do not come on to the plane of observation, but Christ distinctly said
in that word at Cæsarea Philippi, and on these two occasions in these
parables, that at the end of the age the angels will actually come into
human affairs, to carry out His will, and His behests. They have been
visible. They will be again. There are strange and wonderful pictures
of angels, some of them full of suggestive beauty in art. One great
picture, the title of which was, "He was despised and rejected," was
exhibited in London some years ago. It was wonderful, though the
figure of the Christ did not satisfy me. The crowd surging round Him
was typical humanity, but the most wonderful thing to me was the
background, the august and awful figure of an angel watching. Jesus
said when this age comes to its consummation, the Son of man will
send forth His angels. They will deal with this enclosed mass of fish,
and will sort and sift it. Angel discrimination means heaven's standards.

Angel separation means heaven's might at work, insisting upon the standards, and bringing everything to its measurement, at the end of the age.

We often lose sight of this. Even the Church of God is so possessed oftentimes with the activities of the present. Action in the present loses half its significance, power, and value if we lose sight of the fact of the end of the age, and the issue of it.

What is the issue? This our parable does not declare. For purposes of understanding we may refer to the King's previous and fuller statement, in verses 41-43, where we have exactly the same figure of the consummation of the age, and the angels are seen.

In this parable our Lord spoke of what would be done with the things found in that gathered-in net. In the previous parable He went beyond that, and showed what would happen to others, when the angels have wrought their great work of separation. To put those two together, at the end of this age what will happen under angel intervention and ministry? First the cleansing of the Kingdom from all things that cause stumbling, and all that do iniquity,—activities and persons. Think what would happen today, if suddenly all the affairs of the world were halted by the visitation of angel ministers, acting by the order of the King, and they began to deal with everything that caused stumbling to humanity, casting out all those who were workers of iniquity, the bringing of limitation and sorrow to such, not the limitation of sorrow that has in it the element of repentance, but the element of remorse, as witness the gnashing of teeth. Evil persistence to the very end is to be dealt with, gathered up, and cast out by angel ministry.

What our Lord did not say in this parable, but did say in the previous one was, "Then shall the righteous shine forth as the sun in the Kingdom of their Father." That is far more than a poetical figure, describing the blessedness that shall come to the righteous. It is much more than that. It is rather a figure of the influence that the righteous shall exert when all these evil things are removed, and they shine forth in the Kingdom of the Father. They will create the opportunity for goodness, and the opportunity of nations that have never been reached.

Does that not bring halt and shock to some? Surely all this is going on, until all nations have been reached, and all nations have bowed to Christ. Is that our view? It was not His. Never in one of these parables did He teach anything of the kind. He never suggested the work of the Church was to go on and on until all nations had bowed to Him, and kissed His sceptre, and crowned Him. He knew human nature better than that, and He knew all the things that so often have puzzled the Church, and made them at times feel as though everything was failing. He knew. But when that consummation of this age comes, as the prelude to other ages that lie beyond in earth's history, the angels will gather out all these offending things, and the righteous will shine forth as the sun, and that will create the opportunity for other nations.

The parable is of the nature of a look ahead. There are some senses in which today we have little to do with it, for the net is still swinging, and the Kingdom influence is still being exerted, and the reaches of the net are going further and further out, as every great society we call Missionary takes the Kingdom to the peoples of the earth. We have nothing to do with the pulling in of that net. We have far less to do with trying to sort the good and evil enclosed in its meshes.

Yet in other ways this parable is a gracious source of strength as it assures us of a certain process that is going forward which will culminate in an advent, and a clear judgment, in which the King, our Lord and Saviour, through His heavenly servants the angels, will visit earthly affairs, and that gives us all hope when we are inclined to lose it.

> "That can't end worst that began best,
> Though a wide compass round be fetched."

As we lift our eyes for a moment, not to tarry there, because we have our immediate call and business, we look on and see the day when the pierced Hand will manifestly grasp the sceptre, and will call the ministries of heaven to His service, in separating the evil from the righteous, the wicked from the good.

15. The Householder

Matthew xiii: 51, 52.

THIS PARABLE is the completion of the octave found in this thirteenth chapter. "He spake to them many things in parables." So the movement began. At the fifty-third verse, "And it came to pass, when Jesus had finished these parables, He departed thence." Those are the boundaries of this parabolic day in the teaching of Jesus. He spoke many things in parables, and when He had finished His teaching, He departed.

This last parable is not concerned with the history of the Kingdom in the age, but with the responsibility of His disciples during that period. The parable in itself is very brief, and yet full of revealing suggestiveness. It followed a question and an answer. That question and answer must be borne in mind. The question was one which our Lord asked of these men who had listened to Him, and the answer was their reply.

After the delivery of the four parables in public, and the three in private, in that same privacy Jesus said to His disciples, "Have ye understood all these things?" And they answered, "Yea." I believe they were quite honest in their answer, but I do not think they had fully understood. Events proved they had not grasped the real significance of all He had said. But they had gone so far; and however much we may say about their limited understanding, our Lord took them at their own valuation. Immediately He proceeded to utter this parable. That "therefore" is most significant. It leans back upon the question and the answer. Have you understood? Yes, "Therefore every scribe who hath been made a disciple to the Kingdom of heaven," that is who has received his instruction, and has understood all these things, "is like a man that is a householder, which bringeth forth out of his treasure things new and old."

That preliminary setting of the revealing parable marks the method of treatment. First of all note the preliminary requirement as revealed; and then that which is taught in the parable, the perpetual responsibility. If we have understood these things, something must happen, something will result, because every scribe instructed to the Kingdom of heaven, or made a disciple of the Kingdom of heaven, who has been listening to the teaching, and is instructed, is like a householder.

"Have ye understood all these things?" Notice carefully, "*all* these things." In the very way in which our Lord asked the question there is revealed the fact that the parables are mutually explanatory, that we are not prepared for whatever is to follow as to responsibility until we have grasped the significance of all these things, the sower, the darnel, and so all through the seven. They merge, they belong to each other, all are necessary to an unveiling of truth concerning this Kingdom of heaven. Have we understood all of them? Not one of them, but all these things in their interrelationship.

That is the preliminary question, and it is no use going on until we have faced it. He compelled the disciples to face it, and they were honest as far as they went in their reply. But our Lord's emphasis is on the word "understood." To understand is to put together, to comprehend. In the question there is a recognition of the whole drift of the teaching as necessary to the fulfilment of the obligation, whatever that obligation is. "Have ye understood all these things?" In an arresting aside, because He was going straight on to an illuminative word, He said to them "Therefore." Wherefore? Because you have heard the things, and understood them, "therefore every scribe who hath been made a disciple to the Kingdom of heaven is like unto a man."

Here are two synonymous terms, a disciple to the Kingdom of heaven is therefore a scribe. Here our Lord did an arresting thing, though it is possible we may not at first be arrested by it, or notice it. It is that of His use of the word "scribe" at that point. From the commencement of His ministry, and growingly, there was an order of men called scribes, and they were opposed to Him, "the scribes and Pharisees." Who were these men? When our Lord foretold His suffering at Cæsarea Philippi, He said He must go to Jerusalem, and suffer many things at the hands of chief priests, elders, and scribes. That was no mere piece of rhetoric. He was describing the three orders actually then existing in Jerusalem, and among the Hebrew people; the priests, the spiritual rulers; elders, the civil rulers; and scribes, the moral rulers. The moral rulers had been opposed to our Lord throughout His ministry.

As a class the scribes arose in the time of Ezra. There was no order of scribes in Moses' time. The scribes in Old Testament history were the historians, and principally military historians. But in the time of Ezra there arose a new order of scribes, and Ezra was the outstanding figure of that order. He made a pulpit of wood, and stood on it, from which he read the law, giving the sense. That does not merely mean he read correctly, and with clear articulation, though that undoubtedly is inferred. It simply means that he read the law and explained it. There was a great Bible movement, a Scriptural movement at that time under Ezra. So this order of scribes arose. They were men who read the law, and explained it; consequently they became the moral interpreters.

As time wore on these men became more and more concerned with the letter of the law, and they attempted to safeguard it by building a fence around it. That fence consisted of the traditions that were supposed to interpret the law. In process of time it not only shut out the law, but shut men out from it, and men came to misunderstand the law through the traditions and teaching and interpreters, those men whose whole business was to interpret it. So in the time of Jesus

He flung Himself in anger oftentimes against these traditions and these false teachers, the scribes, the official interpreters of the law.

Again another reference. Upon one occasion in remarkable language our Lord quoted from them, calling them the interpreters of the law. He said they sat in Moses' seat. Their business was to interpret the law of Moses, and Jesus set the seal of His authority upon the idea, never upon the men, but upon the idea. Going on, He said Therefore, because they sit in Moses' seat, whatsoever they say unto you do it, only do not ye as they do. Thus He set His seal upon the authority of that order.

Christ had now been instructing His men, His disciples, those representative men who were to interpret the Kingdom of heaven to the world, and He named them by that same name; and in so doing, He transferred the fulfilment of an office from men who had failed to men who were to succeed them. In order to achieve the fulfilment of responsibility, therefore there must be understanding of the King's teaching concerning the Kingdom in this age.

Once again go back to these parables. According to Jesus, this age is to be one of conflict from beginning to end, characterized largely by human break-down and failure. But it is to be an age in which God accomplishes definite purpose both in the world and in human history, and in the creation of an instrument for the ages to come. Said Jesus, Have you understood these things, have you grasped My teaching? If you have a sense of what this age is to be like, you are to go out into it as scribes.

Come now to the parable. Every such scribe, made a disciple himself to the Kingdom of heaven by the teaching of Christ, standing for it, every such one is like a householder.

What is a householder? One cannot interpret this parable by thinking of a householder in London. We use the phrase properly, but it was an Eastern figure which our Lord employed. The word is *Oikodespotes*, to translate that literally, a house-despot. We do not like the word despot. We have no reason to dislike it save when despotism is evil. Then we have not only the right to dislike it, but we have the right to fight it to the end. It is a word that marks tremendous authority, the house-despot. It is a picture of a shepherd, father and king, all which phases are merged into one personality, one at the head of affairs. To illustrate and illuminate, Jesus one day said to these men, "Fear not, little flock, it is your Father's good pleasure to give you the Kingdom." To the Western mind particularly it may look as though our Lord were mixing His metaphors. A merely literary critic might say, This Teacher is confused. He begins His statement with a shepherd and a flock. He forgets it before He has gone far, and it is the man and his family. Then He forgets that, and the picture is of a nation and a king and Kingdom. But we know perfectly well that if the figures merge they do not mix. They reveal the threefold aspect of a head of a clan, or a nation and people. The Arab shiek today at once is the shepherd of his people, the father of the family, and king of the nation; and all these are involved in "the householder." The disciple to the Kingdom of heaven is like a householder. That word "householder" was on the lips of Jesus some ten or twelve times, and almost invariably He used it of Himself. It is the word that marks authority. The disciples were to be scribes, authoritative inter- preters of the moral law.

What then does the householder do? He brings forth from his treasure house. He brings forth treasure. There are two words for treasure in the New Testament. One means that which is laid up, layer on layer, and kept. The other means that which is spent. The difference between a miser and a spendthrift is that a miser says sovereigns are flat that he can hoard them; and the spendthrift says they are round, so that he can roll them, and get rid of them! These two ideas are in the two words for treasure. We find them both in the Sermon on the Mount. Here it is the word which means laid up. The householder is seen as having vast resources. What does he do with them? He brings them forth, and here the Greek word scatters them lavishly. It is a suggestion of bountifulness. He has them heaped up, but he is bringing them out, and scattering them everywhere.

Then comes the remarkable phrase, "things new and old." Notice, He did not say new things and old things; but the same things which are new and old. These scribes, these disciples of the Kingdom, these who have heard and accepted His interpretation, and have understood, are to go out, and they are to be householders, bringing out of their treasure things new and old.

The whole picture is that of an authoritative ruler, lavishly scat- tering out of his wealth the things which are necessary for the supply and government of his household. That is the picture of all those who are instructed to the Kingdom of heaven.

Disciples of Jesus are those seen as the true rulers of the age, as they correctly interpret the Kingdom, and represent Him in it. They have access to the eternal treasure-house, and in that treasure-house there are things new and old. Mark the arresting picture of these disciples of Jesus in the age. We see the age, on the human side, as it will be seen by men of sight. But we see also the Divine side, as it is seen in the purpose of God, having a far wider application than earth or time stretching out into the ages. That is the Kingdom of God, and therefore there is the treasure-house, and these disciples, made disciples to that Kingdom, by understanding that teaching, and that outlook, are to go forth to exercise the true authority. The scribe was the moral authority. So are we to be.

That has been going on for nineteen hundred years. The Church has been doing that very thing. She has been exercising moral authority in the history of the world from Jesus until today. I know how she seems to have failed. Our Lord told us there would be failure. We must however think bigly and broadly enough of history. Every great moral sentiment that obtains in the thinking of the world today has come to it through the Church of God. Yes, failure again and again, but that thing still remains true. The emancipation of womanhood, the emancipation of slaves, the value of children, the bed-rock basis of marriage, all these things have come because of the scribes of the Kingdom, who have been interpreters of its moral law. Theirs is the final authority, not that of kings, and rulers, and emperors, and presidents, and parliaments; but of those scribes who understand the Kingdom, and are made disciples thereto.

What are they to do? They are to "bring forth things new and old." Jesus did not say to them they should bring forth new things, and old things. That is not two orders of things. It is two facts concerning the same things. They are one in essence. The principle is old, the application is new. The root is old. The blossom and the fruit are new. The old things are the eternal things, the eternal verities. The new things are the applications of those eternal things to the passing phases of changing times. "Things new and old." The two are necessary to growth. If we destroy the old, there will be no new. If we find an absence of new, we shall discover that the life of the old has ceased. Take an illustration from Nature. Go into the garden. If that root be dead, there is no blossom, and no fruit. If the old be dead, the new does not appear. Or look at it from the other side. Come into the garden, and if there is no blossom, no fruitage, we know that the root is dead. "Things new and old." The interrelationship therefore is a perpetual test. The new which contradicts the old is always false; and the old which has no new is dead and useless. "Things new and old."

Surely Russell Lowell had that great principle in mind when he wrote those lines that have become hackneyed by quotation, but still are so marvellously true,

"New occasions teach new duties, Time makes ancient good uncouth;
    They must upward still, and onward, who would keep abreast of truth;
Lo, before us gleam her camp fires, we ourselves must pilgrims be,

Launch our Mayflower, and steer boldly through the desperate Winter sea,
Nor attempt the future's portal with the Past's blood-rusted key."

But if we attempt the future's portal with any key except the key
that hangs upon the girdle of the King, we cannot unlock its door, but
the key is always there. That is the old. The unlocked door is the new,
and the Church has been called upon to pass through the centuries,
and will, until the age ends, for evermore meeting new conditions with
the old principles in new applications. Because the Kingdom of heaven
is old, it has ever new applications, new methods, new manners. Men
may change, but the Kingdom of heaven, the Kingdom of God, remains
for ever rooted in the nature of God, and it blossoms fresh in every
generation among the sons of men.

So we can summarize. What is meant by the old? The Kingship
of God. What is meant by the new? The application of the old, nationally, socially, and individually, at all times. That is the responsibility
of all those who are named scribes, those set in authority as householders. The treasure-house is there. The business of such is to bring
the treasure forth, and seek its revealing. For evermore our view of
the age must be His view of it. Then our influence will be His influence, bearing fruit for the Kingdom of God. All the other phases are
there in the other parables, and are manifest throughout the teaching
of our Lord; but this is the great final parable in the octave, of application to us, and of our responsibilities.

16. Parabolic Illustrations

Matthew xv.

IN THIS fifteenth chapter we find a parable, and a parabolic illustration. The parable is in the eleventh verse, and our Lord's explanation occurs in verses seventeen to twenty. Then in connection with
another incident in His ministry we have a parabolic illustration in
verse 26.

It is necessary that we understand the subject which He was illustrating, when He uttered a parable. To do that we must go back to
see the occasion upon which our Lord used these words and this
illustration

There had come to Him a deputation from Jerusalem. By this time He was approaching the end of His third year of ministry. That third year culminated at Cæsarea Philippi, which account is in the next chapter. So He was approaching the end of the central period of public propaganda, so full of interest. Hostility to Him on the part of the rulers, spiritual, moral and civil, which had manifested itself from the beginning, had grown with the passing of the years. Here they sent down to Him a deputation from Jerusalem with the explicit purpose undoubtedly, of somehow entangling Him, or asking for some explanation of things they did not understand, and to which they had most strongly objected in His teaching, and finally as that teaching had manifested itself in the conduct of His disciples.

The whole Hebrew religion at that time was suffering under the intolerable burden of tradition. Indeed, tradition had so covered over, submerged, the law of God that men were not familiar with the law. They were far more familiar with the tradition. How constantly our Lord in speech and action flung Himself against prevailing traditionalism. Here that is what manifested itself. We can hardly realize what that meant then. The whole system of religion had passed under its yoke and incubus, and was in slavery to it. In a previous chapter we have dealt fully with this subject. To give two actual quotations from the rabbis of the time. "The words of the elders are weightier than the words of the prophets." Or another, "Some of the words of the law and the prophets are weighty, others are not weighty. All the words of tradition are weighty words."

It is impossible to go into all the meticulous divisions of these traditions, and how on every hand what was legal by tradition, was supposed to interpret the law of God. Take this case in point. These men had come down from Jerusalem to Jesus, and they had asked Him, Why do Thy disciples transgress the traditions of the elders when they eat bread? They owned they were thinking about the tradition of the elders. They had seen the disciples of Jesus transgress that tradition, ignore it, fail to observe it.

The disciples were eating bread with unwashed hands. There was no tradition that a man should wash his hands before food in order to cleanliness. It was not cleanliness that was in view, but ritual. All these traditions had become impregnated by superstition, and the rabbis were declaring that Shibta, a demon, sat upon the hands of men as they slept, and ceremonial washing was necessary, or food would be contaminated by the presence of that demon upon their hands, while they were asleep! We are inclined to smile at it. But there are people doing things today quite as foolish as that.

That was the hour and atmosphere that drew forth this reply from Jesus. He flung back upon them their own tradition. They had charged the disciples with transgression of the traditions of the fathers. He said, "Why do ye also transgress the commandment of God because of your tradition?" Then He gave them another tradition which they had transgressed. God had said, "Honour thy father and thy mother; and, He that speaketh evil of father or mother, let him die the death." They were saying, "Whosoever shall say to his father or his mother, That wherewith thou mightest have been profited by me is given to God," or "Corban" as in the Old Version. The mystic word can be pronounced upon anything, as "do wrong!" But our Lord uttered this tremendous word, "Ye have made void the word of God because of your tradition." "Ye hypocrites."

Having answered the deputation, He uttered this parable to the multitudes. It was a parable characterised by the greatest simplicity, that could not be misunderstood. He led them to face the fact of the physical organism. He showed them that physical organism deals with physical aliment, that it has no reference to moral cleanness or defilement. Notice carefully, "Not that which entereth into the mouth defileth the man." Then at once linking the thought with that other word, words proceeding out of the mouth, coming up out of the thoughts, they defile the man, because when thoughts are evil, words are evil, and acts are evil. So by the false thinking and heart, the very flesh may be defiled. The sustenance of the flesh can have in it no defiling element. It is not that which enters into a man that defiles him, but that which comes out of the deeper fact of his nature, out of his heart, out of the realm of mind and spirit, mastering the activities of the flesh, thoughts producing acts, reacting in defilement.

The teaching here is important. The flesh in itself is not evil. It does not defile. Paul, and other New Testament writers constantly refer to the flesh as being that against which we have to watch and battle, which is true in certain ways. But the flesh inherently is not evil. That is an old Gnostic heresy which cursed the early Church, and against which the writings of Paul were directed. There is nothing inherently evil in flesh, and therefore that which sustains flesh could not defile. If we take food, it strengthens us in physical powers, because the flesh in itself is not inherently evil, and therefore it is not defiled.

But a man pondering in his heart evil thoughts, may be led by so doing to the expression of words which presently will find further expression in deeds, and those very deeds will defile the flesh. The flesh which is not inherently evil may become contaminated, harmed, and may become the very instrument of destruction and death. But

that is not the result of the food eaten. Consequently to believe con-
tamination resulted, was stupid, to use no stronger word. The observ-
ance of external rules has no power to touch the inward spring of
action. We may observe all the rules, we may sign all the pledges, and
we may not eat that food, nor drink that drink, nor go to that place;
but the inner, spiritual life is not touched by these things.

Paul warned some to whom he wrote against worship of the will,
when he wrote of being subject to ordinances, "Handle not, nor taste,
nor touch." It is a curious thing that these words are often quoted as
giving good advice. Paul said it was bad advice. All that is of no value
to the purifying of our flesh. That is what our Lord was teaching here.

There was profound significance in that word of Jesus to Nicodemus.
I take it reverently beyond the application He made of it. "That which
is born of the flesh is flesh, and that which is born of the Spirit is
spirit." There is a clear distinction. That which is born of the flesh is
not inherently evil. That which is born of the spirit may become so,
and may react even upon the flesh, upon the physical being.

Read again His own explanation. "Whatsoever goeth into the
mouth passeth into the belly, and is cast out into the draught." That
cannot defile the man. "For out of the heart come forth evil thoughts."
He then gave a list of the things by which even the flesh becomes
defiled; but "to eat with unwashen hands defileth not the man."

The parable was for the listening multitudes, in the presence of
those rulers who were hiding the commandment of God, and making it
of none effect by their tradition. It also stands for evermore as a
warning against adding anything as a final authority in life to the law
of God itself. That is the consummate wrong that is being done by the
Roman theologians. Our Roman friends tell us we can read the Bible,
but we must not interpret it. We must accept the interpretation of
those in authority, the Church, as they say. That is what these men
of old said. We have the law of God, but it cannot be interpreted save
through tradition; and whenever tradition, whether of a priest, or a
prophet, or a Bible teacher, is put in the place of authority over life,
we are violating our own spiritual need, and wronging the Word of
God. Only as priest, prophet, or teacher can lead men into the living
presence of the Word is there any value in his work. Everything else
is mere tradition, which ultimately hides the value of the truth of God.

A brief reference to the parabolic illustration. There is no connection between the parable spoken to this deputation, or to the multitudes
after the deputation came, and this story, except that directly after
this, our Lord "went out from thence, and withdrew into the parts of
Tyre and Sidon" (Ver. 21). It was a significant action of our Lord.

He crossed the border line between strictly Jewish and Gentile territory. Tyre and Sidon were outside Jewish territory. So was Decapolis. Our Lord first went up to Tyre and Sidon, and then went down to Decapolis. In Tyre and Sidon this woman met Him, outside Jewish territory, outside the ritual of the Jewish covenant. Here, and in Decapolis He was among those not of the Jewish faith, but among the Gentiles. He had turned from Israel which, for the moment through its rulers, was manifesting hostility to Him. He had gone away, and had entered into a house, and would have no man know it. He had gone for quietness.

Then that wonderful statement is made which flames with light. "He could not be hid." We read elsewhere that upon occasion He hid Himself, and they could not find Him when He was in the middle of a crowd. Why could He not be hid here? Because there was a woman outside the house in trouble. It was to that woman He used that curious parabolic illustration, "It is not meet to take the children's bread, and cast it to the dogs." This is not strictly a parable, but a parabolic illustration. Jesus had crossed the border line into foreign territory. He was in the parts of Tyre and Sidon, which means the environs. The woman came out from thence. The attitude of Jesus toward her was the attitude of the Messiah towards an outsider.

When she cried first of all He did not answer. First He had come out to see her. He could not be hid, and in that first sentence we have a wonderful illumination of everything that followed. He then maintained silence when she cried, and His disciples besought Him to give her what she wanted, and let her go. Then He said, "I am not sent except to the lost sheep of the house of Israel." He was the Messiah of Israel.

Notice carefully here in the outcome of the story how that phrase finds a remarkable interpretation; and in the use of it in all that followed, He turned from the flesh to the spirit. We read it, "the lost sheep of the house of Israel," and we think, as these men did, in the realm of the flesh. He had said He was not sent but to the lost sheep of the house of Israel. Then she addressed Him, not as the Hebrew Messiah, but with the universal title, "Lord, have mercy on me." Then He said this strange thing to her, "It is not meet to take the children's bread and to cast it to the dogs."

Our Lord used an uncommon word for dogs. As a matter of fact it is the only place in the New Testament where it occurs, and it is a diminutive, "little dogs." Behind that lies the whole Eastern picture. The dogs that were an abomination at that time were the wild, half-wolfish, marauding dogs, those in the mind of Paul when he wrote,

"Without are dogs." In those Jewish homes there were little dogs, domestic dogs, pets of the children, who gathered round the board. Our Lord did not use the word referring to the prowling, fierce, marauding dogs, held in horror. He used the word that denoted the little dogs, when He said, It is not meet to take the children's loaf, and cast it to the little dogs.

Then the woman answered, Yea Lord, but these little dogs eat of the crumbs. Whatever we may think of that answer, notice what Jesus thought. "O woman, great is thy faith." What a wonderful process is seen here. When He used this figure, He softened it by the term He employed for dogs. He was sent to the lost sheep of the house of Israel. The loaf is not to be flung to little dogs. But when the woman said, They eat the crumbs, by that word she confessed her complete faith. It was the woman's victory. An old Puritan father has said that in that last word she manifested the perfect wit of a woman. Yes, it was wit, but it was faith-inspired wit, for Jesus said so, "O woman, great is thy faith."

Yet by that last parabolic illustration our Lord reached the climax in a process from the beginning. Outside the covenant He had been feeling after faith, knowing that it was there in the heart of that woman. That is why He had come out to see her. She did not know much about Him, but His fame had spread; but her agony was there, and the germ of faith. He took the method of manifesting it, and in such wise as to say, "So great faith." It was the Lord's victory.

And mark this. He did not go outside His commission. She was one of the lost sheep of the house of Israel. She proved herself by her faith to be the child of Abraham. Those who were of Abraham after the flesh were not all children of Abraham, but those who were of Abraham by faith. Here that illustration is brought into visibility by that apparently harsh answer of Jesus, which was not unkind. It was an opportunity for such a confession of faith, and the demonstration of the fact that the woman had her place, not in the fleshly covenant, but in the covenant of God with His Israel after the spirit, and the children who are of faith.

17. Parabolic Illustrations

Matthew xvi.

THE SIXTEENTH chapter contains no parable, but five suggestive parabolic illustrations, of weather forecasting, of the leaven in a new setting; and closely together, three parabolic illustrations of a great theme, rock, gates, and keys.

Look first at weather forecasting. We think we live in an advanced age, because we have weather forecasts. Evidently they had them in the time of our Lord. "When it is evening ye say, It will be fair weather, for the heaven is red; and in the morning, It will be foul weather today for the heaven is red and lowring." Jesus knew about weather forecasting, and He employed it.

Note the subject which He intended to illustrate and illumine when He made use of that particular figure of speech. The Pharisees and Sadducees had come to Him requesting a sign from heaven. On other occasions they had asked a sign, but at this time they were particular. They wanted a sign from heaven.

In our familiarity with these words, we may not understand the significance of their conjunction in that statement. The two great parties in the Jewish State at that time were divided philosophically, theologically, politically, and socially. They had no dealings with each other and were constantly in conflict. "The Pharisees and Sadducees came," a coalition formed for the one purpose of trying Jesus. They came "tempting Him," that is, trying Him, testing Him. These men had nothing in common. They were all the time at daggers drawn. The Pharisees were the ritualists in religion, and the Sadducees were the rationalists. The Pharisees believed that Rome had no right to have any authority over them. The Sadducees submitted to the Roman authority, and insisted upon it. Yet they came now in a united effort to put Jesus in such a position that would reveal the truth of their contention that He was an impostor. That was their purpose. They asked for a sign from heaven, and the very request as it was preferred, showed that they intended not to deny the things He had done, but to cast aspersion upon them.

In the twelfth chapter Matthew has recorded the fact that the Pharisees did not deny our Lord had cast out demons; but they affirmed He had done so because He was in league with Satan himself. Now they came to ask for a sign from heaven. Signs were everywhere, casting out demons, healing disease. Signs had been multiplied. He went about, doing good. As Peter said on the day of Pentecost, He was a Man approved of God by powers and wonders and signs which God did through Him. Signs were everywhere. Yes, but these men said it was possible to account for all the wonderful things He had done, on a low level. They had said the casting out of demons was the result of complicity with the devil himself. Now they came to Him and asked for a sign from heaven, expressing their disbelief that anything He had done had behind it heavenly authority, or heavenly power. There is little doubt they were asking for some spectacular manifestation. Some sudden illumination of the night by supernatural light would have done nothing to convince them; so they suggested some appearance in the heavens, in the midst of the brightness of the day, that would bring conviction; something supernatural from heaven that could have come from nowhere else.

Now note our Lord's reply to them. "When it is evening, ye say . . ." We read next, "*It will be* . . ." That little phrase is not in the Greek, neither here nor in the next verse. The italics mean that the words have been supplied by translators to give sense. Read it bluntly, without the words. "When it is evening, ye say, Fair weather . . . in the morning, Foul weather today." That was something with which they were all familiar. Christ was quoting from their commonplace speech. They had said it often undoubtedly. It must be remembered the illustration is peculiarly Palestinian. It was the aspect of the sky in Palestine; but it is equally true in England today. Many will remember the old saying, "A red morning is a shepherd's warning; a red night is a shepherd's delight." Travelling over the vast expanses of ocean, we always notice whether the morning or evening was red. This was a commonplace figure of speech Jesus used.

Then He applied it. He said to these men that they were intelligent on a certain level, and within certain limitations. They knew how to discern that red morning and that red night. They were significant. As they watched the face of the sky they were clever in surface observation, but they could not discern the signs of the times.

Notice this carefully. He flung them back upon their own request. They had asked for a sign. The signs were all about them. They had observed phenomena, and had come to correct conclusions about the weather. They did not fail in accurate weather forecasting, but they could not see the meaning of the things in the midst of which they were living, "the signs of the times."

Then He told them why this was so. "An evil and adulterous generation seeketh after a sign; and there shall no sign be given unto it, but the sign of Jonah. And He left them, and departed." Why were they blind? Why could they not understand? Why could they not discern the real meaning of the things in the midst of which they were living? They were evil, an adulterous generation. Those were terrible words. They were evil, *poneros*, harmful in their influence, because evil in their hearts. The moral nature was warped, because of the evil of their spiritual nature, which was atrophied.

He then fell back upon that appalling figure of the Old Testament, with which these men would be familiar if they had their own Scriptures, "an adulterous generation." How constantly the great writers of the past had referred to these people under the figure of a marriage relationship. Said Jehovah, "I have betrothed thee unto Me." Again and again the prophets charged them with adultery, infidelity in their relationship to God as their Husband, Master and Friend. Jesus swept the whole of that generation into that description, "evil and adulterous." That was the reason for their blindness. They were evil because they were adulterous. They had been unfaithful to their covenant with God, and the result of that was that they were harmful, evil in their hearts, and hurtful in their influence. Therefore they were blind.

Seeing all these signs, they could not discern them. There would be one sign, full and final, the sign of Jonah. On another occasion He put that more fully when He said, "As Jonah was three days and three nights in the belly of the fish; so shall the Son of man be three days and three nights in the heart of the earth." The ultimate full and final sign of authority would be that of His death and resurrection, and no other sign would be given than that. He turned His back upon them, He left them. They had ability to observe natural phenomena, and to make correct deductions in forecasting the weather; but utter inability to understand the commonplace things of His power and majesty, which had been apparent to them in the course of His ministry. This was because of their infidelity in heart, resulting in an evil nature, and so in spiritual blindness.

No application is needed save perhaps to declare that this always abides. Take the world today with its great advancement which cannot be denied. All this weather forecasting is marvellous, whether a depression is here, or there, and the way it is likely to move. We can discern in England the signs of the weather. But can we discern the signs of the times? Have we caught the significance of the things Jesus, not did, but is doing? If so, remember there is one great sign that brooks no denial. It can be evaded by supposed intellectuality, but it remains the central fact of all history, the death and resurrection of Jesus.

Pass now to the second illustration in this chapter, contained in verses five and twelve, that of the leaven. We have studied that figure before in one of the parables. Take it here as Jesus used it. The subject that He was illustrating here was that of false teaching, and what it meant in human life as to its influence. The Pharisees and Sadducees, in a coalition, were attempting to entrap Him. Now the evil of the teaching of the Pharisees was their attitude toward tradition. That made sin purely external. Here was the reason of our Lord's constant conflict with them. The spiritual and moral conceptions of these Pharisees and Sadducees were radically opposed to Jesus. The teaching of the Sadducees created the right to, and the opportunity for, indulgence in every form of material living. All their policies were based upon that materialistic and naturalistic conception of life. The Pharisees who professed to believe in angel, Spirit, and resurrection, had so covered over these essential truths of life and religion with their traditions, which they suggested were interpreting these things, were really throttling them, smothering them, killing them as to vital power. Our Lord now dealt with this teaching of the Pharisees, and in that connection used this figure of leaven.

What does leaven mean? Let us take a definition from a scientific text-book. It is "a chemical decomposition of an organic compound." Of course when we get away from our Bible we get simplicity of language! An "organic compound," that is life, the organism; but leaven is the "decomposition" of that compound organism. In other words, leaven is that which destroys, it is fermentation. It is something which always breaks up, and ultimately destroys. It is quiet and insidious, but terrible in its working, and yet persistent. As Paul said, "A little leaven leaveneth the whole lump." In his Corinthian letter he referred to those Judaizing teachers who were seeking to superimpose the Pharisaic philosophy upon Christians under the title of Judaism, that is Pharisaism, and he called that leaven.

Our Lord warned His disciples against the danger of their teaching. It is arresting however to notice that when He said, "Beware of the leaven of the Pharisees," even His disciples did not understand Him, and they were materialized by the influence of their age. They thought He was talking about the fact that they had forgotten to take bread on the ship, which called forth from Jesus a word of tender rebuke, "How is it that ye do not perceive that I spake not to you concerning bread?" These men who came and asked for a sign were blind. Are you blind too? Can you not understand? Then He told them what He meant, and then they understood that He spoke of the leaven of the Pharisees.

The value of that illustration to them, and to us for all time is that it lays emphasis upon the danger of false teaching, even though that false teaching be given in the name of religion. The Pharisees claimed to be religious teachers. The Sadducees claimed to be religious teachers, even though their philosophies and theologies were fundamentally opposed. But they were claiming to teach religion. They put upon the teaching of religion a false conception and outlook, and understanding, a leaven which brought about the decomposition of the organic compound. False teaching is a leaven that for ever destroys. There can be nothing more important than that teaching in the name of religion, in the name of Christianity, nay, in the name of Christ, should be according to His outlook, His power, and His will; anything else works fermentation, decomposition, and ruin.

So, having rebuked the seekers after a sign, and revealed the reason of their failure, that they were blind because evil, and evil because unfaithful to God, He warned His disciples against their teaching, using the figure of leaven.

We come to the last illustrations in this chapter, the figures used—rock, gates, and keys. The passage is well known. Simon Peter had just made his confession, expressing, as I believe, not only the conviction of his own heart, but of the whole group about Him. "Thou art the Christ," the Messiah, that is, His office. As to nature, "Thou art the Son of the living God." Jesus responded to that confession by uttering a beatitude upon the man, "Blessed art thou, Simon, son of Jonah, for flesh and blood hath not revealed it unto thee, but My Father which is in heaven. And I also say unto thee . . ." Do not miss the "also." It is significant. Why did Jesus say "also"? Thou hast made thy great confession concerning Me. Now I have some confession to make to thee, some secret to reveal which I have never told you before. He began with Peter personally. "Thou art Peter," thou art *petros,* a piece of stone; "and upon this rock"—*petra,* essential rock;—"I will build My Church, and the gates of Hades shall not prevail against it. I will give unto thee the keys of the Kingdom of heaven." Rock, gates, keys, three illustrations flaming with light, shining in the great declaration.

"This rock." What subject was He illustrating? The fact of His Church, "I will build My ecclesia," different from everything that had gone before, even in the economy of God. The Hebrew nation had been God's ecclesia, His called out and separated people, for the fulfilment of function, but it had failed. Its Pharisaic and Sadducean rulers had been in unbelief to ask for a sign from heaven a short time before. They had utterly failed.

Then has God failed? I hope He will forgive me for suggesting the question. God never fails. Everything may look as though God is being beaten out of His world. He is not. He never fails. If that old economy, which God created, has broken down and failed, then "I will build My Church." It is the great authoritative word of Jesus, declaring that He would establish an institute for the fulfilment of the Divine purpose, and the accomplishment of the Divine end. He used first of all the figure of rock, that He would build upon rock.

Remember that He was talking to Hebrews, to a group of men belonging to that ancient nation which He would presently excommunicate. They would understand the figure He used. Rock. How was that figure of speech used in the literature of the Hebrew people? Turn back to the Old Testament, and look at the occasions where the figure of rock is used in a figurative sense, and there are over forty such. "Rock" is only used figuratively in the Old Testament of God. Upon one occasion, in Deuteronomy, in the Swan Song, Moses used the word as of false gods, putting them into contrast with the true. "Their rock is not as our Rock." Through Moses and the prophets, rock is always used, reserved, not by the intention of the writers, but by the intention of the Holy Ghost, as a figure of God Himself, essential Deity.

"Thou art the Christ, the Son of the living God." "On this Rock," of essential Deity, "I will build My Church." The Roman Church still believes and teaches that the rock was Peter. Our Protestant Churches are saying the rock was Peter's confession. A poor foundation that. In a few days he was swearing he had never seen Him. The Rock is God, and Christ says, "I will build My Church"; I will build back into relationship with the living God human souls, and so create My ecclesia.

What about the figure of the gates? He had swiftly changed the figure of speech, from building to battle. The gates of Hades shall not prevail. What are gates for? To guard the city against the enemy. The gates of Hades shall not prevail. How often that has been interpreted as though our Lord said, My ecclesia is built on a rock so strongly, that Hell cannot overcome it. Oh, no, He will build on rock, and that proves its invulnerability. But now He said, Hell shall not be able to withstand the attack of the Church. It is not a picture of the Church invincible against attack. It is a picture of the Church invincible in attack, so that the very gates of Hades shall not prevail against it. With the eye of a great Commander, the Lord saw the whole Church, and the last enemy, death; and the Church victorious, as she ever has been. No, they are not defeated, our loved ones, defeated in death. They are victorious in the hour of death, over all the power of Hades. The gates of Hades shall not overcome them.

Again another change of figure, from those of building and battle, to that of moral influence. "I will give unto thee the keys of the Kingdom of heaven." Again we can interpret that figure of speech only according to the times. It was perfectly familiar. That great order of scribes for a long time had looked upon keys as the insignia of their office, as the interpreters of the moral law. So He made use of the figure to show that the Church was not only to be built on rock, and therefore invulnerable; not only to be the attacking force against which the force of Hell should not prevail; but that she should be in the world to enforce the laws, in the sense of moral standards; to bind, to declare that which is obligatory; to loose, to declare that which is voluntary. So in these figures used by our Lord, rock, gates, and keys, eternal truths are revealed concerning the Church which He is building.

18. A Parable and Parabolic Illustrations

Matthew xvii and xviii.

IN THESE two chapters we have two parabolic illustrations and one set parable; first the illustration of the grain of mustard seed, and then the parabolic illustration of the quest for the lost sheep. At the end of the eighteenth chapter we have the parable of the two debtors.

It is important that we should remind ourselves of the subject which our Lord was intending to illustrate when He used either parabolic illustration or more set parable, in order not only to understand the parable or illustration, but to put the true limits upon them. It is possible to take a parable of our Lord away from the setting and context, and misinterpret its intention.

We ask then, when our Lord took this parabolic illustration of the grain of mustard seed, what was He intending to illustrate? The teaching arose on account of the disciples' failure on an outstanding and memorable occasion. Jesus had taken three of them away from the group. Nine had been left behind, and to them there had come a man bringing his boy, his only begotten son, demon possessed. The twelve when they had been sent out had all been given authority and power to cast out demons, and they had done this very thing. Here, however, was an occasion when they could not do it. When our Lord came down from the mountain and faced the father, he had said to Him bluntly, "I brought him to Thy disciples, and they could not cure him." They could do nothing.

When the Lord had cast the demon out, and given the boy back to his father, the disciples came and asked Him the secret of their failure. It would be a great thing if the Christian Church today, in its activity, paused long enough to ask Him the reason for its comparative failure. These disciples did so, and immediately He gave them first a direct answer, and then used this illustration to illuminate His own answer. His answer to them was quite simple. "Because of your little faith." Here I like the Authorized rendering better than the Revised, because this does not apply to quantity here, but to quality, "Because of your unbelief," then He illuminated His answer, "For verily I say unto you, If ye have faith as a grain of mustard seed, ye shall say unto this mountain, Remove hence to yonder place; and it shall remove; and nothing shall be impossible unto you."

Our Lord was illustrating the meaning of His declaration that unbelief was the reason of their failure. He took a seed, a grain of mustard. The word there is simple, primary. The word seed always implies that which contains the life principle. If your faith is of the nature of that seed, then things follow. Our Lord had used the same figure in an earlier parable in the thirteenth chapter. He was telling the disciples here that their failure was due to the quality of their faith, their unbelief.

In the Revised rendering here, "because of your little faith," the word little does not refer to quantity. When the disciples said on another occasion, "Lord, increase our faith," it was not an increase in quantity, but a change of quality they sought. And the faith that removes mountains is like a seed which has in it the element of life, which means growth, dynamic. In Nature the ultimate result of the life principle in a seed comes through death. A grain of wheat must fall into the ground and die. So it bears much fruit; and if it die, the life principle begins to appear, through death.

What then is the secret of our failure? Our faith is of a failing, faltering quality. It lacks the principle of life. Applied to the whole situation, we see where they failed. This incident followed upon Cæsarea Philippi, and Peter's confession, and his fear of the Cross. But yesterday our Lord was talking about life, the life of the Church, and its coming glories. They had naturally been exalted and filled with joy. But when He told them of that final and ultimate victory, that He must die, their faith failed. It was not of that living nature that could grasp His teaching. They could not interpret it, and consequently they were paralysed in the presence of the demon. They had failed at Cæsarea in confidence, in faith. Their faith lacked the principle of life. They failed now in the presence of their own work which He had commissioned them to do, and which they had done until this hour.

Follow out the application. The quality of faith is life, faith as a grain of mustard seed. This does not mean that if we have a big enough faith we can go out and say to a mountain, Move, and go into the sea. A living faith never seeks to do anything without having first ascertained that it is the will of God. If we go to a mountain, because we want to see an upheaval, and see the mountain go into the sea, we can talk about our faith as long as we like, and sing about it, but the mountain will stand fast. But if, peradventure, the thing should be that the actual material mountain in the will of God needed to be removed, and we knew it, then nothing is impossible. Living faith fastening upon the will of God, submissive to His will, and seeking nothing out of harmony therewith, becomes part of the Divine dynamic, and no mountains can stand against it. That was the subject illustrated, and that was the mighty illustration.

We come next to the subject of the lost sheep, and the quest for it. What was our Lord illustrating? He used this parabolic illustration of a man who lost a sheep and sought it. He used it again later, when He linked it with the lost drachma and the lost son, as recorded by Luke. Here it stands alone. What was He illustrating? The subject illustrated was finally that of offences, which might be committed against little ones. Here He was limited in His teaching, but not in the essential appearance.

This all grew out of a question that the disciples had asked concerning greatness. Jesus had taken a child, and set him in the midst as the type of greatness in His Kingdom; and when He used this illustration of the lost sheep, He showed the value of that child. The illustration is a familiar one, and needs no elaboration. A shepherd had lost a sheep, and went out after it, and found it.

This is applied to the child. It occurs in that chapter of rare beauty, which is pre-eminently the chapter of the child. The illustration came out of their passion for greatness. Jesus made their enquiry the reason for things He said about the child, in their bearing upon the disciples, and their quest for greatness.

He told them first of all that the child was the type of character in His Kingdom. Except they were turned back again from their manhood with its prejudices and pride, and became plastic and simple and emptied of all pride as a child, they could not enter into His Kingdom.

The teaching is amazing and wonderful. The little child is the gatekeeper, and we cannot pass into His Kingdom, save as we come by the way of the child. He was showing them this, and in words that are terrible He charged them not to cause that child to stumble. He declared that we had no right to despise a little child, and summarized everything by saying it was not the will of our Father that one of these little ones should perish. Notice what a revelation He gave in the context, of the value of the child by the eternal standards. Angels, the Son, and the Father, are committed to them. Their angels always behold the face of the Father. They have constant access to God on their behalf. The Son Who is the good Shepherd, is seeking them; and the Father doth not will that one of them should perish.

It is a wonderful illustration that of the Shepherd, and the Shepherd heart, and the compassion of the Shepherd, that goes out from the field where the ninety and nine are safely gathered, into the desert and the wilderness, and brings back the child. To make that application of it which is scriptural is to cut across anæmic theology today which tells us that the children do not need saving. Such theology forgets the truth declared in the Bible, and illustrated in all human experience that we go astray from the womb, that we were born in sin, and shapen in iniquity. The Shepherd is seeking every one.

> "Then on each He setteth
> His own secret sign."

It is the picture of the love of God, operating through His Son as Shepherd, caring for the little ones. Some expositors try to explain this by saying the little ones means believers. Not at all. The child was in the midst, and His eyes and heart were upon it; and He saw how His disciples were likely to be hindered in work for the children by self-seeking and pride and desire for place. He kept the child in front of Him, and told His disciples what to think of it, under this figure of the Shepherd.

We pass next to that which we describe as a parable in itself, that of the two debtors. What was the subject He was illustrating by this story? Forgiveness, not God's forgiveness, although that is the background by suggestion, but forgiveness among themselves. This

came out of Peter's enquiry, although the enquiry was due to something which our Lord had been saying. There came a moment when
Peter was overwhelmed with a wave of generosity. "Lord, how oft shall
my brother sin against me, and I forgive him? until seven times?"
How many times have we forgiven that man who had wronged us?
We think even today we have risen to the ultimate height of generous
action when we have forgiven a man three times. We have heard
this said, "I forgave you once, twice, but the third time pays for all!"
Peter doubled up, plus one, on our generosity when he said seven
times. Oh blessed Peter, warm-hearted blundering Peter. But Jesus
laughed at him with a fine satire, tender and cleansing, as the flashing of the summer lightning. Seven times? Supposing you try 490!
"I say not unto thee, Until seven times; but, until seventy times
seven." We shall have to live a long time before we have any chance
of forgiving a man 490 times, seventy times seven.

This wonderful parable consists of a contrast of attitude and
activity towards debt. One owed his master, his lord, through his own
fraudulent activity. This is a purely Eastern scene. He owed his
lord ten thousand talents. That does not mean very much to us
here, until we become mathematical. If it were ten thousand talents
of gold, it is beyond computation. If it was a reference to a currency
of silver, the thousand talents of silver was worth two million
sterling. If he owed his lord ten million sterling then here is a picture
almost unbelievable, and yet thoroughly Eastern. The lord ordered
him to be sold, his wife and children, and all that he had, and payment to be made, as far as he could. The man fell down before
him, casting himself upon the mercy of his lord; and his lord forgave
him all the debt, cancelled it, wiped it out.

Then that man so forgiven, went out and found a man who owed
him something. That can be computed in pounds. The amount was
£5. He had owed two million; the man owed him £5. He said, "Pay
that thou owest." The man said, Give me time; and he would not, but
took him by the throat, and cast him into prison. There was such
an inherent sense of rightness in his fellow servants that they reported
the case to their lord. His lord summoned him back, and the end of it
all was that he was wroth with him. The compassion that had been
shown to him had been violated by the activity of the man to whom
he had showed that compassion; and he delivered him to the tormentors
until he should pay all that was due. We may say, that was very
hard. Wait a minute. "So shall also My heavenly Father do unto
you, if ye forgive not every one his brother from your hearts."

How many times shall I forgive my brother? Seven times? Seventy times seven, 490! Do not forget that. Your brother owes you not more than £5, and you owe all of two million, which you can never pay. But God in His compassion forgives you everything; and if you go out to exact the last farthing from your brother, then God has no forgiveness for you. His wrath will fall upon you. His compassions are violated by your inability to be compassionate, and will bring down His wrath upon you.

Notice how the compassion of God shines behind the whole of this. Forgiveness, not because of any worth in the man making his appeal, not because of any worth in the sinner to forgiveness, but intended to produce in the heart of that man a spirit like the Spirit of God. In that light therefore we see the baseness of the failure of the servant. Forgiveness? Who is it that we have in our mind? Have we forgiven? How many times?

19. Parabolic Illustrations

Matthew xix: 11, 12, 24.

THE TWELFTH verse of this chapter contains a remarkable parabolic illustration. Immediately before uttering this, our Lord had said, "All men cannot receive this saying, but they to whom it is given." Then at the close of the twelfth verse He said, "He that is able to receive it, let him receive it." Those words of our Lord show the difficulty of the illustration, and of the subject illustrated. It does show however that the intention of our Master was to reach, not the general crowd, but a limited company, such as were able to receive it.

The word at the end of verse eleven, "All men cannot receive this saying, but they to whom it is given," did not refer to His own saying, but to the statement of the disciples. They had said to Him, "If the case is so with his wife, it is not expedient to marry." In the last clause, His statement linked up with what the disciples had suggested, applying to what He Himself had said, "He that is able to receive it, let him receive it." We see then that this parabolic illustration contained in these words of Jesus, seem to guard it, to fence it off, to show that it was not intended for everyone; and therefore had a particular and limited application.

That being admitted, we ask, what was the subject under discussion? What subject was our Lord illustrating at this point? To put it first quite bluntly, the subject was that of celibacy, of abstention from the marriage relationship. The subject under discussion was consequent upon previous happenings. The question of divorce had arisen. In order to understand our Lord's teaching, definite, and applicable to all time; it is nevertheless necessary to remind ourselves of the conditions obtaining in all the Jewish world at that time, and opinion held then on the subject of divorce.

It was one of prevalent and almost bitter controversy between two great theological schools within Judaism. Hillel, that great teacher who had passed on twenty years before our Lord began His ministry, but whose opinion was widespread and tremendous, interpreting the finding of Moses in Deuteronomy (xxiv: 1), had declared that the meaning was this: "A man may lawfully divorce his wife for any reason that might render her distasteful to him." He was interpreting the law that if a man, after marrying, found some blemish, he had the right to write the wife a bill of divorcement, and send her home. It is a long time since Hillel died, but men are trying to bring this up again today! On the other hand, stood the theological school of Shammai, that declared there was only one reason for divorce, and that was unchastity.

Those two schools were bitterly opposed, and when they came to Jesus with the question, it was the result of that wide-spread difference of opinion and dispute. The Pharisees came to Him, "tempting Him, and saying, Is it lawful for a man to put away his wife for every cause?" We see at once what lay behind the question.

Notice carefully our Lord's answer to that question. Both teachers, Hillel and Shammai, appealed to Moses as final interpreter, but differently. When they came to Jesus He said, "Have ye not read, that He which made them from the beginning, made them male and female, and said, For this cause shall a man leave his father and mother, and shall cleave to his wife." Any detailed examination of the passage is unnecessary; but they raised the question, with all the background of theological controversy. He went from Hillel and Shammai, beyond Moses, to God. He took the whole question back into the region of original Divine purpose and Divine intention. That was the first line of His answer.

Then He clearly declared that there was one reason for divorce, and only one; and that, to use the word of our translation, was "fornication." Thus He really set the seal upon Shammai's view, rather than upon Hillel's. He went on, and interpreted that. It was at that point the disciples showed they had been under the influence of

Hillel in their thinking. Divorce had become simple, and cheap, and easy; and any man whose wife was distasteful to him could obtain a divorce. So they said to Jesus, If that is the standard, it were better for a man not to marry. It is rather a revelation of degradation in their thinking. They were Christ's men now, but they still had very much to learn and understand.

Then came our Lord's remarkable reply. He admitted the possible accuracy of their view. He said, "All men cannot receive this saying, but they to whom it is given." As though our Lord said, You may be right in the presence of existing conditions, and of the original Divine intention, and of this strong law of chastity that permits divorce only for the reason of fornication. If you are right, it is a hard saying, and it may be so. All men cannot receive it, but they to whom it is given. It may be possible, in view of existing conditions, that there are those who take that position. Christ was not condemning them.

Then He gave them this parabolic illustration. It is purely Eastern, and in that way we must understand it. The word eunuch meant guardian of the bedchamber. The peculiarity was that these men had to be unmarried men, and unmarriageable men. Our Lord was looking at the conditions, and said, There are those who are eunuchs from their birth. There are those who have been rendered impotent by the act of man. But beyond those two facts then in existence He saw another. There are those who have taken up this position of celibacy from the marriage relationship in the interest of the Kingdom of God. "He that is able to receive it, let him receive it." Some are born incapable of marriage. Some are created incapable to marry. With them we have nothing to do. We are not living in the East. Then some for the Kingdom of heaven's sake take up the position of celibacy. Our Lord said that was not for every one. Some men cannot receive this, but He recognized the possibility. He said, "He that is able to receive it, let him receive it." In other words He taught distinctly that in the interest of the Kingdom of heaven, celibacy is permitted, but it is not enjoined. There can be no command laid upon a man that he become celibate, if he is to serve the Kingdom of heaven; but if any man out of soul conviction, separates himself from the marriage relationship, so be it, let it be. There is nothing forbidding it; there is nothing to enjoin it, nothing to command it.

That little paragraph stands there, fenced off by the words of Jesus, showing that what is said is not easy to be received, and was only for those who were able to receive it. That does not mean that those able to receive it are lifted on to a higher plane than those not so able; but it does mean that those not able to receive it are not to hold in contempt anyone who devotes himself or herself to the celibate life, in the interests of the Kingdom of God. It must be a matter of personal conscience and relationship for those who are able to receive it.

Then we look down the ages, and look around. How often we have known those who have been able to receive this thing, and have rendered service to the Kingdom of God of a most remarkable kind, because they have been able to receive it. I do not know that it would be historically safe to quote the case of Paul, because in Farrar's *Life of St. Paul* he argues at length that Paul was a married man. He did say, "Have we no right to lead about a wife?" Yet taking the context we see that he said, speaking to the unmarried, "It is good for them if they abide even as I am." In all probability he used it as an illustration of the celibate life. Do not forget, if any incline to the Roman view, that the one who is claimed as the rock of the Church was not a celibate. That does not invalidate either Peter's or Paul's power. There however the great principle is presented to us.

There is another principle at the heart of it, applicable over a wider area. In the last analysis the attitude and action of every individual soul must be personal and individual, and in the presence of God. So the light shines over a wider field than evinced in the realm that our Lord referred to by His use of the figure.

We pass on to another quite different figure of speech found in verse 24. "It is easier for a camel to go through a needle's eye, than for a rich man to enter into the Kingdom of God." Much more should be read and referred to. Our Lord was now illustrating the blighting influence of wealth on personality. Look at the previous verse. "It is hard for a rich man to enter into the Kingdom of heaven." That was the subject under discussion at the moment. The disciples were astonished, for they said, "Who then can be saved?" The subject emphasized was the possible blighting influence of wealth on personality, not inevitably so, nor finally necessary.

The whole subject arose out of the departure of the young ruler. It was then that our Lord said, "How hardly shall they that have riches enter into the Kingdom of God." He did not say they cannot do so. Indeed, presently we shall see that they can. He did not say it was impossible, but that it was hard and difficult. The emphasis of the declaration might have been seen if it had been immediately uttered, as the disciples looked at the retreating back of the young ruler; as he had turned his back upon the revelation Christ had brought to him, because he was one "that had great possessions." How hard it is for a rich man to enter into the Kingdom of heaven. Our

Lord's comment emphasizes in the most superlative way, and almost terrifying degree, the statement He had just made.

But there is something else to be added. Take the illustration as it stands. "It is easier for a camel to go through a needle's eye, than for a rich man to enter into the Kingdom of God." We may say, of course that means it is impossible. Yes, in a certain sense, and our Lord meant to teach that. There is no need to go fully into the matter of the word camel, or eye, or needle. There have been many attempts to explain this passage by explaining it away; that our Lord did not really mean what He said, if He used the actual words. Some of the Cursives there give *Kamilos,* which means rope, instead of a camel. Hort says that was "certainly wrong," and Robertson has ratified Hort's finding. They are both right. Lord Nugent said in his *Lands Classical and Sacred* that the needle's eye referred to a gate with the smaller arch, through which no camel could pass except unladen. That is possible, most possible. However to me it is unnatural, forced, and insufficient. I believe our Lord meant an said exactly this, If a camel cannot go through a needle's eye, neither can a rich man enter into the Kingdom of God.

A friend of mine in the States, a man, a scientist of unusual ability, once delivered one of the most remarkable addresses I have heard, fanciful, but scientifically clever, on this text. He showed it was quite possible to put a camel through a needle's eye. He took a camel, dissected it, analysed it, and reduced it to its elements, down to a liquid, and so was able to squirt it through a needle's eye. I apologize to my distant friend for the blunt way of stating this! I do not know that I am prepared to accept it. Yet there is something here that is of great importance. The saying of our Lord here meant that a rich man is rendered incapable by his own action of entering into the Kingdom of God.

The disciples then said, "Who then can be saved?" another revelation of their mental outlook and attitude. We saw it in their question on divorce. What lurked behind it? Rich men could not enter into the Kingdom, because they evidently believed in the power of wealth to introduce men everywhere. If a rich man cannot go, no man can. We see their faulty thinking. Perhaps they were hoping some wealthy man would join the movement. "Who then can be saved?" As on another occasion they came to Jesus with astonishment, and said, All men are seeking Thee. They were always thinking on a faulty level. He had almost as much trouble with them as He has to do to train us. We are so slow, fools, and slow of heart to believe. That is the background here.

Mark the tremendous significance of what our Lord said. He replied to them, saying, "looking upon them, With men this is impossible; but with God all things are possible." Everything depends upon the preposition employed there. "With men," *para*, by the side of, in the company of. "With God," *para*, by the side of, in the company of, in fellowship with. "With men it is impossible." With a rich man hampered by his riches, overwhelmed by them, mastered by them, depending upon them, imagining with the disciples that they constitute some right of entrance into any possession of privilege, it cannot be done, said Jesus. With men, not by men. If a man is only looking out upon the level of his fellows, if only acting with men, if his thinking is mastered by human views, and he is struggling under the mastery and co-operation with others to enter the Kingdom of God, it cannot be done, it is impossible. But with God nothing is impossible. All things are possible if that man ceases to look to himself as a human being, or to his fellows in association with him, trying to find entrance, if he cuts himself off from them, and comes into definite contact with God, if he begins by submission to God, and continues in fellowship with God. Nothing is impossible to that man.

This all began with the coming of the young ruler. Do not forget our Lord looked upon him with great affection. Mark tells us that "Jesus, looking upon him, loved him." That was after he had declared he had kept all the commandments on the second Table of the Decalogue from his youth up. He had come asking what he should do to inherit eternal life, this man with great possessions. Jesus had told him, "Thou knowest the commandments," and in quick succession had flashed upon him in brief wording, the essential light of the six commandments that marked the interrelationship between man and man. Man *with man*. He had said "All these have I kept from my youth up." Do not say he was lying. He was not. He told the truth. Looking at Jesus he said he had a clean record by the test of the law, the commandments that marked relationship with his fellow-men, "with men." But he was outside the Kingdom.

Then Christ said to him, "One thing thou lackest, go, sell all that thou hast, and give to the poor." That is initial, preliminary, "And come, follow Me." Who was speaking? The One Whom the young ruler had addressed as "Good Master"; and when He said that, Jesus said to him, "Why callest thou Me good? There is one good, that is God." We are shut up to an alternative. Jesus meant, either, I am not good, or He meant, I am God. We do not accept the view that He meant, I am not good. One thing lacking, that is life. One thing thou lackest, follow Me, follow the One Who stands before you in the place of God, and then all things are possible. You can enter into life. You can find your way into the Kingdom of God.

The case in question was that of a wealthy man. The final application of Jesus is to far more than the wealthy men. It is to every man whether rich or poor the truth abides. "With men," if our thinking is mastered by human opinion or action, in seeking human co-operation; if endeavour is halted within the paralysis of our own human nature, we cannot struggle our way into the Kingdom of God. But if on the other hand we are "with God," all things are possible, even the passing through the needle's eye of the camel.

20. The Labourers in the Vineyard

Matthew xx: 1-16.

THE FIRST sixteen verses of this chapter contain the parable of the labourers in the vineyard. We ask, What was the subject our Lord intended to illustrate when He made use of this parable? To take the parable out of its context and study it alone is impossible. John Ruskin went hopelessly wrong when he wrote "Unto this last," and thought he was interpreting the parable, which he did not understand.

Observe first the boundaries of the parable. The final verse of the nineteenth chapter reads, "But many shall be last that are first; and first that are last." The sixteenth verse of chapter twenty reads, "So the last shall be first, and the first last." In the first verse we have the dictum of Jesus, and in the second, an interpretation of the dictum. The great dictum is uttered, "Many shall be last that are first; and first that are last." The parable is given in illumination and illustration; and then our Lord gathered everything up and said, "So," in that way, "the last shall be first, and the first last." Those are the boundaries.

We go a little further back and ask, What was the particular occasion of this dictum of Jesus? What made Him say, "Many shall be last that are first; and first that are last?" That came as the result of an answer to an enquiry raised by Peter. How thankful we are for Peter, and all his questions. In verse 27, "Then answered Peter and said unto Him, Lo, we have left all, and followed Thee; what then shall we have?" It was because of that question our Lord uttered this dictum, and it was because of that dictum, resulting from that question, that our Lord gave this parable.

So again we must go back a little further, to the story of the young ruler, to whom Jesus had said, "Go, sell that thou hast, and give to the poor, . . . and, come, follow Me." He had turned his back, and gone away sorrowful. The man who had great possessions, a clean record, a fine temperament, stood confronting Jesus, and heard that word, that he lacked control external to himself. Jesus called him to submit himself to Him, but he went away. He clung to his possessions; and Jesus interpreted that as we saw in our previous study, "It is hard for a rich man to enter into the Kingdom of heaven. . . . It is easier for a camel to go through the needle's eye, than for a rich man to enter into the Kingdom of God." Peter now said, "Lo, *we* have left all, and followed Thee; what then shall *we* have?" What is to be the gain of this renunciation, after we have done it? As though he had said, Master, Thou hast called the man to a great renunciation. He has turned his back, and gone away. "We have left all, and followed Thee." What is the use of it? What shall we gain?

The Lord gave him a wonderful answer to that question: "Verily I say unto you, that ye which have followed Me, in the regeneration, when the Son of man shall sit on the throne of His glory . . ." He was looking on to something in the future, and telling them what they would gain in that future order that should be set up. They would gain authority as His administrators in that Kingdom; and not only so, but "everyone that hath left houses, or brethren, or sisters, or father, or mother, or children, or lands, for My name's sake, shall receive a hundredfold, and shall inherit eternal life." It is a very wonderful answer, that of Jesus. They would gain authority, friendship, eternal life; but do not forget that "many shall be last that are first; and first that are last."

So the Lord first answered that question of Peter's, and then uttered that word of warning. The parable is the illumination of the word of warning. Literally He said, "Many shall be last first, and first last." The words *that are* are in italics and are not in the text, "The last first, and first last."

What then is the subject He was illustrating? Service, and its reward. The teaching of this parable is applicable only to the disciples of Jesus, with regard to their service.

What is the figure? First, a man who is a householder, and who has a vineyard. It is his vineyard, his property. Notice carefully that the picture the Lord draws here is of a man with a vineyard, his property; and he hired labourers to do his work in his vineyard. It is interesting here that the Lord took a day, twelve hours. "Are there not twelve hours in the day?" Here they are. He went out early, at the third, the sixth, the ninth, and eleventh hours. The owner, the master went out, and hired labourers at these intervals during the passing day. They were all called by the Master. There is no word in this parable of men asking for work. The labourers were not seeking work. They were outside the vineyard; but he called them inside, and set them to work; and they all came in, when he called them. Many were called early. They went in and worked. At the third hour they went in, and at the sixth, and ninth, and eleventh hours, when he called them. It is an Eastern picture of a householder, a vineyard, and work to be done in a vineyard. He went out, and the labourers went in to work, when they were called. They did not ask to go. They agreed for a penny. It was a bargain. It was a contract. Then the day closed after the eleventh hour, and the last hired did one hour's work only. Having agreed with the first, he paid the workers according to the agreement. We are not told he made any agreement with the rest, but he paid them according to his own will. He gave every man a penny only, to those last who worked only one hour he also gave a penny.

We can understand the murmuring; but if we also are inclined to murmur at the story, it is because we have not yet caught the real significance of the parable, or what Jesus was intending to teach. First of all the master dealt with the last men as unto the first. The first "supposed that they would receive more, and they likewise received every man a penny." We agree that a bargain is to be kept, a contract is sacred. If you agree with me for a penny; if justice is done, have you any right to object to my generosity? Has not this man a right to do what he wills with his own? That is the only question that arises, as to whether this householder had a right to do what he liked with his own. The implication of the question of Jesus was that he had such right.

Yet the teaching of the parable shows that the right is invested in something else. So we come to that teaching. It must be found in the strict limits of the context. There is no question of salvation here. It is wholly one of service. Moreover, these men were no lazy loiterers. They all entered the vineyard when they were called; and that is specially emphasized in the case of the last called.

Other parables have other aspects of service. There is the parable of the Pounds, and that of the Talents. In our thinking we often confuse these. The Labourers, the Pounds, and the Talents all have to do with different aspects of service. In the parable of the Pounds, every man received a pound, and our Lord was showing common opportunity, created by a deposit received. In the parable of the Talents, He was showing how varying gifts create responsibility. What then was He teaching here? That payment is according to fidelity to opportunity.

That covers the whole ground. That is the whole meaning of the parable. That fellow who went in at the eleventh hour never had a chance before. He was not called; but when sent, he went in, and was paid on the basis of the fact that for one hour he was faithful. The man who went in early, and served through all the burden and heat of the day was faithful to his work. The parable therefore illustrated the payment of reward to fidelity of opportunity. It does not mean that if a man has his opportunity, and does not take it, and wastes the fleeting hours, he will get the same reward as the man who has toiled through all the livelong day. Our Lord was simply emphasizing this one matter, fidelity to opportunity.

I wonder if we have really grasped that yet. What opportunity has God given you? I do not know. I am not asking for any answer, except in your own soul. He gave to D. L. Moody the opportunity of a waiting nation, of two nations, and when his day's work was done, he had his penny, because he was gloriously faithful to his opportunity. There is a woman somewhere among the hills and mountains, poor, struggling, striving, but she has two children, and she puts her life into the business of training them for God. We do not know her. We never heard of her, not even in the columns of the religious press, but she has gone. Her children have grown up; she has gone on. She got her penny! The penny is nothing. Our Lord took a denarius, a trivial amount even for labour, to emphasize the similarity of reward, on the basis of fidelity to opportunity.

Now then, "Many are called, but few are chosen." These words are omitted from the Revised Version both in the English and American revisions. It is wholly a matter of MSS. If we retain them, we should not read "chosen" there, but "choice," which word carries the idea far better. "Many are called, but few choice." These men were all called, and according to the parable they went and did their work, and got their penny. Said Christ, Yes, there are many called, but they are not worth their salt, they are not choice; they will not get their penny. "Many are called, but few are choice."

Has He called us into the vineyard? Well, if He has, we have only one thing that ought to fill our souls with Divine anxiety. That is that we do the job He gives us, and according to our fidelity will be our reward.

21. *The Cursing of the Fig-tree*

Matthew xxi: 18-22.

IN THE chronological sequence of the life of Jesus we now reach a new realm in His teaching and work. This incident of the cursing of the fig-tree, and the remainder of the parables and parabolic illustrations in Matthew, were uttered in the last days of His life on earth.

He had now arrived in Jerusalem for the final scenes, and it is important that we recognize at the beginning that His teaching was largely denunciatory, and His actions administrative. By this time His teaching to the crowd and the multitudes generally was over. Presently He would gather His own disciples around Him, and give them His final teaching. His actions now were administrative, the actions of a full and supreme authority.

What we celebrate and call Palm Sunday, and speak of as the triumphal entry of Jesus to Jerusalem, was really a threefold entry on three separate days. Mark tells the story of His first coming. It was on a Sabbath day when He entered the Temple, and looked round about upon all things, and said nothing. He turned His back, and went out. On the next day, our Sunday, the first day of the week in the Jewish calendar, He came again, and cleansed the Temple. When He first entered the traffickers were not there. It was the Sabbath. They had taken their places again on the next day, when He cleansed the Temple. Then on the Monday, their second day of the week, He came again, and that was the great and dramatic day of controversy with the rulers. That word is used with care and determination. It was a dramatic day. There is nothing in the life of our Lord comparable to it in certain respects. It was a day in which He, though rejected by the rulers, chief priests, scribes and Pharisees, nevertheless entered the city and the Temple, gathered those men about Him, and compelled them to find verdicts on their own condition, and pass sentences on their own failure. That is a summary of events, details of which we come to in the parabolic illustrations. In these days this cursing of the fig-tree occurred, which was unquestionably a parabolic act, and concerning which our Lord gave an interpretation. The whole paragraph must be taken in its entirety, against its background, to understand the things I have referred to as existing.

We see at the beginning of the chapter how Jesus had now come up to Jerusalem for the official rejection of the Hebrew people; not their rejection of Him, but His rejection of them. If we study carefully that story of the threefold entry, we shall find He entered in every aspect of authority. He entered as the King, as Prophet, as Priest. All through the story we see the august and splendid and glorious dignity of Jesus. Oh, yes, His enemies were there in their robes and their phylacteries, all opposed to Him; but He moved with majesty into the midst of them, and dealt with them until there fell from His lips that final sentence addressed to the nation through the rulers, "The Kingdom of God shall be taken away from you, and shall be given to a nation bringing forth the fruits thereof." That nation was then rejected from the office it had held for the interpretation and revelation of the meaning of the Kingdom of God. They were rejected, and the Kingdom was taken from them, because they had failed to bring forth fruit. The Kingdom of God was taken from them, and given to a nation that should bring forth the fruits of that Kingdom.

After the entry on that first day, and the cleansing of the Temple on the second day, having spent the night in Bethany, He returned to Jerusalem, and on the way He destroyed the fig-tree.

This action had created difficulty in the minds of many. One is almost amused at the way some people seem to be puzzled. The rank and file seem to understand it better than the expositors. Going over expository literature it is interesting to find what difficulty has been created. We must bear in mind this is the only miracle of judgment that Jesus wrought. We may say, What about the destruction of the swine, when they swept down the steep place into the sea? Yes, that is certainly true, but in the case of the Gadarene swine, the objective was not judgment, but the delivery of a man. There was judgment incidentally. But this was a case in which Jesus, passing along, exhibited His power to destroy, not to save; and it is the only case on record. There can be no doubt whatever that it was a parabolic action, especially if we put ourselves back into the mental mood of the disciples who were with Him; and with all reverence, into His own mental mood. When He destroyed that fig-tree, there were wider meanings in the action than the mere destruction of the tree.

Let us look at the story a little carefully in two ways, first facing these difficulties, and then enquiring what were the immediate and

permanent values of this action of Jesus, according to His own interpretation of it to His disciples.

Three difficulties have been suggested. First, that His action in
destroying that tree was an act of injustice. Mark tells us, "It was
not the season of figs." People have fastened upon that, and have said
if it was not the season of figs, it was an act of injustice to destroy
the tree, because no figs were on it.

Then it has been objected that it was an angry action, because
He was hungry. He was hungry, and no figs were there; and so in
anger He smote the tree with His power, and destroyed it. It is interesting to see people think that was wrong. One wonders where they
learned it was wrong, if they did not know Jesus! The very objection
grows out of a consciousness of the mind and the heart of Jesus.
Still there is the objection which has been definitely raised.

The third objection is that it is not in harmony with His methods
as they have been revealed.

We need not tarry with these objections. First of all the charge
that it was an act of injustice. What are the facts about these fig-
trees? The usual time of figs there in the East was certainly June.
and I think we can say without any argument, this cursing happened
in the month of April; so Mark says it was not the time of figs, not the
time of the full usual harvest of figs. But there was a kind of first
ripe fig, before the time of figs, often found on certain fig-trees. In the
prophecy of Isaiah, in the course of the 28th chapter, describing the
desolation that is coming, he said, "The crown of the pride of the
drunkards of Ephraim shall be trodden under foot; and the fading
flower of his glorious beauty, which is on the head of the fat valley,
shall be as the first ripe fig before the summer; which when he
looketh upon it seeth, while it is yet in his hand he eateth it up."
That is an allusion to a fact of Nature, with which all dwellers in that
land were familiar. On certain fig-trees ripe figs were found before the
summer, which was the time of figs; and whenever figs were so found,
it was before the leaves appeared, when the trees were just burgeoning
out. The figs were found growing on the stems and on the branches,
before the leaves came.

But when Jesus came to this fig-tree, He found nothing but leaves.
There should have been no leaves at all. It was a false development,
so there were leaves, but no fruit. It was a tree of false development.
The leaves suggested its fruitfulness, but no fruit was there. There
the tree grew by the wayside as they travelled along. Jesus, being
hungry, came up to it, and looked at it. Leaves were on the tree before
the time, but no fruit; a false development of show and appearance.

with no reality of fruitfulness. It was upon that condition that our Lord based His word, "Let there be no fruit from thee henceforward for ever"; and at the word of authority, the tree immediately withered away. So much for the charge of injustice. It was the cursing and destruction of a tree that had failed.

What about this suggestion of anger? There is not a sign of personal vindictiveness in the whole story. Notice carefully a simple matter, but it is important. The disciples were not surprised at the effect produced upon that tree. They were surprised at the quickness, the suddenness of it. That is what amazed them. There was no suggestion on their part that such a tree should be destroyed; but that with the spoken word, the leaves withered and crumpled, and the tree was dead. That is what amazed them, the speed with which it was carried out. There is no suggestiveness of the vindictiveness of Jesus, but the astonishment of the disciples. The tree was faulty, a failure; but they were surprised at the swiftness of the judgment.

Again we are told that the action of destroying that tree was not according to the methods of Jesus. Let us think again before we say that. So many people have the idea that our Lord is known only as the meek and lowly Jesus. He was meek. He said so. He was lowly. He claimed to be so. But He was infinitely more. He was majestic with a majesty that appals us the nearer we get to Him, and His wrath was terrific when it blazed forth in words that at the distance of nearly two millenniums scorch us as we read them. We remember when He read Himself in, at the synagogue in Nazareth, He read, "The Spirit of the Lord is upon Me. . ." We have all noticed where He stopped. He ended with the words, "to proclaim te acceptable year of the Lord." Then He closed the book and sat down. If we open the book, the Hebrew version, we are not helped very much; but if we take our English Version, and open the book, where He stopped there is a comma, and nothing more. What is the next sentence? "The day of vengeance of our God." That is the whole prophecy concerning Him. The Spirit of the Lord was upon Him to preach the acceptable year of the Lord, and the day of vengeance of our God. To be quite technical, only a comma, but that marks a pause of at least 1940 years. That day of vengeance has not come. It is coming. Some of us seem to see the clouds sweeping up the sky now. It is coming, the day of vengeance. But in the method of Christ, there is not only the acceptable year of the Lord; there is the day of vengeance.

Take another illustration from Matthew, where the quotation is made concerning Him. It is said, "A bruised reed shall He not break, and smoking flax shall He not quench," and we constantly quote that to show the gentleness of His method. We have no right to do so. Finish the quotation.

"A bruised reed shall He not break, and smoking flax shall He not quench, till He send forth judgment unto victory." The acceptable year of the Lord is the day of His grace. The day of vengeance of God is the day when He will break the bruised reed, and quench the smoking flax. Do not think falsely about the methods of Jesus. For a moment here there flamed into the view of His disciples a retributive act of Jesus in the realm of the material, as He cursed that fig-tree.

What did it mean? We need to take the whole paragraph, and to notice first of all His condition. In the morning He returned to the city, and "He hungered." How do we interpret that? He had been in Bethany, which may not necessarily mean that He was in the town of Bethany, but in the neighbourhood. During that last week in the life of our Lord, He never slept in Jerusalem. He went up there on successive days, but at night He left the city, and went away into loneliness. Martha, Mary and Lazarus were in Bethany, and we can hardly conceive of His coming back from that hospitable home hungry on the physical level.

Yet I think He was hungry on the physical level, which was a symbol of a deeper hunger possessing Him, the hunger for the doing of the will of God, the hunger for the redemption of humanity; yes, let us say the drastic thing, the desire, the hunger for His Cross. He knew the failure of the nation, and the reason of their failure. He knew that they had now become apparently a fair fig-tree—to use the figure which was one of the symbols of the nation,—but He knew also that upon that fig-tree leaves were flourishing, but fruit was absent. He was hungry, hungry for the things of God, hungering for the accomplishment of the Divine purpose. The material hunger was there, but in the perfect unity of His Personality, the material hunger was the sacramental symbol of the spiritual hunger.

Then He found that fig-tree, saw its unutterable failure, and He cursed it, and destroyed it. He did that which was a strange thing. Strange? Yea, verily. I go back once more to Isaiah to the 28th chapter at the 21st verse. The prophet is still speaking of the judgments to fall, and he said this, "For the Lord shall rise up as in mount Perazim, He shall be wroth as in the valley of Gibeon; that He may do His work, His strange work, and bring to pass His act, His strange act." What? Judgment, destruction, the strange act of God. That is, something foreign to the desire and the heart of God. God willeth not the death of any sinner. That does not prevent the death

of the soul that fails. "His strange act." Jesus is walking towards Jerusalem on one of His last journeys, and there is a false tree, emblem
of the nation; and He acted in "His strange act." He was on His
way to national judgment, which the next two parables will make
clear.

Look again, and notice that when this was done, the disciples
spoke to Him, and they said, "How did the fig-tree immediately
wither away?" Notice, not, Why didst Thou do this? but, What
brought about that strange swiftness of result?

The Lord did not answer that enquiry. He did not tell them how
He had done it, but He did reveal why He had done it, and He did
reveal what the principle was, that found illustration in that destructive act:

"Verily, I say unto you, If ye have faith, and doubt not, ye shall not
only do what is done to the fig tree, but even if ye shall say unto this
mountain, Be thou taken up and cast into the sea, it shall be done. And all
things, whatsoever ye shall ask in prayer, believing, ye shall receive."

We ask, Where is the connection? It is in the revelation of the
reason of the failure of the nation. He had now passed away from
the fig-tree. There the tree stood, withered, blighted, blasted; because
it gave a false appearance which was untrue to reality. There it was,
and while the disciples were wondering at the power that had wrought
so swift a destruction, He took them to the heart of the trouble
He was facing. What was it? Why had that nation failed? For lack
of faith in God. He took those simple words, and yet so sublime, telling
them that if they had faith and doubted not, it would not be a
withered fig-tree, but a mountain in front of them, barring progress,
which could be moved into the sea, "All things, whatsoever ye shall
ask in prayer, believing, ye shall receive."

Then He revealed the principle. Lacking faith, the nation was
perishing, notwithstanding its outward appearance of life. Possessing
faith, though everything seemed to be against them, they might come to
power. The cursing of the fig-tree and the destruction was a parabolic
and symbolic act, and our Lord interpreted it to us.

As we consider this story, we are impressed with the absolute
oneness of Christ with God; and we see His ministry of mercy merging
into one of judgment. But that judgment is exercised in strictest
justice, vindicated by mercy. The power in which His own followers
are to cast out the obstacles which are in the way of God's coming
into His Kingdom is that of faith. Men of faith co-operate with God,
and God operates through men of faith.

22. *Two Sons and Husbandmen*

Matthew xxi: 28-44.

W E HAVE seen that the parabolic miracle of the cursing of the fig-tree was judicial and denunciatory. This paragraph contains two parables which were uttered on the day of the third entry of Jesus to Jerusalem. He had entered the city as the King, and had looked round about on all things, and turned His back upon them. He had entered as Priest, and cleansed the Temple, for a brief period restoring it to its true place in the economy of God. He now came as the great Prophet, with the message of God, and this time the message was judicial. That was His purpose in coming.

These things should be stressed, because we need to be delivered from any false thinking about the final things in the life of our Lord. We might be apt to think, and perhaps naturally, of Him as being hemmed in by His enemies, caught, and by them put to death. That is an entirely false view of the situation. Never in all human history was anyone less hemmed in by His enemies than was Jesus.

The story beginning in this passage is a remarkable revelation of this. In all literature there is no more dramatic passage than this. From the standpoint of the watching angels, and heaven's observation, we see a most amazing thing. He is seen coming up, gathering round about Him the rulers who had utterly failed in the economy of God; and compelling them to find a verdict upon their own conduct, and to pass a sentence commensurate with the verdict they themselves had found. He did this by the simple method of telling them stories, and asking their opinion on them.

He began first, "What think ye?" He told them a story, asked their opinion, and the opinion they gave was perfectly accurate. Then He told them another story, and again He asked their opinion, and they gave it, and it was quite correct. Thus, with a master hand, and by the use of simple illustrations of parabolic nature, He reached down into the deepest things in the lives of these men, and they pleaded guilty, and chose their own punishment, without knowing what they were doing, until He had finished. Then they saw He was speaking about them.

There are two parables here, that of the two sons, and that of the husbandmen. What was the subject illustrated in both of them? The verse preceding the parables says, "And when He was come into the

Temple, the chief priests and the elders of the people came unto Him as He was teaching, and said, By what authority doest Thou these things? and who gave Thee this authority?"

That was the challenge of the rulers. Their opposition to Him had been growing. It began at the beginning of His ministry. It had grown more and more intense, and things had happened on the previous day. He had cleansed the Temple, driven out the traffickers, interfered with vested interests which were permitted by these very rulers; and they now came to Him. This time it was not a casual question, asked by one of their number. It was a question asked officially. They asked Him two questions. What were they? "By what authority doest Thou these things? and Who gave Thee this authority?" Literally the first question was, In what authority doest Thou these things? and the second, Who gave Thee this authority? It was a direct challenge on the part of the authorities to Jesus concerning His authority.

While this is not our subject, we need the background to see to what it led. Our Lord now asked them a question. "I also will ask you one question." They had asked Him two. "I also will ask you one question, which if ye tell Me, I likewise will tell you by what authority I do these things. The baptism of John, whence was it? from heaven or from men?"

Look at that question. They had asked Him for His authority. He took them back to that mighty ministry, with the effects of which they were all familiar, the ministry of John. They knew as well as He that John's ministry had culminated in the prediction of the Messiah. Vast multitudes had heard, and they had heard John as he had identified this very Jesus, and said, "Behold, the Lamb of God." Now, said Jesus, Was John's baptism and mission authorized from heaven or not? Or was it of men?

They were on the horns of a dilemma. If they said, Of heaven, then their question about Jesus was answered. If John was right in declaring He was the Messiah, the authority of Jesus was from heaven, then why ask Jesus for His authority? Notice what they said. They did not yet see the implication of the question. They began talking, and reasoning among themselves, saying, If we say, From heaven, He will say, Why do you not believe Me? If we say, From men, we fear the multitude, for all hold John a prophet. Their reasoning was false. They missed the point of His question. Their whole concern was to set themselves in a right light with general opinion. If they admitted the authority of John was derived from heaven, then Jesus would ask them why they did not believe Him. We see the contention. They had not believed, and they knew He would ask them why. If however they said what they wanted to say, His authority was from men, then they would have all the multitudes up in arms. So we see them halting between expediency and convenience; and whenever a man halts there, he is doomed and damned, unless he repent.

Our Lord then gave them two parables, each based upon the song of Isaiah, in the fifth chapter. "Let me sing for my wellbeloved a song of my beloved touching his vineyard. My wellbeloved had a vineyard in a very fruitful hill." They all knew that song of Isaiah. They were all familiar with that writing, and Jesus based His two parables upon that old-time song, and that in a remarkable way.

Take the first parable. The story told to them was that of two sons, and their opinion was asked concerning it. The story of the two sons, carefully considered, is seen to be the condemnation of their methods. The second parable, that of the husbandmen, is a condemnation of their motives.

The figure employed is that of two sons, both receiving a command to work in the vineyard. One said, I will not go, but afterward he repented, and went. The other said, as we render it, "I go, Sir." There is no word "go" there in the Greek. It would be awkward without it, but really it is an emphatic "I." "*I*, Sir." The picture Jesus drew was that of two sons in front of the master of the vineyard, and he said to the one, Go and work in my vineyard, and he said, I will not go; to the other he said the same thing, and the other said, "I, Sir." He was putting him into contrast with the man who said he would not go. That was his decision. Certainly I will go, Sir. "I, Sir."

We know the sequel. The man who said "I will not," repented, and the word means more than a change of mind. It means sorrow. He became sorry. He thought the matter through, and he went, and did his work. The other man who had emphasized it, by putting himself into contrast with the brother who would not go, did not go. Now, said Jesus, there is the story. Which of them is the true son of the father? Which of them did the will of the father? Oh, the first, they said. Oh yes, they knew, they agreed; and they were perfectly right.

Then our Lord made a remarkable application. He took them back to John. He had asked them about the baptism and mission of John, and his authority. I have asked you whether John's ministry was from heaven or of men, and you have said you did not know. That was their final finding, "We know not." Look back and see publicans and sinners, the rebellious crowd, on the one hand; and these very rulers, professing allegiance to God, on the other. Two sons. The publicans and harlots, and the rebellious say, We will not go; we will not yield to God. The rulers say, *We* will yield to God. We remember the prayer in the Temple, O God, I thank Thee I am not as other men are, or as this publican!

Then said Jesus, Under the preaching of John the publicans and harlots have repented; they have believed. You, the rulers, believe not, yet you refuse the signs of the publicans and harlots who are believing, and are doing the will of God. These outcasts, these publicans, these harlots, these rebellious ones who have defied God, and said they would not obey Him, have repented, and obeyed. You who wear the robes and livery, and recite the confession, and declare your loyalty, are failing to do the will of God. So our Lord compelled them to find a verdict against themselves.

How eternally true we know this to be. The publican, the drunkard, the harlot, the sot, the profligate who repents and turns to God, becomes God's son, God's child, God's instrument. Those men and women who name the Name, and wear the sign, and are disobedient and rebellious in all the deep facts of their life, are not the children of God, are not the sons of God.

But He had not finished. As He had condemned their method, now He turned to their motives, and the figure again is quite familiar. A man who was householder planted a vineyard. Mark the words, how He still quoted from Isaiah. He "set a hedge about it, and digged a winepress in it, and built a tower." It was the proprietor's perfect provision made for fruit to be gathered from his vineyard; and the husbandmen were those to whom he gave responsibility for the cultivation of the vines and vineyard, so that fruit should be brought forth to meet the proper requirements of the possessor. That was their responsibility.

Now, He said, in this case, when the time of fruit came, he sent his bond-servants, his servants, his slaves, his messengers to gather up the fruits; and those husbandmen stoned them, and killed them. Then he sent others, with the same result. At last,—and is there not mighty power and tremendous force in this, coming from the lips of Jesus?—at last he sent unto them his son. "But the husbandmen, when they saw the son, said among themselves, This is the heir; come, let us kill him, and take his inheritance. And they took him, and cast him forth out of the vineyard, and killed him." That is the story.

"When therefore the lord of the vineyard shall come, what will he do unto those husbandmen?" Again, they were so intrigued by the story, they had forgotten their hostility to Jesus. They saw the truth, and became vehement in their reply. "He will miserably destroy those miserable men, and will let out the vineyard unto other husbandmen, which shall render him the fruits in their season." They had passed sentence upon themselves. It was they, the rulers of the people, in the long succession, who for centuries had failed to yield the fruit of the vineyard. It is impossible to avoid the sentence.

For an interpretation of this, implicated and involved in the words of Jesus, we go back to Isaiah. There the vineyard instead of bringing forth grapes, brought forth wild grapes, and he explained his song, "For the vineyard of the Lord of hosts is the house of Israel, and the men of Judah His pleasant plant. And He looked for judgment." Change the word, not to improve it, but to interpret it. "He looked for justice, but behold, oppression; for righteousness, but behold, a cry."

Isaiah, in the Old Testament, tells us what the fruits were for which God looked in that nation of His. They were to bring forth in the world justice and righteousness, instead of which they had brought forth oppression, and created a cry of the oppressed. That is what these men had been doing; and the culmination of their false rule and government of the people had come in the case of the Son Himself. He knew what they were about to do. They were going to cast Him out, and kill Him.

When they had found their verdict, and passed that sentence, He passed His sentence. That is found in verse 43. He first quoted to them the Scripture about the rejected Stone being the Head of the corner. He pronounced the sentence of utter and absolute excommunication upon the whole Hebrew people, "Therefore say I unto you, The Kingdom of God shall be taken away from you, and shall be given to a nation bringing forth the fruits thereof. And he that falleth on this stone shall be broken to pieces; but on whomsoever it shall fall, it will scatter him as dust." There is the judgment.

The marvel of this is that He compelled these men to find a verdict, and pass a sentence. They who had failed to till and manage the vineyard of the Lord, so that the fruit for which God was seeking should be brought forth, they who had said, I go, and yet had failed and they who had stoned the prophets, and such as were sent unto them, and were now preparing to cast out the Son and kill Him—there was only one thing to be done, that they should be miserably destroyed, and the vineyard taken away from them, and given to others. The Lord repeated the verdict as He pronounced the appalling sentence of excommunication.

These parables, and others to follow, reveal the King's authority. That authority is demonstrated by the line of His accomplishment, of the revelation of truth, His recognition of the Divine rights, His restoration of a lost order. That was the purpose of His presence in the world. To these men who were not convinced, there was no argument of any avail. If they were not prepared to be honest enough to face the fact that the baptism of John was from heaven, and consequently his identification of Jesus proved the authority of Jesus, there was nothing else to be said to them. To men who were not honest, there was no argument of any avail, and those who refused the evidences that were so simple and patent and clear were rejected.

As Jesus told these stories to those rulers, and they found out what He was doing, their anger was stirred to yet greater depths. We learn therefore that ancient privilege is always unavailing when it departs from immediate and present responsibility. The King's new teaching here was a return to fundamental intentions, and He showed how the rulers of the people had failed, and declared that there should be another nation that would not fail, but would bring forth the fruits of justice and righteousness, for which God is ever seeking in His vineyard.

23. The Marriage Feast

Matthew xxii: 1-14.

THERE is an intimate connection between the 43rd verse in the previous chapter, and this parable. That verse read, "The Kingdom of God shall be taken away from you, and shall be given to a nation bringing forth the fruits thereof." This chapter begins, "And Jesus answered and spake again in parables unto them, saying, The Kingdom of heaven is likened unto a certain king, which made a marriage feast." The linking of those two verses help us to see the immediate significance of what our Lord was saying, and to discover the fact that it had a wide application, wider perhaps than we have been accustomed to think.

This chapter begins in a strange and arresting way. It says, "Jesus answered." Answered what? No question had been asked Him. There is no account of anything that had been said immediately to Him. Yet Matthew, going straight on with his account, says, "And Jesus answered." Again we go back and look at the verses at the close of the previous chapter. The 44th verse reads, "And he that falleth on this stone shall be broken to pieces; but on whomsoever it shall fall, it will scatter him as dust. And when the chief priests and the Pharisees heard His parables, they perceived that He spake of them. And when they sought to lay hold on Him, they feared the multitudes, because they took Him for a prophet. And Jesus answered," that is, He answered their attitude, answered the question in their minds, which had now become a conviction, perhaps suddenly and startlingly so.

Our Lord had spoken the two parables of the sons and of the vineyard; and they had expressed their opinion upon the stories He had told them; and by so doing they had found a verdict against themselves, and passed sentence upon themselves. Then they suddenly awoke to the fact of what they were doing, and their anger was stirred, and they would have liked to kill Him. And the Lord answered. It was the result of their frame of mind. It was an answer to this mental attitude of those who were His enemies, of those rulers whom He had now come to Jerusalem thus to condemn.

These were the final days in the life of our Lord on earth, and these parables all move in that realm. On this third day, He was there in the Temple as the great Prophet of God, the King, and Prophet, dealing with the nation in august majesty and dignity. The two parables we have considered had dealt with responsibility. Now He gave them a parable which dealt with privilege. In the former two parables, labourers were in view, and the vineyard was the background. Now guests are in view, and the background is a marriage feast. In the former, two commandments were laid upon men to fulfil obligations. In this, an invitation is offered to men to accept hospitality. So there is that difference between this parable and the two former, though they are all linked together.

As He had been dealing by parabolic illustration with the fulfilment of the responsibility of the rulers, and consequently of the nation, He now gave to these selfsame rulers a parable which dealt with the refused invitation, which had come through His ministry. Still further, glancing at the whole of these fourteen verses, we see their structure. The parable He now uttered was, in a remarkable way, predictive. He was looking over the whole fact of His own ministry, to the ministry of His servants that should follow to the end of the age. That is clearly seen if we study this carefully. Three invitations are offered. The marriage feast is in the background, to which men are asked, but there are three distinct invitations.

The account of the first invitation is in verses 2 and 3. The call was given, and those invited would not come. In the second invitation (4-7) the call is renewed, and we have the response of indifference and hostility. Then the third invitation, commencing, "Then saith

He to the servants," runs to the end of the parable. Our Lord was referring to three events, resulting from His own mission.

The first was that of His own mission. The second referred to His mission as it would be carried on by His servants, and that ended with judgment and the destruction of the city, a literal prediction of what happened a generation after, when Jerusalem was destroyed. The third invitation applied to the period from the destruction of Jerusalem to the consummation of the age in which we are now living.

If we apply this parable in detail, this first section has no application to us now, save as we look back and learn from what happened. The second section, also has no application to us, except as we watch and see what happened. But we are living in the third section, and our responsibility is revealed in that part of the parable. The first invitation was the call that had already been given, in the ministry of Jesus. The second invitation was the call which was repeated by His servants, from the time of His death to the destruction of the city. The third began when He sent out no longer to them that were bidden, but into the highways and byways, that all might be called in. There is perspective in this parable, and in that sense it is distinctly predictive.

Glance at the three sections. "The Kingdom of heaven is likened unto a certain king, which made a marriage feast for his son." The marriage feast is a figure of speech, and here our Lord was using an Eastern picture. We need not go into any details. We are not concerned with them, save as we remember that the figure was borrowed from the Old Testament ideal of God's relationship with man. The Old Testament symbolism was often strange and wonderful. Hosea speaking the words of God to the people, had said, "I will betroth thee unto Me for ever." Our Lord now took that symbolism of the betrothal and marriage when illustrating the Kingdom of heaven.

In what sense can that be said to illustrate the Kingdom of heaven? We have seen in the previous parables how they had failed to fulfil responsibility, and that judgment would follow later. Now our Lord turned definitely from responsibility to privilege. The Kingdom of heaven which He had come to proclaim, and to be proclaimed, and which He is still continuing to proclaim; He likened it to a marriage feast, something characterised by all joy, gladness, and merriment. So the Kingdom of heaven.

This Gospel of Matthew is peculiarly the Gospel of the King. Jesus is seen therein as King. When He first came to His work, He enunciated the laws of the Kingdom in the Sermon on the Mount. After that He gave an exhibition of the benefits of His Kingship and the Kingdom of God in the wonders He wrought (viii-ix. 35). In those chapters we see Him moving in every realm of human dereliction, material, mental, moral; healing the sick, casting out demons, forgiving sinsick souls. First the laws of the Kingdom and then its benefits. From that point we see Him constantly enforcing the claims of the Kingship of God. Keeping that in mind, then imagine a community wholly and absolutely yielded to those laws, and sharing in the benefits of the power of that Kingdom, because themselves obedient to the claims of the King, seeking first the Kingdom of God. Imagine that community, what have we? The best answer is to let Paul speak. "The Kingdom of God is not eating and drinking." What is it? "Righteousness, joy, peace." Those are the issues of the Kingship of God, when it is recognized and yielded to. The Kingdom of God is not a place of sombre gravity and dread solemnity. It is that, but it is infinitely more. It is the place first of righteousness, then of joy, and of peace. Like the marriage feast, it is filled with gladness and song; to use a word the father used when the prodigal came home,—merriment. The privileges He offered men were all there in the Kingdom of heaven. He had been revealing that Kingdom, calling men into it. The king sent his servants to call to the feast with the son.

What happened? They would not come. Here our Lord declared the national response. Of course individuals were answering the invitation. There were those within the nation who had heard, who had seen the joy, and blessedness; the righteousness, joy and peace of the Kingdom, and had yielded to it so far as the light had come; that little band of disciples, and the larger band seen in the upper room later, and the five hundred brethren at once to whom our Lord appeared in Galilee. There was the elect remnant of the nation. But He was dealing with the nation and their rulers, and with the national outlook, and response as revealed through those rulers. They would not come. So our Lord here declared, on the human level, the failure of His own mission. He, the Son, had come to bring men into that marriage feast, the marriage of men with God, that issues in righteousness, joy, and peace; and they had refused it. "They would not come."

"Again." There is tremendous force in that word. Following through the historic sequence, we know what they did with the Son. We saw that in the previous parable. "This is the heir; come, let us kill him, and take his inheritance." He knew He was on His way to that death. The Son Himself was cast out, and cast out to death. But there was no failure from the Divine standpoint. The failure was of the nation to accept the invitation to enter into the glad joy and peace and merriment of the Kingdom of God.

Again, beyond His rejection, He sent forth other servants. The apostolic age began, the preachers went forth everywhere, as Mark says. We know all the story. They were still to go to them that were bidden, to the people who had rejected Him; even to the rulers who had rejected Him, the privileged, bidden people; and they were to say, "Behold, I have made ready my dinner; my oxen and my fatlings are killed, and all things are ready; come to the marriage feast." Here is an account of the sending out of invitations to come into all the blessedness of the Kingdom again, after the first apparent failure. We see them going, and as we watch them, they are going with the same message. Notice the simplicity, and yet the sublimity of it. What were they to say? "All things are ready." "Killed," is a figure of speech here, which meant that God had done everything to provide for the joy, peace, and gladness of humanity in the proclamation of His Kingdom. He had done everything. By the time when these went out, the Cross was accomplished, and the hatred of men was transmuted by His grace into something that provided for that very righteousness, joy and peace. "All things are now ready."

Go back again to those that were bidden. Go even to those who would not come in the days of My own ministry, as though the Lord had said. Give them another opportunity. Go to them that were bidden. Tell them that all things are ready, that everything is done to create the joy, happiness, gladness, singing and rapture of My Kingdom; and bid them come.

What was the response? Again we necessarily go back to the centre of things where Jesus exercised His ministry. Our Lord said that the invitation would be treated with indifference by each one. "They made light of it, and went their ways." Mark the process, "one to his own farm, another to his merchandise"; and then by definite rebellion. Then the ill-treatment of the messengers, and their beating and casting out. All that happened in that earlier apostolic age. Jesus clearly revealed what the result would be of the second refusal by those who were bidden.

Then "the king was wroth, and he sent his armies, and destroyed those murderers, and burned their city." That happened a generation afterwards. As the Lord God Almighty in the past had girded Cyrus for the carrying out of the punitive action against His own people, so surely He girded the Roman armies, under Titus, as they swept upon the city that for the second time had rejected the call; first the actual call of Jesus, and secondly the call of Jesus by the Holy Spirit, through the messengers. The King was standing there, talking to these rulers, and He clearly saw the things that were about to happen.

What then? "Then saith he to his servants, The wedding is ready, but they that were bidden were not worthy"; because they were blind, they did not see; and they were evil and self-centred, turning every one to his own way, and ill-treating the very messengers of the king because they were blind to the meaning.

What is to be done now? "Go ye therefore unto the partings of the highways"—a great phrase that,—"the partings of the highways." The words were uttered by our Lord in that Roman world, celebrated for its highways. Perhaps nothing more remarkable was done by that Roman empire than the building of those highways. We have them still here in Britain. They beat out from Rome over all the known world, and along them Roman cohorts passed, and Greek merchant-men travelled. They were the great media of travel throughout the known world. Therefore go there to the partings of the highways. Overleap the boundaries which are merely geographical. Those who were bidden, who had the privileges of nationality, and who, lived in the land where My ministry was conducted, are not worthy. Their city will be destroyed. It will be burned with fire. Then the larger invitation will begin. Go to the partings of the highways, and as many as ye shall find, bid to the marriage feast. When the bidden were demonstrated unworthy, then the invitation to the marriage feast, to the benefits and beneficences of the Kingdom of God, were offered to all men. Go where the highways part, where they divide. Stand where the crowds will press and throng and cross each other; and into those highways pass, calling men everywhere to this great Kingdom.

Moreover He said, "Those servants went out into the highways, and gathered together all as many as they found, both bad and good; and the wedding was filled with guests." That does not mean that there was to be no further reference to moral conduct, or standing in the Kingdom. But if men in the highways have no character, no moral standing, if they are bad, call them in. If they are good, by the standards of the world, true to the light in them, and in that way they are good, call them in, good and bad. The servants brought them in, guests of the King, admitted to all the great privileges of the Kingdom of God.

That solemn word of Jesus at the end shows how true it is that there is moral discrimination in the Kingdom, notwithstanding the use of the word "bad" there. We must interpret that by this. "When the king cometh in to behold the guests," to inspect them, "he saw there a man which had not on a wedding garment, and he saith to him,

Comrade, Friend, how camest thou in hither not having a wedding garment?" A man had found his way in, but he lacked the true insignia of relationship. He was violating the true order of that Kingdom. This man has been described in modern parlance as a gate-crasher. It is a very suggestive description. Yes, he had gone in, and the fact he had not on a wedding garment showed indifference, carelessness, or objection. He was not of that company. He had not a wedding garment.

Matthew says, The King "saw there a man which had *not* on a wedding garment." Then he said, "Friend, how camest thou in hither *not* having a wedding garment?" The little word *not* appeared twice over, but it is not the same word on those two occasions. The first word, *Ou* simply marks a fact; he had not it on. But when the king asked him the reason, Jesus used a slightly different word for "not" *Me,* which suggested not merely the fact that he lacked the wedding garment, but that he did so definitely, of his own thought, and will, and intention. When the man came in not having a wedding garment, and the king talked to him, he said, It is not only a fact that you have not a wedding garment; you did not intend having one. Your "not" is the *not* of definite willing. You are determined *not* to have it on. Your presence in here is the supreme sign of your rebellion against the order set up, of which this marriage feast is the great symbol. "And he was speechless"; he had nothing to say.

Then follows the terrible sentence. "Cast him out into the outer darkness," where there shall be sorrow and rebellion; "there shall be the weeping and gnashing of teeth." This was His revelation. That is the continuity of sin. "Cast him out into the outer darkness."

The Kingdom of God has its responsibilities. They rest upon all of us who profess to belong to that Kingdom. The vineyard and the two sons revealed to us our responsibilities. This picture shows us all the glory and beauty of the Kingdom, resulting from its presentation by our Lord Christ.

We ask, How does this apply to us as to responsibility? The fruit of the Kingdom of God as the Kingdom of heaven. I do not want to waste time discussing the difference between those terms. There is no difference, except that the Kingdom of heaven—a phrase Matthew mostly used, and used as employed by Jesus—expresses the result. The Kingdom of heaven is the realisation of the Kingship of God. We are praying that His Kingdom may come on earth as it is in heaven. When the prayer is answered, we have the Kingdom of heaven. The measure in which it is answered in our life, in the community of souls loyal to Him, that is the Kingship of God. The Kingdom does not merely mark a territory, but it marks the fact of authority, and the exercise of it; the Kingdom of God sought, yielded to, realized. Then look abroad, and the result is the Kingdom of heaven. Are we realizing it?

That drives us back to another question. How far are we really submitted to the Kingdom of God? If we are, we know what it is to live in the Kingdom of heaven, righteousness the foundation, joy the result, and quiet peace the issue. It is the marriage feast. The bells are always ringing, and the music always sounding.

But there is a stern necessity for the wedding garment. The call is to all, but there must be the wedding garment. Jesus ended with that strange and wonderful word in connection with this parable, "Many are called, but few chosen." Many years ago, at a great meeting in London, Moody was speaking on this parable. Sitting on the platform by him was one of the great scholars of the Church, and a theologian, a mighty man. When Moody got to that point in his address, "Many are called, but few are chosen," he stopped, and said, "Hold on, what does chosen mean? He turned to Dr. L, this scholar, and said, "I would like to read it like this, Many are called, but few are choice. Dr. L said, "You are quite right, Mr. Moody, that is the whole intention of it." It is good to have such an authority. Jesus did not say, I am calling people, and choosing some, who are the chosen ones, those who accept the call. Those who do not accept, will return to their own imaginings and their own affairs. Those who obey, and fulfil the responsibility of the vineyard, and accept the invitation, will go in as guests in the festive house of God, to the feast which He has spread in His great Kingdom. Many are called, but few are chosen, choice in that sense.

This is a great vision, sweeping over the centuries. Our Lord saw the Kingdom not only as a vineyard, having to be cultivated, but as a feast, a marriage of merriment, and of peace.

24. Parabolic Illustrations

Matthew xxiii.

IT is important to have a general sense of the whole movement of this chapter, for against that background we find illustrations our Lord used in the course of His discourse. We are at once reminded of the inevitable solemnity of the occasion. This chapter records the final hours of Jesus in the Temple. After this discourse He left it, to go back no more. His word had excommunicated the Hebrew people, not from salvation, or the possibility of it, but from the office they had held by Divine appointment, of being the instrument through which the Kingdom of God was to be proclaimed and revealed among men. He had uttered His final, Kingly, Divine word of excommunication when He said to the nation through the rulers, "The Kingdom of God shall be taken away from you, and shall be given to a nation bringing forth the fruits thereof."

This 23rd chapter is a continuous discourse, and we observe it falls into three distinct parts. The first part was addressed to the multitudes and His disciples. Notice the opening words of the chapter. He was still there in Temple precincts. The crowds were all round about Him. Nearest to Him were His own disciples, and in the first twelve verses He addressed Himself to the disciples and to the crowds. As we read, it is easy to see the part intended for the multitudes, and the particular part intended for His own disciples.

Beginning at the 13th verse, still in the same situation, the disciples and the multitudes still there, and the rulers with whom He had dealt in the earlier chapter; He began to address Himself directly to those rulers, and those in authority. That section beginning at verse 13 ends at verse 36.

The third section was addressed, out of His heart, to the city of Jerusalem, as He saw it. There it was, represented by the rulers. There were multitudes of Jerusalem folk gathered in the Temple, and unquestionably others. There was the city of Jerusalem itself, built round about that Temple, and He addressed Himself to the city as the mother of the nation. That is in verses 37 to 39.

In all the record of the words of Jesus we have nothing quite so full of terror as His discourse that day to the rulers. It is noticeable that He pronounced upon these rulers, scribes, and Pharisees an eightfold Woe. It is significant when He began His public ministry, and enunciated His great ethic in the Sermon on the Mount, He began with an eightfold Beatitude. Now to the rulers specifically, definitely, those who had been hostile to Him from the beginning, and whose hostility had grown upon them He pronounced an eightfold Woe. Take the eight Beatitudes and Woes, and they stand over against each other; and we can see how they answered each other in the most wonderful way.

In the course of that discourse He employed certain illustrations. In the first two movements He made use of six parabolic illustrations and then when addressing Jerusalem, unveiling His heart, He made use of one. All these illustrations were in the realm of denunciation, all uttered on the same day, in the same place, in the same discourse; and then a parabolic illustration unveiling His heart.

Whereas the illustrations themselves are brief as to words, they are graphic beyond degree, and as a clear and sharp lightning flash they lit up the things He was saying, whether of denunciation, or of the unveiling of His heart.

Take the words briefly. "They bind heavy burdens" (ver. 4). The picture is common, but it is very graphic. "Blind guides" (ver. 16). Again an illustration, but the picture is absurd, though graphic. "The gnat" and "the camel" (ver. 24). The picture is grotesque, and therefore graphic. "The cup," "the platter" (ver. 26). The picture is disgusting, and so graphic. "Whited sepulchres" (ver. 27). The picture is appalling, and very graphic. "Serpents," "brood of vipers" (ver. 33). The picture is terrible, and so graphic. Then "a hen" and "her chickens" (ver. 37). The picture is simple, and therefore graphic. That brief reference to each descriptive phrase, each parabolic light marvellously illuminated what He was saying.

Take that first word. "They bind heavy burdens." The picture, common at the time was that of an overladen beast of burden, of a horse, or an ass, upon which burdens were placed all too heavy for it to carry. In this country a draft-horse should never be expected to pull more than its own weight. I was once standing by a friend of mine, a member of my church, a great contractor, as he was superintending some of his work. He saw a draft-horse laden, coming up; and I saw him look at it. I wondered at the fierceness in his eyes. He stopped it, and said to the cartman, "What load is on that cart?" He said, "Two tons, sir." He replied, "Keep that load down to a ton; no horse can pull more than its own weight." The figure here is that of a beast of burden, with a weight put upon it that it has no right to be carrying; and, indeed, in the last analysis, cannot carry. It will sink beneath it. Jesus said to those rulers, that was what they were doing, overloading these beasts of burden, abusing authority by putting upon men burdens they could not possibly carry.

It is wonderful what our Lord said in that connection. He said, These men, scribes and Pharisees, sit in Moses' seat. The word "seat" there stands for authority. It is the word *cathedra*. Today we say men speak *ex cathedra*, that is, out of the seat of authority. Jesus said these men sat in Moses' seat. He really said they had seated themselves in Moses' seat. That is the force of the Greek word. The whole order of scribes had arisen, not improperly; indeed, Jesus set

His imprimatur upon it as being permissible. But it was not a Divine appointment originally. They set themselves in Moses' seat, that is, they were there to interpret the law as given to men through Moses. "Therefore," put emphasis upon the "therefore," "all things whatsoever they bid you these do and observe." But they had said so many things that men could not do; they had bound burdens on men that they could not bear. They had added to the law multiplied traditions, crushing the soul, and making men turn from the law, and from God.

Did the Master mean if they sat in Moses' seat the people were to do anything the rulers told them? No; when they spoke according to the law, then they were to be obedient. But He said to the rulers that their whole method of tradition, superimposed upon the law of God, men could not carry. "Woe unto you, scribes and Pharisees, hypocrites." Why? They were putting these burdens upon men, but were not carrying them, and they would not help. He did not mean they would not help men to carry them, but they would not carry them themselves.

In that connection He went on to show the disciples what they were to do. In the 13th chapter He had appointed His disciples the new scribes, the moral interpreters. "Every scribe who hath been made a disciple to the Kingdom of heaven is like unto a man that is a householder, which bringeth forth out of his treasure things new and old." They were scribes. His disciples were His new scribes. He was denouncing these scribes who had bound burdens upon men, who had become taskmasters, cruel even in their enunciation of law. Notice now what He said to His disciples. Do not be called Rabbi. Do not be called Father. Do not be called Master. All these words indicated their mission, and reveal the value of their teaching. They were servants. So He was sending forth His own disciples. He was sending them out on that great mission; and it was that of service, not to bind heavy burdens upon men, but to serve men for the lifting of burdens and bringing of release.

Then in the 16th verse He said, "Woe unto you, ye blind guides." Again in verse 24, "Ye blind guides." There is another parabolic illustration, absurd and therefore graphic. One blind man is trying to lead blind men. The guide who should know the way, and be familiar with it, and lead others along it, is himself blind. He does not see the way at all.

Our Lord was illustrating the fact that these men had given interpretations of the law, and of the ritual, which inverted order, proving that they themselves did not see. They were making the gold more valuable than the Temple. They were making the gift more valuable than the altar, forgetting it was the Temple that sanctified the gold, the altar that made sacred the gift. "Blind guides!" They could not see themselves. Their spiritual vision of relative values had faded, and yet there they were, teaching the people, and because they did not see, their teaching was utterly false.

In close connection He went on. "Blind guides, which strain out the gnat, and swallow the camel." What a grotesque idea it is. The picture is one of a man with a goblet. He is about to drink, and there is a gnat, and he is particular to get it out; and there is a camel, and he swallows it. It is intended to be grotesque, and to show exactly what these men were doing. "Woe unto you scribes and Pharisees, hypocrites!" It is a picture of most glaring inconsistency. Observe in passing our Lord did not say it was wrong to tithe mint and anise and cummin. As a matter of fact He said they ought to do so. But the trouble was, while they did that, and got the gnat out of their drinking goblet, they were neglecting essential values, and swallowing the camel. "Woe unto you scribes and Pharisees, hypocrites!"

We come next to the cup and platter. The picture is graphically disgusting. Certainly nothing could be more loathsome than a dirty cup inside, when the outside was clean. But our Lord used the figure intelligently. It *was* disgusting. They were very careful that the outside was clean, but it did not matter what the inside was like. The commonplace reaction of every man and woman is that it is disgusting; yet that is exactly what these men were doing. They were eager about the maintenance of an external appearance, which was a lie, because within they were full of every form of corruption and evil. I am not staying to apply these things. I am leaving the Holy Spirit to do that. These are all perils for us all the time.

Then the figure of a "whited sepulchre," a peculiarly Eastern figure, a burying place, in which only corpses are placed, and are covered over, and whited. The picture is appalling and graphic. In that Eastern country it meant anyone buried, and people walking across the place where corruption was going forward, were in danger. It is not by external whiteness and cleanness that we are in danger of deadly infection. The rulers, scribes, and Pharisees were whited sepulchres. They were practising a deceit which had in it a terrible menace to others. They were concerned with an external appearance which veiled an inward corruption. Men and women incessantly crossing their pathway, attracted, at least not repelled by all the white appearance, nevertheless were inhaling the deadly germs of their own wrong and corruption. "Whited sepulchres!"

Once more, "Woe unto you, scribes and Pharisees, hypocrites! . . .

serpents, ye offspring of vipers," the spawn of vipers. The picture is terrible. Serpents, the offspring, the brood, the spawn of the viper; the keen eye, the poisonous bite. Jesus said, That is where you hypocrites belong, to that realm of dire peril to men. He gave the reasons. So in all these we hear Him in that last discourse within Temple precincts, uttering these terrible Woes, and by illustration showing their reason, and revealing the truth about these men.

Come to the final illustration. "As a hen doth gather her brood beneath her wings," simple, and yet graphic. It is one of the most beautiful pictures of motherhood that can possibly be imagined. It is not necessary to dwell upon it. We have evidences of it in all our villages, hamlets, and farmsteads. We have seen the mother hen, when the sharp cry of a hawk is heard, suddenly gather all the little ones under her outspread wings. There is no need to enlarge upon it. It is such a wonderful picture. Jesus said as He addressed Jerusalem, the great centre and mother of the national life, which was under the influence of the hypocrites, the scribes and Pharisees, which had scattered her children, and driven them out into all the places of deadly peril, "O Jerusalem, Jerusalem," what that hen does for those chickens I fain would have done for you. "How often would I have gathered thy children together, even as a hen gathereth her chickens under her wings." The whole illustration thrills and pulsates with the Motherhood of God. I did not say Fatherhood. That is a great truth, but the other truth is as vitally revealed in the Bible. "As one whom his mother comforteth, so will I comfort you." Those are God's words. Jesus took that great figure of Motherhood, in its simplest ritual manifestation, the picture of the hen and the brood, and He said, That is what I want, that is what I came for, that is what I fain would have done.

"Woe," uttered eight times over. It was necessary because of human choices and misrepresentations; but that was not what His heart desired. He would have gathered them as a hen gathers her brood beneath her wings.

So among the last sentences in that Temple, even after the pronouncement of His Woes upon the rulers who had misled the people, He unveiled His heart. Yet that was the prelude to His ultimate sentence. "Your house is left unto you desolate." He had often been in that House. If we treat the word as local, as certainly it was, while referring to far more, to the whole dynasty and economy, He had often been in that House. He was going out of it, and as He went He said, "Your house is left unto you desolate." In the course of the ministry He had called that Temple, "My Father's

House." He had called it "My House." Now He called it "your house," and it is desolate.

Yet while that was the sentence, it was the penultimate sentence, and the very last word is this, "For I say unto you, ye shall not see Me henceforth, till ye shall say, Blessed is He that cometh in the name of the Lord." Thus through the appalling gloom of desolation there shone a light that spoke of a day of restoration when they would say, "Blessed is He that cometh in the name of the Lord."

The main thing is His description of those rulers. The key word, "hypocrites," was uttered six times over, perhaps seven. As we see Him thus denouncing hypocrisy, we observe all through His passion for righteousness, and we find in the unveiling of His heart His compassion for the worst. His passion for righteousness never destroys His compassion; but His compassion never destroys His passion for righteousness.

25. *Parabolic Illustrations*

Matthew xxiv.

IN THE parabolic illustrations and parables which remain to be considered in this Gospel again we find ourselves in a changed atmosphere. The illustrations throughout the three previous chapters have moved in the realm of judgment and of denunciation. In this 24th chapter our Lord had left the Temple and the city of Jerusalem, never to return until He was taken back as Prisoner.

As they passed out of the Temple, His disciples drew His attention to the buildings. I wonder why they did so, for He surely knew them. Note His immediate reply. He said, "See ye not all these things? Immediately before this, before they left the Temple, He had declared, "Your house is left unto you desolate." As they went out, the disciples said, Lord, let us show You these buildings. It was unthinkable to them that that house should ever be desolate; but within a generation from that time it was literally true. He now said, "See ye not all these things?" Take a good look at them, because they are going. "There shall not be left here one stone upon another, that shall not be thrown down." Remember the Temple as it then was, for material magnificence there had been nothing like it. The temple of Solomon had been wonderful, but the temple of Herod, from the standard of material magnificence far outshone the glories of Solomon's temple. It was a wondrous structure, and He said, "Not . . . one stone upon another, that shall not be thrown down."

Then they went down from the city. Follow them in imagination along the way they took, across the Kedron, and up the slopes of Olivet. When they came there, He sat, and the disciples came to Him privately, and they said, "Tell us, when shall these things be? and what shall be the sign of Thy coming, and of the end of the age?"— the consummation of the age. I resolutely change that phrase, "and of the world," and adopt the marginal reading, which is correct. They were not asking when the end of the world would be, in the sense of the break-up of the material structure, as some people seem to imagine, even now. No, it was the consummation of the age. Their question really resolved itself into three: first, When shall these things be? secondly, What shall be the sign of Thy coming? third, What shall be the sign of the end of the age?

They were three perfectly natural questions. I do not think they meant to ask three, but one. They had heard Him say the things that were coming to pass. They had heard Him in denunciation declare the tribulations that were coming. Now they said, When is it all going to happen, when? It is interesting how all down the ages men have been busy asking that futile question, When? These men started it. They said, When? and they linked up the things He had foretold with His presence, the sign of His coming, His parousia, His presence again in the world. They felt that His prediction of the consummation of the age involved the winding up of all things, and they believed it would be brought about by His presence; but what they wanted to know was, When? It was a plain question that they asked.

Our Lord answered them. I take now only the beginning of His answer. When they had asked their question, He said, "Take heed that no man lead you astray." We are interested now only in the two things. They said, When? and they did not understand what the things were to which they were referring. They thought they did. They still had their material conception of a Kingdom that was to be set up, that the Roman power was to be destroyed, and the Messiah would reign there, materially. They had no correct vision of the future. I am not criticizing them. We are trying to see how they looked at things. They believed He would bring all this about. They wanted to know how long they, and the world would have to wait. To that the first answer of Jesus was, Be careful, lest you are led astray, for many will come, claiming to be Christ.

Jesus then answered their question. That answer occupies the whole of this and the next chapter. To that question asked by the disciples our Lord gave a longer and fuller answer than He had ever given before, or ever did again, showing there was vital importance in what they asked, even though they were mistaken in their outlook. He showed that there would be a consummation, that these things were to come to pass, showing, moreover, in the course of His answer that they would be connected with His own coming, His own Parousia, His presence. He sat there upon the slopes of Olivet as Teacher, and with that group of men, honestly perplexed, He surveyed all the coming centuries. In this prophecy He uttered definite predictions, looking on down the centuries.

While it is not our subject now to deal with the prophecy, it is difficult to look at the illustrations He used without having the background in mind. As we study carefully we find He broke their question up into three parts, and showed when "these things" would be, that they would not be immediate; and then what should be "the sign of His coming"; and finally showed clearly what would be the nature of "the consummation of the age." This Olivet discourse moved wholly within the realm of prophecy. He was looking on to things beyond His departure. He knew He was going to Jerusalem, to be killed; He knew He was going to rise again; and He was in no perplexity as to the course events would take. He was making no speculation as to the future. He clearly marked the course of events all down that period after His Cross and ascension until the present hour, and beyond it.

Does anyone whisper, When will the end be? I recommend to all such the answer Christ gave to His own disciples, and pray that we may ever put upon the things of God the measurements of His own outlook, in which there was an utter absence of dates, or of the fixing of an hour. Processes, events are marked, the consummation is revealed; but there are no dates from first to last.

The illustrations have to do with that period, and principally with the consummation of the age. We find then in this 24th chapter five illustrations. The first was that of lightning. The second was that of a carcase with eagles gathered round. The third was that of the fig-tree. The fourth was that of a master of the house, and the thief, the burglar; and the last was that of the lord presiding over his household. Let us take each briefly, following our usual line.

Verse 27, "For as the lightning cometh forth from the east, and is seen even unto the west; so shall be the coming of the Son of man." Our Lord had foretold definitely the destruction of Jerusalem. What

He had said about the Temple is involved in what He said, "When therefore ye see the abomination of desolation, which was spoken of by Daniel the prophet, standing in the holy place." That was fulfilled when the Roman armies invaded the Temple. Then the abomination of desolation was standing in the holy place. The Master was looking on to the fall of Jerusalem which came within a generation. He had foretold it, and He was now warning His disciples that the fall of Jerusalem, the wars and rumors of wars before that event, and the actual "abomination of desolation standing in the holy place" were not the signs of His advent. He foresaw all these things, but they did not signify the nearness of His advent; and in that connection He used the figure of the lightning.

The figure is so simple that there is no need of interpretation. Lightning is seen from one arc of heaven to the other. It is patent and self-evident, and He was insisting upon this in connection with His coming, that it will be as clear and as patent as the flash of the lightning across the sky from the east to the west. His coming will have a universal manifestation. We must not forget that the figure is used to show that the fall of Jerusalem, and the trouble immediately coming on the generation, was not the sign of His coming at all. Some believe that He came in connection with the fall of Jerusalem, and that His coming is past. But nothing can be clearer that was not the sign of His coming. When that hour comes, it will be something self-evident to the whole world. Of course the figure He used took in a hemisphere. If we watch the lightning, we only see it in a hemisphere. It goes from east to west, and from the point where it ends as to our observation, it goes on again. This figure, showing that His coming, when it takes place, will be universal, known and self-evident, needs no proof either than its own manifestation.

Immediately following it, we have the words, "Wheresoever the carcase is, there will the eagles be gathered together." The Old Version reads, "For wheresoever." It should read as in the Revised Version. He had talked about the lightning. Then, "Wheresoever the carcase is, there will the eagles be gathered together." What did He mean by that? What was He illustrating? This illustration is in exactly the same realm as the former one, but here with a judgment application. The coming of the Son of man will be as patent as flashing lightning across the sky, but what will it mean? He was referring now to the judgment that was going to fall.

Take the figure of speech in all its simplicity. Vultures, carrion birds, swift birds, detecting the presence of a dead thing, fasten upon it for its complete annihilation. He was looking on to the condition of death that would obtain at His advent.

Do we really believe that? Our Lord distinctly said, "When the Son of man cometh, shall He find faith on the earth?" All exposition that says the victory of the Kingdom will be completely won at His coming is unscriptural. There will be a terrible condition of affairs, and however much we may be perplexed by some of the details, if we carefully read the book of Revelation, we see some of the awful conditions, and fearful blasphemy against all the advancement of goodness, until this culmination in judgment. The world in its final outworking of its choices and inspiration is looked upon as dead; and the vultures represent the last processes of judgment. Where the carcase is, there will they be gathered together.

Pass on to verse 32, to His next illustration, the fig-tree. The coming of the Son of man shall be manifest like the lightning; the coming of judgment when the vultures gather together over the dead, the carrion of a world that has rejected God; and yet notice, from the fig-tree learn this parable. It is interesting to notice in passing that Luke also records the saying, and adds four words Matthew omitted, thar Jesus said, "Behold the fig-tree, and all the trees." So do not lay too much emphasis on the fig tree, although the picture was the symbol of the people and of the nation. Do not imagine the Lord was only speaking of the Jewish people, but of "all the trees." He was taking a simple illustration from Nature. What was it? That there are signs in Nature by which we can know Summer is coming. We need not take the fig tree. We can take the balsam tree. Some of us have seen it blossoming. It is a prophecy of what is coming. We see the burgeoning of the trees, and we know Summer is coming.

Now mark what our Lord says. Lightning, vultures, a carcase; but as a process, leading on to something, summer. "Now is the winter of our discontent," but there is summer time coming; and in a simple and yet beautiful figure of speech, here He returned to the subject of His second Advent, and showed that there would be signs that lead to it, signs that show these things of His own glory manifested, and the things of a sharp act of judgment, destroying the dead carcase, and the sign of Summer. We may know by these things that the summer is nigh.

Go on to verse 43. "Know this, that if the master of the house had known in what watch the thief was coming, he would have watched, and would not have suffered his house to be broken through. Therefore be ye also ready; for in an hour that ye think not the Son of man cometh." Our Lord has returned to the ultimate idea of the consummation. This portion of His discourse had to do largely with the responsibility of His people. To that subject we come more fully in subsequent parables. The subject He was illustrating here was the need for vigilance, alertness, watchfulness; and He took that commonplace illustration of a man, who had a house. He is the master of the house, and the thief may dig through—that is the actual word,—and break in upon it. Now if the master of the house had known when the thief was coming, he would have prevented his breaking through. Therefore watch, for ye do not know when the Son of man is coming.

This is an illustration by contrast, the Lord Himself in contrast with the thief. The idea is that if a man knew when the thief was coming, he would watch. We are to watch, because we do not know, and because we do not know, there is all the more necessity for watchfulness. The Master added three words here, "at every season," marking the necessity for watchfulness.

Then the last of these illustrations is in close connection. "Who then is the faithful and wise servant, whom his lord hath set over his household." This marks the responsibility of those who are watching. It is difficult to get these illustrations placed in relation to the great mosaic of the discourse. We are now looking to the consummation of the age. We do not know when it is coming. There will be signs that mark it near, and those are the signs of judgment, clearing the way for the glory that is to be revealed. We do not know when that event will take place, hence the necessity for watchfulness, alertness, diligence; all which words may be expressed in another;—readiness.

How are we to be ready? Our Lord took the figure of the household where the lord is absent. The servants are left, responsible for the things of that household, and this subject illustrates the responsibility of the watchers. What is their responsibility? "Blessed is that servant, whom his lord when he cometh shall find so doing," watching. How? Giving to each in the household his "food in due season. Verily I say unto you, that he will set him over all that he hath. But if that evil servant shall say in his heart, My lord tarrieth; and shall begin to beat his fellow-servants, and shall eat and drink with the drunken; the lord of that servant shall come in an hour when he expecteth not, and in an hour when he knoweth not, and shall cut him asunder, and appoint his portion with the hypocrites; there shall be the weeping and gnashing of teeth."

What an august majesty of outlook. At the consummation of the age appalling things are going to happen; and there will be the judgment of wickedness. His charge to His own is that they shall watch, be diligent, alert, be ready. Then this little illustration shows that the true test of vigilance for the absent Lord, and expectation of His coming, is right behaviour within His own household. Here His Church is in view, down the ages. A communal relationship must be maintained, and if within that household there are those who are professedly the servants of the absent Lord, who are not behaving as they ought to do to their brethren, we can go on into the New Testament, and to the letters of John especially, and find words that interpret all that behaviour. There can be no watching for the coming Lord on the part of people who are first of all behaving as they ought not, to each other within His household; and who are giving way to riotous excess of living on the earthly plane. There must be the watchfulness, true fellowship and behaviour within the household, until the Lord shall come.

If when He comes, He finds these things have not been so, then mark the almost terrible word, "In an hour when he knoweth not," He shall come, and "shall cut him asunder," put him out, "appoint his portion with the hypocrites," where there shall be sorrow, and perpetual rebellion, in other words, "weeping and gnashing of teeth."

All these illustrations need the context perhaps as none other we have considered. Let us note the vision of Christ, the interpretation of Christ in answer to the questions of His disciples, as He said to them, Take heed, do not be led astray. Do not imagine that the Advent is so near, or that things are coming to a consummation as speedily as you imagine. Many will arise, false christs, and claim that they have come for fulfilment of all things. Do not believe them. Do not go out to the wilderness to them. Watch and wait, knowing that we do not know the hour, but that we know the fact, and are living in the power of it by true relationship with each other within the household of God, and so hasten the coming of the Day.

26. *The Ten Virgins*

Matthew xxv: 1-13.

CHAPTERS 24 and 25 constitute one great whole in the teaching of our Lord, occasioned by a prediction that He had made about the destruction of the Temple, and the question then raised by His disciples, as the result of that prediction. This unbroken discourse of Jesus was uttered, not to the promiscuous crowds, but to His own disciples.

It is impossible to take this parable, or the one immediately following this, without a consciousness of the whole discourse. Our Lord was illustrating great truths in the realm of His predictive discourse, delivered to His own disciples, on Olivet.

The first word of this chapter is important, "Then." There was no break in His discourse. What He now said in this parable followed immediately upon what He had been saying before, when He had used the illustration of the householder, and the wise and faithful servants therein, and those who were unwise and unfaithful in the household. He had ended that illustration by saying those unfaithful and unwise were to have their portion appointed with the hypocrites, "there shall be the weeping and gnashing of teeth." "Then shall the Kingdom of heaven be likened unto ten virgins." He was referring to that time, already referred to in the previous chapter, and the parabolic illustrations of the householder and the servants when the lord comes. "Then shall the Kingdom of heaven be likened unto." In that little word "Then" is the key to the interpretation. When will the Kingdom of heaven be like this? Not today. This parable of the ten virgins is often used as an evangelistic message. Evangelistic values may be deduced from it, but our Lord was not referring to this period, but to the consummation of the period, the time when the Lord shall come.

His discourse included the parabolic illustration of the householder and servants, and this parable of the virgins, and that which immediately and consecutively follows. There was no break. Again we have the word "For" at verse 14. The three parables followed each other, all belonging to the consummation of the age; intended for His own, not for the world outside. In every case there is an absent lord; but in each case the absent lord returns, and it is with this return of the absent lord these parables deal. They reveal certain aspects of the responsibilities of His own while the Lord is absent, in the light of what will transpire when the Lord returns. The parable of the household, the lord absent, his servants left in charge; the parable of the lord as bridegroom absent, certain people left there to wait for him; and the parable of the absent lord, having bestowed talents upon his own, and their response.

A threefold responsibility is revealed in the three parables. They link and merge in revelation. The first parable dealt with communal responsibility, within the circle of His own, concerning their behaviour towards each other. The whole Church is seen there. The second, that of the ten virgins, is still responsibility, but it is the responsibility of individual life that is manifest here. In the next parable, that of the talents, we shall see the responsibility of the Church with regard to imperial matters, the empire of Jesus, and trading for Him in His absence. First, how we should behave inside, communal responsibility, the parable of the householder. Then personal responsibility, what our attitude should be in the presence of the absence of the Lord, and the expectation of His return, the parable of the virgins. Then the imperial responsibility, as He has entrusted to us certain things for which we are responsible, the parable of the talents.

"Then," when the Lord shall come to deal with His people concerning their communal responsibility, as was revealed at the end of the previous chapter, "Then shall the Kingdom of heaven be likened unto ten virgins." What was the subject which our Lord was illustrating? He was looking on to the consummation of the age, created by the coming of the Bridegroom. The parable is a figure of the bride and bridegroom. He is showing here the relation to that consummation of those whose duty is that of being prepared for it. The emphasis here is not on service. The symbols are not those of service, but of life. Everything leads up to that final injunction, "Watch." He has shown what our responsibility is towards each other, that there is to be a love-mastered community. Now, coming closer to the individual application, He takes this parable.

The figure employed is very simple, and Eastern. This Eastern scene was commonplace. Every one who heard Him would understand it. Moreover we must not strain it in exposition. There is no mention of the bride in this story. That may give some pause. It is interesting how many people have tried to find the bride in the story, and have said that the wise virgins were the bride. There may be an element of truth in it. But the figure here is not of the bride, but of the bridegroom. Such an undoubted scholar as Trench, and others, interpret this whole parable as referring to the homecoming of the bridegroom with his bride. Generally however it is interpreted as the bridegroom coming for His bride, and that certainly harmonises with other Scriptures. In that sense it may be said that the five wise virgins represent the true bride of Christ. The figure represents those who waited for the bridegroom when he comes.

We need not go into the particulars of the Eastern picture, because it is so simple and familiar. The Bridegroom is away, and whether He is coming for His people, or with His bride at the moment is not important. There are those who were expected to be waiting for Him, for His coming. These are represented by these virgins. They were all waiting for His coming, they were all expecting Him. They all had lamps, and at a certain moment, they all trimmed their lamps. Here is a picture of the light of that period, fed with oil, needing to have the wick constantly trimmed. That is the figure.

As they waited, "they all slumbered and slept," which does not suggest negligence on their part. It is natural and right. It is rather interesting, that "slumbered and slept" would be better interpreted if put in another way, they nodded, and went right off! That is precisely what this means. They were waiting. It was night. They were waiting for the bridegroom, not knowing when he was coming; and necessarily and properly, they got drowsy, and they all went to sleep.

Then came the cry that told them the event for which they had waited was at hand. "Behold, the bridegroom! Come ye forth to meet him." Then we see that five of them heard the cry, awoke, trimmed their lamps, adjusted the wicks to find their own flame, and they had no oil. Five of them did exactly the same, but in their case there was oil, and the flame shone out in the darkness. Then those who lacked oil turned to those who had it, and said, "Give us of your oil; for our lamps are going out." No, they could not do that. This has been criticised. A good preacher some while ago said the good virgins were a selfish crowd when they said they dare not share their oil. But they were quite right. If they shared their oil they also would be without light. The oil is individual in the case of those burning torches, and cannot be shared. The foolish virgins had to go and find oil, and they went; but it was too late. Those that were ready had entered in, and the door was shut.

What is this picture? Bear in mind that which we have seen already, but which needs emphasizing. It is a picture of the consummation. It is one phase of truth, the hour when the absent Lord returns. The absent Lord is coming back, when men render an account of stewardship. That is seen in the next parable; but here the absent Lord is coming back, and at His coming there will be the revelation of truth concerning those who have supposedly been His own during the period of His absence. The whole Church is here revealed. Yet I would amend that, and rather say it is a picture of Christendom. A very clear distinction should be drawn between the Church of God and Christendom. The Church of God consists of those who have the oil, and whose lights are burning, and who are ready when the Lord comes. Christendom is bigger than that. Here is a picture of the consummation, and the whole of Christendom is in it. Note carefully what we have already seen. There are similarities between the five foolish and five wise virgins, and they are remarkable similarities. They all expected Him. Apparent expectation on the part of the foolish, apparent expectation also on the part of the wise. Of both the foolish and the wise it is said, "They went forth to meet the bridegroom." But of the foolish it is said, "They took no oil." There had been evident carelessness. Of the wise it is said, they "took oil." There had been reality in their attitudes.

Yet there is this tremendous difference. Some had no oil. Others had the oil burning, and what is the appalling verdict at the end? The voice of Jesus saying to those who had lamps, who had expectation, but who had taken up only apparently and outwardly, a form of relationship to the absent Bridegroom, "I know you not." Then those who had the oil went in to the marriage feast, a picture of the sifting of Christendom at the conclusion of the age; an hour when profession, with all its symbols and ritual, devoid of oil and light and power, will have no avail; an hour when if there have been similar provision, and similar symbols, plus the oil that keeps the flame burning, these will be the password, and the passport to the marriage feast.

Everything culminates in that final word of Jesus, in the 13th verse, "Watch therefore, for ye know not the day nor the hour." What then? "Watch." What does it mean by watching? Does it mean that we are for evermore to be talking about the coming of the Bridegroom, and affirming our conviction that He is coming? No, the ten did that. What then is it to watch? We must have that mystic oil that creates a flame and a light.

When we begin to interpret that parable we find once more many suggestions. So great a father of the Church as Origen said their oil consisted of good works. In my judgment that was a breakdown in explanation. Martin Luther said that the oil consisted in faith, living faith. But was not Grotius right when he said that the oil is the symbol of the Holy Spirit? I think that is so. Through the Old Testament oil is ever the symbol of the Holy Spirit. Whether in the lamp, burning in the Holy Place, or whether in the symbolism of such an one as Zechariah; whether in all those anointings of the ancient ritual, the oil was always typical of the Spirit and of power. Our Lord surely used this whole parable in that connection, and for that purpose.

The great word is "Watch." The interpretation of the watching is having the oil supplied. In the supply of the Spirit of God, and the life yielded to that Spirit, and dominated by that Spirit, there is always the oil which provides the light. Yes, Origen and Luther were partly right in a secondary sense, for where the oil is, there is the Spirit of God, there is living faith, and where there is living faith there are living works. But the great necessity is that oil that burns.

"Behold, the Bridegroom cometh!" When? The moment we ask When, we are in danger. "Ye know not the day nor the hour." It may be before this day closes He will put His pierced hand on all these furious world powers, and end them. He is coming to do that. It may be a thousand years, but a thousand years are only measurements of man, and are not in the economy of God. We do not know the hour.

What then are we to do? To see to it our lamps are burning, to see to it that we have the supply of that oil apart from which there is no shining of the light, no flaming light. So the parable of the virgins stands there in the midst of a triptych of parables, showing not communal responsibilities, not responsibility to my brother; not the responsibility for the Master's business in the world; but our responsibility, my responsibility about myself, about my own life. It is no use my coming to you, and asking you to let me have part of your oil. You cannot do it. This is personal and individual. There must be that fulness of the Spirit of God in individual life, which produces the shining of the light, and the burning of the flame. But at the end there will be division, and the Church and the Bridegroom will be revealed, while those who have had lamps, and attitudes, and expectations intellectually, but have made no living response; to them He will say, "I know you not."

27. The Talents

Matthew xxv: 14-30.

THIS parable of the talents is the third of the triptych of related parables concerning the responsibility of His own through the age between the fall of Jerusalem and His second advent. We have already considered the parable of the household and that of the virgins. One fact however is in view in all. All those constituting the Kingdom of God are under His supreme control. The first parable had to do with the household, the Church within itself. It was communal, and revealed the responsibilities of individual members towards each other, of care and love, with an absence of all differences and quarrelling, and biting one another. The next parable, that of the virgins, revealed personal responsibility, of having not merely an outward form, but of having life. It teaches not merely a general expectation of the coming of the Lord, but of having oil, so that the light is burning.

We come now to the parable dealing with responsibilities of the widest nature, the imperial responsibilities of the Church. That at once reveals the subject which our Lord was intending to illustrate when He used the parable of the talents. The word imperial is used resolutely, though in some ways I do not like it, because in history it has bad connotations. The word has come to us from that act in the history of Rome when one man seized absolute authority by military power, and became imperator of the whole of the Roman empire. Things imperial meant the mastery of a people by autocratic and military power. Yet because of its true use it has its own and rightful place in this connection. Jesus is the only Imperator; not Cæsar, nor the kings of time, but Jesus alone. The word connotes a King and a Kingdom; and the idea contained in the parable, which our Lord was illustrating, the truth He was enforcing was that of the prosecution of the interests of the King by the subjects of the Kingdom, during the period of His absence, as to bodily presence.

He is not absent in the sense of spiritual power. We know what it is to walk and talk with Him, and to hear Him talk to us. We know the real presence of the living Lord. Yet in historic sequence, this is the period of His absence. He was in the world for one brief generation of a little more than three and thirty years, the great period in human history to which everything else led up, and from which everything else of value had proceeded, and is proceeding, and will proceed. But He is coming again. No one who believes in the New Testament can deny that. The statement is clear that He Who came, is coming again to the world. All through this Olivet prophecy our Lord was looking at the world, and His Church from that standpoint of their being in the world, when He, as to bodily presence, was absent, going into a far country, and after a long time, coming again.

This parable must not be confused with that of the pounds in Luke's Gospel. The emphasis in the two parables is entirely different. What then was the figure used here? One characterised by the uttermost simplicity. The 14th verse opens, "For it is as when a man, going into another country." In the Revised Version the words "It is" and "when" are italicised, which means they are not in the Greek, but have been put in by translators to give smoothness to the statement. Leave them out for a moment, "For as a man, going into another country, called his own servants." That links the parable closely with what had preceded it. Our Lord did not tarry between the parables. We look back then at the parable of the virgins, and the whole impact and value is found in the final charge of Jesus in verse 13. "Watch therefore, for ye know not the day nor the hour. For as a man, going into another country, calleth his own servants, and delivereth unto them his goods." He now illustrated the necessity for watchfulness, but in another regard. So He takes this simple figure; "a man," He says. With all justness we may say, a king. It is the picture of a man who has a country of his own, under his own control. He is the lord, the master, the king. In that country this man has servants. The word He used all through here was bond-servants, slaves. Paul always spoke of himself as *doulos*, the bond-servant of Jesus Christ, that is, the absolute property of his Lord, all his life forces belonging to his Lord, himself at the disposal of his Lord. That is the picture here.

Moreover this man has goods. They belong to him. Change the word, wealth, or substance, but not substance stored, but something to be dealt with, to be offered for sale. It is a commercial figure connected with a king, the man who owned a country, and who had servants in it, he possessing goods in the country, substance. The picture our Lord gives here is of that man leaving behind in the country which is his own, these very servants to whom he has distributed talents, according to their ability, and leaving them there to trade for him, to carry on his business in his absence, to represent his goods to those who were left behind, and to put his goods at the disposal of others. That is the very simple picture which our Lord used. After a long time he comes back, and has a reckoning with the responsible servants he has left behind, and three illustrations are given; to one, five; to one, two; and to one, one talent.

Look at the picture again. What is the teaching of it? That in the absence of the Lord He has delivered to His servants His goods. He called them His own servants. Mark the emphasis on authority and possession, "His own servants," and He "delivered unto them His goods." The implication is perfectly clear. The goods were left that they might be used for the glory and enrichment of their absent Lord. He had goods. The servants were responsible for their use in order to bring wealth to Him. Really the relation and suggestiveness of these pictures are full of appeal. Goods, our absent Lord, and His goods. What are we to sell in this world? Do not quarrel about the word "goods." We may say God's gifts are without money and price. But the figure stands good. The apostle used the same figure in a great passage in which he told us, not to redeem the time, but to buy up the opportunity; and in that little word the apostle used of buying is the figure of the market-place, and merchant-men sitting by their wares, watching for the opportunity, and buying it up. That is the idea here.

What are the goods? The whole fact of the mission of Jesus in the world, the Gospel; and not merely the fact historically, but the fact in all its vital power, of the manifestation of God to men in Christ, the fact of a ministry full of the revelation of the possibilities of humanity in Jesus, the fact that He went to His Cross, and bore the sin of the world, the fact that He proved His victory in His dying, by His resurrection, the fact that He ascended on high, and received gifts for the rebellious, the fact that He is the living Lord, and waiting to come in and take possession of human souls, and change them and remake them after His own image and likeness. The goods! The great merchandise of the Church of God is concerned with things that belong to the Lord Himself, not with their own things, not with their own enterprises, not with their own merchandise; not with their own organizations; but with the goods, the wealth of Jesus, purchased at infinite cost, and now offered to the sons of men, offered to the whole human race. He has left these goods with His servants while He is away.

That leads one to an equally careful though brief consideration of this word "talents." He gave one five talents. He gave another, two talents. He gave one, one talent. What does "talent" mean? The popular use of the word suggests ability. We say of some one, That is a talented man, or a talented woman; and we are describing someone who has some gift, some ability. That is not the meaning of the word here. It is not a question of whether we have something to

teach the world in our own personality. The word means something
quite other. This word *talantos,* which we translate "talent" is a noun
rather of quantity, not a revelation of quality. It is a noun of quantity,
representing the Lord's possession alone. The five talents were His,
part of His goods, and so with the two and the one. They did not
belong to these servants at all. It is not a question of the fitness of
His people, but one of the riches of His grace, provided for humanity
in quantity.

One man was given five talents, another two, and another one.
Why did one man have five, and the other two, and yet a third, one?
Why the division? We are told, "To each according to his several
ability." We now come to the question of ability. Talents were given
according to ability. There is a tremendous principle involved in
that. This does not mean that the man with the five talents had a
bigger opportunity than the man with the two; or the man with the
two than the man with the one. The personal possession of responsibility of some part of the King's wealth depended upon the ability
of that particular person to use it. God will give one man, Christ will
give, the king will give a man so many talents, because he has the
ability to use that particular amount of the wealth that is committed
to him. It means this, He will never call a man to preach who has no
natural ability for preaching. I am afraid we often do. He never does.
Behind that wonderful little expression, according as each man had
ability, is a revelation of natural fitness, the ability of the personality
as preparation for the reception of a supernatural gift, and that is
always so. If a business man has that ability, he will receive responsibility according to that ability, which is his natural ability, the natural
baptized, empowered, by the supernatural. Do not be led astray by the
five, and the two, and the one, as though the first marks some element
of greatness, and a kind of inferiority in the next case, and a greater
inferiority in the third. Not at all. The man is taken into account.

Go to the epistles, and when Paul dealt with gifts, he says, To
some was given thus, and others so; and among the lists, he says,
"He gave some helps," not tongues, or preaching, or teaching, or
exposition, or actual ability, but just "helps." Thank God for those
in the Christian Church who are helps. But it is according to ability;
and there is no reflection on the last man because he only received
one talent. It was according to his ability. The great principle illustrated is that of his disbursement of his goods to his bond-servants.
That they may fulfil the responsibility of carrying out his enterprises
during his absence, he gives to each man severally as he will, five,
two, one; according as a man was able to use the five, or the two, or

156 PARABLES AND METAPHORS OF OUR LORD

the one. According to his several ability; the natural creating fitness for the supernatural.

Then the Lord showed how these men used these things. The one who had five produced other five, a hundred percent. The one who had the two produced other two. How much is that? Fifty percent? No, a hundred percent. The second did as well as the first. The man with the one had a wrong estimate of his master, which was entirely false, as an excuse for inactivity. He took his talent and hid it in a napkin and buried it, and he said he did it because his lord was hard and unjust, reaping where he did not sow. Inactivity! One talent committed to him. If he had traded with it, and that talent had produced one, then it would have been as good as the man with the two, or the man with the five talents. It would have been one hundred percent. But this man had done nothing with his lord's possession. Nothing was brought to the lord by the use of his talent.

The issue is perfectly simple and plain. Notice carefully two verses. Verse 21. "His lord said unto him, Well done, good and faithful servant; thou hast been faithful over a few things, I will set thee over many things, enter thou into the joy of thy lord." Verse 23, "His lord said unto him, Well done, good and faithful servant, thou hast been faithful over a few things, I will set thee over many things, enter thou into the joy of thy lord." There is no difference of a word. They show what Jesus said of the man with five talents, and of the man with two was exactly the same. The approbation of the two men is identical, "Well done." "Well done." My masters! Jesus will never say "Well done" to anyone unless it has been well done.

Then mark it well, "enter thou into the joy of thy lord." Share with Me in the joy that comes from thy use of My goods in the world, the substance that I entrusted to you. So do not be foolish enough to wish we had five talents if He has given us two, or that we had two when He has given us one. Have we got one? Has He entrusted us with one? Have we got some portion of the Master's goods that is our special responsibility for other men, one, two, five? Then see to it we make full use of His goods entrusted to our care. The whole story teaches us this that the final question is not one of greatness of opportunity, but faithfulness, fidelity to the opportunity that has been granted.

We need not tarry with the man with the one talent, although it is a very tragic story. He lied about his lord, and the lord refuted that lie by repeating it to him. One cannot read the words without catching the note of irony, of satire, as he spoke to him. "Thou wicked and slothful servant." Then come the words of refutation. Is that what you knew, that I reaped where I did not sow, and gather where I did not scatter? Is that your estimate? Well, if you think that way, you might have put my money to the bankers, and at least I should have had interest on my return. It is so conclusive, and so revolutionary.

These were all the servants of the lord, and it is possible to have five talents, and bury them, and the two talents, and bury them as did the man who had the one talent. He did not bury it because he only had one. He buried it because in his own soul he had a false thought about his master. Then he lied at the end, and gave it as an excuse; and the lord said, Take it away from him, and give it to the man who has ten talents, and cast him into the darkness outside, the darkness that is outside the Kingdom of responsibility.

It is important that we keep these three parables in connection with each other. They reveal the threefold responsibility of the Church. First, communal responsibility, right behavior among all its members, the ending of all malice and unkindness;—to use the figure—beating one another. Then the personal responsibility, that we have far more than a name, far more than a torch, far more than a wick which can be dim, if it has become encrusted. We must have oil that keeps the light burning. Finally, imperial responsibility, our responsibility for the goods of the Lord, for the enterprises of Christ in the world. In each case the responsibility is defined by our relationship to Him. True to Him, the household is always at peace. Waiting for Him, the lamps are always burning. Working for Him, the Kingdom is hastened, and the glory is brought to His name.

28. Sheep and Goats

Matthew xxv: 31-46.

IN THESE parabolic illustrations of the sheep and the goats we shall principally be concerned with all that our Lord was intending to illustrate by those figures. They occur in this third and last section of the Olivet prophecy. In order to correct interpretation we must first remember the relationships between the sections, and to the whole message of the Gospel in which it is found. Secondly we must be careful not to read into this part of our Lord's prophecy, and especially into His parabolic illustration, any of the things which are not truly found in it. We are in danger of doing this, especially with regard to this story and illustration. When those safeguards are observed, we shall be free to catch the true meaning of the remarkable passage, and to examine the process which it so vividly describes.

The parabolic figure of sheep and goats here is used in application to finality. Finality of what? That question will be answered as we look carefully. Consider the relation of this section (xxv. 31-46), to the whole of this Olivet prophecy. In answering His enquiring disciples He had first looked down the coming age and uttered a prophecy specially dealing with the Hebrew people, which found its culmination in the destruction of Jerusalem, fulfilled within a little more than a generation after He had uttered the words. Then in the second section (xxiv. 45-xxv. 30) our Lord was specially dealing with the responsibilities of His Church between the first and second advents. We have seen these responsibilities, communal, personal, and imperial. Now in the last part of the prophecy He deals with the nations. It is not the Hebrew people as a nation. That nation He had rejected from its place in the economy of God. It is not now the spiritual nation, the Church, with which He had been dealing as to responsibility. It is now the nations of the world. In this last section He is looking on to the consummation, and the things that will happen then with regard to the kingdoms of the world.

In each of these sections of the prophecy His second advent was evidently in His mind. It is always there, recurring. The first section ended with the charge, "Be ye also ready, for in an hour that ye think not the Son of man cometh." The second, in three pictures, deals with the return of the absent Lord. The Lord of the household comes to enquire into communal responsibility; the bridegroom arrives to meet those who have expected him; and the owner of the goods comes for a reckoning with those who have received talents.

Now this section commences with the reference with which the others close. "But when the Son of man shall come in His glory." He is dealing now with the second advent as the starting point, and giving the happenings immediately connected with that advent. He describes the effect of His second advent on national affairs in this world.

Notice how Matthew, this remarkable chronicler of the King, has proceeded, and here reaches a great climax. This is the Gospel of the Kingdom, and of the Kingdom of heaven. The opening movement presents the King. From that there follows the description of the King's propaganda. His enunciation of an ethic, the sermon on the mount; the exhibition of the benefits of the Kingdom, as He moved amid derelict humanity, healing need, whether physical, moral, or mental; and then enforcing His claims in opposition to those of His foes. The hour was coming when He was moving towards rejection, but He was moving towards an ultimate victory. It is that ultimate victory that is here revealed in this final section of the Olivet prophecy. In Matthew, the ultimate victory is not seen in heaven, but on earth. That does not mean the ultimate things are not the heavenly things, and things in the ages to come. They certainly are, but that is not the theme here, and it is not the theme in this particular discourse.

The laws of the Kingdom, in the sermon on the mount are for earthly conditions, not for heavenly. They do not apply to a heavenly state, and condition of a life after this. They all apply to the present life. As we watch the King moving in Kingly power and compassion and majesty amid derelict humanity, that does not mean an exhibition of the powers of the Kingship of Jehovah in the heavenly realms that lie beyond. It is an exhibition of His power on this earthly level. So as He enforced His claims all the way, they consisted of His claims upon the earth. That prayer which we designate the Lord's prayer moved on two realms. The first had to do with man's relationship to God, and the second, man's necessities on the earth level, and man's interrelationship on the earth. He taught His disciples to pray, "Our Father, which art in the heaven, Thy name be hallowed, Thy Kingdom come, Thy will be done on earth as in heaven." The passion of that prayer does not ask that men may find their way to heaven one day, but that God may win the earth, and that the earth may find itself in the Kingdom of God. The earth is in view.

In this gospel of Matthew (xxvi-xxviii) we have the final mission and commission, and again I take a slightly altered translation, which is more accurate. Mark the voice of the King. "All authority is given unto Me in heaven and on earth; go ye therefore and disciple the nations." Disciple whom? All the nations. As they come under the influence, and obey it, then "baptizing them into the name of the Father and the Son and of the Holy Spirit." But it is "all the nations." It is on the earth level. Do not imagine that takes any dignity and glory from this. It does not interfere with the larger meaning of the work of Christ, as it includes the ages to come, to use Paul's poetic language, "unto the generation of the age of the ages." Have you ever sat down in front of that, and tried to measure it? The first concern of our King is the establishment in this world of the order harmonising with the heavenly order.

All this is of supreme importance to our understanding of the events to which this prophecy refers. Certain events must be excluded from our thinking. This is not a picture of the Great Assize, not of the great white Throne. That account is given in Revelation. "I saw a great white Throne, and Him that sat upon it, from Whose face the earth and the heaven fled away." Then the dead are raised, and stand before Him. There is nothing here about a great white Throne. The Son of man is here, not so much as the final Judge, but as the King in authority. Earth and heaven are not fled away here. The earth level is in our view. There is no resurrection of the dead. The nations referred to are living nations. Our Lord was looking on, as He had done all through His Olivet prophecy, to the consummation of the age, showing what it will mean in the case of the nations.

What then are the facts revealed? First of all we see the Son of man on the Throne of His glory, and it is a regal throne. He is the King. "The King shall say"; He is speaking of Himself as King, when He comes with His angels, at the consummation of the age. He is coming. When He comes, He will sit on the throne of His glory. Watch the movement with sanctified imagination, and draw the picture. He is seen assuming the reins of earthly government, and doing it openly. By doing this He is eliminating all other rulers. No other ruler is in sight. There is no king, president, or dictator in sight; but He is gathering all the nations. It is not a question of multitudes of men and women. It is a great gathering of nations, and He is seen administering the affairs of an earthly kingdom. This is the picture of the initial process of the new administration of earth's affairs. Not the great white Throne, not even the Judgment Seat of Christ, before which all believers must appear. As Paul says, we must all appear before the judgment seat of Christ. When we appear under that glance of fire, then all that is unworthy will be destroyed, and the fire will burnish to beauty everything holy. This is a picture of the King enthroned, laying His pierced hand upon the world affairs, and bringing them to finality, as He moves toward the establishment of the Kingdom of God in this world.

What do we see at the centre of everything? The Son of man on His throne. Here our minds necessarily go back over all the ground. The title "Son of man" was His own familiar designation of Himself in the days of His flesh. That is the first thing we see; the Son of man enthroned, exercising His authority. Then all the nations are gathered around that Throne, which again means, not necessarily that all the people of all the world are so gathered into one spot, although that would not be difficult. All the population of the world could stand together on the Isle of Wight, for instance. That is only a passing reference. When we think about the League of Nations, that does not mean all the nations are gathered together at Geneva. The King is seen calling together every nation, possibly through its representatives. While not stressing it, it is worth noting. All the nations are there, and are gathered. There is the cancellation of differences. Old national lines which have characterised us are obliterated. Whatever the forms of government may have been, and however they may be changed, when the Son of man sits on the Throne of His glory, they will all be arraigned before Him. The very gathering suggests His authority.

Take this parabolic illustration. If the gathering cancels the old lines of division, there immediately follows a new division, a new separation. The nations are not treated on the basis of race, or of political position, or occupation, or achievement, or failure, and disaster. They are divided into sheep and goats, a division of the nations, a new separation. The old national lines are obliterated before the King; to His right and left hand, sheep and goats.

Look next particularly at the sentences and the verdicts. To those on the right he says, Come, enter the Kingdom. That is not heaven; that is the new order on earth; when the prayer that we pray that the Kingdom of God may come on earth as in heaven, is answered on the earth level. Enter the Kingdom, not heaven, but the earthly order.

But on what basis? He now comes to that word so full of infinite meaning. "I was an hungered . . . I was thirsty . . . I was a stranger . . . I was sick . . . I was in prison." The astonished people on the right say to Him, When were these things so? Now mark His answer with great care. It is the same answer, by contrast, to those on the right and on the left. They say, "When? . . . When?" "Verily I say unto you, Inasmuch as ye did it," or "did it not," "unto one of these My brethren, even these least, ye did it unto Me," or "ye did it not unto Me." What a marvellously revealing thing to say.

But let us understand it. Some say He was talking about the Jews. That is a strange view. Go back in the Gospel to an earlier period (xii. 46) "While He was yet speaking to the multitudes, behold, His mother and His brethren stood without, seeking to speak to Him." While He was yet speaking, "But He answered and said unto him that told Him, Who is My mother? and who are My brethren? and He stretched forth His hand towards His disciples, and said, Behold, My mother and My brethren! For whosoever shall do the will of My Father which is in heaven, he is my brother, and sister, and mother." We cannot confine this scene of infinite majesty to that small and foolish idea that He was talking about the Jews when He said

"My brethren." Who are "My brethren"? He had told us who they
were. Those who do the will of His Father. He was including all Jews,
all Hebrews who did the will of His Father, but He was including
all Gentiles also. He is looking down this whole age from the standpoint of our responsibility; and He sees them going out, His spiritual
brethren, His Kin, mother, brother, sister; multitudes of them bringing His strength and comfort and help in every way; and He says at
last to the nations, I came when they came, and I came through suffering. I have passed down the age in these My brethren, and if you
have failed to receive them, you have failed to receive Me; and in
failing to receive them and to receive Me you have proved your
unfitness for the newly established Kingdom of God. Thus to those
on the left hand He has said exactly the same thing, only from the
other side. Thus He was showing that nations will be admitted to the
inheritance of the Kingdom of God, established upon the earth, upon
the basis of their attitude to Christ Himself, as He has been represented to them through His people during the whole period.

Look at this more particularly. That is how the nations are to
be judged. It is Pilate's question asked over again from the national
standpoint. Pilate said, What shall I do with Jesus? It is the question
for the nations. What are they doing with Jesus? What are they
doing with His message? What are they doing with His messengers?
What are they doing with all the spiritual forces and moral powers
that He has set at liberty, and which are at work through His people
in the age? Upon the basis of that, His judgment will be found for,
or against them. The tremendous thing in that great division is that
the righteous shall enter upon age-abiding life, and the wicked upon
age-abiding fire. It is a national division.

We must stop there, because there He stopped. We can go beyond
it, and try and find out what it means. It is the initiation of that
Kingdom in human history. It is not finality. Finality is never reached
until this has first taken place. He will be the Dictator. If I am asked
today, Do you really think this is coming? I answer, Certainly it is
coming. If I did not believe it I would lose all heart and hope. I am
sure it is coming. When? No, my friend, you must not ask that, because He has told us distinctly—He told these disciples in this prophecy,—we are not to know the When.

This section of the prophecy then describes in broad outline, and as
an underlying principle, how the King will personally—to quote words
He used in the earlier parables,—"gather out of His Kingdom all
things that cause stumbling, and them that do iniquity"; and thus

prepare for that new era, in which, again to quote His words, "the righteous shall shine forth as the sun in the Kingdom of His Father."

This picture flashes its light back upon the previous section, and reveals part of our responsibility with new force and power. Within the household we are to be obedient to the absent Lord, and love one another. As individuals we are ever to have lamps trimmed and burning, waiting for the Advent. As His representatives in the world we are to prosecute His commerce with the talents He has committed to us. Or in brief, witnessing for Him, and so creating the opportunity of the nations, in the work of the Christian Church, and thus preparing the way for that final discrimination when the Son of man shall come in His glory.

29. The Growth of the Seed

Mark iv: 26-29.

IT is certainly an arresting fact that this parable is only recorded by Mark, and it is peculiar therefore to His Gospel. He records others of the parables, and some of the parabolic illustrations found in the Gospel of Matthew.

A certain amount of wonder and speculation is permissible, providing it is not carried too far. Why has only Mark given this parable? I do not know, but one does wonder, especially because of its remarkable value, a value that no other parable had which Jesus uttered concerning the Kingdom. It assumes the teaching of the other parables, and so is arresting that Mark has recorded it. Perhaps it specially impressed Mark because of his own character. His was an interesting personality. Paul and Barnabas had a difference of opinion concerning him, so definite a quarrel that they parted company. Paul may have been right that Mark was vacillating, that when he went back at Pamphylia, there was some element of weakness in his character. To give a personal opinion, if Paul were right, my sympathy is with Barnabas. He kept Mark with him, and gave him another chance. That is a better attitude. Perhaps this parable therefore gripped Mark, and came back to him in after years, that marvellous parable revealing the necessity for patience, first the blade and then the ear, and then the full corn in the ear.

We do not know why only Mark has recorded this parable; and moreover, there is nothing to show definitely when it was uttered. Undoubtedly it was given on that first day of parabolic discourse. The 30th verse begins, "And He said, How shall we liken the Kingdom of God? or in what parable shall we set it forth? It is like a grain of mustard seed." There Mark records one of the parables Jesus gave on that great day of parabolic utterance, recorded fully by Matthew in his thirteenth chapter. Mark does say, "With many such parables spake Jesus the word unto them, as they were able to hear it; and without a parable spake He not unto them; but privately to His own disciples He expounded all things." So it is possible that this little parable was spoken on that self-same day. It is even possible that it was spoken on the first day of parabolic discourse between others that are closely related to it, possibly after the parable of the sower that went forth to sow, and before the parable of the wheat and the darnel, showing the two sowings going forward; and so leading on to that of the mustard seed, which Mark also records. More than that cannot possibly be said, except that we pause to notice the similarity of the basic ideas in this group of parables. In every one of them is the seed containing potentialities, but needing to be sown. In every one we have growth, development, consequent upon sowing, and in every one there is harvest, the result of the development, consequent upon the sowing.

The central matter in this little parable is that of growth. Sowing is recognised. Harvest is also recognised, but the teaching concerns the process between the sowing and the harvest. If we have all those parables in mind, and remember how our Lord had likened the Kingdom under these changing and yet similar figures of speech, we are prepared to approach this. Following our method, let us look at the figure which our Lord here employed.

It is a perfectly natural one, and therefore absolutely necessary. A man sows seed. Notice how our Lord says this. "So is the Kingdom of God as if"; "So . . . as if a man should cast seed upon the earth." Then, when this man has sown the seed, he goes on with his ordinary life. There is nothing reprehensible in this. It is "as if a man should cast seed upon the earth and should sleep and rise"—two periods of time, "night and day." Night for sleep; day for rising, which means activity. What is the man doing in the picture? He has sown his seed, and then he goes on with his ordinary life. Quite properly he goes to sleep at night, and rises in the morning. He carries on.

Meanwhile, what he has done in sowing the seed, is being carried forward without his help. "And the seed should spring up and grow, he knoweth not how." Mark that carefully, for we shall return to it in another connection. What does happen? The earth beareth of herself." The man is doing nothing. He cannot do anything. He has done something. He has sown the seed, but there is no more he can do yet. He goes to sleep, and goes on with his ordinary life; but all the while in that period, when he can do no more, something is going on. The seed is springing and growing; he does not know how, and it "beareth fruit." "The earth bringeth forth of herself."

What is he to do? Watch. "First the blade." We have all seen this in the country; and that goes on, until we see the ear, and that goes on until we see "the full corn," ripeness and maturity. All this time, the man who has sown the seed is doing nothing with regard to what he has sown. He has done his duty. He has sown the seed. He goes to sleep, and he rises, in night and day, but there is no cessation in the activity resulting from what he has done, though he is not now acting. The result of what he has done is that the seed is springing, growing, developing, and it is coming quietly, first the blade, then the ear, and then the full corn in the ear. There are certain laws and forces inherent in the seed and in the soil. In the seed is a principle of life. That principle is in every seed. There are forces of life in the soil, and these forces of life in the soil, in co-operation with the forces of life in the seed produce a result, and produce it quietly; and presently, "First the blade, then the ear," and then the full growth.

Take the whole, and see a wonderful co-operation between man and Nature. Nature cannot sow, and it cannot reap. Man cannot give the increase. The figure is everything in this parable. It carries its own lesson. The marvellous forcefulness of this grips us. In the first great parable, the sower went forth to sow. Whereas the one Sower was the Lord Himself, He is not the Sower here, because the figure says that the man does not know how the growth is going on. He cannot help it, and cannot do anything about it. That is not true of the Lord. It is true of us, and of everyone called into co-operation with Him in sowing seed. We know what the seed is. We have had the figure in other parables. The seed is the Word.

We have a wonderful figure here. We need not go to the East for this. We can look at it in our own land anywhere. A man goes forth to sow, and when he has done his sowing there is no more he can do. He must wait, but there is no cessation of activity. There is an activity resulting from his sowing. The seed he sows has fallen upon the soil, and the earth brings forth fruit of itself. Then presently,

"He clothes the smiling fields with corn."

How do they come? Not golden harvest yet; but "first the blade," and what a wonderful picture it is, a field, when that first blade is appearing, the shimmer of its emerald green from end to end. Watch it, until presently the ear is at the head of every stalk. Wait a little while longer, and it is ripe. Then the man comes back, and does something. Then he puts in his sickle. Now the earth cannot produce a harvest unless the seed is sown; and the man cannot produce a harvest unless he sows the seed; but having sown the seed he has to wait, and wait patiently for all those processes of Nature which result presently in germination, growth, development, and finally harvest.

What a wonderful parable it is, in the midst of the rest. We cannot understand it in any true way unless we keep it in relation to the others, especially the first, the one Sower going forth to sow. In Matthew's account of the Kingdom parables, the seed sown was the Word of God incarnate in human lives. When Luke gave the account of that parable, as I believe on another occasion, he distinctly said the seed is the Word of God. But whether the Word in essence, or the Word incarnate in human beings, men and women, sons and daughters of the Kingdom, the great principle is the Word of God. Do not forget, "So is the Kingdom." Here we see those who are His, carrying out this self-same work of scattering the seed. "So is the Kingdom." That is how it begins, how it always begins.

The application is evidently to us in this sense, because He is not ignorant as to the *how*. This man does not understand, but the great revelation of this parable is our Lord's teaching about the Kingdom, and about Himself as the Sower, and about the Word of God, the life principle out of which all the true activities and results must grow.

This parable therefore teaches first of all the necessity for sowing. That has been said in other ways in looking at the figure. There must be this sowing of the seed. The earth will produce no harvest of itself. What harvest? The Kingdom of God, His rule, His reign, His triumph over all human affairs. For the bringing in of that harvest the seed must be sown. That is the first teaching. The man casts seed upon the earth. The earth produces no harvest from itself.

Then to me at least this is always the true impact of this parable, the necessity for patience, because of this inability in the actual realm of life. We can take the life principle of the Word of God and scatter it. That is our duty, whether we do it by preaching or teaching or living, which is potent also. We can do that, sow the seed, and that is all. Paul may plant, Apollos water, but it is God Who gives the increase. We need to be reminded of this. That does not say that man has nothing to do. It only reveals the point at which man's doing must cease, and in which he must exercise patience. Man can help or hinder. Man helps by ploughing up the fallow ground by all those processes that prepare for the scattering of the seed. In a thousand ways we can help. All that is preparatory to the one thing, the scattering of the seed. We can hinder. Man can even in his folly trample upon the blade as it appears, and crush it out ere it have time to develop. All that is admitted. Interference may be destructive, but man cannot produce a harvest. Man cannot produce a harvest even by the sowing of the Word of God. In a sense his very sowing is preparing for harvest, but all this is an unveiling of the necessity for standing still, and being patient. The co-operation of life forces outside himself produces harvest.

Let us be very practical about that. Are we not in danger of wanting to see results too soon, and too quickly from our sowing? Have we learned the secret of the husbandman who hath patience as he waits "for the precious fruit of the earth," that great declaration of one of the epistles concerning God. We are all in danger of doing what some of us did when we were children, when we were given a little plot of garden. We dug it and got the soil ready; we planted our seeds, and in a week or two we were digging them up to see how they were getting on! We are very much given to digging up what we have planted, instead of resting content to scatter the seed, and leave it to the forces of God to bring in the harvest.

And yet there is a necessity for reaping. When the full harvest is there, when the manifestation is there that the sowing of the seed has produced this process of development, the blade and ear and full corn, then the harvest. In that sense we may take this parable and apply it as to the Sower, as to the Lord Himself, although primarily it was intended for those working for Him. He has patience, and waits for the precious fruit of the earth, and how patient He is. But the harvest will come. Then His sickle will be put in.

I am more concerned with the application of the parable to ourselves, and the first of all to our work. We do want harvest. Jesus said, "The fields are white already to harvest." What fields? Fields that others have sown before us. We may never reap from our sowing here, it may be, or perchance we may. But the fields are white with the sowing of those who have gone before, in a myriad ways; and whereas we may always be sowing, we may always be putting in the sickle to reap. But that which we reap has not come suddenly. That also had its sowing, and it is the development through blade and ear until that harvest came. As Jesus looked out He saw harvest everywhere, "The harvest is plenteous, but the labourers are few." "Put in the sickle," He said on two memorable occasions; and so is it today, and so it is everywhere.

What is our relation to this whole process within the work of the Kingdom of God? First of all activity, sowing the seed. Let us be very careful we are sowing the right seed, and the only seed that will bring forth the fruit of the Kingdom of God in this world, the seed of the Word of God. I should not like to say that conviction about that has gone out of date; but it has weakened within the processes of the last generation or more. Whatever opinion I may have of it does not matter finally. There is no doubt however that He is calling us to a tremendous work, the supreme sufficiency of the Word of God. Let us see to it that we are sowing the right seed in life and in teaching.

What next? A sense of our helplessness in the matter of the germination of the seed. No, we cannot do that. We scatter it, and then we stand aside. To quote it again. Paul may plant. Paul must plant, and Apollos may attend to irrigation, as he waters. I go further, and say he must do it. But there is a process that Paul cannot help in, and that Apollos cannot serve. It is God's work; and it is great to learn to be patient with God.

Then in conclusion we may apply it to individual life. Do not be impatient about your own life. I know it is almost a dangerous thing to say because some people are careless. On the other hand I meet so many people who are impatient with themselves when God is patient with them. Do not forget, first the blade, and if that is there, life is there; and if life is there, there is the promise of growth and development. Do not be impatient. Do not dig the blade up to see what is happening. Leave it alone. Then the ear, and that proves the process is happening, and we wait a little longer, and there is the full corn in the ear. No, not on a sudden, in a moment is this great work of the Kingdom of God completed in any human soul. Yes, suddenly, in a moment it begins, when the seed falls upon the soil. Let us recognise then that which makes it grow and develop is the action of God. Let us see to it we do not hinder that, but yield ourselves to the life forces that are ours by faith in the Word of the living God. Let us wait for the full ear, and the richness of the harvest.

Part II

30. *The Two Debtors*

Luke vii: 41-43.

LUKE is rich in parables and parabolic illustrations peculiar to his narrative. There are no fewer than eighteen.

In order to understand the subject our Lord intended to illustrate when He used this parable of the two debtors we must have its setting. The story is well known. In it we see three persons; Simon, who invited Jesus into his house to dinner; the woman, who as Simon would have said, invaded the sanctity of his house; and Jesus.

We give attention first to Simon, and notice what he was thinking in his heart. We understand the cause of his thinking, and find that in the parable the Lord was revealing the reason for what Simon saw that perplexed him. There was no cordiality in the invitation which he extended, because when he received Jesus, he neglected all the common courtesies of an Eastern home. He brought no water for His feet, no oil for His head, he gave Him no kiss of salutation; all which were things of common courtesy in an Eastern home. He simply asked Him to come in, and Jesus went in, and sat down to meat.

Then Simon saw a very strange happening. Luke with fine delicacy employs the phrase "a woman . . . a sinner." The word is the synonym for a harlot. Simon saw a prostitute, to use the blunt word, suddenly cross his threshold. There is no need to emphasise the fact that she had never been there before. No man like Simon, cold and dispassionate, moral, upright, and conceited, need be afraid that kind of woman is coming near him! Simon saw her come in and go round the board, and stooping behind Jesus shed tears over His feet, then with loosened tresses of her hair wiping them, smothering them with kisses, and pouring on them precious ointment. Simon saw this, and it perplexed him.

Now what did Simon see? He saw this woman manifesting and giving evidences of great devotion, and of affection towards Jesus, and he associated what he saw with what he knew of the woman. He knew who she was, knew what her story was; and when he saw a woman of that character come into his house, and give evidences of

171

tremendous affection for Jesus, and devotion to Him, he measured the action by what he knew of the woman.

Jesus accepted those evidences of affection and devotion. He allowed her to do what she did. He did not forbid her. Simon said if He were a prophet He would have known who and what manner of woman she was. That was Simon's outlook. Jesus accepted it. Simon associated what he saw with what he knew of the woman. Jesus accepted the devotion and affection because He associated these things with what *He* knew of the woman. The whole story shows what Simon knew, and what Jesus knew. Our Lord presently asked Simon if he really knew the woman. Notice the two little sentences. Simon said, "If He were a prophet He would have perceived who, and what manner of woman this is that toucheth Him." Presently Jesus said to him, "Simon, seest *thou* this woman?" Then He proceeded to show the woman to Simon, and He did so by comparing her with him, and He showed—to put the matter bluntly—that by comparison with her, Simon with all his boasted morality, was as coarse as sackcloth, and she was fine as fine-spun silk. That is the background.

What was Jesus showing by the use of this parable? He was showing that this woman was a cleansed woman, a forgiven woman. He did not pronounce forgiveness then, but as something already accomplished. The tense of the verb is, "hath been forgiven." He was showing Simon this one thing, for I believe He was trying to reach the soul of Simon. This leads us to the parable, which teaches that moral cleansing is the inspiration of devotion, and of beauty. That summarises everything at the beginning as to the circumstances under which the parable was spoken, and the subject which the parable was intended to illustrate.

Take the parable, remembering the narrative. Jesus said, "A certain lender," and the word is a money-lender. They existed then, and still exist. "A certain money-lender had two debtors; the one owed five hundred pence, and the other fifty. When they had not wherewith to pay, he forgave them both. Which of them therefore will love him most? Simon answered and said, He, I suppose"—and the word there suggests a rather supercilious attitude—"He, I suppose, to whom he forgave the most." The Master said, "Thou hast rightly judged."

Look then at this figure our Lord employed. It is strictly a commercial one, money, debtors, and creditors; and in each case the inevitable conclusion is that the debts had been incurred through need. This money-lender had advanced to one fifty pence, and to the other, five hundred. The proportion of fifty to five hundred is the important thing. To translate into the English equivalent is not easy.

There were debts, and the degree of obligation is marked by the difference in the amount, between fifty and five hundred. It is a commercial picture, quite usual, happening often enough in that country, still happening too. The advance had come from the same source, and it had gone to two people in the same condition of need, and they were both still in the same condition that they had nothing with which to pay. They were both bankrupt; they owed the debt, but they could not pay it.

Then our Lord introduced into His parable something extraordinary, almost unusual. What is it? That the money-lender forgave them both. Do not miss that, because there flashes a light of the Divine, there beams the glory of the grace of God. Keep to the figure for a moment, the cancellation of obligation in both cases, the fifty wiped out, the five hundred wiped out! It was a purely gratuitous act on the part of the creditor, on the ground only of the bankruptcy of the debtors. I think Simon must have been astonished when he heard the story at that point. The creditor cancels the debts of the debtors, which was something quite unusual; and from that fact He asked this question, Which of them is likely to love him the most? He did not use the prerogative which was his, and take the usual course of events, which follows a personal indebtedness to a creditor. He cancelled the debts.

What had Simon to say to that? What he would say is so obvious. I think with a touch of superciliousness he said, "I suppose, he to whom he forgave the most." Quickly and sharply came the word of Jesus, "Thou hast rightly judged." The greater the obligation the greater the sense of gratitude when the obligation is cancelled. We see much of infinite beauty gleaming in this wonderful parable. I see in the parable itself, in the mind of our Lord, a tender satire for Simon. I think He was accepting Simon's valuation of his own degree of guilt at fifty, and that of the woman at five hundred. He took figures that revealed the working of Simon's mind. Simon was a Pharisee, and therefore an orthodox Jew. Simon would have admitted he was a sinner, but would thank God that he was not such a sinner as that woman. How wonderfully things persist. Our Lord said He would take him at his valuation. You are the fifty pence sinner, and the woman the five hundred pence. Ten times she owes as thou dost. On his valuation He took him; but as a matter of fact, there are no such degrees in sin. Sin is rebellion against, and unlikeness of God, whether the form be that of the hypocrite as Simon was, or the form of a fallen woman, such as the one who came into his house. The essence of sin was rebellion against the law and will of God, and contradiction of the heart of God. That is sin, and there is no such thing as degrees of guilt. Or even if we should admit degrees, then considering this whole story, Simon's sin was greater than the woman's, for do not forget this, that the sins of the spirit are always more heinous than the sins of the flesh. The sins of the spirit, pride, self-satisfaction, are more deadly to human life than the sins of the flesh ever were, or can be. So the parable Jesus used.

What does the parable teach us by implication? I begin at the heart of it. First of all, the bankruptcy of all men when they stand in the presence of God. We are all His debtors, but we have nothing to pay, not one of us. In the words of our hymnology, often sung,

"Nothing in my hands I bring."

Why not? We have nothing to bring. We have nothing with which we can pay the debt we owe to God, consequent upon a violated law, and sin in our lives, whether of the spirit or the flesh matters nothing. This parable, sharp-cut as a cameo as we ponder it, brings us face to face with the fact that the sentence on every one of us morally is that we have nothing to pay, nothing sufficient to meet our obligations.

Then if that is the great central truth, by implication there is another amazing thing. There is forgiveness for all. He forgave them both. Behind that there is so much that cannot be said, but must be remembered. I do not know who this money-lender was, but even the parable of Jesus fails, as all parables do, to utter the ultimate truth. He forgave them both. Mel Trotter has said an arresting thing. "We are all redeemed, but we are not all saved," an important distinction. When Jesus died, He did not die for me alone, but for the world, and the Cross provided redemption for the world, that which makes it possible for God to forgive. "He forgave them both." This money-lender lost not much more than 550 pence, more than £55 in our currency all told; but in order to provide humanity's need in its deep necessity, in its bankruptcy, God gave His only begotten Son. That is not in the parable, but it is implicated. "He forgave them both," forgiveness for me, for you, and that by an act of God; very costly to Him, which was all of grace. We have no claim upon God right-eously. Our only claim upon Him is that of His heart, His love, and His grace; and neither the heart, nor the love and grace of God can ever act at the expense of holiness. That is where the Cross came in. It was the means by which He made possible the forgiveness of God, granted to both of them, the fifty, and the five hundred sinner, what-ever the degree of guilt might have been.

Then we glance at the direct teaching. He teaches that moral cleansing is the inspiration of devotion, that love is not a mere passing human emotion. It is a great devotion, and it springs out of moral cleansing. No man knows what it is to love Jesus who is not conscious of His cleansing power from sin. It is interesting that all through this story the word for love is the highest, *agapao*, love intelligent, informed, devoted. She loved much, and her love sprang from the fact that her sins which were many, had been forgiven. A cleansed heart becomes a loving heart. Moral cleansing sets free from a sense of bondage. It restores spiritual perception, and is of such a nature that such a woman will violate her own inclination or prejudice. Nothing else would have persuaded her to go into that man's house, but she went in. Luke is careful to tell us that when she knew He was in the house, that brought her in. She trampled on all her prejudices when she went in, because she was spiritually cleansed, she was set free from the bondage of fear. What cared she for the opinion of Simon? She knew the relationship between her Lord and herself.

Then I look at her again, and learn from the whole story, in the light of the parable, that such devotion, resulting from moral cleansing, is the secret of restored beauty. That is what our Lord tried to show Simon, that the actions of the woman were characterised by beauty. Her tears, her kisses, her nard, were beautiful things; and they were brought by a woman whom Simon looked upon as soiled and spoiled, smirched, and cast out and reprobate. So she was, until Jesus met her. But then at once all the graces of womanhood blossomed into beauty and into fine expression. That woman was nobly born, because she was born again; and the only men and women of noble birth are those born from above, morally cleansed, freed from all the bondage of tradition and fear, and blossoming with grace and beauty. All this was seen in a desire to serve her Lord, and the tears and kisses and nard were the sacramental symbols of the devotion of a woman whom Jesus had forgiven in the name of God, and delivered. His last word to her was this, "Go in peace." So we have rendered it, but it is really, "Go into peace." There was a future before her. Probably she never did get back into communion with Simon and his crowd. Very likely she would be looked down upon by some of the moralists who knew nothing of the grace of God. What did it matter? The Bible never names a woman of this kind. In great beauty, names are withheld; but the personality is seen. Two debtors, both forgiven, but the one who was conscious of the value of the gift manifested it in her devotion; and so went in peace.

31. The Good Samaritan

Luke x: 25-37.

THIS is commonly known as the parable of the good Samaritan. We cannot entirely ignore all that lies round about it; for our method of dealing with our subject has been that of first discovering the subject our Lord was intending to illustrate by the parable, or parabolic illustration He used; secondly to examine the figure itself; and finally to gather up the teaching resulting.

We have called this a parable. I wonder if it was. Our Lord did not say so actually. He may have been quoting an incident; something that had actually happened. Unquestionably things like this did often happen on that road from Jericho to Jerusalem, for it was infested with robbers. To what then was Jesus referring when He told that story, whether giving a piece of history, or using a parable? He was showing two things; first, the relation of law to life; and secondly, the responsibility created by law.

The story is a beautiful one, merely as a story. Taken as the writer of a hymn took it, it is typical of the work of our blessed Lord, and it is full of beauty. Exactly what happened, and why did Jesus tell this story?

Jesus used the parable in answer to two questions asked by one man. The first question was this, "What shall I *do* to inherit eternal life?" The Lord answered that with a statement. Then the lawyer asked the second question, "Who is my neighbour?" The story was told to answer that question. The lawyer was one whose official business it was to interpret law. He was of the order of lawyers, or scribes. Those are synonymous terms. His whole business in life was that of showing the relation of law to life. In those times, if men had a difficulty, they consulted a scribe, a lawyer, to know what the law said on this matter of behaviour in life. This was the man who came to Jesus. He said, Give me a law that will so condition life that it will be full-orbed, eternal life. Eternal life does not mean long life merely; it is full life. Eternal life is high and deep, broad as well as long; the life of the ages would be an accurate rendering of the great phrase "eternal life," so often occurring. That was the phrase he used. He asked Jesus for a law, "What shall I *do*?" When we ask a man what we shall do, when we ask a teacher what we shall do, we are asking him to state some law, to give us some commandment, to give us some instruction. That is the realm in which the story moves.

This was a request for a law conditioning life, in order to its fulness. What this man wanted was life in its fulness. I think he was perfectly sincere. This is not the only time when Jesus was asked that question. It is the great question that in some form or another comes ever and anon from a human soul. Life, give me life. Give me a law that shall condition my life so that it shall be full-orbed and perfect. "What shall I do that I may inherit eternal life?"

Notice the method of the Master at that point. He looked at the man and said, "What is written in the law, how readest thou?" That phrase was a technical term, constantly used by the scribes and teachers and lawyers. They would consult one another about some subject or condition, and one would say to the other, "How readest thou?" Jesus said, You have asked Me for a law conditioning life. What is written in the law? How do you read it. He flung the man back upon himself, and upon the things he already knew, and the things with which he was familiar. He called him to a recognition of those things he knew perfectly well, and he proved he knew them, because he gave Jesus the right answer, the only answer, the complete answer. Jesus told him so. He said, "Thou hast answered right. This do, and thou shalt live." That is the law that conditions life, said Jesus.

Then we come to that which immediately introduces us to the story. It was a question concerning the responsibility created by law. The lawyer asked his second question, "And who is my neighbour?" It is most arresting that he fastened upon that part of his own answer. What had he said? "Thou shalt love the Lord thy God with all thy heart, and with all thy soul, and with all thy strength, and with all thy mind, and thy neighbour as thyself." Said Jesus, That is quite right; do it, and you shall live. The man replied, "And who is my neighbour?" He did not ask any question about the first commandment; he only asked about the second. Again I see the manifestation of a remarkable intelligence in this lawyer. There was no question to him as to Who God was; but there was a chance of backing out of a difficulty by trying to find out who his neighbour was. Do not forget that this lawyer belonged to the rulers and teachers who said that no Gentile was a neighbour. There is no need to make any long quotations, but in their writings they distinctly said no Gentile was to be treated as a neighbour. Neighbourliness belonged within the covenant people. That was the distinct teaching and these men knew it. Was there any lurking suspicion in his own soul that some thing was wrong? "Who is my neighbour?" Luke tells us very carefully he said this to justify himself. To justify himself with whom? With the crowd standing round? I do not believe it. With whom? With his own conscience. He was dodging an issue. Then the Lord told this story, and that is the background which is all important.

Look at the story itself. There are three things standing out, every one of them demanding attention. As our Lord spoke, the picture grows before us. We see a road along which travellers journey, and certain events happening thereon. That is so simple, every child can understand it. If we have something a child can understand, we have something fit for the philosophers!

Glance at the picture, and do not forget that our Lord was show-ing this man what the responsibility was, created by the law which conditions life, in order that life may be full. He was illustrating responsibility. Look at the road. Luke is careful as he says it was a road "going down from Jerusalem to Jericho," a geographical accuracy. The road did go down. The boundaries are there, Jerusalem and Jericho. Jerusalem, the city of history and religion, the great centre of privilege. Jericho, beautiful in situation, a city of palm trees, but a city that had been under a curse of God for centuries. The book of Joshua tells us this. Strangely enough by this time Jericho had become a priestly city where priests dwelt when not fulfilling their courses in Jerusalem. The road lying between these two cities was a rocky and dangerous gorge, a pathway haunted at the time by marauding Beda-win. It is so yet. It was on that very road in 1820 that an Englishman, Sir Frederic Henniker was stripped and slain by the descendants of these very men who robbed and wounded the man in this story. There was the road, and yet it was used by priests and Levites. I am inclined to think they had an immunity from attack of these brigands because of some superstition surrounding their calling. But they constantly travelled up and down that road.

There we are face to face with the story. A road about fifteen to twenty miles long, connecting the city of privilege with the city of commerce as it was then, unsafe for travellers; and yet traversed by religious people. I present that to all social workers. The road had no business to be unsafe. What had they done? They had done nothing. It may be they had attempted to exterminate these robbers, but had failed, had tried hard to drive them from their lurking places, and had failed. That is the road Jesus showed. It was quite familiar to them all, and perhaps with a great deal of trepidation, used by travel-lers, except perhaps by priests and Levites, preserved by the super-stition of their calling, by the brigands.

Now see the travellers. First here is an unknown man going down from Jerusalem to Jericho. We know no more about him. Whether he had been in Jerusalem for worship, I cannot tell. More likely he had been there for business. Most likely he was a man carrying certain forms of wealth about his person, of which the robbers knew. He travelled down that road.

What else? Robbers, brigands, brutal men, selfish men, devoid of all pity as long as their own ends were served. They travelled along that road.

Who is this other traveller we see going down? A priest. There is nothing to tell us which way he was travelling, whether coming from Jerusalem to Jericho; or going up to Jerusalem from Jericho. By chance, that is, by coincidence, he went by and passed that man lying there. A priest, either going home, having completed his ritual obligations in the temple of God, or else travelling up to Jerusalem, to fulfil his ritualistic observances in the temple of God.

But there is another man going along who is a Levite, shall we say, a secondary priest, one who served the temple, but had no direct function as the priest. He was in the same condition. He was on the way to complete, or had completed his religious obligations. Two representatives of religion travelled along that road.

Who is this other man? An unknown Samaritan, belonging to another nation. I wonder where he was going, and what he was doing upon that road? I cannot tell. I am permitted to wonder many things I cannot answer. He was on the road. It is possible he was crossing it, to take another road that led up to Mount Gerizim, for his worship. It is even possible he was coming back from Mount Gerizim after worship. He was an unknown man, a Samaritan. That robbed man was a Hebrew. That priest and Levite were Hebrews. The robbers we cannot tell what they were racially, probably Arabs. But this man had no dealings whatever with Jews. We are told Jews had no dealings with the Samaritans, and the other thing is equally true, the Samaritans had no dealings with the Jews. This man, travelling along, the robbers in hiding, a priest, a Levite, an unknown Samaritan, all travelling that road.

With the happenings there is no need to tarry; the attack of the marauding robbers, the man overwhelmed, robbed, stripped; and in order that there should be no chance of his following, beaten until so far as the robbers knew, there was no life left in him. The priest chanced to pass that way. There is no equivalent for "chance" in the text, except that the word means a coincidence. He passed that way, and he saw, but he did not stop, but at once passed on. The man was a Jew who was lying there bruised. That did not matter. The priest's religious observances were too important, or else, having performed them, he might gather defilement; and he could not do anything, so he passed him.

The Levite, more callous than the priest, went and looked at him, and examined him, and then he too passed on. The man was still left there, half-dead, bleeding, broken, bruised, robbed, helpless.

Then this travelling Samaritan came by, and immediately his heart was touched. He was filled with compassion. But he was a Samaritan, and this was a Jew. What did he care? The man was suffering. He might have said he did not have any dealings with Jews. But it depended upon what condition they were in. This man was suffering. He went to him, leaned over him, and poured into his wounds oil and wine, wonderful remedies of the time and place, bound him up, picked him up, and put him on his beast. I do not know how far away the inn was, but he had to walk, while the man in his feebleness rode. He took him to the inn and gave the host sufficient money to cover expenses for several days at that time and that place; and moreover, gave him an I.O.U. for anything over, "Whatsoever thou spendest more, I, when I come back again, will repay thee." He passed on.

We never see him again, but Jesus said to this lawyer, You have asked Me, Who is my neighbour? In effect you have asked what responsibility is created by those laws you have quoted, love to God and man. Tell He, which of these was neighbour to that poor fellow? I do not want to be unfair to this lawyer, but it always seems to me there was a little superciliousness in his answer, but he gave Jesus the right answer. He did not say, the Samaritan. He would not take that name on his lips. He gave the right answer; and quickly, sharply, like the flaming of a lightning's flash of God, Jesus replied, "Go thou and do likewise."

What a picture, what a parable. What does it teach? First that the purpose of law is always the conditioning of life. It is so with our human laws, faulty as they all are. It is pre-eminently so with the Divine law. If God has given man a law, it is in order that man may know life, and eternal life in all its glory and fulness. The purpose of a law is healing and healthing, to use an old Anglo-Saxon word. There is an Old Testament name for Jehovah, Jehovah-Ropheka. Expositors say that means the Lord Who heals. It really means the Lord that healths, and to health is not to make well, but it means to keep well, so that one is never sick. When we read in Revelation the leaves of the trees are for the healing of the nations, it is really the healthing of them, the keeping of them from being sick. That is the purpose of law. But supposing we become sick and are bruised and wounded and stricken, then the purpose of law is to heal to health. Those are the functions of law.

What does this story reveal as to the breakers of law; first the robbers who attack, but secondly and principally, the religionists who neglect? Not those brigands, those bandits, those robbers, were more guilty; but that priest, and Levite who left the man to bleed and sob his life out to death, without ministering to him. That is breaking law. It abides so to this time. All robbers who take, or by any means rob humanity of its riches, strip it, and leave it half dead, and broken, and bruised, are breakers of law. That is equally so if we pass by on the other side of that wounded man, that broken woman, that spoiled human nature. That is what our Lord was teaching.

Finally He teaches us what the keeping of law means. Its inspiration is compassion. "He was moved with compassion." That is the first thing said about the Samaritan. What he did came out of his compassion. Take the New Testament and go through it, and look for that word "compassion." It is always used about Jesus, or by Jesus, and never about anyone else, except as He used it in this case. Compassion is the inspiration of keeping law.

What is the activity, if that is the inspiration? Personal service. The binding up of wounds, the pouring in of oil and wine, the lifting of the man to a beast that carries him, or makes provision for him. Those are the responsibilities which law creates. We can spell them in one little word of four letters LOVE. That does not make it easier!

32. *Parabolic Illustrations*

Luke xi.

IN THIS chapter there are three parabolic illustrations demanding attention. Whereas they are separate illustrations, they are concerned with the same subject. The first concerned the friend at midnight, the second concerned the father and his child; while the third that of the strong man and the Stronger than he, is in some senses separated from the first two. Studied carefully however it will be found there is a close connection between all three.

The parable of the friend at midnight is peculiar to Luke. The illustration of the father and the child is also found in Matthew, but must be glanced at again, even though previously considered, because

of its association with the parable of the friend at midnight. The
illustration of the strong man and the Stronger is also to be found
in Matthew, but we omitted it when surveying that book, because
the account of Luke is more detailed.

Take the first two together; that of the friend at midnight, and
that of the father and his child. What was the subject our Lord was
intending to illustrate? The answer can be given in a word—Prayer.
This chapter in Luke opens, "It came to pass, as He was praying in a
certain place, that when He ceased, one of His disciples said unto
Him, Lord, teach us to pray, even as John also taught his disciples."
It was out of that request that the Lord's teaching came, and in that
connection these two illustrations were used.

Why did these men ask to be taught to pray? Notice they did not
ask to be taught how to pray. That is rather arresting. It is often
quoted as though they asked to be taught how to pray. That is not
what this man asked. He said, "Lord, teach us to pray." He knew
how to pray. The Lord had given special instructions concerning prayer
in His Manifesto. This disciple had heard it unquestionably, and had
received instructions how to pray. This man wanted to know, not the
method, but to find the secret of praying; two very different things.
There are many people who know how to pray, but they do not pray.
I cannot say they listened to Him at prayer. We have no means of
knowing whether He was praying aloud, or in silence. They were
round about Him. They came to Him as He was praying in a certain
place. Here in all probability He was praying alone. *Alone* does not
necessarily mean they were not with Him, because they were with Him,
and yet His prayer was alone. On an earlier occasion in Luke's record
it is said that when He was praying He was alone, and His disciples
were with Him. We might change the word "alone" and say, apart,
but His disciples were with Him.

It has been affirmed, and I agree with the general statement, that
Jesus never did pray with His disciples as though He were on a level
with them. He always prayed alone. It is certainly well to remember
that the word employed for His praying was never the word that
indicated their prayer. It was a word that indicated fellowship and
familiarity. He never came as an empty-handed pauper to pray. These
disciples had watched Him praying, and when He had ceased, one of
them, unquestionably affected by what he had seen, and perhaps heard,
asked, "Lord, teach us to pray." Then there was a flashing side-light
upon John, "even as John also taught his disciples." There is a suggested contrast. John had taught his disciples to pray. It is quite
evident he had devoted himself to the prayer-life, and he had taken

time with those disciples of his early and mighty ministry to teach them to pray. Yet these men saw in Jesus something different. They were not content with what they knew as the result of John's teaching. "Lord, teach us to pray."

Out of that request, that searching desire, Jesus answered, and in two ways. He first gave them a model of prayer with which we are all familiar, an abbreviated model, but a full one in another way. Then He turned to the illustrations of the friend at midnight, and of the father and his child.

First there came the model. He began by saying, "When ye pray say, Father." Everything is there. We must keep that in mind when we come to the illustration of the father and the child, "When ye pray say, Father."

Having given this abbreviated model of prayer He then proceeded to His illustrations. The first moved in the realm of human friendship. Notice the recurrence of that word *friend*. It is an account of friendship. A request was preferred by a friend to a friend, on behalf of a friend. A man had come to call on him at midnight, a very awkward hour it may be admitted at once; and he had nothing to set before him. He had a friend in some dwelling nearby, and so he made his way to the house of his friend, to ask him for help for this other friend. The awkwardness of the hour may be some excuse for the aciton of the man in bed with his children. Notice what he objected to. He objected to being troubled. Keep the emphasis there. Therefore on the basis of friendship he made a refusal. The house was locked up, he was in bed, and did not want to be troubled. That is the story.

But evidently this man who went for a loaf meant to get it. He kept on. Said Jesus, This man would not be troubled on the basis of friendship, but was disturbed, and so rose and acted because of the importunity of the man who was asking. That is the word. That word importunity is very interesting. It is the only place in the Greek New Testament where it occurs. Importunity means impudence. That is the real meaning of the word. It comes from the Latin *importunas,* which means troublesome. Because the man was importunate enough, this man who would not be troubled on the basis of friendship, was troubled in another way, by impudence. What for? To make the troubling cease. He only gave him the loaf to get rid of him, to save himself further trouble. He who would not be troubled on the basis of friendship, got up and found the loaf and gave it to the man, so that he went back home with something for his friend. That is our Lord's illustration.

Then He went on to the second illustration. "Of which of you that is a father shall his son ask a loaf, and he give him a stone? or a fish, and he for a fish give him a serpent? or if he shall ask an egg, will he give him a scorpion?" A father and child. Take the figure of speech first. A father never mocks a child's request. Our Lord here very remarkably recognised that one element in human nature that abides, in spite of all human nature's failure and breakdown. It is instinctive care of the father for the child. There may be some fathers who do not care. That I admit. But take the general outlook on life, and how marvellously that is evidenced. Even though men themselves may be depraved, they have not lost the father heart in relation to the child. That is the picture. Jesus took it for granted, and He only asked a question. Can we imagine if a child asks for bread, the father gives a stone, or for a fish, a serpent, or for an egg, a scorpion? We need not change the figures today in this country. They were all familiar things then and there, bread, fish, and eggs, the very things children needed, and were likely to ask for. Our Lord took these familiar things, and the one thing He was impressing upon those who listened was that the father never mocks the child's request.

What had these illustrations to do with prayer? The first was an illustration in the realm of contrast. Often expositors and preachers have said this teaches importunity in the matter of prayer. It teaches nothing of the kind. It teaches that there is no need when we are dealing with God, to hammer and hammer at a door. God is not asleep, a sleepy man who does not want to be troubled, and therefore refuses; and is only persuaded to get up in order to escape trouble for Himself, by getting rid of the seeker. That is not the picture of God. It is intended to be a contrast. The record reads, "Because of his importunity he will arise, and give him as many as he needeth. And I say unto you, Ask, and it shall be given you; seek, and ye shall find; knock, and it shall be opened unto you." We do not have to keep on knocking. The door is open. "Teach us to pray." "When ye pray say, Father." Understand that "Father" implicates friendship, and understand that your Father is not as this man who on the human level was a friend of the man asking help. God is quite different from that. He does not need to be importuned.

Again, "Which of you that is a father." You father, and "thy Father." The two illustrations merge, shining upon each other. God understands the need, and directly the soul applies to Him, the answer is given. There is no need for begging and praying and hammering at heaven's gate, as that man did at midnight. I do not believe there is any necessity to persuade God to do something for us, or to keep on asking. We may say, We have asked Him, and He did not give us anything. We should rather say, We wanted something we did not need, and our Father did not give it to us. With all reverence take those words of Jesus surrounding them. Supposing a son does not ask for bread, but asks for a stone, would the father give it to him? A fine old English phrase comes to me, I trow not! Supposing he asks a serpent, will a father give it to him? I think not. Supposing he does not ask for an egg, but for a scorpion. The father will say, No, certainly not. We need not keep on hammering. God knows, and His gift is always based upon His Fatherhood, and upon His love. There is no need for being importunate as the word suggests. This is the only case in the New Testament in which that word is found, and it is rightly rendered. There is no need for importunity with God.

Then comes the story of the father and the child to illustrate what God is. We may rest assured if we ask, it is given. Mark the contrast. In the first illustration the man would not give. He did not want to be troubled, but at last did give to save himself further trouble. You are different, said Jesus. When you ask, having said, "Father," it is given; seeking you find; knocking, there is no need for hammering, for the door is open. It was a great old Hebrew who said of God in one application, "He is ready to pardon," and He is always ready and waiting. Do not forget what I illustrated, by turning those illustrations round. When I go to Him, and ask for a stone instead of bread, or a serpent instead of a fish, or a scorpion instead of an egg, or we have asked Him for something; because He knew we did not need that, later on we find when we asked a stone, He gave us bread; and for a serpent, fish; and for the scorpion, an egg.

Luke here records something that had happened previously, but unquestionably he has recorded it here because of its application to the teaching Jesus was giving on the subject of the relation of the Holy Spirit. He will give the highest gifts. Matthew records Him as saying "good things." Luke records Him as saying "the Holy Spirit," the highest, the best, the one great gift humanity needs for its regeneration, and for all its life.

Then Luke went back, to tell how on one day they charged Jesus with complicity with Beelzebub, the devil. They acknowledged His was supernatural power, but that it was of the devil. It was then that Jesus spoke to them very severely, sternly, solemnly; but He rebutted that argument. He claimed that what He did, was done with the finger of God. There is no contradiction in the two things. The terms are synonymous. Jesus said what He was doing was not done under the power of the under-world of evil, but in the power of the Holy Spirit. In saying that He used this wonderful illustration. A strong man fully armed guardeth his own court, and his goods are in peace.

That is Satan. Satan fully armed, guards his realm, and we cannot interfere with his goods. But when the Stronger than he shall come, that is, the Son of God, the Lord Himself; He shall overcome him, and take from him his whole armour, and divide his spoils. That was His illustration.

Then to those who were diabolically criticising Him He said, "He that is not with Me is against Me, and he that gathereth not with Me scattereth." In other words, our Lord there claimed to be the Stronger than the strong man armed, and that He was Master over the strong man. As our beloved friends of the Salvation Army sing oftentimes,

> "Jesus is stronger than Satan and sin,
>   Satan to Jesus must bow.
> Therefore I triumph without and within,
>   For Jesus is saving me now."

That is the whole fact, and that is what He was claiming, that He was mightier than all the forces of evil. It was a remarkable phrase our Lord used there. He takes from him his whole panoply, his whole armour. That Greek word only occurs in one other place in the New Testament, where Paul was writing to the Ephesians, "Take the whole panoply of God." We take that text and preach sermons, and rightly so, to show how we are armed. We are to wear the same panoply, but do not forget it is God's armour. It is the armour that has made Him, is making Him, and will make Him invincible against all attacks. The Stronger than the strong came against the strong man, and took from him his panoply, because His own panoply was stronger. He was claiming authority over all evil forces, and to be stronger than all of them. That Ephesian passage (vi. 6-11) is worth careful study; the armour which God wears is invincible over all the forces of evil.

So in this realm of teaching, in which the thought of the Spirit is found throughout, He was showing that by the Spirit He overcame, and He had just told His disciples that His Father would give the Spirit to those who asked Him, so that we may be more than conquerors, the highest answer to which is not in the initial, but the continuous filling of the Spirit of power.

33. *The Rich Fool*

Luke xii: 13-21.

THIS parable also is peculiar to Luke, and in common with others peculiar to his record, this familiar story has made a profound impression. It is almost startling in its clarity, and supreme in the light it throws upon life. Those two men seen in the background of the story must be considered, for they were both involved when our Lord spoke the parable. We must also remember its supreme note, that it has to do with life.

Immediately preceding the parable itself, our Lord was speaking to a man, and said, "Who made Me a Judge or a Divider over you?" Then Luke says, "And He said unto them," not to the man who had spoken to Him, but "unto them." What does that mean? To whom? It may be said, to the disciples, and we should not be wrong, for undoubtedly they heard what He said. Or it may be He was addressing Himself to the large crowds surrounding Him at the moment, for there were such. The commencement of the chapter reads, "In the meantime, when the many thousands of the multitude were gathered together insomuch that they trode one upon another, He began to say unto His disciples first of all, Beware ye of the leaven of the Pharisees." So He was surrounded by multitudes, and His disciples were there; and He was in the midst of giving them definite and specific instruction in view of the hostility which was growingly manifest against Him, and He knew would be manifest against them as His representatives and followers in the days to come. He was charging His disciples not to be afraid of hostility, of them that kill the body, and after that had no more that they could do. Taking the whole of His teaching, we find He spoke of God's care of sparrows, and arguing from that His care of them.

In the midst of this teaching a man interrupted Him. To that interruption He replied, and then "He said unto them." The disciples certainly heard, and unquestionably the greater crowd heard what He said, but I believe "them" referred specially to the man who had spoken to Him, and the brother about whom he spoke. "Take heed, and keep yourselves from all covetousness; for a man's life consisteth not in the abundance of the things which he possesseth." That is the theme, life. It was to illustrate life, and its application to the case before Him, and to His disciples, and to the multitudes listening that He uttered this parable.

This man asked Him to intervene between himself and his brother in the matter of the division of an inheritance. We do not know all lying behind that request according to the law and custom of the time; but it was certainly possible that a man could wrong another, and in all probability that was the case here. We are not to suppose the man was wholly in the wrong, so far as the division of an inheritance was concerned. While Jesus was talking to His disciples, He had talked about God's wonderful care of sparrows and His children, this man suddenly broke in. It was quite evidently an interruption, almost a rude one. The man was evidently not thinking about what Jesus was saying. There was no relation between his request and the teaching of Jesus at this point; indeed the request was quite alien from it. If this man had been listening to His teaching, and had accepted it in any sense, he would not have spoken. There was a fretting and fuming against the wrong as he spoke, and perhaps on the human level it was a wrong. At any rate he appealed to Jesus to bid his brother to divide the inheritance with him.

Our Lord's refusal was a sharp one, and was in the form of a question, in which He revealed the fact that He was not in the world on the business of judging and dividing inheritances, which were wholly of the earth, and human, on the material level. Then to the listening multitudes He made that tremendous declaration, "A man's life consisteth not in the abundance of the things which he possesseth," and then He spoke the parable. He was illustrating the meaning of life, what it really is, to people who were largely thinking of life in the terms of the material, and the earthly, as evidenced by that interjection. They were thinking in the terms of things. Keep His word in mind, "Things." How largely our life is conditioned by things. What things? Just things, that is all. Half the trouble in life is that we think there are things we do not possess which we would like to possess. No, said Jesus, that is not life. A man's consisteth not, is not held together, is not made entire and complete by things, even though there is an abundance of them.

So we reach the parable itself. It is very simple. Look at the figure Jesus employed. "A certain man." The first thing that impresses us is that he was, on the material level, a fortunate man. He was rich, and he was successful through diligence. There is no hint here of fraud. There is no suggestion this man added wealth to wealth by fraudulent procedure. One can always expect wealth to bring more. Moreover he was a thoughtful man. He was sagacious. Jesus portrays him, "He reasoned within himself." In the presence of his multiplied prosperity, when his land was bringing forth more and more, and wealth was piling up, he took time to sit down and think. A sagacious man withal. What is this I hear him saying? "My fruit, my barns, my corn, my goods, my soul." He has listed them, and he has prefaced every reference to that possessive pronoun "my." "A man's life consisteth not in the abundance of the things which he possesseth." "My fruits . . . my barns . . . my corn . . . my goods," and of course the appalling and arresting thing is "my soul."

Look at him again. There is nothing vulgar about this man according to our common standards of vulgarity. What is he thinking about? What is his goal, his aim? "My soul, Soul, thou hast much goods," material possessions. What will be the outcome of having goods? Oh, the tragedy of it, "Eat, drink, and be merry." That is the most vulgar thing that can be said about life; goods the possession of the soul, in order that the personality may eat and drink and be merry. One cannot read this story without feeling how appallingly revealing it is of life as it is being lived today in multitudes of cases. Here is the picture of an entirely sensual man who imagines his soul can be fed with goods, and that the one object of everything else is to eat and drink, and be merry.

Yet look at him again. He is restless, and his satisfactions which are anticipated, are postponed until tomorrow. Tomorrow he is going to say to his soul, Eat, drink, and be merry. What is wrong with this man? So far there is not a word about God. "My fruits." Where did they come from? "My barns." Where did he get them? "My corn." Whence came it? "My goods," yes, all my possessions, and "my soul." Back of the fruits, the corn, the goods, and back of the soul is God. That is what is the matter with him. He is not recognising God; he does not know Him.

Then comes the dramatic part of the story that breaks in like a clap of thunder. "But God said unto him." The Revision has softened it in translation. I like the Old Version because it is exactly what it means, "Thou fool," in spite of your wealth, and your diligence and success and sagacity; because you think you can be satisfied with goods! "This night shall thy soul be required of thee." But it is "my soul." No, it is not; and therefore neither fruit nor barns nor corn nor goods belong to you. If you do not possess your own soul, you possess none of these things to which you are looking to satisfy your soul. You do not possess your soul. God shall this night require it of thee "and the things which thou hast prepared, whose shall they be?" We can see this man that night going out. His hands cannot handle shekels any more. He cannot go and see to the gathering of the fruits into barns any more. He has passed over, and all these things are still there, and the satire of eternity for the folly of time, "Whose shall they be?" Why are you piling up things for men and women to wrangle over when you are dead? They are still doing it! What a wonderful story this is.

We need not say much about it. Here our Lord was dealing with life. A man's life consisteth not in fruits and barns and corn and goods. He may have them in abundance, but they do not hold life; they do not make it consistent. A man's life does not consist in those things. He can have them and multiply them and store them; but that is not life. Our Lord used a word here for life. The man talked about his soul. They are two different words here. The man's word referred to his personality, and he used the word *psuche,* soul. That is only mental. Paul writing of personality, gave that full and final analysis of it, "Your whole spirit (pneuma), soul, (psyche), and body." (soma). There is the tripartite mystery of human personality. This man did not talk about his spirit, but his soul, the mental side of him. It is a wonderful side through which we have appreciation of all things of mental activity. "My soul," my mind; and he thought that was his essential life. It is not. The psychic is always the mental consciousness. Paul wrote in one of his letters about the "natural man." We should be perfectly correct if we translated that "the psychic man"; that is his word, the man who lives in the mental only. The psychic man can be mastered by the flesh from beneath, and become fleshly; or he can become mastered by the spirit, and become spiritual.

When our Lord spoke of a man's life He did not use either of the man's words. He used the old and familiar word, *zoe;* that is, the simple word for life, any life, the life of the butterfly, or of the beast, the angels, the archangels, or the life of man, and the life of God. In Greek literature they had another word for life, *bios,* and they spoke of *bios* as of higher development; and *zoe* as the animal and lower side of it. We are still doing this. We talk of biology, and mean the higher form; and zoology, and go to the Zoological Gardens to study it. Yet mark this well. The word Christ used was the word that refers to life, essential life, not spirit only, not mind alone, and body; but all, that principle that creates the difference between death and life. Whenever we read the phrase "eternal life" in the New Testament, this is the word used. It is very wonderful how Christianity took a word in Greek literature which had been degraded to something lower, and made it the supreme thing; life that is supreme. That is what our Lord said, "A man's life." This man was talking about his psychic nature, the mental apprehension. Life is more than that. That essential thing cannot be fed with goods. "A man's life consisteth not in the abundance of the things which he possesseth." *Zoe* is far more than *psuche*. That is only the mental and psychic side, and any man who is living there, however highly he trains it, however erudite his mentality may be, so that he may have the right to be known as an eminent scholar in the realm of the mental, if he has shut out God, and has no contact with Him in fruits and barns and corn and everything, then he is living on a low level, and is not living at all in the true sense of the word; for "a man's life consisteth not in the abundance of the things which he possesseth."

Then what about life? Life is under the control of God, and its earthly period is marked by God. God will break through somewhere. "But God!" Whether it is to enter upon the fulness of life, or whether it is to pass out into the darkling void, God is always there. He may be unknown, and it is an awful tragedy when He breaks in as He broke in upon the life of this man. Remember possession is never complete. Everything we hold is leasehold, rather than freehold. The lease runs on until God says, "Thy soul is required of thee." The one supreme fact in life is God, and it is a tragedy of all tragedies when He breaks in upon the soul unmindful of Him, with a "but," and declares "Thy soul is required of thee."

The parable applied to both those brothers. They were both characterised by selfishness, the one who gripped and held, and the other who coveted and wanted to grip and hold. So our Lord warned them against the sin of covetousness, and after the parable He said, "So," like that man, "is he that layeth up treasure for himself, and is not rich toward God."

34. The Watchful Servants

Luke xii: 41-48.

THERE are senses in which this paragraph is not an easy one with which to deal. While not exactly obscure, we need to give careful attention to certain details, in order not to miss its chief value.

The parable in its fulness is peculiar to Luke. Other parables have moved in the same realm. In the 24th and 25th chapters of Matthew we considered three, one communal, having to do with inter-relationships within His Kingdom; one personal, dealing with the supply of oil for lamps; and one imperial, concerning the talents entrusted to His own. When considering the first of these in Matthew, we postponed a full consideration, because the teaching here in Luke is fuller than that given in Matthew. Matthew recorded briefly this parable as our Lord uttered it in the Olivet prophecy. Luke gives it as our Lord had uttered it in an earlier part of His ministry.

This parable has a value all its own. What was our Lord intending to illustrate? Notice how the record begins. "And Peter said, Lord, speakest Thou this parable unto us, or even unto all?" What parable? Certainly not the one we are now considering, because He had not then uttered it. Immediately preceding that question is a parable Jesus had been uttering, and the question of Peter concerned the application of that previous parable, which dealt with the subject of fidelity to an absent Lord. Matthew Henry once said, "Thank God for Peter. He was always asking questions." His questions always brought forth wonderful answers. This was a perfectly fair question, "Speakest Thou this parable unto us, or even unto all?" It is one that faces us as we consider the parable. This present study is the answer to the question about fidelity to an absent Lord. The "us" referred to the twelve chosen apostles, representatives of those who should be the successors in the long history. Is the teaching of that parable restricted to such, or does it apply to all? Whether the "all" means all men, or all disciples we cannot say. Peter was definitely seeking to know if our Lord's teaching was intended to lay responsibility on the apostles, and those who should be called after them to certain definite spiritual authority within the Church of God, or whether it applied to all the Church. That is the background of the parable.

Notice how our Lord answered it. He did so by asking a question which, in a sense, He did not answer at all. Peter said, Who is that teaching for? Is it for us, or all? Jesus said, "Who then is the faithful and wise steward, whom his lord shall set over his household?" The question is open. Does what He is now going to say apply to a special company, called to specific service, or does it apply to all? Our Lord left it quite open. In effect He said, What I have said applies to every steward in the household who is faithful and true, whether in a special sense called to ministry, or not. I think in the last analysis the supreme value of the parable is for such, but it applies to others as well.

The picture our Lord here drew was of a household, which we must interpret by the East. There the household is a very different thing to what it is here. The household was composed of a lord, a master, the supreme one over all those who constituted the household, a despot not in any bad sense, but in a good sense, signifying complete and unquestioned and unqualified authority. Then in the household there was the office of stewardship, those under the lord who were the representatives of the lord. They were stewards of the property of their lord. A steward not only had charge of these things, he was responsible for their administration in the household. In the Eastern countries too the position of steward was often held by slaves, bond-servants. In this story the word used for servant is *doulos*, bond-slave. Those who were representatives of the ruler, the lord, were in complete surrender and subservience. That was the household.

Now in that household the responsibility that rested upon those who were stewards, being bond-servants, was that of watching over the life of all in the household, and of feeding all in that household. In the teaching of Jesus, taking the figure, we see that it was applicable to all in a household. Every bond-slave was in some measure the steward of the property of his lord, and every bond-slave was responsible to the rest in the household for the administration of the will of his lord, and the feeding of each other. Yet there were those in such households who were in special positions of government and authority over the affairs. That is the picture.

What were the possibilities lying within that fact of stewardship in the household? Simply, fidelity on the one hand, and failure on the other; those faithful and those unfaithful. Reasons for infidelity on the part of stewards within the household are suggested. The lord is absent, he is not there. There may be those who postpone his return, or declare, "He delayeth his coming"; and are therefore careless in their watching for him; the result being that they do wrong to each other. They "begin to beat the men servants and the maid servants," ill-treat them, and give themselves to carousing. That is infidelity. The Lord's teaching is that presently when the lord comes himself, he will deal with these stewards. He will deal with those who have been faithful, and set them in authority over all other things; associating himself completely with them in dominion. With those unfaithful, they will receive condemnation. He "shall cut him asunder." The Old Version had it, "cut him in sunder." The Revised Version has changed it. The judgment will be discriminative. Those who knew and wilfully disobeyed their lord's will will be beaten with many stripes; and those who disobeyed, and yet did not know the lord's will, yet were guilty, and did things worthy of punishment, will be beaten with few stripes.

If the story is taken in all its simplicity, we see what this teaching really is. There is a sense in which this parable is applicable to all in the household. That is a great phrase, "the household of God," which is the living Church. Every member of the Church is responsible for the other. The one sentiment which is for evermore denied at the door of the Church is the sentiment that is never recommended by the lips that first used it, "Am I my brother's keeper?" We should remember that. Yet there is the attitude, the peril, the possibility of an attitude in those words, "Am I my brother's keeper?" That is not true in the Christian Church. If it is true, then there are stewards who are failing. We are all responsible for each other in the great household of God.

Yet it is true according to New Testament teaching, that God has called by the Holy Spirit, and set apart certain within the Church who are in specific sense in oversight. That is the meaning of the word *bishop*. Bishop and presbyter are synonymous terms in the New Testament. They meant those who have oversight. That is what the writer of the epistle said, "Remember them that had the rule over you." Who were they? Those "which spake unto you the word of God." These orders of Christian ministry emerge clearly in the New Testament. We have mixed them terribly, and yet their essential values remain, those who are called upon "to watch in behalf of the souls" of "the household of God." Whereas the application of this parable of Jesus is unquestionably to all, I cannot study it without being convinced that its special application is to those whom we today call ministers. We are mistaken if we think ministers are servants of men. We are servants of the Lord, and "your servants for His sake," in His interests. There are great words in the New Testament,—bishop, teacher, pastor; and they all mark the fact of a position of responsibility in the Church of God concerning that Church.

The great underlying thought here is that of a revelation of an atmosphere in all this teaching of Jesus, that of fellowship in the household in the absence of our Lord, the fellowship of the Christian Church. The Lord used that distributive method in order to show that it applied to all, those who take the position of bond-service, or stewardship; whether specially or generally, but specially to those who are called. In the book of the Acts we have that wonderful story in the 20th chapter of Paul calling together the elders of the Church at Ephesus, and talking to them. Take a few sentences that fell from his lips. "Take heed unto yourselves, and to all the flock, in the which the Holy Ghost hath made you bishops," that is, overseers, "to feed the Church of God, which He purchased with His own blood." So Paul said to the elders at Ephesus, and it reveals the very thought of responsibility.

In Peter's letter we find the same great truth (I.5:1), "The elders among you"—presbyters—"I exhort, who am a fellow-elder, and a witness of the sufferings of Christ, who am also a partaker of the glory that shall be revealed." How did he charge them? "Tend the flock of God which is among you, exercising the oversight, not of constraint, but willingly, according unto God; nor yet for filthy lucre, but of a ready mind." Mark this, "Neither lording it over the charge allotted to you." It is interesting to note that the word "Charge" is the word *cleros*, from which we derive our word clergy. This is the only occurrence of the word in the New Testament. The clergy therefore according to the New Testament, are not the special ministers of the Church, but the rank and file of the members. The Church members here are in the clergy, and the minister is not! The clergy means the laity. It has to do with the inheritance, and the elders are not to lord it over the clergy, but to make themselves "ensamples to the flock." "And when the chief Shepherd shall be manifested, ye shall receive the crown of glory that fadeth not away."

Those two references show how the teaching of Jesus has special and first-hand application. To every brother in the ministry, and Sunday School teacher, and those preparing for this sacred work, it is borne in upon us as we study these words of Jesus, that we feed the flock of God.

It may be said, Surely the picture cannot be a true one, that within the household were those beating their menservants and maidservants, and eating and drinking, and becoming drunken. It is rather startling. But consider the history of the Christian Church. Again and again within the Church, on the part of those supposed to be stewards and fellow-watchers, this very thing has literally taken place; the beating, and beating to death, in the supposed interest of Christ Himself. One of the things that gives me cause for hope and rejoicing today is that there is far less of it than there was, when I was young. I can remember the extreme bitterness manifested to those who were of the household of God by others, and how men mauled each other. They are still doing it. There is an awful possibility of being in this fellowship, and so failing that our treatment of our fellow-men is utterly antagonistic to the spirit and genius of Christianity. Study the history of the Church to see to what I am referring.

What then are our duties? Paul said, Watch, and also, Feed the flock of God. Peter emphasised it. There is to be mutual ministry within the Christian Church, that of helpfulness, a mutual ministry on behalf of the other *douloi*. In the Church it is specially true. It is philosophically true of the whole race, but in the Church it is specially true, "No man liveth unto himself." It was also written, every man lives for his Lord, but this applies to his fellow-member too. When the function is fulfilled, then we find the blessedness; and when it fails, there must be discipline and punishment.

"Lord, to whom sayest Thou this? Unto us or to all?" To both, to all, to any who become members of the household, bond-slaves of the Lord, and stewards, serving each other in the things of the Kingdom of God.

35. The Barren Fig-tree

Luke xiii: 6-9.

THE PARABLE of the barren fig-tree is again peculiar to the Gospel according to Luke, and is one that has become familiar. Again care is needed to discover the subject which our Lord intended to illustrate. The figures of the fig-tree and the vineyard were prominent nationally at that time. One might be familiar with the song of the vineyard in the fifth chapter of the prophecy of Isaiah, without realising that this parable as to method is closely connected with it. There is no doubt that in the mind of our Lord thoughts of Isaiah's song are to be found, and that His parable in certain ways was an adaptation of that song of Isaiah.

This parable might be applied to the nation of Israel, and to God's dealing with that people. While not denying that there may be such an application, unquestionably there is that implication, if that be all, we do not really understand at what our Lord was aiming. So we must give attention to the context of His parable.

In doing so we see at once the application was individual rather than national. The larger application is of course involved, but the national entity has to be measured by individuals, and its strength measured by the individual unit. As it is true that every chain is as strong as its weakest link, and no stronger; and every fortress is as strong as its least guarded gate, and no stronger; so the nation is as strong as the individual. If it is weak individually, the weakness of the national life is created. So there is the closest relationship between the national and individual application.

However we are concerned to know why our Lord, at this point, used this parable; and also to mark the relationship of all that lies round about it. To find the answer we go back to the previous twelfth chapter. It is one continuous narrative, the two chapters being linked.

Luke is careful to show at the beginning of chapter 13, that what Jesus was about to say, happened at the same time. In verse 54, in chapter 12, we find Jesus speaking to the multitudes. To summarise there, He was rebuking the people because they were unable to discern the times in which they lived. He recognised their mental ability. He said they were weather-wise, but were entirely ignorant as to spiritual things. "Ye hypocrites, ye know how to interpret the face of the earth and the heaven; but how is it that ye know not how to interpret this time?" He was charging them with spiritual incapacity and misunderstanding of life.

Then "at that very season," so begins chapter 13, there were people who came to tell Him something that Pilate had done. He had mingled the blood of some Galileans with the sacrifices they had offered. The Galileans were a hot-headed crowd, and were often in some political difficulty, and it is quite evident there had been some trouble. At the time perhaps some religious festival was going forward. They were offering sacrifices, and Pilate had sent down a punitive expedition, and had slain them, mingling their blood with their sacrifices. They came and told Jesus the news. When? Immediately "at that very season," when He had rebuked them for ignorance and inability to discern the times.

Why did they tell Him that at that time? Note His reply. He said, "Think ye that these Galileans were sinners above all the Galileans because they have suffered these things?" Was that what they were thinking? Was that how they were looking upon life? Was that their interpretation of things? Were they thinking that those Galileans were sinners above all because they suffered these things? Were they imagining that a swift judgment was evidence of profound sin? "I tell you, Nay." They were wrong. They misunderstood life; "but except ye repent, ye shall all in like manner perish." Did that mean that Pilate would slay them too? They were looking upon the slaying of those people as though they perished. That is not the deepest meaning of perishing. They were slain by Pilate, but they could perish without being slain by Pilate, and they would, unless they repented of their sins.

Then transferring His thought from Galilee to Judaea, He continued, "Or those eighteen, upon whom the tower of Siloam fell, and killed them, think ye that they were offenders above all the men that dwell in Jerusalem? I tell you, Nay; but, except ye repent, ye shall all likewise perish." That is the context of the parable.

He had rebuked the multitudes for their spiritual insensibility to the time in which they were living; and they, desiring to show

Him that they were not such fools as He imagined, said, We do understand things. We know that because Pilate killed these Galileans this catastrophic judgment falling upon men proved that they were sinners above all. Our Lord gave them a parable to correct their false thinking about life; and revealed once and for all, the truth about human life, whether individually or nationally. Keeping here to the individual application, He gave parabolic illustration of the truth concerning human life, as against the foolish superstition in their minds of which they had given evidence, as they reported this story about Pilate and the Galileans.

Even today there is a tendency to say some catastrophe is the judgment of God upon people, because of their extreme wickedness. We have no right to say such a thing. People said that the earthquake in San Francisco, and the fire that followed, was the judgment of God on that city. Nothing of the kind. God does not deal with men like that now. That is not His method. Here in this parable we see the truth concerning all life, and though we may never be slain by Pilate's soldiers, or be crushed by the falling of houses in an earthquake, we may perish unless we repent.

Look at the parable. What a marvellously clear and succinct revelation it is. It is a simple and human story. What is the picture presented? First we see a proprietor, and his rights are revealed. "A certain man had a fig-tree." It was his, planted in his vineyard. It derived all its resources from his soil, his property. There are three rights of the proprietor, taking the picture simply.

There is first the absolute right of the proprietor to his own property. It was his soil. It was his vineyard. It was his fig-tree. It belonged to him.

Secondly we see, growing out of the absolute right, the moral right of expectation. Why did he give that fig-tree room in his vineyard? Because he expected figs, fruit. If a man plants a fig-tree in his garden, he expects figs. We can change the figure. If a man plants an apple tree in his garden, what does he do it for? Apples. The moral expectation is perfectly justifiable.

But in this parable there is another right, a punitive right of the proprietor to destroy that which fails. That is what the proprietor said to the vinedresser, the one in charge of his vineyard. For three years I have sought fruit on this fig-tree, and found none. My right of expectation has been trifled with, and thwarted, in spite of my patience for three years. Cut it down. Who will gainsay his right to do it? His right was created not merely because it brought forth no fruit, but because it cumbered the ground. That means two things.

Another tree, occupying that same space and soil, will bear fruit, and because it is robbing the soil of its riches, and bringing forth no fruit, it is ruining the soil. Those are the proprietor's rights as we look at the picture. There is no need to make any application.

Now in the parable there is interference, gracious, beneficent, but just, made by an intercessor. What does he ask? An opportunity to provoke that failing tree to such action as shall produce the fruit. "Let it alone this year also till I shall dig about it," disturb it; "and dung it," fertilise it. That is the plea of the intercessor. Is that all? No, "If it bear fruit thenceforth, well." That is what thou hast been expecting. If I can make it produce fruit, that is everything; and if not, then there is no quarrel between the vinedresser and the proprietor. "If not, thou shalt cut it down."

As we look at the fig-tree, what is the revelation? Everything depends upon the fulfilment of the proprietor's moral right to fruit. If a tree bears fruit, it will still keep its place; and functioning according to the intention of the proprietor, he will be satisfied. If it fails, in spite of the intercessor's plea, and his ministry, there is only one thing to do. A fruitless tree must not be allowed to cumber the ground.

Here the truth concerning life is revealed, whether it be individual or national matters nothing. The first fact is, the rights of God. Are people tired of hearing that? I thank God that it is being said with new emphasis again today. A man has no rights apart from the rights of God. The only right man has is to be damned! That is not the only thing. We have no right to expect anything, except for the mercy and grace of God. God's rights are the absolute rights of proprietorship. We are His by creation. We have no power of personality that is not created by God. Any essential power of personality is the result of Divine creation, and we are in His vineyard. This world is His. We have lived in it so many years. We have breathed His air. We have known His sunlight. We have benefited by His laws. Here we are, living in His world, His creation, His property, and deriving all the resources of personality from that which is His.

Has He any moral right of expectation? What does He expect? When looking at the fig-tree I used the word of the parable, and said we could change it to suit this Western clime in which we live. What did that man want from that tree? Figs. What is God looking for in man? What is He looking for in me? A man. What is He looking for in you? A man, a woman, a youth, a child. When He said, "Let Us make man," He is looking for the realising of the meaning of our own life, according to His own creation. Suffer me an illustration, often used. When a boy in Sunday School we used to sing,

> "I want to be an angel,
>   And with the angels stand.
> A crown upon my forehead,
>   And a harp within my hand."

Surely there was never anything more stupid taught to children than that! I am not an angel, thank God. God never intended us to be angels, and He never intends us to be. He does not want angels when He makes men. He wants men. Someone may say I am lowering the standard. No, I am not. What is a man? We have only one answer. Jesus is the revelation. That is what God wants when He comes into His garden seeing fruit, from you, from me; likeness to Jesus. There is another of childhood's hymns I have not given up singing even now,

> "I want to be like Jesus,
>   Meek, lowly, loving, kind."

That is what God wants. A man looks for figs from his fig-tree. God looks for humanity from His humanity, and He has that moral right of expectation.

If we fail, who will deny His right to destroy, to cut down. That right is inherent in the meaning of humanity. A man who is not realising that Divine ideal is cumbering the ground. It may be, my dear Sir, somebody living where you are living would exert an influence of fruitfulness, and would benefit humanity; and you are taking up space, you are cumbering the ground. You are taking God's resources, and prostituting them to base uses. Because you are not fulfilling the meaning of your own life, has He not the right to say, "Cut it down"?

Then of course the great Lord Who uttered the parable is revealed to us as the intercessor. Mark carefully this one supreme fact. The ground of the plea of the intercessor is not pity. We do not understand it if we talk merely of pity. It is not a case of the woodman sparing that oak because of the beauty of its foliage. If there are no figs, if there are no apples, if there is no humanity, Christ is not interfering, or asking God to let us off, or making excuse for failure. No, He has received the right to dig about it and dung it, to disturb and fertilise the life, to come into contact with the barren fig-tree and make it fruitful.

Then, if in spite of all He does for us, there still is no fruit, then He joins with the proprietor in the verdict of doom, "Thou shalt cut it down."

What is the test then of life? Fruitfulness, according to the Divine intention. No, God is not swooping down upon people and proving they were dreadful sinners, by some calamity. He is expecting fruit. Oh wonderful imagery and matchless grace, He is introducing Himself as the vinedresser. He is waiting and able to take the deadest tree and make it live again, a fruitless human life, and make it blossom with beauty, and bear fruit.

> "But if we still His call refuse,
>   And all His wondrous love abuse;
> Soon must He sadly from us turn,
>   Our bitter prayer for pardon spurn.
> Too late, too late, will be the cry,
>   When Jesus of Nazareth has passed by."

It behooves us to turn from all the false thinking of man about life, and its conditioning; and to find out God's thought, and its revealed purpose now and for ever, from this parable of the barren fig-tree.

36. The Great Supper

Luke xiv: 15-24.

THIS parable was uttered in the house of a ruler. Luke has recorded a remarkable section (xiv-xvii. 10), telling of happenings on one Sunday afternoon in the life of our Lord. I think it was the last Sunday in His public ministry, of which we have any record. This parable was given on that afternoon.

Our Lord had been invited into the house of one of the rulers of the Pharisees to eat bread, and "they were watching Him." The first thing then suggested is that it was an occasion of hospitality, a Sabbath afternoon reception. At that time one mark of the degeneracy of the Hebrew people was that they encroached upon the Sabbath day for social reception. It is a mark of degeneracy today very often, in the Christian Church. Our Lord went to this house. We can go to such gatherings too if we do what He did there. Guests and host were there, and it is evident that the hospitality offered to Jesus, which He accepted when He went into the house, was of a sinister nature; because there was a man there whom no ruler would have asked, except for an ulterior reason,—a man with dropsy. Luke tells us that they watched Jesus to see what He would do with that man. He healed him, and let him go.

Then in that house, which was for the moment a house of hospitality, where guests were assembled, Jesus did the most unconventional thing on record. He first criticised the guests for their bad manners, and then His host for the false principle upon which he had issued his invitations.

As He talked to them, He had spoken about a marriage feast, about dinner, and about supper. It was all in the realm of hospitality. He was there in the house, with a sinister motive in the invitation; and the other guests were there, seating themselves round those three-sided tables of those homes, where there was one place of preeminence. We are told Jesus marked how they chose the chief seats. The word "marked" is a good translation, though it does not merely mean He saw. He watched them. They watched Him, but He watched them; and everything was in the realm of hospitality.

As He criticised the guests and the host, He revealed two principles of social order. He revealed first that self-emptying is the true secret of exaltation. Office seekers were excluded; those wanting the chief places were dismissed. Those not seeking were to have the chief places in social life. Self-emptying is the secret of exaltation.

Then when He turned to the host, He showed that self-emptying is the secret of hospitality. In that story there is one little word, twice repeated. *"Lest* a more honourable man than thou be bidden." That is the danger. When He came to the host He said, Do not call your friends and brethren, or your rich neighbours, *"lest* haply they also bid thee again." But that is generally why we do ask people. We expect them to ask us again. Said Christ, If people act on that basis, they cut the nerve of hospitality.

It was at that moment someone at that feast, said, "Blessed is he that shall eat bread in the Kingdom of God." There are different opinions what that exclamation really meant. Some look upon it as a satirical exclamation. Personally I believe strongly that it was a genuine exclamation of admiration. Some person in that company listened to Him, and saw through the things He had said, things of the simplest, and yet most searching; an order of life quite different to the one with which people were familiar; a new social order altogether, in which the places of honour went only to honourable people, an order of life in which hospitality was completely self-emptied, and never self-seeking. I think somebody saw it, and cried out, "Blessed is he that shall eat bread in the Kingdom of God." It was an intelligent remark. A man saw that the order revealed was the order of the King-

ship of God, and the Kingdom of God. Someone saw the beauty of the
ideal, of a social order mastered by these principles.

We come now to the parable. "But He said unto him." The parable
was an answer to that exclamation, and becomes a most searching
and revealing one. Our Lord took His story from the realm in which
He found Himself, that of hospitality. There in the house the guests
were gathered, bad-mannered; and a host who did not understand
hospitality. It was a social occasion, a feast. So our Lord said, in
effect, Let Me tell you a story. This story was an answer to that
exclamation.

What was the figure employed? It was purely Eastern. A host pre-
pares a supper, and issues his invitations to that supper. All the guests
decline, making various excuses. Surely there was humour in the heart
of our Lord, as seen in the illustrations. The host was angry, and sent
his servants with invitations to new guests, the poor, the maimed,
the blind, and the lame. Notice these were the people whom He had
told His host he should ask, when he made a feast. The report was
made to him, This is done as thou commanded, and yet there is room.
Then the last words of the host, "Constrain them to come in that my
house may be filled. For I say unto you, that none of those men which
were bidden shall taste of my supper."

Taking that as a story, without thinking of any application for
the moment, it is a most unusual one, and our Lord intended it to
be such. Common experience would contradict it, that any host who
had a supper, and sent out invitations, everyone invited should decline
the invitation. Did a thing like that ever happen? Immediately we
are face to face with this fact, that implicated in the story is a recognition of hostility toward the host on the part of those who were
bidden. They began to make excuses. They were only excuses, but
they made them. They declined. They would not come. Why not?
There is only one answer, that they did not like their host. One cannot
argue anything else. The neglect lies deeper than that of a supper table.
There is some objection to the one who sent out the invitation.

Jesus told this unusual story when someone really admired the
ideal of the Kingdom of God. He did not deny what this person has
said as to the blessedness of the Kingdom of God. In His great Manifesto He struck the key-note in the word "Blessed," happy, prosperous,
as the Greek word means. That is the purpose, the meaning of the
Kingdom of God, blessedness. Here in two social illustrations some
man saw the new order, and said, There is the secret of happiness;
blessed is he who shall live under those conditions. Our Lord was not
denying this. What was He doing? He was revealing the human heart,

and was saying to them in effect, Yes, men admire the ideal, but they will not enter into that Kingdom, in spite of their admiration, they are refusing to enter into it. To admire the ideal is one thing. To accept it, submit to it, enter into its laws, is quite another. He was preaching that very Kingdom of God. That was the great burden of His preaching from the beginning of His ministry, as it had been of His great predecessor, John the Baptist.

Take the story as a suggested revelation, bearing the Eastern atmosphere. "A certain man made a great supper." The nature of the Kingdom of God is that it is a gift, offered to man, an invitation to enter into the true order of life, as a gift. Keep the simplicity of the story. In the back of the mind of our Lord He thought of God as a Host, and He has provided, as a gift of His love and grace, the feast of the Kingom. It is a gift of grace.

What is the right of entry? What right had anyone at the feast? None other than the invitation of the host. The whole thing being of grace, no one had any right there, and gate-crashers in the supper are put out. While the invitation constitutes a perfect right to the Kingdom of God, yet at last the host says, None of those that were bidden shall eat of my supper. Why not? Because they refused. Their own refusal was the reason of their exclusion.

Our Lord in a marvellous way gave illustrations of excuses, not reasons. There is no reason amongst them. "They all with one consent began to make excuse." "I pray thee," literally, I pray you have me begged off. What does the first man say? He has bought land, possessions, real estate. We are bound to say that these people on the level of human common-sense, were either liars or fools, every last one of them. Fancy a man buying land, and then going to see it. Still that is what he said. He had to see his possession, real estate.

The next man said, I have bought five yoke of oxen, and I go to prove them. Imagine it! I know it is said we must not look a gift horse in the mouth, but one does so before buying one! This man said he had bought oxen, and now was going to look at them.

Then came that last man. He felt the matter was quite settled. "I have married a wife, and therefore I cannot come."

What have we here? Possession, or wealth; commerce, or labour; emotion, or human affection; and those are the three things that today are keeping thousands out of the Kingdom of God. It was a simple story Jesus told, one that could have been translated into history all over that country side; and He knew it. He said, These men all began to beg off. Why? The man who said he was going to see land, was not truthful. The man who said he was going to look at the oxen he had bought, was lying. The man who said he had married a wife was a fool. Why did he not take her with him? There was some reason behind it all, and so there always is. God's Kingdom is a great feast,

"Come, for the feast is spread";

and the right of entry is His invitation, without money, without price. If we are excluded, it is because we refuse ourselves, and for no other reason; and if we refuse, why do we do so? Get behind the excuses, and whether it is the passion for wealth, or consecration to commerce, or mastery by human affection, there is something else behind that in every case. The underlying reason of refusing to enter the Kingdom is hostility against God. The carnal mind is enmity against God. The carnal mind is the mind mastered by carnalities, by the flesh, by material things. It is wonderful how much can be shut out with an apparently small thing. A man can so put a golden sovereign before his eyes, as that he cannot see the sun or the world; and when men have put other things between themselves and God, the result is they become hostile to God, because they do not know Him, or understand Him.

"Blessed is he that shall eat bread in the Kingdom of God." Who is there who would not be prepared to say that. Who is there who does not admire the ideal, illustrated here by our Lord in its entirety, that Kingdom wherein dwelleth righteousness and peace and joy? Who does not admit it? If we admit it, have we entered? Are we in it? That is what Jesus meant. We admire the ideal, but the story shows what men are doing.

Of course the story had immediate application to the nation, to the fact that when those bidden ones of high privilege through the running centuries, were refusing Him, He was opening the door to the poor, the maimed, the blind, and the lame; and compelling or constraining men everywhere to come in. But the supreme value of it is, Where am I? Am I in the Kingdom? If not, what is the excuse? When next you are alone, and every one else is shut out, find out the reason beneath the excuse.

37. Two Parabolic Illustrations

Luke xiv: 25-35.

TWO PARABOLIC illustrations are found in this paragraph. It is important again that we briefly review the circumstances. The 25th verse reads, "There went with Him great multitudes." Our Lord had left the house of the Pharisee where strange things had happened, and where He had found no congenial atmosphere. The hostility of the host was manifested in the presence there of the man with the dropsy. The behaviour of the guests was at fault, and the principle of the hospitality of the host was wrong, as Jesus had shown. Then in answer to that exclamation of one of the guests, Jesus had spoken that parable of the great supper, the intention of which was to show the reluctance of the human heart. Admiring the ideal, men were not prepared to submit to the conditions. That all happened in the house.

Having left the house, our Lord now used two parabolic illustrations. He had moved away, and started on His journeyings. While He had been in that house, there were multitudes of people outside, who had been waiting for Him. These were the last months of our Lord's public ministry, and by this time, wherever He went, the crowds went after Him, following Him from town to town, and village to village, eager, keen, interested, loving to hear Him, and to watch Him, and wanting to be near Him. In many cases, perhaps the majority, they felt they would like to be connected with Him, enrolled as His followers. They were all waiting for Him, and "there went with Him great multitudes." The moment He came out of the house these waiting people outside were alert; and as He moved away, they went after Him. That is the significance of the next phrase, "And He turned, and said unto them." Upon this occasion He declared the terms of discipleship. It is almost like a fierce wind that blew across that crowd, unquestionably winnowing them. Yes, Jesus was winsome, but there was another aspect to His ministry, as well as winning. He was winnowing, and while He won those crowds, and they were interested, and were coming after Him, just as crowds do today, and are still doing, He turned round, and not this time only, superlatively, but constantly, He said things that blew like a wind of God across that crowd, thinning out those who wanted to be His followers. He gave them the terms of discipleship.

There is a phrase here from the lips of Jesus thrice repeated in this paragraph. "Cannot be My disciple" (verse 26). "Cannot My disciple" (verse 27). "Cannot be My disciple" (verse 33). H was telling them that there were people who, however much they were interested in Him, were like the man left in the house, admiring His ideals, but could not be His disciple. Who were they? I can never read these words without trembling, and wondering whether I am a disciple. If any man were coming after Him, he could not do this unless he put loyalty to Him above the highest and finest and noblest loyalties of earthly love. It was a tremendous saying. He said unless a man do that, he could not be His disciple. Then to interpret what He meant by that saying, He declared, "Yea, and his own life also." Not only earthly loves, high, affectional loves, but the love of self, and the love of life. Then He interpreted that. "Whosoever doth not bear his own cross"—that is failing to love self,—"and come after Me, can not be My disciple." Then finally, to summarise everything, Unless a man "renounceth not all that he hath, he cannot be My disciple."

Then something happened. This passage is only understood as we can see that crowd imaginatively. We need not travel to Palestine where He was at the time, nor need we go back nineteen hundred years to see it. Take any massed company of men and women gathered together today, in an evangelistic service, interested in Jesus, attracted towards Him, and having a feeling that they would like, in some measure, to be associated with Him. Then let the preacher, as the mouthpiece of the Master, declare these terms of discipleship, and then look at that crowd. They will be more attentive than ever for the moment; but if one is keen enough to discern the fact, there is a puzzled, almost restless look, and at last a protesting look, as though they would say, But surely those terms are severe, Cannot it be made easier than that? Cannot we be His followers, and listen to Him and admire Him, and rejoice in His power without such drastic measures? Humanity is just the same today as then. Jesus would say to them today without any reservation, what He said to them in the olden days. That is the background of these illustrations.

What then is the subject He was illustrating? Without any question He was showing the reason why His terms were severe. Men and women were looking into His face and saying, Why be so severe? He used two parabolic illustrations to show them the reason why.

Look again at the illustrations. He said, "Which of you, desiring to build a tower, doth not first sit down and count the cost, whether he have wherewith to complete it? Lest haply, when he hath laid a foundation, and is not able to finish, all that behold begin to mock

him, saying, This man began to build, and was not able to finish."
The second illustration, "Or what king, as he goeth to encounter
another king in war, will not sit down first and take counsel whether
he is able with ten thousand to meet him that cometh against him
with twenty thousand? Or else, while the other is yet a great way off,
he sendeth an embassage, and asketh conditions of peace."

To come now to a technicality. The next verse in the Authorized
Version begins, "So likewise whosoever he be." That is an unfortunate
translation, one that has misled the thinking of men generally as to
the meaning of these two illustrations. The Revised Version has correctly translated the Greek phrase, which never meant "likewise," but
"So therefore." What is the difference? If we read "So likewise," then
Jesus meant that just as the man going to build a tower, and the king
going to war, must both count the cost; so must we if we are coming
after Him. But our Lord said, "So therefore." He never told men to
count the cost. They were to come at all cost, at the cost of earthly
love, and the cost of renouncing everything.

What then did He mean? That He had to count the cost, and that
was why His terms were severe, in the interest of what He was doing.
"So therefore." Note the difference carefully between "likewise" and
"therefore" in that passage. Notice also the repetition three times over
of the phrase, "Cannot be." Behind that "cannot be" were instructions
that proved to men that they were to stop bargaining and counting
the cost; that they were to trample on personal love and ambition
and all possessions. They were to come at all cost. Yet He showed
the necessity of His counting the cost.

Take then, the two figures. First, building, the figure of construction. Building is the great symbol of construction. But He used a
second figure, war, and battle, and battle is destructive. Building is
constructive work; battle is destructive work. He said, If a man wants
to do constructive work, to build a tower, he sits down first and counts
the cost. If he does not do so, the purpose of his building will be frus-
trated, and he will never be able to complete it, and men will laugh
at him. Some buildings have been called some man's folly. Some man
started to build, and he could not finish it, and carry out his purpose.
That was the first figure of speech.

Then a king going to battle, before he goes, if he is wise—and this
is pure political wisdom—he finds out whether every man in his army
is worth two of the enemy. That is a different mathematical formula
of expressing the thought of the text, "whether he is able with ten
thousand to meet him that cometh against him with twenty thousand."
He needs his every soldier to be equal to two of the enemy. That is our

Lord's estimate. Then that satirical word; if the king do not do that, if his men are not of that quality, presently there will be an embassage sent to the opposing forces, asking for conditions of peace—surrender!

Building. If one does not count the cost, there will be failure and laughter. Battle. If one does not take time to find out the quality of the soldiers, there will be defeat; and conditions of peace will have to be asked from the enemy. Those are the two figures of speech. Our Lord had just uttered the terrifying terms of discipleship, and men were inclined to protest. He said to them in effect, You wonder at the severity of My terms. Let Me tell you why they are severe. He used the two figures of speech, and asked them to think the matter through. What did He mean? That He was in the world to build. If any man were going to build, would he not count the cost, whether he could carry out his purpose? That is what He was doing. That was why His terms were severe. He appealed to their own common-sense, to their own experience, and to their intelligence. They were no warriors or kings, but they knew enough of war. What king does not sit down and calculate, on the basis of the quality of his soldiers?

What were the implications? Here our Lord was declaring His purpose in the world. He was here for building and battle. At Cæsarea Philippi, in other language, He had used the same terms in addressing Peter and the rest. "On this rock I will build My Church,"—building. What next? "And the gates of Hades shall not prevail against it,"—battle. The ultimate purpose of His presence was constructive; but on the way to the completion of the work on which His heart was set, there were battles to be waged and won. He had told His disciples that He would build. He had told them He would conduct the campaign victoriously, that the gates of Hades should not prevail against it. Victory was in His mind. The fulfilment of purpose was there. He would build. Now He used the same figures in a slightly different application.

Thus He was telling them that the purpose of, and the reason of the severity was the greatness of His own emprise; and the fact that in order to complete that building and win that battle, He must have resources and men upon whom He could absolutely depend. He was showing them that following Him meant more than personal advantage only. Personal advantage was secondary, and in the presence of His Cross was smitten out of sight as almost unimportant. Oh the terror of it that we have so often made our salvation a kind of fire insurance, a way by which we may escape hell! Following Jesus meant far more than that, and this was what He was showing His disciples. To follow Him was to commit oneself to His enterprises, to stand by Him in the battle, to stand with Him in the battle, until the building is done, and the battle is won.

I will use an old illustration. When Charles Haddon Spurgeon was exercising his marvellous ministry, and building up the Pastors' College, he started a magazine, the title of which was "The Sword and the Trowel." Nehemiah when building the wall of Jerusalem commanded the workers to grasp the sword as well as the trowel, to fight the enemies that would hinder the building. Spurgeon knew that little incident of ancient Hebrew history was symbolic of the action of God through the Jews, and of the mission of Jesus Christ. Jesus came to build; and He came for battle. He had left the house of the Pharisee and found Himself surrounded by thronging multitudes interested in Him. As He started to move away, they came with Him. He turned, and halted them, and said in effect, What are you following Me for? Are you coming after Me? I am in this world to build. I am in this world to battle. You are no good to Me unless you are of the right quality, the right calibre. I do not want followers coming after Me for their own sake. I want those committed to Me and to My enterprises. That was the meaning of the illustrations. He it was Who had to count the cost, not they.

Thus by these very illustrations, by the use of these terms of severity, our Lord emphasized the importance of quality. Quality is always the thing that counts in the Church of God, and among the disciples of Jesus, not quantity. We have such an unholy passion for quantity. We say, Great crowds go to that Church; it is a scene of success. Not at all. It may be that little chapel down in the valley, or on the hill-side, away in the Highlands, or in the valleys of Wales where the two and the three are gathered is of more use to God than the great congregation simply attracted by something less than the highest. It is quality that counts, and He wants quality, men and women on whom He can depend, who are with Him, with sword in hand, and who lay stone upon stone in the mighty building, men and women who will stand there against all opposition.

> "The Son of God goes forth to war,
>   A Kingly crown to gain.
> His blood-banner streams afar,
>   Who follows in His train?"

Let us get to our knees and ask if we are such upon whom He can depend.

After He had uttered these words, the crowds still listening to Him, He ended with that vibrant challenge, marking the supreme importance of what He had been saying, "He that hath ears to hear, let him hear." Which words lead us to the fifteenth chapter, and to our next study.

38. The Parable of Lost Things

Luke xv: 3-32.

THIS familiar chapter of Luke's record contains one of the best known parables of our Lord. One phase of this, that of the lost son, usually referred to as the parable of the prodigal, has made a greater impression on human consciousness than any parable Jesus ever uttered. We do not now dwell upon the details of the parable, but rather attempt to gather its values, asking first, what it was our Lord intended to illustrate here; secondly, looking at the figures of which He made use; and finally gathering the teaching He intended to give on this particular occasion.

This is one parable, with three pictures. Luke uses the expression at the beginning, "He spake unto them this parable." There are stages in the pictures, but there is no break in the parable itself. First then, what was the subject that our Lord was intending to illustrate? Reminding ourselves of the historic setting, this parable was uttered towards the close of that memorable Sabbath day, of which Luke alone gives so full an account. Jesus had uttered His parable of the great supper, in the house of the Pharisee. He had used the two parabolic illustrations of building and battle, illustrating the reason for the severity of His terms of discipleship; and at the end of the previous chapter there fell from His lips those words, "He that hath ears to hear, let him hear." Going straight on with the narrative, Luke says, "Now all the publicans and sinners were drawing near unto Him for to hear Him." He had uttered severe terms, interpreted in the figures of building and battle, showing that He needed those with Him who should stand by Him in His building until the work was done; and in the war till the victory was won; and the publicans and sinners pressed closer to Him; they drew near to hear Him.

But they were not alone in the crowd. "The Pharisees and the scribes murmured, saying, This man receiveth sinners, and eateth with them." He let them come near Him. He did not stand aloof. Indeed, He went so far as to sit down and eat with them. The scribes were the appointed moral teachers and interpreters of the law; and the

Pharisees were the great ritualists and supernaturalists in the realm of religion. Both these criticised Him. The crowds held in contempt by the rulers, were getting near Him, and He was receiving them. The Pharisees and scribes were standing aloof, critical, uttering words of condemnation. We discover then unquestionably, the subject which our Lord wished to illustrate. He was first declaring the meaning and reason of His receiving sinners. That is what the Pharisees and scribes objected to. He received them. The word is a very strong one. He received them to Himself. He took them into close comradeship, and sat down, and had close fellowship with them, and He ate with them. He was trying to show these critical rulers why He received sinners and ate with them. He was interpreting to them the actions they were criticising. It is quite evident that the subject He wished to illustrate was not the manner of His own ministry and method; but rather the attitudes and activities of God in the presence of derelict humanity. When we remember these things, then we are prepared to follow Him, listen to His words, look at the pictures, and gather the teaching.

There are here four pictures, three, and one more. Jesus first drew the picture of a shepherd and his lost sheep. He began by appealing to them, as was so constantly His custom. "What man of you." He told the story of a shepherd who had a hundred sheep, one of which, no reason being given, had wandered and was lost. He declared that any true shepherd, if he had lost one sheep, would leave the ninety and nine, and go into the wilderness, and find it. It was not the first time He had employed the figure of the shepherd. That however is the first phase of this parable.

Then next, a woman and her lost drachma, her piece of silver. As a picture there may be differing opinions as to its intention. One view is that this woman had lost a piece of current coin in the house. She had ten, and had lost one. The story would lose nothing if that were its meaning. I think however that there is something deeper in it. The women of that time often wore upon their brow a frontlet that was called *semedi*. It was made up of coins, in themselves perhaps largely valueless, each one of which might be worth 10½d, or perhaps a little more; but under a shilling. But it was a coin that had stamped upon it the image of authority. Again here scholars differ as to the significance of the frontlet. Some hold that it was a frontlet that revealed betrothal; and again others, that it revealed the marriage relationship. Whether it was of little monetary value or not, it was of priceless value to the woman who wore it. That is evidenced by the fact that she sought it diligently, sweeping the house, until she found it. I cannot imagine a woman sweeping a long time to find a shilling!

But I can imagine her searching diligently to find something which, to her, was a thing of beauty, and adornment, and suggestiveness. However, that is the picture. One coin out of ten, gone. The woman had lost that which perfected the symbolism of her frontlet.

The third picture is familiar and beautiful, that of the father who lost his boy. But there is another. It is the final phase in this parabolic setting forth of Jesus. It is the picture of an unnatural son, who was upright and loyal by all the outward appearances of life, but who had no understanding of, or sympathy with his father's heart; and consequently held his brother in contempt. Undoubtedly there were such, as there always are. There is the merging of four figures.

What does it all mean? What did our Lord intend to teach? First of all, as we listen to Him telling those stories, keeping in mind that crowd of men about Him, and that crowd of publicans and sinners pressing eagerly forward, conscious of their own failure and sin, yet eager to hear Him in spite of the severity of the terms He had uttered; as we listen to Him we gather what His outlook was upon humanity. He saw humanity lost. Whether it was the sheep, or the drachma, or the son, in His view each was lost.

Take the first three phases. What an illustration is there of lost humanity. First, a lost sheep. A sheep is one of the most stupid things. It goes anywhere where it sees a gap. It does not stop to think. It cannot think. A gap appears in a fence, and the animal goes through it, and away it goes, wandering on, until it is lost upon the mountains, and does not know its way back. There are multitudes of people who exactly fit in with that description; lost from sheer stupidity.

How was the piece of silver lost? It was not to blame at all for being lost. There was something lost through the carelessness of others. Mark it well, lost at home, but lost. There are multitudes in our Churches today who are lost at home through the carelessness of others. They are still somewhere about, but they have no purchasing power, and they are making no contribution that is worth while to the great cause. They are lost through the carelessness of others.

When we turn to the picture of the first son, we have a very different story. This is not stupidity. This is not a losing through the carelessness of others. This is deliberate, self-centred pride. This is the lost son, representing those lost because they rebel against all restriction and all order, and vainly imagine that away from God and Christ, and away from the Church, there is freedom, liberty; and they will be able to express themselves. They go to the far country, away from God and Christ and the Church and restriction, and they say, Let us eat, drink, and be merry; and they go, and they are lost! There is tremendous power in every phrase. He went into a far country, and spent his substance, which he had derived from his father. He was spending what his father had given to him. Humanity away from God is expending the forces which God has created in them, and committed to them. Every man who sins with his hand, foot, eye, or mind, is sinning with force that God has given to him to bless him, and to make him. Men are prostituting their gifts, wasting their substance; they are lost!

Then that sentence from the lips of our blessed Lord always seems to have in it a biting satire. "When he had spent all, there arose a mighty famine in that country." That does not necessarily mean there was some physical famine. It may mean that if a man have spent all in London, there is a famine in London! One can be in the midst of plenty, and yet find a famine. He joined himself to a citizen of that country. He was not going home yet; not he! He was going to face it out. And "he sent him into his fields to feed swine." We may not get the force of that, for we are not Jews. He gave him the lowest and most degrading and humiliating thing to do. And "he would fain have been filled with the husks that the swine did not eat; and no man gave unto him." I never read that sentence without thinking all the nobility was not gone from him even then. I know men who, if no man gave to them, they would have helped themselves. He did not. He suffered hunger.

But "he came to himself." It is a great hour when a man comes to himself, when substance is gone, and friends are gone, and the possibility of finding food is gone. There is nothing left. He came to himself, and that is when reason dawned again. He began to think. He was lost. That is Christ's outlook. He was lost through his own deliberate choice and pride.

Yet there is another picture there. Another son is out in the fields doing his work, attending to the affairs of the estate, and very proud of what he is doing. He hears the sound of music and dancing, and makes enquiries, and a bond-slave tells him, Your brother is home. My brother! Notice this, Jesus never called this man a brother. He called the other man his brother, but He never called him the other man's brother. It is a slight matter, but worth noticing. He was lost. He did not know his father. He did not know his father's heart. He was lost in his father's country; duteous, and a man can be lost there, as well as everywhere else. The lost sheep—a stupid thing. The lost piece of silver, guiltless, being lost through the neglect of others. The lost son, rebellious man. The lost son, so concerned with duty that he had no fellowship with his father, with God. The outlook on humanity—lost!

Where is the emphasis? On the word lost in each case, not on the condition of the thing lost. The emphasis lies in agony upon the heart of the one who has lost. The shepherd is suffering more than the wandering sheep. The woman is suffering because the silver is lost. It is the father who knows the depth of agony when that boy is away. It is the father who knows the pain of having a son who does not understand. Lost, the possession gone, the purchasing power of the coin, or its significance from the standpoint of order and beauty, gone. Love deeply wounded by the wanderer, and the hide-bound vanity of self-pity.

If that is the Lord's outlook upon humanity, what is His relation of God? All the stories merge and blend. The lights of the Urim and Thummim are flashing in rainbow splendour through these stories. He first shows that God is mindful of His own, and He has never forgotten. That shepherd did not forget the one sheep, though he possessed the ninety and nine. Neither has God. That woman did not forget the silver, though she had lost it through her own carelessness. And the father had never forgotten that boy. The sentences here are so beautiful. "While he was yet afar off, his father saw him . . . and ran." Is there any lack of dignity to see an old man running? Do not believe it. Why did he not stay and wait and retain his dignity? He could not. I declare that there is no dignity greater than the running of a father to meet his boy. That is God.

But there is more than that, of course. It is a revelation of God acting for the recovery of that which was lost; the journey of the shepherd. The phrase is enough.

> "None of the ransomed ever knew
>   How deep were the waters crossed.
> Nor how dark was the night that the Lord passed through,
>   E'er He found the sheep that was lost."

That is God. The search within the dwelling, is God seeking by His Spirit. The woman is the instrument, but the inspiration is Divine. Then we see the picture of God in the father, welcoming the boy. It is wonderful to see that when the boy got back, he found that which he had left home to find in the far country, and had not found there. He went into the far country to have a good time. Judged by the days in which we live, he expected to have fine clothes, and jewellry. When he got back home, the father called for the best robe, a ring on his hand, and shoes on his feet. He got these when he came home. He lost them in the far country. He expected food, and variety of menu, and he came to an hour when nobody would give him husks. But when he got home, they killed the fatted calf. He went to the far country to be free from restraint, and he found disillusionment. When he came back he found merriment, gladness, restoration.

Then we come to that other man in the field. How we have tried to explain him. What varied explanations have been given. There is no explanation that is final. It has been said that he represented the Jew, and the other son the Gentile. To me that is far-fetched. I am sure He intended an illustration of the men criticising Him, the scribes and Pharisees. But whatever we have said about the elder son, the father did not say anything unkind to him. "Son, thou art ever with me, and all that is mine is thine." He went out and entreated him to come in. He was as concerned about that son as about the one who had been away. All he said to him was in the nature of a tender and gentle appeal. That was the revelation of God that He gave to those who were listening.

Then look at them again, Pharisees and scribes. What did all that mean, or what did He intend it should mean for them? I have no means of knowing if any understood Him. Any interpretation of religion which holds derelict humanity in contempt is the worst form of irreligion. To hold in contempt the unwashed multitudes outside is the most irreligious thing of which a man can be guilty. Such attitude demonstrates ignorance of God, and consequently failure to appreciate the true value of humanity.

What about those publicans and sinners, and those listening crowds. To them it was a message of hope, it was a revelation of love, it was a call to faith. Oh matchless parable, shining with all the glories of the grace of God; rebuking all that religion which is merely devoted to duty, and ethical, and cold, and dispassionate. Oh wondrous parable, wooing the sinner, the failure, and the wanderer back to the Father's heart and home.

39. The Unrighteous Steward

Luke xvi: 1-13.

THERE is a certain unusualness about this parable which has often-times given pause to interpreters and expositors. A superficial reading of it might leave the impression on the mind that our Lord, by using this figure of speech, was condoning a fraudulent proceeding. That impression is impossible, and incorrect by a careful reading of the whole story. We note first then, the subject which our Lord was intending to illustrate; secondly the figure He employed in the story He told; and from that twofold consideration we deduce the teaching for all time.

When our Lord used this parable, what subject was He intending to illustrate? That is an important question, in view of the possible difficulty created by a superficial reading. To see the subject He was intending to illustrate, we must once again go back to the context. We find ourselves still in the last Sabbath afternoon recorded by Luke (xiv-xvii. 10). Here then first notice that the words of this whole paragraph were addressed to His disciples, though not to them alone. That is found in the opening verse of the chapter, "And He said also unto the disciples." He had spoken the parable of the lost things specially to the criticising scribes and Pharisees, but also to the listening crowd of publicans and sinners. Now continuing, without any break, "He said also unto the disciples." That is the first thing to be noticed. That little word "also" is significant, indicating that He was not leaving out those scribes and Pharisees, and the listening multitudes; but He was specially addressing Himself to those close to Him, His own disciples, in the hearing of the rest.

Glance on to the 14th verse of this chapter. We read, "And the Pharisees, who were lovers of money, heard all these things." They were listening, "and they scoffed at Him." He spoke then to His disciples immediately after He had uttered the threefold parable, in answer to the criticism of His attitude towards sinners, by the Pharisees and scribes. Why did they scoff at Him after they heard this parable of the unjust steward; and His application of it? We are told the reason, "they were lovers of money." That lay behind all this criticism of Jesus on the part of all these rulers; "lovers of money." Not money, but the love of it. The Bible never says money is the root of evil, but the love of it. "The love of money is a root of all kinds of evil," is a very profound saying. He was talking in the hearing of these men, to the disciples especially, but to these men also who were lovers of money. That was the motive behind everything, the motive of their criticism of Him, and of their aloofness from the unwashed multitudes and sinning crowd. They were "lovers of money." He talked about money, and began with a story.

We see therefore that the subject illustrated was that of motive, the method in the use of mammon, that is, of material possessions. Our Lord had much in His teaching of the larger life, and the world beyond this, and spiritual verities; but here He was dealing literally with the subject of money; talking to His disciples, but in the presence of men whose master passion was money, wealth, possessions. That is why He told them this story, and applied it as He did.

What a strange story it was. Look at it carefully. It was a story of two rogues. Two? Yes. Who were they? The steward who defrauded his master, and his master who condoned the sin. He was as big a rogue as the steward. If a man condones sin in another he is partner with the rogue, even though the rogue be his servant, if he commends him for his wrong-doing. We must be careful in reading the story. Many have become perplexed when they reach the eighth verse, "His lord commended the unrighteous steward." But it is "his lord, not "the Lord." Our Lord did not commend him. He had no commendation for that action. It is an arresting fact however that his lord commended him.

What do we see? First of all cleverness practised. This steward when he discovered that he was found out, was perplexed at first. He said, "What shall I do?" There is really a note of exclamation here, a sudden discovery in what he said, "What shall I do?" "I am resolved what to do." He was in difficulty. He had been defrauding his master, but when he was found out, he looked at the situation. He had lost his job. "I have not strength to dig." The lack of strength was probably disinclination to work. It often is. "To beg I am ashamed." That was pure pride. Then suddenly,—I know what I will do. I will defraud him a little more to my own advantage, in order that the people who will reap the benefit, will take me in, when the lord, my master, has cast me out. So he proceeded, "How much owest thou unto my lord? A hundred measures of oil. Take thy bond . . . and write fifty." "How much owest thou? A hundred measures of wheat. Take thy bond and write fourscore." I have often wondered why in one case he suggested a fifty per cent reduction, and only a twenty per cent in the other. Probably he knew the situation of those people, that some were better off than others. It was extremely clever. His lord commended him for his wisdom, rather, for his prudence, his smartness. Cleverness practised, and admired! There is no record that the lord reinstated him. He simply looked at what he had done. He was clever.

But Jesus told us why he commended him. Mark the word "for" in the middle of verse eight. He commended the unrighteous steward because he had done wisely, smartly. Why did he do it? "For the sons of this age are for their own generation wiser than the sons of light." There is no word there of approval for the action of the steward or his lord, but there is a declaration that on the earth level, for this age, the sons of this age are wiser than the sons of light. The action of this steward, and that of his lord in admiration were actions influenced by the fact that their thinking was bounded by the age in which they were living, and bounded by their own generation. It was purely selfish; a selfish steward and a selfish lord, both lovers of money, because they were looking at things from the standpoint of the present age, limited by their own generation. The sons of light are those who are not limited in their outlook by the present age, and are not limited in their calculations, by the generations in which they live. The sons of light are those who see far more than the near.

Yet Jesus said,—and this is the arresting, the acid thing,—that for their own age and generation, the sons of the age are wiser than the sons of light. Note that intended contrast of our Lord. There they are, the sons of the age, of their own generation, with limited outlook, a certain rich man and his steward. They saw nothing before their birth, and they did not see that very clearly, but they knew it was a fact; and they saw nothing beyond the end, and they were not very much concerned about that. They were living in the age, in their generation. That was the limitation.

The sons of light are those who see far more than that. They see far more than the near. Peter when describing certain people, wrote in one of his letters, "seeing only what is near." What a condemnation that is. I commend to thought the word of the Old Testament, "The eyes of the fool are in the ends of the earth." People say it means that a fool is a man who, instead of attending to things near him, are engaged in things in the ends of the earth. That is not what it means. He is a fool because he sees nothing beyond the ends of the earth. He is bounded by the material. He is acting as though the earth were all, and the generation everything, and the age in which he is living is the only thing that matters. The sons of light see beyond. They see the earth, they see the near; but they walk in the light. The Light is now shining upon men, the One Who said, "I am the light of the world; he that followeth Me shall not walk in the darkness." They see the near, but they always see more. They put upon today the measurements of eternity, upon the dust the values of Deity, upon the age the measurement of undying ages, upon the generation, "the generation of the age of the ages." Sons of light! It is a descriptive phrase.

If that contrast is seen, what was our Lord doing? While He had in mind those critical Pharisees who were lovers of money, He also saw the group of disciples round about Him, and His words constituted a rebuke. He was rebuking them because of their absence of acumen in the highest things. Look at this rogue. See the cleverness with which he manipulated things. But said Jesus—and He spoke with infinite knowledge and understanding,—on the earth level, within the boundaries of the age and the generation, they are so bounded; but they are more astute, more filled with acumen than the sons of light, who are supposed to be living with the measurements of eternity placed upon all the things of time.

We cannot finish there, because all He said in immediate connection has its bearing. He then gave them instruction on the right use of money, of mammon. Notice first with great care the nature of mammon. The word mammon here signifies material wealth. We are justified in saying money, because that is the symbol of wealth. He said to those listening to Him, Make friends by means of the mammon, or money of unrighteousness, a phrase that needs careful understanding. Mammon He called the wealth that was possessed by that rich man, the thing that the rogue had been trafficking with to his own advantage, "the mammon of unrighteousness."

What is "the mammon of unrighteousness"? What is the meaning of *unrighteousness* there? Not wickedness, but the absence of wickedness; not goodness, but the absence of goodness. In other words, the mammon of unrighteousness is neither moral nor immoral; it is non-moral. Mammon, or money is an instrument, an agent for good or for evil. Everything depends on how it is used, and how we use it depends upon how we think in our deepest life. Nothing reveals the thinking of a man more clearly than the use he makes of money. Our Lord had one thing to say. Make friends to yourself by means of it. That is an alteration from the Authorized rendering. He never told men to make friends of mammon, but to make friends by means of it. So use money as to make friends. Friends? Yes. A man may say, I have got some money, but I want it for myself. Is he using it for himself alone? Christ said, Do not use it that way. Make friends by means of it. So use wealth as to gather friends.

Then mark how He swept out beyond the age and the generation. "That when it"—the mammon a man has made use of—"shall fail, they," the friends made by the use of it,—"shall receive you into the eternal tabernacles." He is beyond the age and the generation. He is looking at the vastness of the life that lies beyond, and He is saying plainly, So make use of money as to make friends who will greet us on the other side of the line that divides between this life and the eternal ages. Make friends by means of the mammon of unrighteousness, for it shall fail. It always does. We can use it, and it is still there, but we have used it, whether we have got it, or someone else. We that use it, and the others that get it, will die on the earth level; and then, as Jesus in another parable said of the rich fool, "Then whose shall these things be?" Oh that wonderful list of wills and bequests in our papers. I would fain write that word of Jesus over every such list. Men die, and leave a hundred thousand, twenty thousand, five thousand, ninety pounds! "Leave!" What had they done with it when they were here? Were they so making friends that they were met by them on the other side? Many call the hymn doggerel, but there is a truth in it.

> "Will anyone there at the Beautiful Gate,
>   Be watching and waiting for me?"

Have we done anything with the wealth, the means we have, to get ready for that day that lies beyond?

See how He linked the now with the forever, the present with the eternal. When He had made that direct application to the use of money, and had shown the true use of it, He gave the principle of fidelity; faithful to the much, in order to be faithful in the little. If we want to be faithful in the little things, the mammon, we must be faithful in the big things, the much of eternity and God, and relationship thereto.

Then He gathered everything up in that sentence that stands for ever blazing in light. "Ye cannot serve God and mammon." How this comparison of Jesus remains true. How much there is in the world to prove its truth today, that the sons of the age are more acute, are more business-like, have more acumen than the sons of light. Many a fine business man on the earth level, honourable and capable, becomes a fool when he enters into the business of the Christian Church. If all the acumen and business ability of the members of the Christian Church were consecrated in the light as they are dedicated to the earth level, there would be no Missionary Society problems, and no other missionary problems. It remains true, sons of light are failing to walk according to the light, lacking wisdom, and there is no more revealing symbol than money, and the use men make of it.

Many years ago I remember in the home of a very wealthy man, who was a Church member and a Christian, one morning at Family Prayers he was eloquent and tender as he prayed for the salvation of the heathen, and for the missionaries. He was startled beyond measure when the prayer was over, one of his boys, a lad of ten, said to him, "Dad, I like to hear you pray for the missionaries." He answered, "I am glad you do, my boy." And the boy replied, "But do you know what I was thinking when you were praying, if I had your bank book, I would answer half your prayers!"

Two motives. The one, love of money, which is love of self, and forgetfulness of the needs of others. The other, love of man, which is always the outcome of the love of God. How are we using anything God has committed to us? Is the true passion of life, love of self, or love of man, because we love God?

40. The Rich Man and Lazarus

Luke xvi: 19-31.

THERE is a sense in which even the Christian and instructed heart would fain pay no attention to this story. There is something in it from which the mind instinctively recoils. If that be our reaction, we do not recoil from it any more than God does. That picture of the condition of the human soul beyond the narrow span of this life is not a picture of what God wills for the human soul. It is a part of that which was described by one of the ancient prophets as "the strange act" of God. It is a revelation of things eternal and necessary; and the Biblical Revelation would play false to human experience and understanding if it veiled some of these things from our eyes, because of reluctance to consider them.

The question arises as we approach this story, was this a parable, or was it the record of an actual event? Some believe that it was such a record, and that it should not strictly be treated as a parable, because Luke does not call it such, and because our Lord began with an apparently definite statement, "There was a certain rich man." He did not name him, but continuing, He did name the beggar. It is the only case in all the parables where He used a name. It may be this was a statement of an actual case, which He had seen, and which perhaps those listening to Him, had seen. I do not dogmatise, but that position applies equally to the story of the unrighteous steward, which we have considered. Jesus began then in exactly the same way, "There was a certain rich man." He did not name him, or his steward. That is the only difference in the method between this parable and that. But if these were actual cases known to Jesus, that He used them parabolically there can be no doubt whatever. We shall therefore consider this story as parabolic, whether from actual life, or an imaginary picture, as so often, does not really matter.

What was the subject then He was intending to illustrate? Consider quite simply the figure He employed, and from those two things attempt to deduce the special teaching.

In reading this story there are two perils we must avoid. We have no right to leave anything out of the story that is in it. Secondly we have no right to read into it anything which is not found therein. These two principles are vital. Some have been dogmatic on the question of duration, which may be suggested. There is nothing here to warrant any such position. Going as far as our Lord has gone, we consider first the story only, and we ask, What subject was it Jesus was intending to illustrate? He never told a story without a purpose, and that purpose is always discoverable in the context. Looking back at the 14th verse we read that "the Pharisees who were lovers of money, heard all these things." What things? The teaching He had been definitely and specially giving to His disciples, which found its culmination in His command, "Make to yourselves friends by means of the mammon of unrighteousness," and when it, the mammon fails, they the friends made, shall receive you into the eternal habitations. He had uttered that culminating dictum, "Ye cannot serve God and mammon," and when the Pharisees heard these things, because they were lovers of money, they laughed at Him, "they scoffed Him." The Greek word is a strong one. It means not merely that they smiled, but with ribald mockery, they laughed at Him, mocked Him, at the idea of the relation between material and spiritual wealth. That led to this story, though not immediately, for in the verses preceding the 19th, we find that He unmasked their motive and their method, unmasking the reason why they laughed at His interpretation of the relative values between material wealth and spiritual, between mammon and the fear of God; and the reason was as He said, that they lived in the sight of men, instead of in the sight of God.

Then continuing, He showed how they were unfaithful in much, in great things, and consequently they were not to be trusted in the very little. Again there is the contrast between the spiritual and the material, between the eternal and the temporal, between the much of life in its vastness and all the ages, and the very little of life conditioned in dust, on the material level. He told them men unfaithful in the much were unfaithful in the little, and the relation of the much to the very little, of the spiritual to the material is the relation of time to eternity; and so the relation of money and its possession to the life that lies beyond. That was the occasion of the story. In connection with those solemn and revealing words, He said, "There was a certain rich man."

In this story we find the one occasion when our Lord stretched out His hand, and drew aside the veil that hangs between the now and the hereafter, and allowed men to look and see not merely what lay beyond, but the intimate relationship between the now and the then, between the here and the hereafter.

Take the story quite simply. Jesus drew a contrast between two men living on earth, on two entirely different levels. The one was wealthy, living in luxury and ostentation. It is significant that there is not a thing against this rich man, measuring him by the standards of time. We are not told that he was vulgar, though he was terribly so, as every man is who is living only on the level of the dust. No court of law in England would have put this man on trial. The things we usually classify as vulgar sins are not in sight. There is no suggestion that he was living a depraved life, but he was rich. That was not wrong. He was clothed in purple and fine linen. Those are small expressions, but in the East that meant the elements and things manifesting his riches. They spoke of abounding wealth. Even when it is said that the beggar was laid at his gate, the word used is *pulon*, which means a gate full of artistry and exquisite beauty. He lived there in wealth and luxury. The revealing word of course is this, "faring sumptuously every day." A marginal note says, "Living in mirth and splendour every day." There is only one word that conveys that in English, flamboyantly. What does that mean? Living ostentatiously, in abounding wealth, dressed in purple and fine linen. We are told that a robe of fine linen was worth six times its weight in gold. These simple statements are intended to show a man on the earth level, lacking nothing, enjoying everything, and especially enjoying the fact that he possessed, and could show it in ostentatious living, flamboyant living. We are told that the beggar lay at his beautiful gate, and would fain be filled with the crumbs that fell from his table. Possibly he was, but certainly the rich man knew nothing about it, or if he did and suffered it, there was no credit to him. When we allow beggars or paupers to have things we do not want any more, there is no credit to us, rummage sales notwithstanding!

What about the other man? There is no more poignant picture of abject poverty than that man, living in hunger, evidently lacking the necessities of life, and the nourishment of the body, so that he was full of sores. We are not told how he came to be there. There is no dealing with social conditions. They were there, or that man had never been in that position. There is no blame attached to circumstances and en-

ironment, and none is suggested as attaching to the man. As a matter
f fact, the issue, when he crossed over, proves he was a godly man,
hat he believed in the God of Abraham. Poor, weak, so far down, that
he rough pariah dogs had pity on him, and with healing salve, licked
is sores. There is no contrast more remarkable than that of two men
n the earth level.

But our Lord had not finished His story, and those two men had
ot finished. Something came to them both. What was it? "The beggar
lied." "The rich man also died." They both died; and all the ostenta-
ious splendour of the rich man could not buy off the rider on the pale
orse, when he approached his beautiful gate. He died. And the beggar
ould not escape, had he so desired to do, the lot that was common.
Ie died. That is how it ends for all, you Pharisees, publicans and
inners, Christ might have said. Death is coming. Now draw the veil
nd look beyond. Is there any difference? Yes.

What did He say about the rich man when he died? He "was
uried." Was the beggar buried, we ask? I do not think so. A beggar
f that type, completely destitute, alone, covered with sores, at last
reathing out his spirit in all his poverty, in those times was not
uried. Almost inevitably the cleaners passed the dead body, unknown,
nclean, and hurried him away in the early dawn until they came to
ophet, Gehenna, the rubbish and refuse heap of fire, where they flung
he body in. That is a known fact of the time, and the very fact we
re not told he was buried, leads us to suppose such an end for him.
he rich man was buried, on the earth level, and one wonders how
uch the funeral cost! I have no doubt it harmonised with the kind of
fe he had lived.

Is that all? No, that is not all. What about the beggar? In Hades
e was "comforted." Our Lord used a Jewish figure of speech, Hades,
he place of departed spirits. The rich man was in Hades. So was the
eggar. They were both there in Hades. That is not Hell, the place of
orment. The rich man was in Hades, in torment, and the beggar was
n Hades and was comforted; one great realm that of the departed
pirits, clearly divided as Jewish theology taught, and we believe. On
ne side, to use a geographical expression, the spirits of the evil, the
pirits of the lawless, of the rebellious, those who have forgotten and
ebelled against God. On the other side, the souls under the altar, a
Iebrew figure of speech used in the Apocalypse; souls in Abraham's
osom, the souls of the righteous, who on the earth level trusted in
od, and were obedient to God, and walked in the ways of Jehovah.
hey both passed into Hades, but their experience there was different.

The beggar was comforted. That is a great word, *parakaleo*. He was

called near. The rich man was tormented, that is, in anguish, and th
root of the word means the uttermost dejection, sinking. The one ma
was called near to Abraham's bosom, and to the God Who he ha
served. The other man buried and banished, sinking with the treatmer
and the torture resulting from his neglect of God. That is the pictur

What has this story to say to us? Take the simple plain facts. B
that picture and that story our Lord insisted upon the fact first
existence beyond the article which men call death. Dying is the end
earthly and conscious opportunities and activities. Beyond that, how
ever, personality and consciousness continue, whether it is that of th
rich man, or the beggar. Crossing over the boundary line that we spea
of as death, they are not extinct, and they are conscious. That is th
first tremendous truth that is taught by the story.

The next is that the conditions beyond, result from life as it
lived on the earth level. The one had left behind him the things i
which he gloried and boasted and had paraded. All the flamboyar
living was over. It was left, the purple and the fine linen, to the moth:
and the wealth to quarrelling relatives, if we are to believe humanit
is the same, and it is. He went out into eternity a pauper, and a paupe
stripped. The little left, he lost the much that was never possessed.
was too late to gain possession. The other man crossing over was draw
near to the much, near to the spiritual, near to the eternal, near to th
heart of the God of law, Who is the God of love, drawn near to realit:
drawn near to God. The condition beyond was the result of the metho
of life here.

One more thing, and perhaps the most arresting of all. We hav
the conversation as Jesus described it, between this rich man an
Abraham. We hear that haunting cry, as the rich man said concernin
his brethren, "If one go to them from the dead, they will repent.
Then this startling and amazing answer of Abraham as recorded b
our Lord, "If they hear not Moses and the prophets, neither will the
be persuaded, if one rise from the dead."

In other words. Life is never affected by the miracles, if it is nc
affected by the moral. Does that seem a little hard to believe? Does
not seem as though if Lazarus had been sent, those brethren woul
have repented? All the facts of the case are against it, and prove th
truth of what Jesus said. A little later on, another man bearing th
same name, Lazarus, was raised from the dead. What effect had it o
these men? They tried to kill him. Finally Jesus Himself was raise
from the dead. What effect did it have? None upon those who wer
living on the earth level, save as they repented and turned. They pu
Him to death, and when He was raised from the dead, they becam

usy trying to put to death all those who followed Him. A tremendous
ruth this. The spectacular, and the miraculous will not have any effect
pon the life of men and women if the moral has failed to appeal.

41. The Unprofitable Servants

Luke xvii: 5-10.

THE SUBJECT of this parable is that of unprofitable servants. In
close connection with it, however, our Lord used a parabolic
llustration, that of the grain of mustard seed. Notice at verse seven
he use of the little word, "But." "But who is there of you." That
hows the connection, and that the parable must be taken with the
arabolic illustration.

We consider then first the subject our Lord intended to illustrate;
econdly glance at the figures employed; and finally attempt to deduce
he teaching from the consideration.

What was the subject illustrated when our Lord used the figure of
he grain of mustard seed, and the parable of unprofitable servants?
Whatever He said was in answer to an appeal of the apostles. The
equest came specially from the twelve, whom He had chosen and
ppointed to be with Him, and whom He had sent forth; whom He
vas training throughout His ministry for their responsibilities in the
lays that lay ahead. "The apostles said unto Him, Increase our faith."
What followed was an answer to that appeal, which appeal had fol-
owed teaching He had been giving them. At the commencement of this
eventeenth chapter He had told them that it was impossible but that
ffences should come, and had warned them with great solemnity "Woe
unto him, through whom they come! It were well for him if a mill-
tone were hanged about his neck, and he were thrown into the sea,
ather than that he should cause one of these little ones to stumble.
Take heed to yourselves; if thy brother sin, rebuke him; and if he
epent, forgive him. And if he sin against thee seven times in the day,
nd seven times turn again to thee, saying, I repent; thou shalt forgive
im. And the apostles said unto the Lord, Increase our faith." The
equest that came from them was an intelligent one, born of their sense
f the tremendous urgency of His commands at this point, and of the
lifficulty to human nature that they would encounter, in attempting to

obey them. They did not feel they were equal to that high level t
which they were to attain. "Increase our faith." I think intelligence i
marked in the fact that what they asked for was an increase, not c
love, but of faith. It was an apprehension on their part that life coul
only be equal to the demands of Jesus by faith, by that activity c
the human soul that takes hold upon the invisible. "Increase ou
faith." It was a great thing they said to Jesus.

That being admitted, we listen to Him as He answered their re
quest. The answer cannot be studied without seeing that our Lord wa
recognizing the reason for the weakness of which these men were cor
scious. He knew, He always knows, and always deals, not with ou
request upon the surface, but with what lies behind it. That is wha
He was doing here. They did not need their faith increased; they wer
not needing quantity, but quality. If they had faith as a grain c
mustard seed. He detected that, lying behind their request for a
increase of faith which should enable them to fulfil the severity an
sternness of His demands, was a hope that if they could gain thi
power, some increase of faith, there would be some reward followin
it, there would be some virtue in it, some benefit, following such a
attainment that would come to them. This He knew, so His reply i
parabolic illustration and parable was based upon a recognition of th
reasons for their weakness, and these were the subjects that He illus
trated. Faulty faith results from wrong motives. True faith issues i
right motives.

Take the two figures. First, a grain of mustard seed. In the para
bolic discourses of Jesus in Matthew xiii, He used the same figure i
another application, and with another purpose. He then said of th
grain of mustard seed, "which indeed is less than all seeds." He nov
took this very little thing, and said to these men their faith should b
like it. What is the principle involved in that? What is there in a grair
of mustard seed? In the previous parable He had said the seed, leas
of all the seeds, grew. There we are face to face with the principle
which is that of life. He was insisting upon the life principle in th
grain of mustard seed, and because of that, in its development, it wil
produce results.

There was an interesting picture in a recent paper of a curiou
growth, of an enormous piece of statuary split in two, because a seec
had been dropped there, and as it developed and grew, its roots goin
downward, gathered force, and it had split the masonry, and finall
the statue. No application was made of it. It was simply a curiou.
picture. However it is interesting, in the light of an old story of a
granite tomb in Italy, where a man was buried many years ago, whc

was flippant in his agnosticism to faith and to Christianity especially. He had given instructions that a slab of granite weighing many tons should be placed over the place of his burial, so that there should be no chance of his body ever coming up, if there was any resurrection! They placed his body in the grave, and placed the granite slab upon it. But a bird passing over, dropped a seed, just an acorn fell there, before they placed the granite slab. The oak tree in time split that granite slab! That is all. We can make the application. The life principle is mightier than any other force. It is there in the grain of mustard seed. Our Lord took it as an illustration of a certain subject; a life principle, capable of growth, and therefore exercising force, producing the most unexpected results.

Then He said, "But who is there of you," and He gave them this picture of labourers, as perhaps we should call them, plowmen, or shepherds keeping sheep, rendering their service. It is an Eastern picture in its terminology. The word used for servant is *doulos,* slave. Slaves are doing their work in the fields, and at the close of the day they still have duty to perform, as they come in from their plowing, or watching over the flocks. Jesus said, What happens? Does the owner of the fields, flocks, ploughs and slaves, invite these men to sit down and have their evening meal? Does he not rather tell them to carry on and do their evening work, and prepare his meal; and when he has eaten, they can take their places at the board? Such the simple picture as He drew it, so well understood by those standing around Him. He asked them this question, Do you say, Thank you? Are we halted as we read that? Are we inclined to say, Of course we say, Thank you? We do, and very often too, but we never need do so. There is nothing in inherent justice that demands that we should thank anyone for service, which is merely the rendering of an obligation, and the doing of a duty. We do say, Thank you; but there is no inherent necessity. At this point Jesus was using the figure that slaves do not sit down first to eat, but only when they have done their duty. The master does not thank them for what they have done. There is no need that he should. If we want to be thanked for doing our duty, that shows our hearts were not in the duty.

How curious to bring those illustrations together, and yet how close together they are. What is the teaching? Take the first illustration of the grain of mustard seed. Men facing the demands of Jesus, feeling how tremendous they are, intelligently feeling it, conscious of their own weakness, in all sincerity said to Jesus, Increase our faith. The plea is not over. People are still praying for an increase of faith. It reveals a false thinking on a true line, an outlook that is conscious of weakness, and has grasped the value of faith, and asks for an increase. Our Lord said, You do not need more faith, but faith of a different kind and nature. It is not a question of quantity, but one of quality.

Then what is faith? Faith is that which has in it a principle of life. We may define a living faith by saying three things about it. Living faith is first conviction concerning the fact of God. It is secondly the experience of relationship with God. Thirdly and consequently, living faith is absolute submission to the will of God. Faith in God is far more than conviction that He exists. Thousands of people believe in the existence of God, but they have no living faith, no faith like a grain of mustard seed, with the principle of life and force at its very heart. There must be conviction of God, but there must also be relationship with Him, the going out of the soul towards Him in faith. That means—and here is the point of supreme emphasis—submission to Him. Jesus said to those men, If you have faith as a grain of mustard seed, you would say to that sycamine tree, Be rooted up, and be planted in the sea, and it should be done. There is no doubt that where He said this, there was a sycamine tree growing, and He pointed it out. There was another occasion when He used, not the sycamine tree, but something far bigger and bulkier—a mountain. It is the same thing, whether the tree planted in the soil near to them, or the mountain towering its head above Galilee. He said if we had faith as a grain of mustard seed, we would say to the tree, Be rooted up and planted in the sea; or we would say to a mountain, Be removed and be buried in the sea.

We ask, But is that so? Yes, if we have faith with the life principle in it. I am emphasizing a truth that is fundamental; first, conviction of God; secondly, relationship with God; and then obedience to God. We cannot exercise faith in God in doing anything that we do not know to be the will of God. We shall never say to a sycamine tree, Be rooted up and be planted in the sea, unless we know God wants that sycamine tree rooted up and planted there. We shall never say to a mountain, Be removed, and go into the sea, except we know it is God's will that mountain should be removed and cast into the sea.

That is where we break down in faith, and that is why we are still asking for an increase of faith, thinking if we had more, we should be better able to meet its demands. But no, it is a life principle, and that is belief in God, having relationship with Him, being submitted to Him.

Let us test our praying by that. We say, We have prayed, and we have believed in God, and we have relationship with Him; and we wanted this great mountain barring our way, removed. We want it moved, but we do not seem to have faith. Does God want it moved? Is it His will that the sycamine tree should be rooted up from the place where it is growing and flourishing, and perish in the waters of the sea? That is the supreme question. These men wanted more faith. He said, If ye had faith like that grain of mustard seed, with its life principle, that principle is always that of seeking and acting wholly and only within the will of God.

Then going on, without any break, our Lord said, "But who is there of you." One is halted for a moment to ask what He meant by this. There can be only one answer. We want more faith, so said the apostles, and so we would say. Why do we want more faith? We want a faith that will enable us to do these impossible things. Supposing we get it; what effect is that going to have on our own characters and natures and lives? There was an occasion when these men were sent out, and they came back with great rejoicing, because of the victories they had seen. Coming back rejoicing, they had said to Jesus, "Even the demons are subject unto us." He said to them, Do not rejoice in that. De not be proud of that. Rejoice not that the demons are subject unto you. Rejoice rather that you are the burgesses of heaven from where Satan has already fallen.

De we see the subtle peril that is revealed here? Any increase of faith producing the ability we think, to do great things, creates a peril for the soul, that of satisfaction in service, and the expectation that the service shall be recognized with reward. We sing,

"We will ask for no reward,
Except to serve Thee still."

Do we mean it?

Yet here is a wonderful thing. Take that little parable, and then turn back a page or two in Luke, and with this parable of Jesus in mind, listen to Him. He was talking to servants who were faithful, and He said, "Blessed are those servants whom the Lord when He cometh shall find watching; verily I say unto you, that He shall gird Himself, and make them sit down to meat, and shall come and serve them." That is the very thing He had told them they had no right to expect, but He had already told them He would do. On the earthly level the lord of the slaves first secures his own meal and sustenance, and does not thank them because they are only doing their duty. Jesus said, That is your position so far as you are concerned. Yet He had already told them He would do that very thing; that at the last He would make them to sit down to meat, and come and serve them.

We should remember that action is completely of grace. We have

no claim upon Him that is legal. We have no right of expectation o:
the basis of service for anything in the nature of reward. Yes, He wil
make us to sit down, He will gird Himself, and He will serve us; bu
even then, in the habitations of the blessed that lie beyond, when w
enter into all that to which our loving hearts are looking forward, w
shall never be allowed to forget that everything we receive is of Hi
grace, our Lord and our Master. We are His servants. We ought to b
and must be faithful; but do not let us look on and say, Now we hav
done very well; we are going to have a reward for this, and we ar
taking it. We have no right to expect it. We shall have it, but by Hi
grace.

42. *The Unrighteous Judge*

Luke xviii: 1-8.

IT IS an interesting fact, perhaps of no great value or importance
that this parable and the next, that of the Pharisee and the publi
can, are the only two recorded parables of our Lord in which th
reason for giving them is first stated, before the parable was spoken
"He spake a parable unto them to the end that they ought always t
pray, and not to faint." Again at the ninth verse, "He spake also thi
parable unto certain which trusted in themselves that they wer
righteous, and set all others at naught." Those are the statements o
the reasons for these parables.

Both parables had to do with prayer. The first is a revelation o
the attitude of God towards human prayer. The second, that of th
Pharisee and publican, is a revelation of the attitude of man in prayer
Taking our usual method in these studies, we consider first the subjec
illustrated; secondly, the figure which our Lord employed, deducin
from that twofold consideration the essential teaching of the parabl
then, and for all time.

What was the subject illustrated? "He spake a parable unto them
that they ought always to pray and not to faint." Notice the sligh
alteration, which is an important one, from the Old Version, whicl
read, "He spake a parable unto them to this end, that men ough
always to pray, and not to faint." We now read, "He spake a parabl
unto them, that they ought always to pray." Apparently a sligh
difference, but it was not a general statement for humanity at large

but a particular application for His own people. He was talking to His disciples. A little more of the context therefore is important.

What had He been saying just before? The record is in the end of the seventeenth chapter. At the 22nd verse we read, "And He said unto His disciples, The days will come, when ye shall desire to see one of the days of the Son of man, and ye shall not see it. And they shall say to you, Lo, there! Lo, here! go not away, nor follow after them; for as the lightning, when it lighteneth out of the one part of heaven, shineth unto the other part under heaven; so shall the Son of man be in His day." He described to them the conditions which would obtain; as in the time of Noah, men went on with the usual habits of life, they ate and drank, and married; as in the time of Sodom, in the days of Lot, they ate and drank, bought and sold, planted and built. The ordinary life in the times of Noah and Lot, godless lives. Suddenly the Divine interference; so shall it be in the days of the Son of man. He had been giving His disciples instructions on that great subject, and had told them in that day, of two men in one bed, one would be taken and the other left. The one taken is for judgment. The one left is the one not judged. He ended by saying to them, "Where the body is, thither will the eagles also be gathered together. And He spake a parable unto them to the end that they ought always to pray, and not to faint." That is the setting. There are no time notes. It is not certain that what our Lord said in this parable was spoken immediately at the time of the teaching in the previous chapter, but Luke does record these parables closely upon His teaching concerning that consummation of judgment; when the Son of man comes in that way. Evidently underlying is the consciousness, because of the conditions obtaining, and continuing to obtain, so that even in the hour of coming judgment, life will be as it has been, eating and drinking, marrying and giving in marriage, buying and selling, the whole godless activity going on; because of that, life for His people must always be strenuous and severe.

If as Christians we are having an easy time, and enjoying life, we are poor Christians. The Christian life has always been lived in the presence of gigantic forces opposed to it, and to Christ, and to God. Life goes on, and so it will. To go back and use the word of the ancient prophet, God is governing. He will "overturn, overturn, overturn, until He shall come Whose right it is"; and in that interval there can be nothing but severe and strenuous life. Because of that, His disciples ought always to pray and not to faint. That is the subject illustrated by this parable.

Granted the severity and strain of life in the midst of unparalleled and rampant godlessness, how are we to go on? How shall we carry on? We ought always to pray and not to faint. In the use of those two expressions our Lord sharply but clearly defined two possibilities for life under such conditions; prayer, is one; fainting, is the other.

Look at them a little more particularly. To take these two ideas and put them thus, if we pray we do not faint; if we faint, it is because we do not pray. The two ideas are mutually exclusive, and in the midst of such conditions we shall either faint or pray. Then we get the force of His command. We ought to pray, and not to faint. To put it in the other way, for the sake of emphasis, we ought not to faint. How can we help fainting? We ought to pray. That is a great word, "they *ought.*" "He spake this parable to the end that men *ought.*" When we read "ought" we mean something we owe, we are in debt; something that is due, and we can pay it. These disciples of His in the midst of these conditions, which will continue until He comes, they owe it to God, and to the world, they owe it to themselves never to break down, never to faint, always to pray.

We might stay there and say a good deal about it; but see how our Lord emphasized the teaching, by the use of this parable. Look therefore at the figure in all simplicity, quite apart from the teaching. What is the picture our Lord drew? "There was in a city a judge." Probably here we have again some actual happening, perhaps many such. Do not forget the time in which our Lord uttered it. Then all that region was largely under the jurisdiction of Herod. That meant it was a reign of injustice and wrong, terror and oppression; and undoubtedly this is the picture of one of the inferior judges under Herod's jurisdiction, one supposed to preside over a court before whom disputes should come, and he was to judge. The word here of the woman, "avenge me," is an unfortunate translation. What she said to the judge was, Do justice for me; avenge, in that sense. She was not asking for wrath to be poured out, but for justice. She was appealing for justice to a judge who was supposed to be there to administer it.

Our Lord gave us the character of this man in these words, he "feared not God, nor regarded man." Attempting to interpret the thought, he was a man submitted to no high sanctions. He was not religious, and he was not humanitarian. Again, to put that in another way, he flaunted both the tables of the ten commandments, the first that revealed relationship with God, and the second that revealed relationship with our fellow-beings. He did not care for one or the other. To state it in the terms Jesus employed when asked which was the great commandment; here was a man who cared neither for God, nor his neighbour. He did not love, fear, or care about God. And man?

No, he was not interested in man either. That is the picture of the judge as Jesus sketched it.

Then there is the picture, again a commonplace one, of a widow seeking justice. We are not told what lay behind this story, or what the cause was. She had been wronged somewhere in the matter of justice and equity. She had an adversary. The word is a legal one. She wanted simple justice. Legally she wanted redress. That is the picture of the woman. She went to the judge. We are told "she came oft unto him." She came again and again with the same simple request for justice. Do me justice in the matter of mine adversary. She was pleading with the one who dispensed justice, for justice, and for nothing else.

Look now at the judge. "He would not for a while," that is, a good space, an indefinite period. But she came again, and kept on coming. Then there came action, in which the judge did what she wanted, did justice, avenged her of her adversary. Why did he do it? What a revealing story it is. First of all "he said within himself." It is wonderful how a phrase sometimes circumscribes things, and shows tremendous facts. Mark the daring, "He said within himself, Though I fear not God, nor regard man." He affirmed his position. Christ had said that of him at the beginning. Here he said it himself. He said within himself, he was not going to be compelled to do anything, because he did not fear God, nor care anything about this woman. He was not thinking about God, nor of her.

What then was the reason for his action? Look at him, "Because this widow troubleth *me,* I will avenge her, lest she wear me out by her continual coming." Quite literally, "lest she give me black eyes," "lest she bruise me." He cared nothing about God nor man. All he cared for was just himself. He did not want to be troubled. If this woman keeps on coming I shall get bruised. Poor man! What an appalling revelation; no fear of God, no fear of man, but fear for himself. He did justice because of a woman's importunity, and his fear that if she kept this up, he would suffer still further personal inconvenience.

What was our Lord intending to teach these listening disciples by that picture? The common answer to that question is that our Lord intended to teach the importance of being importunate in prayer. He intended to teach exactly the opposite. That may be challenged by those who quote and love the idea of knocking and knocking, and asking and asking, and praying. That may have its value, but that is not what our Lord was teaching here, but exactly the opposite. The whole teaching of the parable is intended to be one of contrast between the judge and God, and therefore contrast between the actions of the judge and the actions of God.

Everyone agrees that the contrast is suggested between the judge and God. They are not so sure of the contrast between the actions of the judge and the actions of God. All the judge was, God is not. All that God is, the judge was not. The judge had no sense of high sanctions. Life is always on a low level when self is the inspiration. Self is always animal and beastly when lived alone. No, he had no care for God; no care for man. He had no sense of God, and made no response to high sanctions. With profound reverence, God is exactly the opposite. God is bound by these very sanctions.

> "God nothing does nor suffers to be done,
>   But you yourself would do
> Could you but see the end of all events
>   As well as He."

He is bound by the very sanctions this man ignored, by Himself and by man and man's necessity. He is bound by the sanctions of His own Being. There are things He cannot do because they would deny the truth concerning Himself, His righteousness, His holiness, His justice, His compassion; and God cannot be unrighteous, God cannot be other than holy. God cannot be unjust, and God cannot fail in mercy. He is bound by the sanctions of what He is in Himself. We see the contrast between that judge and Himself.

He is bound by the sanctions of human necessity. That needs no argument.

> "He hath loved me, He hath loved me,
>   I cannot tell why,"

says the old hymn. I know why! He could not do any other, and be the God He is; and in all human history, His law, and everything else has been conditioned by His bending and bowing over humanity, and seeking to serve it. He cares for man, and He is bound by the sanctions of human necessity and human interest.

But now mark the difference. There is just as great a contrast, necessarily, between the actions of the judge and God as between the character of the judge and God. Mark the judge; indifferent delay for a while; but when he acted, his action was in order to escape personal suffering and annoyance. Now look at God, and mark the declaration that the Lord made here about Him. God shall do justice to His own elect, which cry to Him day and night. That does not mean a perpetual wailing on the part of man, but it means the continuity of necessity through the ages. He is long-suffering over them, and He will avenge them speedily. The judge delayed, was indifferent, and did not give at all until he was forced by the necessity created by his own desire not to be worried. If we go to God, He will act, and act speedily. Behind that we have a revelation of God. That revelation is made in Old and New Testaments, and specially in Christ Himself; that God's action is at cost to Himself to secure justice for those who need it. The man's action was to escape annoyance. God's action is motivated by His willingness to suffer all things for humanity, for "God was in Christ, reconciling."

So Christ is saying, We ought always to pray, and when we pray, there is no need for us to keep on as though God were unwilling to listen. He is always listening. We have no need to keep on as though God were reluctant. He is never reluctant. There is no need for us to persuade Him.

Finally, lay the emphasis on the word "always," "always to pray." Not words necessarily, not words at all; but an attitude of life, "always to pray." The life characterised and mastered by the forward, onward looking. That is the meaning of this word "pray." The forward wish, the life that is content with the will of God, and discontented with everything that contradicts that will, that is praying. We ought always to pray. If we live and pray so, there will be no fainting. The Lord fainteth not, neither is weary; and those who put their trust in Him are borne up above all the turmoil and the strife, and they do not faint.

Notice how He finished. "Howbeit when the Son of man cometh, shall He find faith on the earth?" That last sentence swung back to all He had been telling the disciples at the end of the previous chapter. It is the return to the subject of the coming of the Son of man. He had told them when He comes, things will be going on as they had been, that He would break in on all the godlessness, when He comes in judgment. Now He reverted to it. "Howbeit when the Son of man cometh, shall He find the faith on the earth?" It does not mean that He will not find faith, but He will not find the faith established, victorious. That is in harmony with the teaching that this age is not to be consummated with a perfect victory of faith upon all the earth; but it will be broken in upon by the advent of the Son of man; and until then, men ought always to pray, and not to faint; and they can do that because God is what He is.

43. The Pharisee and the Publican

Luke xviii: 9-14.

THIS is one of the best known and best loved parables of Jesus. It is interesting to observe that those parables of our blessed Lord which have taken hold more profoundly generally upon the heart of man, are found in this Gospel of Luke, the chronicler of God's second Man, and the last Adam. He, a Greek writer, portrays Him in all the perfection of His human nature. That may account for this appeal of some of his parables to the human heart.

An honest consideration of this story shows that it is indeed the word of the Lord, quick and sharp, dividing asunder. It is a very searching, as well as comforting story. Like the previous parable, it is concerned with the subject of prayer. In that we had a revelation of God in the matter of prayer, as He was contrasted in His character and in His dealings, with the unrighteous judge. In this parable we have a revelation of human nature in the attitudes, or activities of prayer, in the presence of God.

We consider first, the subject illustrated; then the figure which our Lord employed; finally deducing the teaching.

The subject illustrated is revealed in the specific statement with which the parable opens, "And He spake also this parable unto certain which trusted in themselves that they were righteous, and set all others at nought." We at once see why the parable was uttered. It was spoken to a certain personal and relative attitude. The personal attitude is revealed in the word, they "trusted in themselves that they were righteous." That phrase illuminates the whole situation of the Pharisees, and those closely associated with them. They believed in righteousness, but their idea of righteousness was on a low level. In the great Manifesto Jesus had said, "Except your righteousness shall exceed the righteousness of the scribes and Pharisees, ye shall in no wise enter into the Kingdom of heaven." I do not know that many of them could have said what Paul did in his marvellous autobiographical passage in the Philippian letter. After thirty years of comradeship with Christ, he said, as he looked back at those days, that he was "a Hebrew of Hebrews; as touching the law, a Pharisee; as touching zeal, persecuting the Church; as touching the righteousness which is in the law, found blameless." Perhaps of this man whom we see in the parable, that also could be said. We do not know, but we do know his

righteousness consisted in his devotion to certain laws, and interpretations of the laws; especially in those days to the traditions with which
the laws had been almost submerged, as to their vital applicability.
Our Lord had those people's personal attitude in mind when He spoke
this parable. They were trusting in *themselves* that they were
righteous.

Then the relative attitude of these men is revealed in that pregnant
phrase, "And set all others at nought." The Greek word there might
be rendered a little more forcefully, as in the margin, "the rest." What
a way to dismiss all except oneself! They trusted in themselves, these
people, whom Jesus had in mind, that they were righteous; and accounted all the rest as not counting, as mere ciphers. That attitude is
seen again and again in the Gospels. Once some of these men addressed
the crowd, and spoke of them as cursed, those who did not know the
law. Here is an attitude of life, personally trusting in oneself, believing
one is righteous, and at the same time, setting all the rest at nought.

Luke says specifically in the 9th verse that it was these attitudes
our Lord had in mind. These personal and relative attitudes are seen
in the light of God. Two men were in the Temple, and men were looking at them. The crowds would see them, and form their own opinion
concerning them. Jesus stood quietly there, and said in effect, Look at
those two men. Look at that one man, his attitude concerning himself,
and towards all the rest; and see what God thinks about them both,
the Pharisee and one of the despised.

Now look at the figure employed. Here we are in the presence of
familiar things. Jesus drew a picture of two men in the temple. "Two
men went up into the Temple to pray." They both went to the temple,
and they both went to pray. At that point this story becomes searching.
Isaiah had referred to the Temple, and had called it "My holy mountain," "My house of prayer"; and in the course of His ministry Jesus
referred to it by practically citing Isaiah's words, "It is written, And
My house shall be called a house of prayer." So two men are here,
seen going to the right place, the place appointed, the house of prayer,
with all that that word meant. Look at the two men, and see the
similarity between them. Both of them were going to the Temple,
recognising it as the house of God, the place set apart and ordained
as the place of worship, and going there to pray.

Then we begin to see the difference. What is the first thing about
the Pharisee? He "prayed thus with himself." Oh yes, he began by
addressing God. He used the Name at the beginning of his prayer.
"The Pharisee stood and prayed thus with himself." That is the
emphasis. God he knew. It was the house of prayer, and he knew it

as the place where men come to deal with God, and he began his prayer with a recognition of God.

Luke tells us moreover, that he "stood and prayed." A little lower down we read, "The publican, standing afar off." They were both standing, but the descriptive words are different. The word used by Luke of the Pharisee suggests in itself a static and upright position of perfect security and self-satisfaction. The word *static* as descriptive of his attitude is warranted by the word itself, he "stood." The other man stood, for it was the habit to stand in prayer. But how differently men can stand! A man can stand with the braggadocio of an uplifted chin that tells a great story about him. He can stand with head not lifted, but bowed down, which tells an equally great story. Even in those two different words translated by the same verb in our language, we have the dawning of a great revelation.

This man prayed with himself. What does that mean? Was he alone? Hardly at that time of worship and prayer; and yet he was. He prayed, separated from these others. He knew enough of this man and his habits to know that he would withdraw, perhaps getting as near to the sacred altar as he could, and seek to be separated even in the matter of physical contact of his garments from the rabble, all the rest. He "prayed with himself." But something he did not seem to have recognized was that when he prayed with himself, he was not only separated from the others, he was separated from God; and therefore his prayer rose no higher than the beautiful roof of the Temple, perhaps not so high as that! He was in a circle. He was the centre of the circle, and its circumference. He prayed with himself.

Then he recognized the Deity, approaching Him by using the name, God. His conception of God is revealed in his prayer. "God, I thank Thee, that I am not as the rest of men." I am no extortioner. I am not unjust. I am not an adulterer. I am not "even as this publican." In that prayer can be read all the scorn there was in his heart for men. He was telling God that he had abstained from vulgar sins.

Had he finished? Oh no, he had not. "I fast twice in the week." That was a work of supererogation. The law did not require that, but he had followed the traditions most meticulously in the interpretation of the law. "I give tithes of all that I get!" All that I get, and acquire, I set aside the tenth of everything obtained in the course of my business. This man was talking to God. He began by addressing Him, and he told God that he had abstained from certain vulgar forms of sin, and that he was very careful to observe certain rites or ceremonies.

Why was he telling God these things? Evidently this was his conception of God. He would not have written down what was in his subliminal consciousness. This man thought of God as One satisfied with trivialities, abstaining from vulgar sins, and the observing of certain rites and ceremonies. We may go further and say he thought God was obligated to him, because of these things. He went up to pray, but he prayed within himself. Into the circle of his own self-centred personality he dragged God by name, and degraded Him by what he said.

Look at that other man. Jesus told the story of the publican to fling up into clear and sharp relief the picture of the Pharisee. He spoke this parable to those who trusted in their own righteousness, as this Pharisee did, despising others. He might have left it there, but no. He drew attention to another man, this publican, standing afar off, suggesting a different attitude. The Pharisee was in all probability pressing as near as he could to the altar. This man perhaps was just within the Temple, the holy place. He had crept in, and stood afar off from the place which was central to the conception of the Divine Being. He did "not lift up so much as his eyes unto heaven." With downcast eyes, beating on his breast, the action of confession, then he spoke. "God"—that is the same word the other man had used; but the nominative case was not in his prayer. The other man's prayer was full of it, "I . . . I . . . I . . . I . . . I!" It was the objective case here. It is "me"; "God be merciful to me a sinner." Seven words only. See what he has done. He has drawn a circle, and there are two personalities within it. Who are they? God and himself; "God," "me." That circle that looks so narrow, yet has within it that one sinning man and all the vastness of eternity, for his cry is a real one. One remembers the words of the ancient prophet, in which interpreting the fact of God, God speaks to him and says, "The high and lofty One that inhabiteth eternity, Whose name is Holy; I dwell in the high and holy place, with him also that is of a contrite and humble spirit. To this man will I look, even to him that is poor and of a contrite spirit, and that trembleth at My word." His conception of God is thus revealed. "God be merciful to me, a sinner."

What was his conception of God? That He was holy, One in Whose presence a sinner needs propitiation, for that is his word, Be propitious to me. His sense of God in his prayer was that God is compassionate, One to Whom a sinner could come.

Two conceptions of God. The same name, God; even as we may say God, and mean very different things; even as we may say Jesus, and have very opposing conceptions. The God of the Pharisee is One satisfied with trivialities, and has in some senses a duty to a man because he has abstained from vulgarity, and has kept up certain rites and forms and ceremonies. The other conception of God is of One Who is holy, in Whose presence a sinning man needs mercy; but One to Whom he can come, and with downcast eyes, and beating on his breast, breathe out the sighing of his soul for mercy. That is the picture, and what a picture it is.

The teaching again is self-evident and declared. When Jesus had finished His parable, He had not quite ended. He had something else to say. He had to utter a judgment, to make an appraisement, to pass a verdict. "I say unto you." Take that phrase in the records, and watch when it fell from the lips of Jesus. He used it now. It was the formula of authority. It was the voice of the watching God. Yes, God had been watching and listening to Pharisee and publican, and Jesus now told us the result. He said, "This man went down to his house justified rather than the other." That is the appraisement, that is the judgment, that is the verdict concerning this publican. It is interesting to see some expositors are a little at pains to tell us that Jesus did not mean there, what we now mean by being justified. I admit the men of the time did not understand it in all its fulness; but He knew its meaning. It means exactly what it does in the New Testament. "Being therefore justified by faith, we have peace with God through our Lord Jesus Christ; through Whom also we have had our access by faith into this grace wherein we stand." Only a word, but it is the word of Jesus, with all its meaning; this man went down to his house justified. I think this man came to the Temple again the next day, but he did not come in the same way. He came the first time sin-burdened, knowing his need in the presence of the holy God of mercy. When he went away the prayer was heard; and somewhere, in his house perhaps, confidence possessed him, and I can imagine him coming up the next day, still taking the same attitude, still standing in the same way. There was no strutting or braggadocio but the next day he lifted up his eyes to heaven. This day he could not; but when he came back he knew that he could lift them up. There was no beating upon the breast any more, but perhaps a great, sober Hallelujah—justified!

What about this other man, the Pharisee? There was nothing further to be said about him. He was dismissed. The publican went down to his house justified rather than the other. That is all we know about him. Undoubtedly the Pharisee was there again the next day, but he was left "with himself."

Our Lord gathered up the whole force of the wonderful parable in His last word, "I say unto you . . . every one that exalteth himself shall be humbled; but he that humbleth himself shall be exalted." Where are we when we come into the house of God, and pray? I cannot tell you. You know!

44. The Pounds

Luke xix: 11-28.

THE OPENING verse of the paragraph marks the occasion upon which this parable was uttered. "And as they heard these things, He added and spake a parable, because He was nigh to Jerusalem, and they supposed that the Kingdom of God was immediately to appear." That introduces us not only to the occasion of the parable, but also to the intention of our Lord in its utterance.

Luke said, "As they heard these things." What things? Luke was continuing his narrative. Jesus and His disciples were in Jericho, and they had heard what had happened in connection with Zacchæus, that Jesus had invited Himself to his house. They had seen Him go in, and had waited while He was inside in that private interview. How long it lasted no one can tell. They had seen Zacchæus come forth from that guest chamber with Jesus, and had heard Zacchæus declare the result of the interview as he said he gave to the poor, and restored fourfold what he had exacted wrongfully. Then they had heard Jesus say, "Today is salvation come to this house . . . For the Son of man came to seek and to save that which was lost." They heard these things, and He went on, and added something, spoke another parable. Those are the things referred to, especially the last sentence, "The Son of man came to seek and to save that which was lost."

Luke tells us the reason for this parable. He was nigh to Jerusalem. We are in the last period of the ministry of our Lord. "His face was stedfastly set to go to Jerusalem." He was travelling nearer to the city of the great King, as He Himself called it, coming near to the centre of the national life, and to all the things that were to happen to Him, about which He had been talking repeatedly to His disciples since Cæsarea Philippi. Evidently there was a strong feeling among His disciples that something was going to happen because He was nigh to Jerusalem, and they expected the Kingdom of God immediately to appear, so He spake this parable.

What then was the subject He intended to illustrate? The complete 11th verse gives us the reason of its uttering. "He was nigh unto Jerusalem," and the time of year was near to Passover. There were larger crowds then in Jerusalem than at any other time. Josephus tells us that two million people more than the average and ordinary population came to the city. Jesus was coming up to the city, and they supposed that the Kingdom of God was immediately to appear. It is open to question whether the "they" referred to the disciples or to the multitudes. I think it may refer to both. These were the closing days in the life of our Lord, and there was a spirit of expectation everywhere. There were multitudes that were friendly, and many that were hostile. Yet there was this feeling that a crisis was approaching. Jesus had been up and down in their land, in Judæa, and in Galilee; and now for a long period, nearly six months in Peræa, going here and there, He had been preaching the Kingdom of God; and everyone felt the time was ripe for something to happen. What did they suppose? What did they think? Luke says they "supposed." Take that word and express it by another phrase. It seemed to them, observing the signs of the times, having watched His ministry, and listened to Him, noticing that He would appear in the midst of the multitudes; and by these gathered multitudes it seemed to them that the Kingdom of God was immediately to appear.

How should we understand that? The word for "appear" there is a strong one. It means coming into clear, outward, open manifestation, and there is no doubt that in the thinking of the multitudes, and of His disciples too, when they thought, or supposed that the Kingdom of God was about to appear, they imagined that in this visit to Jerusalem, He would do something to assert His authority, take the reins of government into His own hands, fulfill the common expectation of the Jewish nation about Messiah and the Kingdom of God. To them the coming of the Kingdom would be the breaking of the yoke of Rome, the setting of the nation free from oppression, and the bringing into outward and manifest form that which Jesus had been preaching from the beginning of His ministry, the Kingdom of God. They supposed the Kingdom of God, as they interpreted it, and as they desired it, was at the doors, that the moment had come. The "they" of verse 11 surely referred to the disciples and the multitudes. I am quite sure reference was to the disciples, because even after His resurrection they still had that view, when they came to Him and asked Him, "Dost Thou at this time restore the Kingdom of Israel?" Theirs was a material outlook, and their expectation was of the immediate manifestation of the Kingdom of God in power. They did not understand the nature of the Kingdom of God. He had preached and declared it, and had affirmed its reality. He had announced its nearness, enunciated its ethic; and they were still waiting for something material. As George Macdonald put it,

> "They all were looking for a King,
> To slay their foes, and lift them high.

He came a little baby thing,
That made a woman cry."

Even now the same thing is apparent. They were mistaken in their ideals. They felt He was there for the purpose of setting up that Kingdom. Because of that, Luke declares clearly that He uttered the parable of the pounds.

What was the figure He used. In the course of our studies we have seen a wonderful variety of methods of illustration. He took things near at hand, and persons too, historic incidents. Here is the figure of a man going away to receive a kingdom, and leaving his interests in the charge of his bond-slaves; a man who, when he had started out on his journey to receive the kingdom, was followed by a deputation of his citizens, declaring that they would not have him as king. That idea was familiar then in their current life. Archelaus, Herod the Great, and Antipas, each in turn had gone to Rome to receive a kingdom. They were tetrarchs. Everyone wanted the title of king, and had to go to Rome to get permission for it. Herod went, and he gained that title. It was an empty title, but he gained it.

But the immediate historic background was not Herod, but Archelaus, whose palace was at Jericho. He had gone to Rome, leaving his palace, and the interests of his tetrarchy, or his kingdom as he wished it to be called, to his bond-slaves. He left Philippus in charge, with money to trade for the maintenance of revenue while he was away. While away, a deputation of fifty Jews was sent after him, to make a protest against his becoming king. When they arrived in Rome they were received by a company of eight thousand Jews, and they made their protest, and were so successful that Archelaus never received that title; and afterwards he was deposed from the tetrarchy, and he did not go back there.

Our Lord therefore took a common incident, and used it, of someone going away to receive a kingdom, and that coming of his citizens saying they would not have him. Of course this does not mean that Jesus went away to receive a Kingdom, and did not gain it. When Archelaus came back, he called for an account undoubtedly, and our Lord enlarged upon that. But that is the figure behind the parable. Taking this incident, our Lord applied it in a remarkable way to Himself to show that what they were expecting, would not then take place. He was then going to Jerusalem, and they thought He was going to establish a Kingdom according to their ideas. He wanted them to see it would not be. He was going away to receive a Kingdom, and He was leaving responsibility with His servants for the period of His absence. That was the place of the parable and the figure employed; and that was the purpose for which He uttered the parable. It was to teach them that they were wrong in expecting the Kingdom of God immediately to appear.

What are we to learn from this parable? Some people are expecting the Kingdom of God immediately to appear. I am not entering into any argument as to when He will return. I only declare, we do not know when, and there is no sign of proof that His return is near; at least there is no sign that has not been granted through all the ages. We want to be ready if He comes; and to say, "Even so, come Lord Jesus," and to be led into the patient waiting for Christ, not the impatient waiting, which characterises so many people. Wherever that impatience is manifested, it is due to a wrong conception of what the setting up of that Kingdom will be.

What then did that parable teach those men, and what is it intended to teach us? Three things, the fact of postponement; a period of waiting, and how it should be occupied; and finally, the certain fact of His return, and a revelation then of His action, on His return.

Postponement of His Kingship? Certainly not, but of its manifestation in full power and authority and ultimate victory. That is what was and is postponed, and it is still postponed. The life of our Lord did not begin when He was born a Baby. It stretches out to the past eternity, and on through all the infinite ages. Therefore it is difficult to speak of the life of our Lord in the terms of our calendars and almanacs. He is not going to be crowned. He is crowned. That coronation took place when He ascended on high, after His resurrection. He emptied Himself and became obedient to death, even the death of the Cross; "wherefore God highly exalted Him, and gave Him the name which is above every name; that in the name of Jesus every knee should bow . . . and that every tongue should confess that Jesus Christ is Lord, to the glory of God the Father." In that magnificent passage in Corinthians, Paul says, "He must reign till He hath put all His enemies under His feet." The reign is not postponed until the hour of ultimate victory. He is reigning now, and the time of His coronation was at His ascension.

But He wanted these disciples to see that what they were looking for, which they did not understand, was that the visible and outward victory was postponed; that He was going away to receive a Kingdom. He received it when He was received up, and God set Him at His own right hand, upon His holy hill of Zion, His anointed King.

Then there is a period of waiting, between His receiving the Kingdom in the high court of heaven, and His coming finally to establish it visibly on earth. Here is the heart and centre of our parable. When the king was gone, he gave to his servants; ten of them being named. That is a symbolic reference, and covers the whole ground. He gave ten pounds to ten servants, a pound to each. This parable of the pounds must not be confused with the parable of the talents, recorded by Matthew. The significance of the talents was the varying gifts that may be bestowed. Here in this parable it is equal opportunity. The pound is a deposit, intended to be used in the interest of the passing hour. They were to trade with it. The word used is a beautiful one; occupy, in the sense of trading. The business of those left behind was that they were to take the common deposit, and use it in the interest of the business of the King. They were responsible to trade with His pound; his servants, and his business. Paul in the Ephesian letter urged those to whom he wrote that they "redeem the time, because the days are evil." The marginal reading for "redeeming the time" is a word that marks the activity of the merchants and the market place, "buying up the opportunity." This is not the usual word for redeeming, or for time. The meaning is the opportunity. Our business then according to Paul, is to buy up the opportunity, to prosecute the commerce of the Kingdom of God with such diligence as characterises the success of the merchant-men in the market places of the world. That is the idea.

There is no Christian man or woman without that pound. We may say we have not ten talents, but that is another matter. The pound is something other than the gift. The pound is a deposit, and is the Gospel of the grace of God. We are witnesses to that Gospel. Our business in this world, whether men are saying still, We will not have this Man to reign over us, is to do business with that deposit; so to make use of it that gains other. That is the deposit. That is the pound.

Our Lord says there are different ways of exercising it. One is full and complete. One man at the reckoning said, "Thy pound hath made ten pounds more." Notice he did not say, I have been very successful and persistent, and managed to make thy pound into ten. The pound did it itself. But he had simply fulfilled the responsibility of trading with it, and there were ten.

Another man had not so full, but a partial result—five. Then that other man who had the deposit, did not use it, but took care of it, wrapped it up in a napkin, did not trade with it; and the reason he gave was that he knew his lord was stern, and that he reaped where he did not sow.

The citizens outside that group of servants were in revolt. "We will not have this man to reign over us." They still are. These are the facts. That is what the world is still saying. It is still saying it in its governments, and especially in those which have in past history acknowledged our Christ, where He has been known and presented, and is now dismissed. "We will not have this Man to reign over us."

But He is coming back. About that there is no question. When He comes again He will come as King; not to be made King. Then the Kingdom of God will appear according to this parable. The first activity of His reappearing will be the investigation of what His servants have done with His pound. Where there has been full fidelity there will be fuller responsibility; ten cities to be ruled over. Where there has been partial success, still increased responsibility; five cities. But what about this man who refused to trade? On his own confession our Lord said He would judge him out of his own words, and He quoted them, not to affirm the truth of it, but to show what he thought himself. It was an entirely wrong conception of his lord, and based upon that wrong conception he had hidden His pound and wrapped it in a napkin, and taken care of it. Our Lord asked him why he had not put it in the bank, so that He could have had it with interest; a question saturated with satire. What happened to him? Nothing, except that he lost his pound. It was taken from him, and given to the man most successful. He was deprived of that opportunity. He had missed it. He did not buy it up, and now his own action was unavailing. I do not think it suggests he was cast out himself. He was saved, so as by fire, and there one leaves him.

As to the citizens who had been in open revolt; when He establishes the Kingdom they must be slain and swept out. There comes the hour when Jesus will return and govern the world, and give it its chance. He has great patience, and His longsuffering is due to His patience; but there is the moment of limitation.

We have all got the pound. What are we doing with it? Are we trading with it? Oh my masters, the pounds that are wrapped up in napkins, which if they were used, might increase the glory of the Kingdom of our Lord.

The 28th verse is significant in the light of this parable. He was going up to Jerusalem, and because He was near, they thought the Kingdom was coming. He told them these things, and the 28th verse said, "He went on before" alone. He was still going. But He was "going up." Geographically it was uphill the road that led from Jericho to Jerusalem; but there is more in it than that. Presently He would be received up, and He would receive His Kingdom. And we are left. We have the pound. How are we using it?

45. Rock Personality

John i: 40-42.

IN THE course of our studies of the parables and parabolic illustrations of our Lord, we come now to the Gospel according to John.
Apart from the great allegory of the vine, John has recorded no set
and formal discourse of Jesus. While we have more of the words of
Jesus recorded by John than by the other evangelists, they are rather
of the nature of discussions than set discourses. Even in the Paschal
discourses, He was answering questions which were asked by His own.

Nevertheless, in the course of these discussions we find some remarkable and revealing illustrations. It is arresting also that John
never used the word *miracle*. Where the other evangelists used that
word, John used the word "signs" that indicated the value of the
miracle. It is equally interesting, though not of particular importance,
that John never used the word *parable*. In the Authorized Version it
is said (x. 6) "This parable spake Jesus unto them." In the margin
the Revised has changed that to "proverb." There are two other
instances (xvi. 25 and 29) where the Authorized has rendered the same
word "proverb," which is correct. The difference between the two
words parable and proverb is slight. The word parable, *parabola*,
commonly used in the other Gospels simply means to set by the side of,
or literally drawn together, the similarity shown by an illustration
placed by its side. The word rendered "proverb" in the Revised Version, *paroimis* means to make something like something else. The idea
is similar, that of similitude, whether of a picture, a story, or a saying
matters nothing.

Had we taken a chronological sequence in the teaching of Jesus,
this study would have been the first, for it is the first recorded occasion
of our Lord's use of a figurative expression. In the first five chapters
of this Gospel we have some account of events that happened in the
first year of His ministry. Here we are at the very beginning of that
ministry.

Taking our usual method, we consider three things. What was it
our Lord was illustrating when He used this figure of speech: Secondly,
we look at the figure itself, and what it was intended to convey:
attempting then to gather up from such consideration, the teaching for
all time.

What was the subject He was illustrating? His words were extremely few. He said, "Thou art Simon, the son of Jonah; thou shalt be called Cephas," and John added "which is by interpretation, Peter." The marginal reading is "rock" or "stone." Again we remind ourselves that our Lord was now facing His public ministry. The waiting years were over, and He was commencing His work. He began, as this first chapter of John shows by gathering around Himself a little group of individuals. Five of them are named: Andrew and another, who unquestionably was John, Simon, Philip and Nathanael. Here was the occasion, and the story proceeds with perfect naturalness. There was nothing in the nature of our Lord's work, either here or at any time, of organized propaganda. My mind goes back to a sermon I heard preached by my old friend who has now gone Home, Dr. Len Broughton. He took as his text the words, "As He went," and he gathered up in a remarkable way the occasions when that, or a similar phrase occurred in the story of Jesus. He was doing things "as He went." I think that was the trouble with John the Baptist when he thought Jesus was doing nothing very definite. That still troubles a good many people who think if things are not being done to plan, nothing is being done! Here He proceeded naturally. John saw Him and pointed Him out to Andrew and the one with him; and the two went after Him, and spent some hours with Him in private. One of the two, Andrew, went and found his brother Simon, and Simon was brought to Jesus.

There is no question that of those first five men, Simon, son of Jonah was supremely a representative human being. Perhaps a statement like that needs qualification. All the elements of human nature were present in this man's personality in a remarkable degree. Andrew was perhaps a representative man. John was not. He was a mystic, a dreamer, a poet; a man looking for things not seen, and seeing them; listening for things not heard, and hearing them; feeling after the intangible and touching them. Philip was a quiet and unimpressive man, always willing to be on the edge of the crowd, and showing others in; but this man Simon was just a human.

When he came to Jesus, He said to him "Thou shalt be called Rock." What was the value of that? What was the subject our Lord was illustrating? Without any hesitation I say that He was illustrating there and then prophetically, for the sake of those listening, for Philip and Nathanael, for Andrew and John, and Andrew's brother, the possibility of human nature under His Messiahship. Simon had come at his brother's invitation to see the Messiah. After his interview with Jesus Andrew had found his brother Peter, and has hastened to find him, to tell him one thing only, that was on Andrew's heart, the thing that obsessed his mind and had already constrained his will; "We have found the Messiah."

It is a little difficult for us to grasp the meaning of that. We are so familiar with the word Christ, which is only the Greek form of Messiah, meaning Anointed. We associate it quite properly with our Lord. But if we put ourselves back into the place of Andrew and Simon, and remember that for hundreds of years the one great hope, sometimes flaming and glowing, and sometimes dying into a faint ember, was the coming of the Messiah. They were all looking for Him. Andrew hurried to find Simon to tell him the amazing thing that he had found the Messiah. I think Andrew's feet were hurried by the greatness of the discovery that had come to him. One old Puritan expositor has said there is no doubt that Andrew hurried after Simon, because Simon had been such a nuisance in the family, and he thought it might help him to get him to Jesus early! I prefer however to believe, in spite of the nuisance Simon may have been, Andrew saw the dynamic in that brother of his. While the forces were scattered there were great possibilities in him. That can be dismissed as imagination; but there is no doubt this human was an awkward customer.

Jesus knew the conviction that had come to Andrew that He was the Messiah in that private interview in the house, and He knew that this brother had hastened in obedience to his brother's invitation, to see Him. So He stood in front of him, the Messiah, and to that man He said "Thou shalt be rock," "Thou shalt be called Rock."

That brings us to the figure itself, in that one word Rock, a most significant word. We have touched upon it in other studies, on other occasions. Here we are face to face with the occasion upon which our Lord first used it. What is this figure of rock? Whereas we use the word *kephas,* or *petros,* or our word stone, the idea is the same. We are looking now merely at the material figure of rock. There is a distinction to be found in the 16th chapter of Matthew, where two words are closely connected, cognate words, petros and petra. Of this same man Jesus there said, "Thou art *petros,*" and "on this petra, I will build My Church"; the same general idea is here and a different signification. When Jesus looked at Peter, He did not say, Thou art *petra,* but, Thou art *petros.* The difference is simply this. *Petros* is of the same nature as *petra,* but it is a piece of rock. *Petra* is essential rock, the whole fact of rock. When Jesus said He was going to build His Church, He did not say on a petros, a piece of rock; but on rock, on *petra.*

What is *petros?* There may be geologists here and other learned men, I have no doubt. I am not going to apologize for telling you what rock is. Rock is the consolidation into one, of varied constituents, resulting in strength and durability. There are of course different kinds of rock. Break off a piece of the rock, and petros is in your hand. You may stand or sit down upon essential rock in all its bulk and majesty, and it is the consolidation into one substance of varied constituents, resulting in strength and durability. The constituents in their separation may not be characterised necessarily by strength and durability, but when welded and compounded into one, rock is the result.

Amid all the varieties, take granite. It will be agreed that there is no more perfect illustration of the strength of rock, than granite. What is granite? What are its varied constituents? Quartz, feldspar, mica. Quartz is never characterised by durability and strength, neither is feldspar nor mica. But when these three are compounded together, the strength of the granite is recognised, and its durability. We are not dealing with the question of how it is done. In the main there are two kinds of rock, igneous and aqueous; in the one the result of fire, and in the other the result of the action of water.

Jesus said to this man, "Thou shalt be called rock." There shall be in thee the consolidation of constituent parts into one compounded whole which shall be characterised by durability and strength. Some of us know experimentally what our Lord meant.

Yes, but that does not exhaust the meaning of it. If He employed the figure, the natural figure of rock, there was a spiritual significance in it. This Jew, Simon, was standing facing his Messiah, and bearing Him speak. Whether at the moment he perfectly apprehended the profound significance of that illustration of rock I am not prepared to say. I am sure he did later. Study his letters and that is found out. The Messiah looked at this man, not so much looking at him as through him, and He adopted the language of the literature of the Hebrew Scriptures, which was that of expectation. He had come to fulfil the expectations of that sacred Literature.

Therefore we take up this figure of speech in the Old Testament, and go through it to find the references to rock. There are different Hebrew words translated by that word rock. There is one meaning the same as *petra*, the word *tsur*. Go through the Old Testament, the history, prophets, and psalms, and that word rock is used figuratively, occurring some forty times, beginning in the book of Deuteronomy. It comes out also in the Psalms. The arresting fact is that wherever it is so used figuratively, it is reserved for Deity. I have said Deity, rather than God, and for this reason. There are two occasions only where it is used of false gods, in Deuteronomy xxxii. 31 and 37. There false gods are being put into contrast with the true God. In every other case the symbol is used of the living God, when used in a figurative sense.

It may be argued, What about the reference in Isaiah to a man as the shadow of a great rock in a weary land? Who is the Man? We have no right to apply that to ourselves. It is the great prophetic foreshowing of God manifest in the flesh, the Man a shadow of a great rock in a weary land, and it is full of beauty in that way; but it is always a type of God. Jesus looked at Peter and said, "Thou shalt be called rock." Rock is the symbol of His strength, the strength of the Almighty, the durability of God.

What is rock in the natural world? The consolidation into one of varied constituent parts, resulting in strength and durability. When that is applied to God, it suggests that His strength results from the perfect harmony of all the facts of His Being in the unity of His Godhead. That is why God is strong, changeless, and even the crumbling rocks that seem to us to speak of permanence on earth level, are imperfect symbols of the strength of God.

Jesus said to this man, "Thou shalt be called rock." He told this man that he should be brought to a position and an experience of life in which he should share the Divine nature. Again a statement like that may sound very daring and startling. Not at all. When Peter wrote his letters, he said that we have become "partakers of the Divine nature." The great thought in the word rock here suggests the partaking of the Divine nature that welds the constituent elements into strength and durability; "thou shalt be called rock." That is an attempt to explain or understand the figure of speech.

In conclusion, what do we learn as we listen to this word of Christ? First, Christ's absolute confidence in Himself. God Almighty deliver us from this age that is trying to account for Him on the human level only. Everything He said was final, and superb. Everything He said was awe-inspiring. The first thing I notice when He looked into the eyes of this man Simon, and said, "Thou shalt be called rock," was His absolute confidence in Himself, in His own office, in His Messiahship, in His own nature. Oh yes, He knew man. That is manifest in that first word, "Thou art Simon the son of Jonah." How much lies behind that, we do not know, but we can imagine. We may be wrong, but from all we know of this man after, he had probably been a difficult character to deal with; a man of tremendous possibilities, of marvellous intelligence, of great emotional nature, and of dogged will; and yet as weak as water. Jesus said to him, I know you; I know your father; and I know you. He knew his weakness. He knew his instability. He knew his potentialities; that in that human personality were resident all things that make for greatness. The strength was there only potentially; the durability was not there; but He knew Himself. He knew what He could do with that shaly, shifting sort of stuff. He could transmute it into rock. No word He used ever revealed more His confidence in Himself, "Thou shalt be called rock."

That is the implication in what Jesus said to this man of processes. He did not say Thou art rock, but "Thou shalt be called rock." When the hour came at Cæsarea Philippi when he had passed through three years of partnership with Jesus, and at last had found the Messiah in a new way, he said, "Thou art the Messiah, the Son of the living God," and Jesus said, "Thou art rock." He had arrived. There was a great deal to be done with that bit of rock, a good deal of tooling and chiseling before it became a fitting stone for the eternal habitation, but he was rock. At the beginning, "Thou shalt be called rock." Yes, He knew His own ability. He knew His own power. He knew what He could do with a man like that; and upon the basis of that knowledge and His own perfect self-confidence, He made the prediction, "Thou shalt be called rock." Processes, yes, but he arrived.

Of course the one thing that comes to the heart in conclusion is this, the worth of human personality. It can be changed from shale to rock, but only in one way. That is the way of the meeting with Jesus, and the yielding to Him, and the trusting in Him, and the obeying of Him. If any man however shifty, however much the friends may say they cannot depend on him, come to this Christ, yield to Him; He will never let him go until he is a human being in the likeness of God, and men can build on him.

46. Angels and Ladder

John i: 47-51.

WE ARE still with our Lord in the first days of His public ministry. Nathanael was the fifth of the group constituting His earliest disciples. He stands out, of course, by reason of our Lord's remarkable description of him; a wonderful revelation of the man, especially falling from the lips that spoke no idle or careless word. As He saw him coming to Him, brought by Philip, before He had any conversation with him, He said concerning him, unquestionably to those who were round about, "Behold, an Israelite indeed, in whom is no guile." That is a remarkable description of the man, linking him up with the history of the ancient people of God, by the use of the name Israel, given to one Jacob in connection with that night, when God crowned him by crippling him, that name that means ruled by God, Isra-el. Jesus saw Nathanael, and said, Here is one who fulfils the ideal of the name, "an Israelite indeed." Moreover, He added that word which I never read without thinking that in the mind of our blessed Lord was the thought of the man to whom the name was originally given. Jacob was characterised by guile, by extremely shrewd cleverness; and by ability to practise a good deal of deceit in his own interests. We know all his clever meanness in dealing with Laban, but I am always glad he proved one too many for Laban.

But here was a man who Jesus said fulfilled the ideal suggested by the name, marking his relationship to all the spiritual values suggested by the name; an Israelite indeed, in whom there was no trickery, no double dealing, a clean, transparent soul, submitted to the authority of God. It was a great definition.

The words we are to consider are the background of the story of Nathanael. They were not however, addressed to Nathanael alone, but to the group. There is a sudden transition from the singular to the plural, in what our Lord said. He first talked to Nathanael, "Because I said unto thee, I saw thee underneath the fig tree, believest thou? thou shalt see greater things than these. And He said unto him," but He dropped into the plural, "Verily, verily I say unto you, Ye shall see the heaven opened, and the angels of God ascending and descending upon the Son of man." There are other occasions in the records, when our Lord did that very thing. We shall find it later on in this Gospel, when He was talking to Peter, He suddenly dropped into the plural, "Let not your heart be troubled." I only emphasize it because the words we are now considering were spoken to the group of disciples round about Him at the time. How many more heard Him, of course we have no means of knowing.

What then was the subject which our Lord was intending to illustrate when He said that to this group of men? Secondly, what was the figure He employed? All that so that we may consider the abiding value of the teaching for us.

Turn to the subject illustrated. Notice the method and setting of the thing Jesus said. Observe first that He opened with that formula, "Verily, verily." Another interesting thing to notice in passing is that John is the only one who announces that Jesus used that formula in that form. No less than 25 times in the course of his Gospel it is found. Our Lord introduced something He had to say by that formula, "Verily, verily." Matthew, Mark and Luke all report Him as saying "Verily," and not one of them uses it twice. We may ask, Which did He say? My opinion is that John was the more acute listener, and noticed the double affirmation, the Amen, Amen, for that is the word. It is the method showing that He had something of tremendous importance to say. The formula always marks urgency. It is as though our Lord had been saying something, and then wished to rearrest attention, and to fasten attention upon something now to be said of urgent importance. It is a great study because wherever it is found, it leads to something of urgency, and occurs as a rule in the midst of other statements. That is the first thing to notice in His method.

Then this is the first occasion on record, considering the life of Jesus from the chronological standpoint, when we find Him using the term "Son of man." We are here at the beginning of His public ministry. That was our Lord's favourite designation of Himself, "the Son of man." It is also arresting how constantly He used it. This is the first occasion, and He always used it of Himself. We never find anyone else using it of Him in these Gospel records. No man called Him that. No demon called Him that. His enemies never called Him that, nor are His friends reported as calling Him that. It was His own name for Himself, with one exception. In John xii. 34, on that day when the Greeks had come to Him, and He was saying things of great import, someone in the crowd said, We know about the Christ, or the Messiah. What dost Thou mean when Thou sayest, the Son of man must be lifted up. Who is this Son of man? Just once the phrase is found on the lips of enquirers, and evidently the very form of the statement shows it was a peculiar designation for Himself. They felt at that moment He was claiming Messiahship. His disciples had confessed Him Messiah, and others knew He was claiming it; and a voice from the crowd spoke, What is Thy view? Who is this Son of man? Notice that voice linked the phrase which He was using with the idea of the Christ, or the Messiah. We know about the Christ. Who is the Son of man?

Then notice again we are observing the method and setting that this was an immediate answer or response to Nathanael's confession concerning Him. Nathanael had said, "Thou art the Son of God; Thou art the King of Israel." Then Jesus, continuing the conversation had said to him, Do you believe because I said I knew you before Philip found you? You shall see greater things than these. Then speaking in the plural, You shall see the heaven opened and the angels of God ascending and descending upon the Son of man. "Thou art the Son of God." He did not deny it, but what He called Himself on that self-same occasion was "Son of man."

Then the setting of Nathanael's confession in the presence of our Lord's supreme knowledge and our Lord's declaration, "Thou shalt see greater things than these," and then His interpretation of that. What are the greater things? To summarise everything, the purpose and issue of His presence in the world, the Son of man; and the purpose and issue, angels ascending and descending upon the Son of man, and the heavens open. Through Him there is this link between the heaven that had been closed, and the earth that had been in ignorance. The purpose then of the subject illustrated was that of Himself, in His incarnation, and as to its purpose.

Look now at the figure employed. It is quite evident that our Lord was referring to something that had happened, and that was recorded in their history. It is found in Genesis xxviii. It is the story of Jacob who became Israel. He was travelling away in disobedience, going away from home to a distant place, as the result of his duplicity of which his mother was the inspiration. He laid him down in a place called Luz, to sleep, and put his head upon a stone. He dreamed a dream, and in the dream he saw a stairway. I do not like the translation "a ladder." The Hebrew word literally means a stair-way, a terrace. And he saw Jehovah in the dream, and He was seen standing not at the top of the stairway, as our translation might lead us to think, above it. No, He was right there, on the earth by the side of Jacob. The ladder, the stairway, was standing. When Jacob woke, he said, God is here; Lo, God is in this place. He saw the stairway, and there is the picture out of the dream. Jacob and Jehovah close together, and right from the place where they were close together in the dream, the sweeping stairway moved up until it was lost in heaven. Ascending and descending messengers of heaven in their order, angels is the true word, which means in the Old Testament as in the New, messengers, were going up, bearing messages. They were coming down, bearing messages. That is the picture.

I believe Nathanael had been reading about Jacob when he was under the fig-tree. I believe he had read of his home-coming when God crippled him to make him Isra-el. That was all in his mind, I believe, and our Lord took as His illustration the first description of him, the things he had been thinking about under the fig-tree, in the place of his quietness and his devotion. Have you believed because you were told I knew you before Philip found you? You shall see greater things. You shall see heaven opened, as Jacob did, when he was going out from home. You shall see heaven open, and you shall see what Jacob saw, angels ascending and descending upon the stairway, and the way shall be the Son of man. The figure He was using was that of the ancient dream.

What did that mean to Jacob at the time? It was a revelation of Jehovah's care for him, of Jehovah's love of him. I stress again the point that how at that moment he was going away from home under a cloud. Nobody can defend his action by which he gained what he felt he ought to have, the birthright from Esau. We do not defend Jacob there. It was his in the economy of God, but we really do not help God, but postpone the realisation of His purpose when by tricks we try to aid Him in bringing it about. So it was for this man. He was going out under a cloud. Of course distances today are so different. Take the map, and look at his journey. The country from which he passed, and the country to which he was going. It meant complete exile from home. One can easily imagine his restlessness that night, and his sense of loneliness, accentuated by the conviction that it was his own wrongdoing that was driving him out. He had this vision, and he found that God was there.

When he awoke, what did he say? "This is none other than the house of God; this is the gate of heaven." But he said something far more than that. He said, "Lo, God is here, He is in this place, and I knew it not." Mark the tenses there. The present conviction put into contrast with the past ignorance. "Lo, God is here." When I laid down last night I did not recognize that. I did not know it. I did not think of God as here. No, probably he thought he had offended God, and that God had abandoned him, and that he would have to do the best he could. But that vision, the Lord standing there, Jehovah manifesting Himself in his dream as there, was close to him; and lo, the stairway and angels going up, and coming down, and Jacob learned that night how God cared. We cannot go on with that, for it is a sordid story. The very next thing we find is Jacob bargaining with God. If You do so and so, I will do so and so. He was a mean soul. Nevertheless that great revelation had come. That was the vision our Lord recalled to the mind of Nathanael when He said, "Greater things," and greater things are included in these. Thou shalt see the heaven opened and angels ascending and descending upon the Son of man.

In that whole scene, and in that use of the figure of speech gathered from a piece of history in the sacred writings, with which Nathanael was most familiar undoubtedly there stands for us for evermore a revelation of the fact of the interrelationship between heaven and earth, that they are not divided, that they are not so far apart, that earth can have dealing with heaven, and heaven in dealing with earth. That was the general lesson taught by the vision of Jacob, and that was the tremendous fact Jesus had come to teach humanity at large.

Mark how the two spheres merge in His own Personality, the Son of God and the Son of man. He belonged to the heavenly abode and the heavenly region and the heavenly order. Yes, but He belonged to the earthly region and abode and order. He was Son of man. Heaven and earth were linked in His Person. And it was an unveiling of that fact that He announced to men through Himself. Through Him the door closed should be opened. The Old Version rendered it, "Thou shalt see heaven open." The Revisers have it, "Ye shall see the heaven opened." The very form in which it is stated suggests the fact the door was shut that man had somehow lost his connection, his sense of relationship with the heavenly world and order. Said Jesus, Through Me that door shall be opened. "Ye shall see the heaven opened," and left open through Me.

Then the angels, what are we going to do with them? I would advise you to do nothing with them, but accept them, and believe what He said. Of course we have got beyond medieval art. Modern art knows nothing of the angels. We have lost the angels in our thinking, and our philosophy. We do not believe in angels. No, we are largely Sadducean! They believed neither in resurrection, angel, or spirit. As surely as you let the angels go, you are likely to let the Spirit of God and the resurrection go. That is the danger. That is where that philosophy leads.

"Angels ascending and descending." He said so, and I think He was remembering the Old Testament story. He knew the Scriptures in His human life. He knew of the angelic visitation and ministry, remembering possibly that very word, "The angel of the Lord encampeth round about them that fear Him." At any rate He said that the ministry of heavenly beings should be maintained between heaven and the earth upon Him, and through Him.

The writer of the letter to the Hebrews had a strong conviction about angels when he said, "Are they not all ministering spirits, sent forth to do service for the sake of them that shall inherit salvation?" The word "ministering" is liturgical, that is the anglicising of the Greek word. The double function of the angels is revealed, in that great word. First they are liturgical. That is their supreme function, that of adoration in worship in the presence of the eternal Throne, and the ineffable glory of God. Go back to Isaiah, and we find that in the vision Isaiah had. He saw the seraphim, and saw them engaged in liturgical service. They were crying out, "Holy, Holy, Holy, is the

Lord of hosts; the whole earth is full of His glory." That is praise, that is worship, that is liturgical service, and the writer of the Hebrew letter says that is their function.

But sometimes that exercise ceases. They are sent forth to minister, to do service to those who are heirs of salvation, the ministry of angels on behalf of such. Again that is seen in that very passage of Isaiah. He saw that vision of the angels, heard their anthems, and then it was he cried, Lo, I am a man of unclean lips. Then one of them was sent forth to catch from the altar the live coal, and touch the lips of the sinner, and cleanse him. They are sent forth to minister.

This is not out of date. There are very many things we know for certain that we cannot prove. My last word is that of testimony. I am sure we are surrounded by angel ministry, "angels ascending and descending upon the Son of man." The angel ministry had largely ceased until He was near, then coming again, in the Temple one appeared, to Zacharias, and another to Mary. They have not appeared often. I do not say they never do, or never will; but I believe we are compassed about with a cloud of those who serve us through Jesus Christ.

47. The Temple of His Body

John ii: 13-22.

THIS parabolic illustration was brief in utterance and yet so pregnant in its meaning that it demands careful and close attention. It is found in a few words in the 19th verse, "Destroy this temple, and in three days I will raise it up."

The occasion was that of our Lord's first visit to Jerusalem at the commencement of His ministry. He had come down from Cana where the great sign had been wrought. He had travelled down with His Mother, and His brethren to Capernaum, and He had stayed there "not many days." The Passover feast was about to be observed in Jerusalem. He travelled up there, and it would seem that He went directly to the Temple, for that is the first thing we read.

We are told what He found when He arrived there, the desecration of His Father's house, that desecration taking place in the Gentile courts. It is well to remember that, because those who bought and sold and changed money, would not have allowed that in the courts strictly set apart to the Jew. It was a sign of the times that they felt the Gentile courts were only of value as they might help the Jew as he came up to his worship.

Notice our Lord included everything in His description, "My Father's house." That included the Gentile courts where this business was being carried on. We know what He did. He cleansed those courts. It is a graphic picture, told in simple yet sublime language by John. He did the same thing again at the close of His ministry. Here He made a whip, a scourge of small cords. It is futile to discuss whether He struck anyone. It is so foolish. Do you think He did, says someone? I do not know, and I do not want to know. Personally I believe that with that symbolic scourge in His hands, He advanced upon that crowd, and there was a majesty in His mien that they saw something of His might. If He hit anyone, I am sure it hurt them, but I am not careful about that. This anæmic view of Jesus that He would not hit a man, is not true. That however is the background. He cleansed the Temple, and drove out the animals, and overturned the tables of the money-changers, and sent the whole crowd out. He said to those in charge of the doors, "Take these things hence; make not My Father's house a house of merchandise." Do you suppose He spoke with any other voice than anger, when He said that? If you imagine so, you have a different view of our Lord from my own. He cleansed the Temple.

It was that occasion that led up to the word we are to consider. We are told that the Jews, the rulers, those in authority, representing the Hebrew people, came to Him, and demanded a sign, and they did it in this way. "What sign shewest Thou unto us, seeing that Thou doest these things?" What things? The things He had been doing, driving out the animals, setting loose the birds, rolling over the coins, and sending the traffickers out of His Father's house. They said, Give us a sign.

Now the demand for a sign was one that He would give them evidence of what right He had to do the things that He was then doing. It was a challenge as to His authority. Wherein was His authority? In what was it vital? He had come without apology, apparently only a Peasant, garbed in home-made garments, and He had gone into the sacred precincts, and had destroyed for the nonce at least, the vested interests permitted by all the hierarchy of the priestly caste; indeed from those traffickers, Annas and others were making vast profits. He came and swept it all out. They wanted to know what was His right to do this. It was a challenge as to His authority, although they did not on that occasion, according to the record, use the word, authority. Later however, in the same Temple, they used the word. Matthew records it in his 21st chapter, Mark in his 11th, and Luke in his 20th. They all record the fact that the rulers came to Him, and asked, "By what authority doest Thou these things?" In the fifth chapter of John's Gospel (v. 27), when our Lord was dealing with these rulers, said of His relationship to God, "He gave Him authority to execute judgment, because He is the Son of man."

That was the whole question that was raised here. He did these things by some power that was irresistible. What right had He to do them? What was His authority? What they asked for was a sign of His authority. That was the background. Following our habit, we first consider a little more particularly, the subject illustrated when our Lord made use of these words; then look at the figure employed when He said, "Destroy this temple"; and finally, necessarily, the teaching deduced.

What was the subject under consideration on the day that our Lord said, "Destroy this temple, and in three days I will raise it up?" He had been challenged concerning His right to exercise authority, that was evidently kingly, that was also priestly, to say nothing of the prophetic office. He had been challenged as to what right He had to usurp the position of a king, and of a priest, and to interfere with the orderly and permitted arrangements of the Temple. That was the subject.

The parabolic illustration that we are taking does not declare His authority, does not declare its nature, but as a sign it reveals it. That is what they wanted, and that is what He gave them. In those mystic words He intended to illustrate His authority, and the supreme proof of that authority. It is a great question, that of the authority of our Lord. Take the thought and watch it through. These men were challenging Him there. They doubted that He had any adequate authority, and in order to find out, as they thought, they wanted something to prove it. If an adequate proof of authority could be found, the nature of the authority would be revealed. That is what our Lord was doing.

What was the figure He employed? He said, "Destroy this temple." He used a word that everyone sees, and that men then saw, referred to the place where He was. He had gone up to the Temple. He was in the Temple, and their minds instinctively went out to the Temple. It was the centre of national and religious life. They had not forgotten the deep things of their own history. The Temple was the very dwelling place and Throne of God. In that place He used that figure,

"Destroy this temple." The marginal reading here is sanctuary, and that is an attempt to show a distinction. What was the sanctuary?

The temple was Herod's, and the word temple covered all the precincts, all the courts and buildings of that wonderful and marvellous temple, which as Jesus stood in it then, was not finished. These men said presently, "Forty and six years was this temple in building." No, they said, "Forty and six years has this temple been in building." It was not finished until ten years after the crucifixion. They were still building some parts of it. It is a rather long time, as we build today; but they built well in those days. The word temple, *hieron* covered the whole fact. But Jesus did not use that word that covers the whole fact, when He said "Destroy this temple." That is why the revisers have suggested a change, and have put the word sanctuary in the margin, in which they are justified. The word He used was *maos*, which means the Holy of Holies. The real ideal of God was in the tabernacle with its outer court, the holy place, and then the veil, and the Holy of Holies. Broadly that pattern had been adopted in the building of every successive temple, and it was still there. There were the outer courts, and the holy place, and the Holy of Holies, and that was the *naos*, that was the sanctuary, the centre of the whole temple. Jesus at this point used the word that referred not to the whole temple, but to the inner sanctuary.

I know when they replied to Him they said, "Forty and six years hath this temple been in building," and they used the same word He used but evidently they were referring to the whole structure, because they did not take 46 years to build the Holy of Holies. He had not said so, He had said the *naos*, the Holy of Holies, the sacred centre of everything; destroy that. We know, because the evangelist has told us, although He used the terminology that referred to the place that He was in, and they understood He was referring to the place; He was not referring to it. "He spake of the temple of His body."

Here then our Lord was using a figure of speech, employing it of His body, the Holy of Holies, the dwelling place of God, the place of the Divine revealing, the centre where God and man met by His appointment. All that applied to the material temple, but He was thinking of His own body. Of that He said, "Destroy this temple, and in three days I will raise it up. So the subject illustrated was that of His authority; and the figure He employed was that of His body.

What did He say about it? Mark first of all that He did not say, I will destroy, but He told them that they would. It is an imperative. He challenged them; He dared them. He knew whereunto all their hostility to Him would run, and how it would end. He saw the issue, and that unbelieving and questioning rebellion that was manifest in the challenge as to His authority. He saw it all, and He said, Destroy this temple, this body of Mine. It was an imperative. He challenged them; He dared them. He knew what they were doing. "Destroy this temple." That is the first thing.

We pause to remind ourselves how terribly they distorted that saying of Jesus at the end. When on trial, Matthew records that false witness was borne, in that someone said, "This Man said, I am able to destroy the Temple of God, and to build it in three days." He never said anything of the kind. Mark tells us that the false witnesses said, "We heard Him say, I will destroy this temple that is made with hands, and in three days I will build another made without hands." Again, He said nothing of the kind. The memory of that saying at the beginning they were not careful to be accurate in what they said then. We only refer to it, to draw attention to what He said. "Destroy this temple," this *naos*, this body in which God is dwelling, and which is His appointed meeting place between man and Himself, dissolve it; that was the word, "destroy it," then what? "In three days I will raise it up."

What did He mean? There can be but one answer to it. He meant this. You ask Me for a sign, demonstrating My authority. There is one sign, which will demonstrate it absolutely; My death, which you will bring about on the bodily plane. My resurrection I will bring about in the power that is Mine. The sign they asked for was His death and resurrection. They did not understand Him. His disciples did not understand Him. John is honest enough to tell us that after He had risen from the dead they understood what He had said. The secret of His authority is demonstrated by His death and His resurrection.

Later on we have the same thing with other wording. Matthew has told us "certain of the scribes and Pharisees answered Him, saying, Master, we would seek a sign from Thee." Listen to His answer. "An evil and adulterous generation seeketh after a sign; and there shall no sign be given to it but the sign of Jonah the prophet; for as Jonah was three days and three nights in the belly of the whale; so shall the Son of man be three days and three nights in the heart of the earth." Those two great facts of His death and resurrection constitute the sign and the only sign of the authority of the Son of man. In having the sign of authority, He revealed the nature of His authority, His right to cleanse the temple, His right to heal, His right to do whatever He did was vested in the mystery of His death, and the marvel of His resurrection. If it is said today, and it is terribly true, there are multitudes of people who are seeking a sign, and questioning His authority, they constitute an evil and adulterous generation. That sign abides.

If any ask for proof of the final authority of Christ as King, and Priest, where is it found? Not in His teaching, great and vital as it was and is; not in those signs that we speak of as His miracles, marvels as they were; not in the example of His perfect life, radiant and beautiful in holiness as it was. No, the thing that proves His authority is His death and His resurrection. Not the death alone. Of course there is no such thing as resurrection if there is no such thing as death. The death was brought about by the evil heart of man. The resurrection was brought about by the almighty power of God. These two things together.

They constitute the abiding sign of our Lord's authority for the world today, for this age, for this city, for this nation. What authority has Jesus Christ? Give us a sign of it. Go back to Calvary, and the empty tomb in Joseph of Arimathea's garden and we shall find it. That is the sign of His authority. His system of ethics is not a revelation of His authority. We have laws, and an ethical system, and call it Christianity. It is not Christianity. We can have a psychological approach to the problems of the human mind, but it is not Christianity. Christianity is vested in the absolute final authority of Christ, and the sign of it is His death and resurrection.

We turn to inspiration, and listen to Paul. Read again that fifteenth chapter of his first letter to the Corinthians, wherein every word is of infinite value. Out of one paragraph (14-19) take the threefold movement, beginning, "If Christ hath not been raised, then is our preaching vain, your faith also is vain." "If Christ hath not been raised, your faith is vain; ye are yet in your sins. Then they also which are fallen asleep in Christ have perished." "If in this life only we have hoped in Christ, we are of all men most pitiable." It is when we have considered the "Ifs," then we pass to the great affirmation, "But now hath Christ been raised from the dead"; and that resurrection being the answer of the power of God to the evil that is in men's hearts that put Him on His Cross, is the sign of His present and eternal authority.

48. The Wind and the Spirit

John iii: 8.

OUR LORD was still in Jerusalem on His first visit there according to the records, during the period of His public ministry. It was on that occasion that Nicodemus, a ruler, and the teacher in Israel sought an interview with Him. There is significance in the phrase that he was "the teacher of Israel." To use a phrase of these times, he was the popular teacher, a man greatly sought after, as I believe because of the eminence of his intellect, and his acquaintance with the Holy Scriptures. I think that is what our Lord meant when He said, "Art thou *the teacher* of Israel, and understandest not these things?" Be that as it may, he certainly was a teacher and ruler. This was the man who sought an interview with Jesus.

The first 21 verses of this chapter give us the story of that interview. Some believe that the words of our Lord recorded in this chapter ceased at the fifteenth verse, and that the paragraph commencing, "For God so loved the world," constituted John's interpretation of what our Lord was saying. Without arguing about it, I reject that view, and am convinced the words in verse 16 fell from the lips of our Lord Himself. In the midst however of the story of the interview with Nicodemus, our Lord used two illustrations, one from Nature, and the other from the history of the nation of Israel. The one from Nature was, "The wind bloweth where it listeth"; the other from the history of Israel, with which Nicodemus would be familiar, "As Moses lifted up the serpent in the wilderness." We are now concerned with the first of these, considering the second in our next study.

The wind and the Spirit. Following our usual custom, we first ask, what was the subject illustrated, an important matter; then look at the figure employed, that of the wind; finally, necessarily, the teaching to be deduced for Nicodemus, for us, and for all time.

What was our Lord illustrating when He said, "The wind bloweth where it listeth?" It was the illustrative part of His answer to a question of Nicodemus. Nicodemus had said, "How can a man be born when he is old?" The declaration that Jesus had just made, and gave rise to the question of Nicodemus was this. Christ had declared to him that the Kingdom of God demands a new personality. He told him that no man could see it unless he was born *anothen,* from above; a new personality. In the second part, just after this illustration He said that except a man were born anew, from above, he could not enter into the Kingdom of God.

Those are the two declarations. Christ said that the Kingdom of God, in order to its apprehension and its experience, demanded a new personality. Nicodemus had come up, as I think with great honesty, for I hold a brief for Nicodemus. I always dislike those who say he was cowardly, because he came to Jesus by night. Not at all. He was no fool. He wanted to have Jesus all to himself, and that was the time to find Him, when the crowds were not there. He was a man of great intellectual ability; and he came up with that assertion, which was a great assertion, "We know that Thou art a Teacher come from God; for no man can do these signs that Thou doest, except God be with Him." In spite of the clear understanding that characterised his outlook, and his conception of truth concerning Christ, Christ crashed across it the word that discounted all his cleverness, though it was on a high level as He said, "Except a man be born from above, he cannot see the Kingdom of God."

Later on, to trespass upon the next part of the story, He said, "Except a man be born of water and the Spirit he cannot enter into the Kingdom of God." Two things are necessary, first of all understanding, and in order to understanding there must be a new birth and a new personality; and secondly, experience, entering into it, and in order to that there must be a new birth, a new personality.

If there is anything that the world needs to hear anew today it is that one thing, that all human cleverness is of no use in giving a man to see or understand the Kingdom of God; and certainly apart from a new birth, which results in a new personality, he cannot experience the Kingship of God, and know the deep meaning of it all.

It was because our Lord had said that, that Nicodemus replied, and it was a great thing, he said, "How can a man be born when he is old?" Then he illustrated what was in his mind in the realm of the physical. Nicodemus did not consider the physical as being the whole of personality; when he spoke of a man he did not merely think of his body. He was a Pharisee. He believed in the spiritual side of man's nature. How can a man, an entire man, be born when he is old? To show the incredulity of it, the impossibility of it, as it seemed to Nicodemus, he used the physical as an illustration. "Can a man enter a second time into his mother's womb, and be born?" When he first said, "How can a man be born when he is old?" he was thinking in the realm of personality in its entirety. He was thinking unquestionably of all the past thinking of it in his own personality, that he was the result of all the years that had gone. All the processes of the past were merging in the I am of the present. How can a man undo the past? How can a man be born, begin, start, when he is old? With great force he illustrated from his standpoint, Can a man "enter a second time into his mother's womb, and be born?" Can the physical be taken and pulped back into embryonic stage, and be born again? If that cannot be done with the physical, how can it be done with the whole of personality? That was the question. Do not go away and speak of the ignorance of Nicodemus. It was an important question. It was a tremendous question.

How did our Lord answer that? This leads to the illustration, "Verily, verily, I say unto thee, Except a man be born of water and the Spirit, he cannot enter into the Kingdom of God." Then Jesus corrected the mistake that Nicodemus was making in attempting to illustrate the whole of personality from the physical standpoint. "That which is born of the flesh is flesh; and that which is born of the Spirit is spirit." That verse is constantly used I think, in an improper way. Some read that and think that Jesus said that the flesh is inherently and entirely evil, and the spirit is other than that; yet what is born of the flesh must be flesh, and what is born really of the Spirit is good. Nothing of the kind. He said in effect, You have asked your question. You have used an illustration in the physical realm. Nicodemus remember that the laws that govern the flesh and the laws that govern the spirit are not identical. I see your difficulty, as though our blessed Lord had said to him, in the realm of the flesh. No man can enter into the Kingdom until he be born again. That is the law of the flesh. That which is born of the flesh is flesh. Nicodemus, when you come into the realm of the Spirit you are coming into another realm. Things which cannot be in the realm of the flesh perhaps, may be possible in the realm of the spirit. "That which is born of the flesh is flesh; and that which is born of the Spirit is spirit." "Marvel not that I said unto thee, Ye must be born from above." Stand in the presence of the thing you do not understand, but do not marvel. You do not understand it. Your illustration in the realm of the flesh is well taken, and is true but stay, there is a realm of the Spirit, and things may take place in that realm of the Spirit beyond your understanding. Do not marvel because you do not understand. That was the occasion of the illustration. He has lifted the question of Nicodemus away into another realm, a higher realm of life and personality, which is the realm of the spirit. "The wind bloweth where it listeth, and thou hearest the voice thereof, but knowest not whence it cometh, and whither it goeth; so is every one that is born of the Spirit."

Our Lord was illustrating the fact that the operation of the Spirit

is not an operation of the flesh. He charged this man not to be surprised for the necessity declared in the realm of the spirit· and then
He took this illustration.

Now look at the figure itself, the wind. The margin of the Revised
Version suggests we might read there "The spirit breatheth where
it listeth." There are those who have taken that view, and seem to
think Christ was speaking all through of the operation of the Spirit.
While understanding that view, to accept it is to have broken down
the analogy. There is no contrast in illustration here. If He is speaking of the Spirit, then He has gone into the realm of statement, and
not of illustration. Moreover, to take it in that way, "The Spirit
breatheth where it listeth, and thou hearest the voice thereof," that
cannot be said, because we never do hear the sound or voice of the
Spirit. It may be quoted that on the day of Pentecost there came a
sound from heaven, as of the rushing of a mighty wind. Yes there was
a wind, and the Spirit, but notice, it was like it. There was a sound,
but the fact was of value. It was that which attracted the city outside,
and the miracle of tongues which needs no repetition to the end of time.

The word "wind" is *pneuma*, I admit this is an unusual use of it.
The word occurs in more than 150 passages in the New Testament;
20 of which are in this Gospel of John. It is always rendered spirit,
except here, and on one other occasion, when in the book of Revelation
we read that one beast had power to communicate life, or breath, or
spirit to an image. On these two occasions we have a different rendering. It is a word used of God, of man, and of demons. The word in
itself means quite literally, apart from its high value, a current of air,
a breath, a breeze. The root of it is in that passage in Acts, "a mighty
rushing wind." Here there can be no doubt whatever that our Lord
used the wind, the breath, the breeze as illustrating the fact of the
work of the Spirit. There is no question that our translators were
right in rendering it *wind* in the text, not as in the margin.

It is interesting though not important, that possibly Jesus and
Nicodemus were on the house-top together in the night. Possibly they
may have been within the house in some upper chamber or room in
a house-top. It may have been as they talked, the wind at that moment
was sweeping over the city. If they were in the house, probably they
heard the sighing and the soughing of the wind going up the narrow
streets of Jerusalem. Whether on the house-top, in the house, or in a
garden as my beloved friend Dr. Jowett believed, the one thing Jesus
did here, as He was so constantly doing, was to take hold of something close to Him, the meaning of which the one to whom He was
speaking could not but be conscious. "Consider the lilies," He said,

and they were there. Wheat and tares, and everything else. So here with the wind. There on the house-top, there was the reality which Nicodemus must have been conscious of. The wind was blowing. The sound demonstrated the fact. Nicodemus heard it, whether sweeping over the house-top, or sweeping through the narrow streets, or in a garden; there was no escape from it. Nicodemus, you know that. Can you hear the wind? Now Nicodemus, tell Me where it came from, where it began? Where is it going? Nicodemus could not tell Him that. "Thou knowest not whence it cometh, and whither it goeth." Someone said to me some time ago, Of course that story has gone by the board. We do know where the wind has come from, and where it is going! Well, it may look like it, but it is never so. We may read about depressions and we will, but can we explain perfectly how the depression is caused? Scientists may be sure they know all about it. Are they quite sure? I will use the Scot's phrase and say, "I hae ma doots." If we follow the weather reports on the radio, we find they do not know always. Let the pleasantry be forgotten, and take this fact. Nicodemus heard the wind blowing over the housetop. The sound demonstrated the fact of the wind. I will tell you what you do not know, Nicodemus. You do not know whence it came. You do not know whither it is going. You are in the presence of a reality demonstrated. You are in the presence of a mystery inexplicable.

I wonder if there is any need to say any more. What a marvellous illustration. Keep it against its background. Remember Nicodemus' false question, his false illustration; our Lord's correction of it, and His insistence upon the spiritual fact, a new personality by the birth of the Spirit. Carefully notice one thing in this. "The wind bloweth where it listeth, and thou hearest the voice thereof, but knowest not whence it cometh, and whither it goeth; so is everyone born of the Spirit." It is of the utmost importance that we get the reality of the terms in their right relationship here. Jesus did not say the wind blows where it will, and so is the Spirit in His action. It was not a comparison in the ultimate between the wind and the Spirit. They are both there. It was a comparison between the man Nicodemus, and that other Man. Thou hearest the sound thereof, and by that thou knowest the reality; but thou canst not tell whence it cometh or whither it goeth. Thou standest in the presence of mystery; so is every one that is born of the Spirit. Nicodemus, thy relation for the moment to this natural phenomenon is exactly the same relation a man born of the Spirit bears to that phenomenon. What is the similitude as to the wind? The wind is a demonstrated fact. There is a mystery in its operation. As to the Spirit, to the man born of the Spirit the fact is equally demonstrated by the results. So as thou art listening to the wind, not being sure of it; so he that is born of the Spirit knows it, incontrovertibly by its operation. As thou canst not tell whence or whither the wind cometh and goeth; so every man born of the Spirit has to recognise the mystery of the operation. He may not be able to explain whence or whither. He may not be able to unravel the tremendous mystery of the rebirth of personality in the realm of the spirit; but he knows the fact. The fact is there, and the mystery is there.

Now to summarise. This illustration consisted of a reinforcement and an appeal to employ the same activity in the things of the Spirit as in the things of Nature. In the realm of Nature we recognise the fact. We are conscious of the mystery. Do the same thing in the realm of the Spirit. Act on the fact, and in accordance with it, recognising all the while the mystery of the method. Our Lord only spoke of one demonstration of the wind. It was that of the sound, of a voice. That was what they were conscious of there in the night time. There are other demonstrations of the wind. One is power. We know the power of the wind; still we do not know whence it cometh, or whither it goeth. The mystery is there, but the fact is there. So is everyone that is born of the Spirit. Our Lord is really saying in effect, Nicodemus, if you will act in the realm of the Spirit as you do most honestly in the realm of Nature, where will you find yourself? Take the realm of Nature, and take the wind. Apply the old and familiar formula, Obey the law of the force, and the force will obey you. Obey the law of the wind, and the wind will fill the sails of the vessel and carry it across the waters. If you obey the force, and the force becomes your servant, you still do not understand the mystery. In the realm of Nature no man stands debating a mystery, and neglecting the force. That is what Christ was saying in the realm of the Spirit. Obey the law of the Spirit, and the Spirit will obey you. Obey the law of the spiritual life, and the result will be that all the forces of that life will demonstrate the reality of that birth which is the birth from above, which is the birth of the Spirit.

We can take that tremendous statement and turn it round in another way, Disobey the law of the force, and the force will destroy you. That is always so. Disobey the law of the wind, and the wind will wreck your vessel. Obey the law of the force, and it will obey you. It is true of electricity. It is always true. Obey the law of electricity and it becomes your servant, lighting your buildings, driving your vehicles, and all the things it is doing today. But disobey the law of that force, and it will blast you like the lightning of death.

It was no light thing Jesus said, and it was a tremendous illustration. Nicodemus, you hear the wind. You know the fact of the wind because you heard just now the voice of the wind; but you are standing in the presence of a mystery. Nicodemus, you must be born of water, which is the action of repentance, and the Spirit, which is the action of regeneration. Though you do not understand the mystery, obey the law, and the force will become your servant; and even though physically you cannot enter into your mother's womb and be born again, yet in the great mystery of personality central to which is spirit always; you can be born again, be born anew, be born from above, and find that new personality through which you shall understand and experience the Kingdom of God.

49. The Lifted Serpent

John iii: 14.

OUR PREVIOUS study was concerned with the illustration of the wind and the Spirit, by which our Lord illuminated His answer to the first question of Nicodemus, "How can a man be born when he is old?" Nicodemus then spoke again, and Jesus employed the illustration of the lifted serpent in His answer to that second question, "How can these things be?"

We pause here to notice that there was an essential difference between the two questions which Nicodemus asked. The first was, "How can a man be born when he is old?" It was not a flippant question, but a serious one, revealing the fact that this man was thinking. He did not deny what Christ had suggested as to the value of a new beginning. Jesus said, "Except a man be born from above he cannot see the Kingdom of God." Nicodemus did not question that for a moment. What he did question was the possibility of the thing suggested. How can a man be born all over again, as though the first had never been. He is what he is as the result of all the years that have gone. How can he start again? It was an honest question, an intelligent question, but it was one revealing a great deal of doubt as to the possibility.

After our Lord had used that marvellous simile of the wind and the Spirit, in which He summarised by telling him that in natural things he did not refuse to act because there was mystery present, that he took hold of that which was patent and could not be denied. The blowing of the wind which he heard, he acted upon it, though there was mystery. He could not tell whence it came or whither it was going; so is every man born of the Spirit. Every man that is born of the Spirit obeys the law of the force, which cannot be denied, although he cannot understand the mystery of the activity.

When Nicodemus heard that, he then asked this question, not how the thing happened, but how can the thing be brought to pass? He was still in the same realm of difficulty. The word he used is a very suggestive one, *genesthai*, not how can this happen? but How can it come to pass? I may take Nicodemus' question, and render it a little more fully than in our Versions. It might properly be rendered, By what power can these things be caused to be? It is not a question of there being, but of there becoming. The first thing is incredible. Now if there is a law of the Spirit, how does it work. How can these things be brought to pass?

It was in answer to that question that our Lord used the illustration of the uplifted serpent. We may now proceed with the same three lines of consideration. First, the subject illustrated. Secondly the figure He employed. Finally of course the teaching deduced for us and for all time.

What was the subject that Jesus was illustrating when He used that historic figure? For a moment look at the twelfth verse, in which Jesus said, "If I told you earthly things, and ye believe not, how shall ye believe, if I tell you heavenly things?" We are apt to read that as though our Lord meant, I cannot tell you the heavenly things. He did not mean that, for He immediately proceeded to tell Nicodemus the heavenly things. That is what He is now doing. He had told him the earthly things, the necessity on the earth level for a new personality. He had illustrated that by a natural figure of speech, the blowing of the wind. He had told him earthly things, and Nicodemus was still in doubt. He could not understand. How would he believe if He drew aside the curtain, and revealed the heavenly things. The earthly things declared were those of necessity for a man to be born from above, starting anew on the earth level. Nicodemus you ask how that can be brought about? The answer is that which brings you face to face with heavenly things; the action of heaven that makes possible the earthly experience. Our Lord dealt with that from this point on, the action whereby a man can by the reception of a new life from above, escape from his past. That is what had puzzled Nicodemus at first, how he could not only see but enter into the whole experience of the Kingdom of God. The secret of the life which liberates a human soul, and enables it, how that life is provided straight away, "As Moses lifted up the serpent in the wilderness, even so must the Son of man be lifted up; that whosoever believeth may in Him have eternal life. For God so loved the world, that He gave His only begotten Son, that whosoever believeth on Him should not perish, but have eternal life. For God sent not the Son into the world to judge the world; but that the world should be saved through Him."

Those are the heavenly things. The earthly things, the necessity for the recreating of personality, the liberation of the soul from the accumulation and influences of the past, and the enablement of the soul with a new life to enter upon the Kingdom of God experimentally; these are the earthly things. You ask for the heavenly secrets. How will you believe if I do tell you? And the great declaration comes, with the sixteenth verse, always taken in very close connection with the fourteenth and fifteenth, and also with the seventeenth.

Notice how those two verses (16.17) begin; "For . . . for." That follows after the verse, "As Moses lifted up the serpent in the wilderness, even so must the Son of man be lifted up; that whosoever believeth may in Him have eternal life. For." Everything now beyond the illustration is in the heavenly realm. "For God so loved," and then "For God sent not His Son to condemn, but to save." Those are the heavenly things. Whereas we are not considering those verses at any length, we are bound to recognize them from the standpoint of the Divine action, and the consequent human responsibility.

So we come at once to the illustration. "As Moses lifted up the serpent in the wilderness." Having first used an illustration in the realm of natural phenomena, He now used an illustration in the realm of historic record. Nicodemus knew the Old Testament. He was the teacher of Israel, and he knew the Scriptures. We are familiar with it. The story is in Numbers xxi, the account of how Moses lifted up the serpent in the wilderness.

In looking at this figure, what did this uplifted serpent mean? Why did Moses lift up that serpent in the wilderness? Because the people had been guilty of definite and positive rebellion against God. There is one little sentence in that 21st chapter of Numbers that tells the whole story. "They spake against God." That is the history behind this incident. The people definitely and wilfully rebelled against the Divine government. "They spake against God," and this story in Numbers tells us that as the result of that rebellion there was a punitive action of God. There came to them the fiery serpents, and the deadly bite, and the terrible anguish and suffering.

But we have not reached the lifted serpent. That is only the background. Why was the serpent lifted? It was lifted because the people had rebelled against God, and because as the result of their rebellion they were suffering punishment. That was why.

Now, said Jesus, as Moses lifted up that serpent; and we go back with the simplicity of children to the story in Numbers, and say, Why did Moses lift it up, and what did it mean when it was lifted up? First, he lifted it up by the authority of God, by the authority of the very One against Whom the people were in rebellion. "They spake against God," and that God Whose authority they were insulting and denying, arranged for the uplifted serpent.

Why was it lifted? To give those who were suffering as the result of their own rebellion, an opportunity for return to the government of God. Let us get hold of that first. I know there is something else. What were they to do? Moses was to make a serpent of brass, and lift it on a pole. What were they to do? Look at the serpent of brass. It sounds almost foolish. It is not. Is there any healing in that serpent of brass? No, not so; no healing in it. Then why look? Because God's authority commanded it. His authority had been insulted. His authority ordered the elevation of that serpent, and men were to look, and there could be no look which was not the result of yielding to the Divine authority in a new start, a new beginning. The God contemned is now obeyed by those who look. There were hundreds who looked. It was a speculative look. There were those who did not look. We do know if they did not look they died by the poison of the bite. But the look was a yielding to a Divine command, and that is all. The work of the eyes had nothing in it of value. There was no healing in that uplifted serpent; but in obedience to a Divine command. So Moses lifted up the serpent in the wilderness; first upon the authority of God, and secondly to create for suffering men and women through their own sin an opportunity of return to the government of God that they had refused, by obedience to His command as they looked.

Of course the third thing is involved in what we have said. That demanded repentance, a change of mind; an activity that grows out of a changed mind. If men and women in that camp heard the proclamation that God had appointed the lifted serpent, with the act of every head turned toward that serpent was the head of a repentant man; indicating a change of mind, no longer speaking against God, but obeying God.

Finally of course on the fulfilment of these conditions a way of healing and of new life was provided for those smitten, stricken and afflicted through their own sin. That was the story in Numbers. Moses lifted up the serpent on the authority of God to create a point at which man who had spoken against Him and was in rebellion, and consequently was suffering, could turn back, and by looking be healed and restored, in glorious simplicity of obedience to the command.

Yet the sublime wonder of it. Every head turned was the head of some one who was repenting and now obeying the Divine command; and as and whenever a head was turned in obedience, expressed in the look, life and healing followed.

Nicodemus, you know your history. You have asked about heavenly things. Let Me begin by taking you back to a page in your history, as though Jesus had said, that well-known story of the serpent; and there you will see heavenly activity creating the opportunity for earthly activity; and when the heavenly activity and the earthly come into touch with each other, there is the way of life. "As . . . so."

So we stand back as it were from the illustration, and at once see the greatness of it. There is revealed and suggested in this story in the wilderness the background of human need. What is it? Man perishing by reason of his rebellion against God. That is the whole story of this world's agony and failure. That is the story of the failure of your life and mine. That is the story of the failure of all social relationships. That is the story of failure in national life, and international relationships. All in the last analysis is in rebellion against God; and perishing is the result.

There is only one hope either for the individual or for the nation. What is it? A new beginning, a new birth, the communication of a new life which will liberate us from all the bondage of the past, and enable us for all that lies ahead of us. I go back twenty years for my illustration, to those dark and terrible years. How constantly it was repeated in writings of men who perhaps would not claim what we would claim, of confidence and belief in the Christ of God; but over and over again we were told that what the world needed was a new spirit. It is wonderful how all unconsciously these men simply repeated what Jesus said, "Ye must be born from above." There is the background. Nicodemus was there, and Jesus was talking to him, and as He used this illustration, at the time showing the background in the history of men and women perishing by reason of rebellion, with no hope whatever; then something happened so that they should be healed, and have a new element in life. So we see the condition of the world, and humanity.

Now in the foreground, our Lord told him the story of the Divine action. "As Moses lifted up the serpent in the wilderness, even so must the Son of man be lifted up." "Lifted up"? Everyone knows what He meant, "lifted up, was He, to die."

That is what He meant. It is a great expression. We find it again upon the lips of Jesus (viii. 28). He was talking then to His enemies "Jesus therefore said, When ye have lifted up the Son of man, then shall ye know that I am He, and that I do nothing from Myself, but as the Father taught Me, I speak these things." And once again, we have the phrase on the lips of Jesus in the twelfth chapter, in that marvellous word, "I, if I be lifted up from the earth, will draw all men unto Myself." He used the expression then when He was looking at the Cross, and more than the Cross He was looking through to the victory. So He said to Nicodemus, "The Son of man must be lifted up."

So we are brought face to face with the Cross in a remarkable way by reason of the illustration. The serpent was lifted up by the authority of God. So was the Son of man. The lifting up on the Cross of Jesus was not finally the act of man. It was the act of man's sin; but He never had been lifted up except again to quote from Peter, in his first Pentecostal sermon, He had been "delivered by the determinate counsel and foreknowledge of God." Behind that Cross I see the eternal Throne. In that Cross I see the action of the eternal authority. That which man has condemned and rebelled against is acting in the midst of all the ruin, created by his rebellion, for the recovery of man from those results; by the authority of God creating an opportunity for man to return to the Divine authority. That is what it always means. It is so wrong to think we become Christians to escape the bit of the fiery serpent, or hell fire. Yes, we do; but to become a Christian means we get back to God, yielding to the authority which has been contemned, and against which man has rebelled.

That demands repentance, but it provides life, and healing for all who will be obedient to that command.

> "There is life for a look at the Crucified One,
>   There is life at this moment for thee.
>   Then look, sinner look, unto Him and be saved;
>   There is life in that moment for thee."

But there must be the look. There must be the bending of the neck. There must be the submission of the life to the authority of God. There must be a return to the Throne of government which will be found to be the Throne of grace. We never know the grace until we submit to the government. "As . . . so."

Notice carefully, how this reads. "As Moses lifted up the serpent, . . . even so *must* the Son of man be lifted up; that whosoever believeth may in Him have eternal life." We are still on the earth level?

No, we are going on to the heavenly level now. "For God so loved the world that He gave His only begotten Son, that whosoever believeth on Him should no perish, but have eternal life. For God sent not His Son into the world to condemn the world; but that the world should be saved through Him." A marvellous illustration, so simple, the historic incident, and yet so thrilling with the fact of the Divine power and the Divine authority and the Divine grace. If man rebels, punishment must come; but even when he is suffering, God finds the remedy; and the Son of man given of God, and sent by God is given in order that through that action of God and His Son, man may have life indeed.

50. Living Water

John iv: 1-15.

OUR LORD used this illustration in circumstances widely different from those we have previously considered. We cannot help being arrested by those differences at the commencement. Jesus was not now in the city, but in the country, when this conversation took place, about a mile from Sychar. He was in Samaria, not in Judaea, and we hear Him talking, not to a ruler, the teacher of Israel, but to a woman, and withal, a sinning woman.

The whole story is full of fascination, because of the remarkable things He said to this woman. The story is full of surprises, because He said to this woman, just as she was, things we could have imagined He would have reserved to say to far more advanced disciples.

During the course of the things He said to this woman, He made use of this parabolic illustration of living water. We take our usual course of consideration; first, the subject which He was intending to illustrate; then, the figure He employed; and finally the teaching to be deduced.

Look at the picture. We are all familiar with it. Jesus was sitting tired, weary, as our beautiful word accurately has it, wearied with His journey, and He sat thus, that is as He was, tired, by the well. The disciples had gone away to buy—as the Old Version had it, and I like the word—victuals. The Revised Version says, food. They had left Him to buy food, and He was there alone when this woman came. That is all we know about her. Jesus is seen sitting in the presence of a woman, and the deepest fact concerning her was perhaps one evident to no one but Jesus. She was conscious of it, and yet hardly understood it. He sat in the presence of a thirsty woman, a woman degraded. She was there carrying water pots from at least a mile away, coming to Jacob's well from the city of Sychar. The carrying of water pots marked the fact that she had sunk so low as to be acting as a slave. She was degraded even as to her social position. Whatever it may have been in the past, we know nothing, except some lurid facts which Jesus brought to light presently. We have a revelation on the human side in what she said, "Sir, give me this water, that I thirst not, neither come all the way hither to draw." Tired, thirsty, degraded; and as we know a woman who, through her own fault had burned herself out. There was nothing left. "Go, call thy husband." "I have no husband." "Thou saidst well, I have no husband; for thou hast had five husbands." We know the rest. We see the past of passion, and an attempt to satisfy the deepest cravings of her nature along that line; and she was now there with her water pots, degraded to the position of slavery, utterly disillusioned, degraded and dissatisfied.

The old days had all gone. Whatever glamour there had been in them had faded out. Whatever excitement of the senses she may have passed through during those previous years of her life, they had burned themselves out, and there was nothing left save the drudgery of a slave. We can take those three words, degraded, disillusioned, and dissatisfied, and express them in the one word with which I started—thirsty.

Jesus knew that. He knew the thirst of that woman's life. Perhaps it was a thirst that never expected to find anything that would quench it. It seems probable that she had gone beyond the region of hope of any satisfaction, and therefore she was cynical. That is seen in the way she talked to Jesus. She was cynical of heart and callous, and yet deep down within her, there were elements that were religious. She knew certain things, and Jesus precipitated all these things from the under-world of her life to the surface as He talked with her. He was talking to a woman outside the covenant of Israel, a Samaritan, held in contempt by all the Jews, who were Jews only after the flesh. He was face to face with a thirsty woman, and offered Himself to her, as being able to quench that thirst, and that meant able to lift her from the degradation into which she had fallen, able to give her, who had become disillusioned, an entirely new outlook upon life, able to come to the deep, scorching, burning, restless dissatisfaction, and bring her complete satisfaction. That is what He was doing;

and that is the subject illustrated by the living waters. That is the great theme.

Jesus used this illustration of water. Following that method that so characterised His teaching, taking something that was right there, something under observation, something with which she had connection. He began by asking her for a drink of water; and when in surprise she said, How do You come to ask it of me, You a Jew, and I a Samaritan, then He said this amazing thing to her, using the figure of the water. Notice the word water occurs no less than eight times in the course of the conversation.

Water,—a great essential of human life. What are the things necessary to life on the material level, the natural? I will state them in the order of importance, from the least to the greatest. The first is food, that is the least important, but it is essential. We can certainly live forty days without eating. It is interesting the occasions of fasting recorded in the Bible for forty days. But more important than food is water. How long can we live without water? Scientists tell us seven days, and no more. Of course the most important is breath. How long can we live without breathing? I will not attempt an answer! We need to breathe, that is the first thing. We need water, and we need food. But this illustration was taken there, the second in importance as an element of life—water, that is the figure.

Look at the figure. There is more than that in it; only I would remind you that thirst is a beneficent warning of danger. Thirst in its demand, is a search after deliverance from the danger. A man with no consciousness, no thirst for spiritual things is in dire danger. Thirst is beneficent. It is a warning, and it means a clamant cry for that which will obviate the peril. It was not merely water in this figure of speech; it was the place of water. Notice how the well plays a part all through here. Now for a small technicality, which is worth noting. In the narrative there are two entirely different words, both translated *well*. It is significant. Look at verses 11 and 12. The woman is talking, and she says, "The well is deep . . . our father Jacob, which gave us the well." That was her thought and conception, which was perfectly true. That is the word *phear* which means a hole, or cistern. She was thinking of the accumulated water there in the well, in the cistern. Now look at verses 6 and 14. In the sixth verse John says, "Jacob's well was there." That is not the same word, and John says "Jesus sat thus by the well." That is not the word that the woman used on the other occasions. Go on to verse 14, Jesus is speaking, and He speaks of "a well of water." That is not the same word *phear*. The difference is this, that the word that John used in writing the narrative, even of the same place of which the woman spoke as a cistern, John did not call it that. He said By the spring Jesus sat, by Jacob's spring; and Jesus also used that word spring, when He said "a well of water." There are two words here in the figure of speech.

Our Lord then used the words that suggest not an accumulation of water in a hole, a well, in that sense, a cistern; but a spring. Take the other word in the figure of speech, as Jesus used it, "living water." What is living water? I am not thinking of the spiritual realm merely. There was living water there in that sense, or that well would not have been in use after the long centuries. Jacob had given it to his sons. There it was, an accumulation of water; someone drew out, and the cistern remained and filled up again, why? Because there was living water there. What then is living water, as distinct from cistern water? It is water always flowing, as distinct from water gathered up, and kept. There is a beautiful phrase in the Old Testament on the material or physical level, where we are told in the book of Genesis that Isaac's servants digged in the valley "and found there a well of springing water." That is the same thought, living water, water always coming up, always passing on. We shall consider the figure again later on, in another and wider application. Now we are simply looking at the figure.

Living water is water always bubbling up and flowing, always coming. Water in a glass by our side, is excellent, but it is not living water; it is stagnant, it is collected. Water ceases to be living when it is gathered, and stored and kept. Jesus used that as a figure, living water; not the well in which there is an accumulation of water, but a spring that keeps the well full, however much water is drawn from it.

What a wonderful figure of speech, living water. Jesus is confronting a thirsty soul, and is using the illustration that is close at hand. The woman called it a well. He spoke of a spring, of that which had brought the water into the well. She had come far to draw the collected water. Lifting His illustration on to the realm of personality and the spiritual, He said to her that He could give her water that would be living water, water always coming, always springing, living water. The whole thing is so patent, we need not stay long with the teaching. Christ confronts man's deepest need, his thirst. That underlying consciousness of dissatisfaction expresses itelf in a thousand ways. All the restless feverishness proves it; the failure of all things material to satisfy the deepest craving of the human soul. That is thirst; and the world is crowded with thirsty souls. How many have tried so many things, but degradation has come, and disillusionment has come, and dissatisfaction is abiding, a perpetual irritant, a burning fever. They hardly know what it is they want. There it is, all the restlessness of the age, of which jazz music is one of the symptoms, restless, shivering of the body, symbolic; all the rest less writhing of the spirit; all man's thirst. Man is wanting something that he has not, and the utter failure of all attempts on the earth level to satisfy that craving. The world is thirsty.

Now listen to Christ's claim as made to that woman, and through her as a representative to all humanity. "If thou knewest the gift of God, and Who it is that saith to thee." "If thou knewest the gift of God," what did He mean? What is the gift of God? Living water? Oh no. That is not what He meant then. That is His gift. What is the gift of God? The same thought was in the mind of Jesus when He said to Nicodemus, "God so loved the world that He gave His only begotten Son." Oh yes, "If thou knewest the gift of God, and Who it is"; God gave His Son. "If thou knewest Who was speaking to thee, the One God has given His very Son, of His own nature and being." "If thou knewest thou wouldest ask of Him, and He would give thee living water."

Keep this on the spiritual level of the necessity of mankind. Our Lord was quoting freely the Jewish Scriptures of the Hebrew people. Jeremiah had said, "My people have committed two evils; they have forsaken Me the fountain of living waters; and hewed them out cisterns, broken cisterns, that can hold no water." And later he said, "O Lord, the Hope of Israel, all that forsake Thee shall be ashamed; they that depart from Me shall be written in the earth, because they have forsaken the Lord, the fountain of living waters." And yet one other instance, this time from Zechariah. "It shall come to pass in that day, that living waters shall come out from Jerusalem; half of them toward the eastern sea, and half of them toward the western sea; in summer and in winter shall it be." Living waters! It was an old figure of speech from the Hebrew prophets, and these living waters were waters that proceeded from God, and when men turned their back upon living waters and made cisterns, they found they were broken, and yielded no water.

Jesus said to this woman with that great Hebrew figure of speech, living waters, unquestionably in mind, If you had known the gift of God, you would have asked of Me, and I would have given you living water, that which shall completely quench thirst, so that you would never be thirsty. But those living waters shall be in you, springing within you, springing up, a beautiful word. I am often inclined to change the translation, not to improve it, but to help in understanding it. The word translated springing up means leaping up. The word only occurs here, and twice in Acts (iii: 8 and xiv: 10) when it tells of the lame man at the Beautiful Gate leaping. It is a figure of joy and gladness, leaping up. Springing up, yes, bubbling up, perennially full and fresh; laughing up. That is what He is prepared to give to humanity. That is what He can give to the human soul thirsty, parched, feverish, distracted, disappointed; water that will be not outside, stored in a cistern, but in him a spring in himself, leaping up, bubbling up, springing up unto eternal life.

The story goes on. We know how it ends. What has the story to say to us? The challenge of Jesus abides, and the promise of Jesus abides. "If thou knewest Who it is." There is so much there. Half the trouble today is half the people do not know Who Jesus is. The moment He is made anything less than what the New Testament reveals Him to be, the Son of God, and God the Son, well, we shall not know Who He is, and we shall not ask Him for living water, and we shall try and satisfy ourselves in other ways, it may be in religious ways. People have gone up to Keswick year after year, to get filled up. Poor souls. Whatever they get will become stagnant before they leave Keswick. Oh no, we cannot get it that way.

> "I tried the broken cisterns, Lord,
>   But ah! the waters failed!
> E'en as I stooped to drink, they'd fled,
>   And mocked me as I wailed!"

Jesus is challenging us, "If thou knewest!" Do we know? Then we ask, and He will give the living water so that we shall be able to say,

> "I heard the voice of Jesus say,
>   Behold, I freely give
> The living water, thirsty one,
>   Stoop down and drink, and live.
>
> I came to Jesus, and I drank
>   Of that life-giving stream;
> My thirst was quenched, my soul revived,
>   And now I live in Him."

51. The Lamp of Prophecy

John v: 35.

THIS is a very remarkable parabolic illustration used by our Lord. The subject as announced, is intentional, for it marks the true theme and value, the lamp of prophecy. Peter described "the word of prophecy" as "a lamp shining in a dark place."

John was more than a prophet. We have our Lord's warrant for that statement. Said He to the people, "Wherefore went ye out? to see a prophet? Yea, I say unto you, and much more than a prophet. This is he of whom it is written.

> Behold, I send My messenger before Thy face,
> Who shall prepare Thy way before Thee."

So in that sense he was more than a prophet.

But he was distinctly a prophet, perfectly fulfilling in his public ministry, the prophetic office. We remember that Peter said on another occasion "To Him" that is to Christ, "give all the prophets witness." If that applies, as verily it does to all the prophets, the record of whose ministry and whose words we find in our Old Testament, it is perfectly true that all their prophesying found culmination in the ministry of John. He was the last of the long line of the Hebrew prophets, coming after a silence of four hundred years during which no authentic prophetic voice had been heard, Malachi having been the last. Yet in his message he gathered up all the foretelling, all the hopes and all the aspirations of those prophets who had given witness to the Christ. He was the forerunner, the immediate forerunner of the Christ, and therefore the culminating word of the long line of prophets.

In this way this illustration of our Lord applied specifically to him; "he was the lamp that burneth and shineth." We follow our usual custom and consider three matters. We enquire, What was the subject illustrated by our Lord. Then we will examine the figure itself; in order that we may deduce the abiding teaching.

Let it be said first of all that these words of verse 35 may be taken as parenthetical. By that I do not suggest that they are unimportant. He had been talking about John and at that point He said of him, "He was the lamp that burneth and shineth." What then was the occasion? What lies round about that statement? What had led our Lord to speak of John? It was a great occasion when He made a claim which the rulers understood in one way; when they had challenged Him as to His right to heal on the Sabbath day and make a man carry his mattress on the Sabbath day, He had made use of those tremendous words, "My Father worketh even until now, and I work." We are not considering their value in their setting, save to refer to it. They said He had made a man break Sabbath when He had restored a man to power to keep the Sabbath. When they said in effect, He was making a man break the Sabbath, He said, again in effect, God has no Sabbath while man suffers. What they understood Him to do was to make Himself equal with God, when He said "My Father worketh . . . and I work." They were quite right, but it stirred their anger, and they fain would have killed Him on what they conceived to be the ground of His blasphemy in making Himself equal with God.

Following that, we have His discourse, this wonderful message that He bore to them on His authority, on His relationship with God, on the fact that He was speaking by Divine authority, thus vindicating the claim He had made of being on an equality with God; and He sternly rebuked their unbelief. In the midst of this He referred to John. That then is where these words occur. John's ministry was well-known. The whole countryside had been influenced by it, and these men had gone with the multitudes to hear him. Jesus reminded them of that.

They had sent to John, and he had told them. Moreover they had rejoiced for a season in his ministry, in his light. Having said that to them, He pointed out to them how John His forerunner had borne witness to the truth when he had proclaimed Him. He reminded them they had listened for a while to John, and had rejoiced, and almost in an aside, He said of John. "He was the lamp that burneth and shineth."

So with all our knowledge of the ministry of John in mind, and our recognition of the fact that he fulfilled the prophetic office, and of what our Lord said of him, which was equally true, that of all who had exercised that office of the past, and of all who were to be called upon to exercise that office in coming days, here is the description of the prophetic office, "a burning and a shining lamp."

We come now to consider the figure in its deepest values. What was this figure Jesus used? The lamp. Scholars are all agreed in what may not be quite patent to the ordinary reader, that when Jesus used that word "the lamp," not a lamp, although that might quite well have been said; there was a great definiteness in it. So careful a scholar as Westcott emphasises the fact that Jesus was taking something quite familiar to them, that which they could see in any house; that the definite article, "the lamp" points to the familiar household object. That is the figure, that of the lamp burning. Our minds go wandering there helpfully. We remember that Jesus said, No man lights a lamp, or a candle, the same word, and puts it under a bushel. There He took the same figure. It is the ordinary, everyday figure of the lamp, shining in the house, and giving light.

Look at that lamp for a moment. We recognise first that it has no light in itself, but it is a centre of light, when the illuminating essence is supplied, and ignition takes place. It is always so. It is so even today with the lights round about us. It is very remarkable how underlying principles do not change. Of course when Jesus was talking the lamp was the light, with the wick and oil. I am old enough to remember that was the illumination in my home in boyhood, just a lamp, with wick and oil. But that lamp never lighted the house. Then I am still old enough to remember when the lamp was superseded by gas. They put in all the fittings, and some of them were fearfully and wonderfully made, brackets on the walls and chandeliers. But look at them, there is no light. The bracket and the burner give no light. Now the very homes who used that method, have electric light, and no one knows exactly what it is. What do we do? We wire our buildings, and put in fixtures, and bulbs, or something else, but there is no light in them. The lamps do not light the building. The light comes when some illuminating essence is supplied, and ignition takes place. In the old days ignition took place with the tinder box. The tinder was struck on flint until a spark smouldered, and you blew it, and touched the wick with it, and by that fire it became a centre of light. It is the same with the gas burner. The tap was turned on, and it was touched with fire, and the room was lit, the house was lit. Now we have gone beyond all that. We do not have to touch anything with fire ourselves. We do not have to put a match to the gas burner, but we just press a lever, and there is a flash somewhere of fire, and there is light. But there is no light in the lamp, gas burner, or bulb. Something more is wanted.

Still look at the lamp. What brings the light? Burning, always burning, always fire. There is no light apart from fire, from the sun to the wax vesta there must be burning. Burning in the case of the lamp with the wick and the oil, burning always means consuming. While it burns it is being consumed, and by the consuming of the oil, touched with fire upon the basis of the wick, light is given, and it is not consumed. If that consuming process fails, if it becomes overcharged with charcoal, or fails to supply the oil, the light is snuffed out. We must have burning, and burning means consuming. Whatever we see in a lamp is transitory. It is not going on all the time. Presently it will consume by itself, burning; and out goes the burning, shining.

But because burning, shining, and so illuminating, and always by the process of burning. That was our Lord's figure. Said He of John "He was the lamp that burneth and shineth." I would venture to suggest the introduction of a little word there. "He was the lamp that burneth and so shineth." There is no shining without burning; and any burning that does not issue in shining falls back into ashes, and the light ceases. John was the lamp that burned and shined.

The teaching deduced is so simple and on the surface that we do not tarry with it. Take it in the case of John. The greatness of his work, and the marvel of it, was not something done out of himself, but through himself, and all the influence he exerted in that marvellous ministry as the forerunner of Jesus was not the result of anything in himself. It was the result of an oil that was there, supplied to him. Here without being fanciful at all I take the figure employed in the Old Testament as the figure of the Holy Spirit. Yes, what a great work he did, what a marvellous work; but a work which was consuming, and therefore transitory, and must presently find its end. It did find its end. I am using the word in its true and beautiful sense. He burnt himself out into the essential light; and there was the greatness of his word at the end; "He must increase . . . I must decrease." Yes, he decreased; but Jesus our Lord tells us how he was burning, and therefore shining. That is the true function of the prophet.

It has been the function of the prophet in every age. Go back through the history of these marvellous prophets, those we call mistakenly major and minor, the prophetic utterances, and it is true that they were never self luminous. Their light was derivative. We hear them again and again as we study them saying, "Thus saith the Lord," and they were shining. They were lights in dark places; and indeed, the prophetic ministry is always characterised by darkness round about it. Apart from the darkness there is no call for the prophetic ministry. The prophet is always shining in a dark place; but he is shining because he is burning. He is being consumed, and in the consuming process light is shining and flashing everywhere. "To Him bare all the prophets witness." What high honour, and what grave responsibility. It is the responsibility of a lamp well trimmed, supplied with oil, burning; and there responsibility ends. The issue of the fulfilment of such responsibility in the prophetic office is always shining, the scattering of light upon the darkness.

In a familiar passage Peter said on the day of Pentecost, quoting one of those old Hebrew prophets Joel,

"And it shall be in the last days, saith God,
 I will pour forth of My Spirit upon all flesh;
 And your sons and your daughters shall prophesy,
 And your young men shall see visions,
 And your old men shall dream dreams;
 Yea and on My bond servants and on My bondmaidens in those days
 Will I pour forth of My Spirit; and they shall prophesy."

The gift of prophecy will fall upon all. That is what Joel foretold. That is what Peter claimed to be fulfilled. There was a day when men ran unto Moses and complained that certain were exercising a prophetic gift that were not as was supposed—to use a phrase not Biblical but modern—in regular orders. You remember what Moses said. "Would God that all the Lord's people were prophets." The centuries ran on and on, and the prophetic gift was being exercised to Malachi's time; and then silence for four hundred years, reborn in John; fulfilled in Jesus to the very ultimate limit of all truth, caught up by those whom He called and trained. And on the day of Pentecost the Spirit fell upon the whole assembly, not upon Peter and James and John and the twelve alone, but upon the sons and daughters, upon the bond-slaves and bondmaidens; and they were all prophesying. That is the great ideal.

How terribly we have lost it. But the fact remains. There is no Christian man or woman, a child of God by the marvel and supernatural wonder of the new birth but is called to prophecy. Prophecy is infinitely more than prediction. That is the smallest element in prophecy. It is forthtelling, it is the proclamation of the way and will of God about the past and the present, as well as about the future, and we are all called upon to be prophets. If we are to fulfil the prophetic office in any measure, we must be lamps burning, and so shining. We are lamps, no light in us, or of ourselves. The lamp may be very ornate, and the gas fitting very beautiful, and the electric fitting may be very charming; but they are no good in themselves. There must be the communication of the element of light, touched by fire into radiance; then the burning and the shining, a lamp in a dark place.

52. *The Bread of Life*

John vi: 35-58.

T HE VERSES 35-51 of this chapter in John are really not adequate.
At least the first 59 verses are required. It is preeminently a
chapter about bread. The Greek word *artos* occurs some 21 times. In
verses 11, 13 and 26 the rendering "loaves" is a translation of the same
word. That is simply a mechanical statement of the fact stamping the
nature of the chapter. All the vastness of the teaching given and implied
is beyond the purpose or possibility of this study. In our next study
we shall return to it, considering the figures of flesh and blood.
This subject of bread is related to that, for this is one great discourse.

We are now concerned with the parabolic illustration of bread, of
"the bread of life," which Jesus used upon this occasion. Taking our
usual method, what was the subject which He illustrated; secondly
what was the figure He employed; and consequently, what is the
teaching to be deduced from that meditation?

It is always important to know what our Lord was intending to
illustrate or illuminate. We bear in mind that bread had brought the
crowd together. The day before they had been supernaturally fed
with bread, literal, physical bread. The lad with the five loaves and
the two small fishes had been there; and Jesus had taken those five
loaves and had blessed them, and broken them, and multiplied them.

" 'Twas spring-time when He blessed the bread,
'Twas harvest when He brake."

So they had been fed. Because they had been supernaturally fed on
the previous day, the crowds had come together. That is what brought
them back. We are not unfair to them in saying that, because Jesus
said to them, in verse 26, "Ye seek Me, not because ye saw signs, but
because ye ate of the loaves, and were filled." They ate loaves yesterday, and they had come back today. Whereas it does not say so in so
many words, they hoped for another manifestation of power. They
did not take any cognizance of the sign it was intended to signify.

It was with this attitude Jesus was dealing when He made use of
this figure of speech. He said to them (ver. 27) "Work not for the
meat which perisheth, but for the meat which abideth unto eternal
life, which the Son of man shall give unto you for Him the Father,
even God, hath sealed." So He rebuked their materialism of effort. Do

not work for the meat which perishes. They had worked, some of them, pretty hard, in the hope of a meal that day. They had gone all round the lake. They had put out a good deal of effort to get there, to find Him. They did not want to understand. They were not seeking for interpretation. The sign did not appeal to them. The thing that brought them there was the fact of their full bellies yesterday. He rebuked that, and called them to another kind of effort, of output, of strength that resulted in the meat that did not perish, that would bring them to the place of meat that endureth to eternal life. That is the subject which our Lord was illustrating.

Now look at the figure in itself, bread, the bread of life. We are not touching the spiritual level yet; though in dealing with the figure of course we begin to see into the spiritual significance. Stay however with the figure. The bread of life was a common phrase. In verse 27 He referred to "meat." Here He referred to bread, "the bread of life." Meat of course was the familiar word, *Brosis,* which means food. It does not mean flesh, but all sorts of food. Do not put out your energy to obtain the food that perishes; but put out your energy to obtain the food that sustains the life which is eternal.

What was the meaning of this word bread? In that Eastern country in those times, and very largely today in that particular neighbourhood, bread as we understand it, made of meal, is primary food. It is always considered so. All other articles of food were looked upon as accessory; permissible, but unnecessary. Bread was the principal food, and was looked upon then as having a sanctity all its own. Go to the East today, and it will be found whether among Arabs, Jews, or other members of that land, they never tread under foot a piece of bread. However soiled it is, however smirched or contaminated, they never put their foot on it. An Arab walking down one of the highways, seeing a piece of bread would be careful not to put his foot on it. He would be careful to pick it up, and put it in a niche in the wall for the pariahs. The reason is because there is still a great and peculiar sense of the element of sacredness in bread, because it comes from God. That is true of the East, where Jesus was speaking, and of the thinking of the people to whom He was speaking. Bread stood for necessary food.

In Genesis 3:10 we find it said, "In the sweat of thy face shalt thou eat bread." That did not merely mean an article of food made out of barley or wheat meal; but it meant food; and from there, all the way through the word bread refers to food generally. So it does here. The emphasis is laid upon that peculiar food which was the general source of sustenance in the East. Its sanctity was always remembered, because of its symbolism in the East.

Bread always stood for hospitality and for fellowship; and men in the East broke bread with one another, the one providing it offering hospitality, and those partaking, were united in fellowship. While we are not yet dealing with the spiritual things, they are shining through. Our Lord used a figure of speech. They had referred to the manna, and He had taken it up and dealt with food.

Again, "bread of life"; and still staying in the realm of the figure, what is this? What is the word for life there? It is the Greek word *zoe*, not *pneuma*, spirit; not *psuche*, the mind, but *zoe*, that is, the vital principle; life reduced to its simplest terms, and to its simplest fact. We read "eternal life," and the word is always the same, *zoe*. Here is a wonderful fact that in the teaching of our Lord, and that of all His apostles, they took hold of the word *zoe* and lifted it on to a higher plane than it then occupied in the thinking of men. The Greek word meant life, human life, as well as the life of the lion, and of the mouse. That is the word here, "the bread of life"; the vital principle in our human race, which constitutes the race as differentiated from races. We talk about the Anglo-Saxon race. Where did we really come from? Many races are represented here. For the time being we call ourselves British so as to cover all the English, Scotch, Welsh, and Irish. That is a race. Cross the Channel, and we find races, and they are very different; but the differences are all physical or mental, not spiritual. The vital principle is the same, whether Teuton, or Aryan, or Semetic, or what-not! The bread of life is its sustenance, which maintains the life principle.

It is wonderful how we can change and reduce some of the things at which we have been looking today. Food, what are the things we really need? Protein, carbohydrate, fat. In recent years we have added another—vitamins. We never heard of these when I was young, but they were still there, and they were very important in the forming of bone. The figure our Lord used was the bread of life, food, that sustains vitality.

Our Lord said, "I am the Bread of life," and the claim is very significant, being the first of the great "I ams" that John has recorded for us. There are eight occasions upon which our Lord took the great name of God as revealed to Moses at the burning bush. Then as though the revelation could not be made, it had recoiled upon itself, and reasserted itself in august and dreadful majesty, "I AM, THAT I AM." So God spake to Moses. He had asked, "Tell me, what is Thy name?" For many years the great declaration was left in all its majestic splendour; and Jesus came and took hold of it, and linked it to simple symbols that men might understand. This is the first, "I am the Bread of life."

The figure too is interesting in relation to the necessities of life. When considering the subject of the living water we said that the three essential things to life were breath, water, and food. A man can live forty days without food; and about seven days without water. He cannot live seven minutes without breath. John in bringing the story before us has led us over the ground in which we have seen Him meeting these essentials. In the third chapter, when talking to Nicodemus He spoke of breath. The wind bloweth where it listeth. So the Spirit. In chapter four He made the promise to the woman of water, living water, springing up. Now here we reach food, absolutely essential to life. We come along the line of illustration by that gradation;—breath, water, food.

Necessarily therefore, having looked at the figure, we are bound to face the essential teaching. When Jesus said, "I am the Bread of life," He was facing the hunger of man in his essential life which is not physical, which is not mental, but which is spiritual. Human life is essentially spiritual. Do not take that word spiritual, and make it mean good and holy and true. It does not necessarily mean anything of the kind. It refers to essential nature. It may be false and untrue in its activities; but the essence of human life is spirit. To quote once more. When Paul was on Mars' Hill he said God had made of one every nation to dwell upon the face of the earth. We have the word there, "one blood." That is perfectly true. Submitted to chemical analysis, there is no difference between the blood of the negro and the blood of the white man. But Paul did not say that. The essential oneness of humanity is not in its blood, nor in its mentality, but in its spiritual nature. Get down underneath the physical, the glorious sacramental method of revealing the spirit, and receiving in the spiritual consciousness; and get underneath the mental, the processes of thought; what is it that is thinking, or doing, that looks through the eyes, and listens through the ears? The spiritual thing; and that is what Christ is speaking of. He is addressing the hunger that lies in the human heart.

This great theme cannot be dealt with adequately. It can only be done suggestively. Is man hungry today, in his deepest life? He is, and there are three great proofs of that hunger.

The first is the quest for God; the second is the search for man; and the third is the struggle against sin. These things are universal. They are not confined to one race; they are racial.

The quest for God is universal. All idolatries witness to the fact that the human heart is feeling after and knowing God. The human search for man is equally a revelation of human hunger. Man's quest for individuality, personality in its perfection and realisation. So many of these eternal truths are sobbing and sighing through the writings of men, and the thinkings of men without their understanding them. All the struggle we read about, all the attempts, all the high aspirations to make men fit. What do we mean by being fit? Think it through, this quest of men for fitness, and the quest for man in his social relationships and international relationships. First the quest for God, and then the search for man; and always resultantly, the struggle against sin. We may change the word if we will. Struggle against failure, against imperfection; the consciousness that we have missed the mark; that is the word for sin in the New Testament. Humanity everywhere is missing the mark, and man everywhere is against it. I am not talking about his folly, his foolishness, his wickedness, his rebellion. I am speaking of his hunger, and that hunger proves his quest for God, his search for man, and his struggle against sin.

But hunger is not bread, though it declares the need for it. Therefore hunger never becomes bread. The quest for God never means the finding of God. The search for man never means the realization of the meaning of humanity. The struggle against sin never brings victory over it. Hunger never becomes bread. Unless bread be found, hunger issues in death, inevitably and invariably. Christ stood confronting all this, and He said, "I am the Bread of life," a statement of august majesty; "I am the living bread," I am the bread that has come down out of heaven for men.

Think for a moment, what does He do? Man is engaged in the quest for God, Christ reveals God. Man is engaged in a search after man. He interprets man, and shows man what man really is. Man in rebellion against sin, failure, whatever he calls it, struggling against sin, He comes to save from sin, to break its power, wipe out its pollution, and the profound reason why, He is the bread of life. God is seen confronting humanity, and bringing within its reach that which shall satisfy all its hunger, end its quest in victory; answer its search in a perfect revelation, and deliver it from its paralysis and pollution in sin and power. So Christ says, "I am the Bread of life."

We are Christian men and women. Do we believe that? Have we proved it? Do we know that He is the Bread of life to our souls? Can we truthfully say,

"Thou, O Christ, art all I want."

All hunger satisfied, God found, man interpreted, sin mastered? If we can, then keep the discourse in connection with the physical miracle, and do not forget that when Jesus fed those people, how He had done it. He had asked and had obtained bread from a lad, through His disciples; and He had said to those disciples, in the presence of that hungry crowd, physically, "Give ye them to eat." They brought to Him what they had, which was absolutely inadequate to meet the need of the hungry crowd. He took it. He blessed it. He brake it. They carried it. So the hungry crowds were fed. He is still saying, "I am the Bread of life," "Give ye them to eat."

53. Flesh and Blood

John vi: 53-58.

OUR LORD's use of the terms "flesh and blood" in parabolic illustration is admittedly startling. So it appeared to many of His disciples at the time. John tells us that "Many therefore of His disciples when they heard this, said, This is a hard saying, who can hear it?" The word "hard" there had a very definite significance, which is hardly conveyed by our translation. The Greek word *skleros* means rough, in the sense of being objectionable. We really get nearer to what the disciples said if we substitute that word. "This is an objectionable saying, who can hear it?"

Moreover the use of the figure was divisive. It created a crisis. It was a climax definitely in the course of our Lord's ministry. As we have said, John records, "Upon this many of His disciples went back, and walked no more with Him." It is quite evident that what He said was of a very startling nature, greatly mystifying those who heard it and even His disciples listening very much upon the surface of things, said, This is too much, this is a hard saying; this is a rough saying. This looks foolish. Indeed they were so much offended, many of them, that they went back, never to return to Him. It was a divisive word.

To us also it does remain a startling illustration. While not entering into any controversy such as has gathered around this saying of Jesus, suffice it for us to dismiss the idea that this saying of our Lord has anything to do with what we call the Holy Communion. It has been applied in that way largely by certain theologians of whom we speak with respect, but from whom we profoundly differ. Our Lord was not referring to the Communion here at all, not even in a secondary sense. But seeing that a great deal of controversy has waged around this saying through the running years of theological consideration, at least it behoves us to consider this carefully, and pray for the help of the Spirit to an understanding of what our Lord really meant.

So taking our usual method, we consider first, what was the subject He intended to illustrate, for it was an illustration. Secondly we pause with the figure itself, which He employed. Necessarily therefore from that consideration of the subject and figure we proceed to deduce the teaching which He gave.

What was the occasion upon which our Lord made use of these figures? They were connected with the discussion which has run through this sixth chapter on the subject of bread. We have considered that wonderful figure of speech, "the bread of life," and that Christ claimed He was the Bread of life. This follows on directly. The bread of life is the sustenance of life, the food of life; and Christ said He was that bread. Now therefore, whatever He says about flesh and blood here, He said in close connection with that subject of bread, and must be concerned with the same theme, that namely, of the sustenance of life. So much for the occasion.

What was He illustrating? Again we can gather into a brief sentence the answer to that enquiry. The intended revelation of the flesh and blood was that of how man could partake of the living bread, "I am the bread of life," "I am the living bread which came down out of heaven; if any man eat of this bread, he shall live for ever; yea and the bread which I will give is My flesh, for the life of the world." How can men receive that bread of life? By eating His flesh and drinking His blood.

That brings us at once to the figure. Once again we admit the startling nature of it. Let us pause with it as a figure of speech merely, flesh and blood.

The word employed for flesh here is a very familiar one to readers of the New Testament Greek, the word *sarx*. It is used in differing ways and forms; and it caught a distinctly theological sense, and was used oftentimes in that way by the apostles, by Paul especially in his writings. But get behind all that to the word. What is the flesh? It is the material side of personality, the body as differentiated from the spirit. Yet when that body is dead it is no longer flesh. Flesh demands that life be there; but it is pre-eminently personality embodied;—flesh.

What is the significance of blood? However much the disciples may have been shocked as they listened to our Lord, we all know the sanctity of blood according to the whole of the Hebrew teaching under which the disciples had been brought up. We can summarize it all in one word, simple, sublime and final, in the Old Testament; "the blood is the life." We are still in the realm of the body, and yet the blood, in its mysterious and mighty work within the body, is the element of life. Have we anything the matter with us? It can be diagnosed quite simply, our blood is not acting properly, there is some clot or hindrance. The blood is the life. It is also material, on this level; the flesh and blood.

But now notice another thing. We must get back into the atmosphere of the time. The separation of one from the other in this statement implies death. If the blood be taken away from the flesh, that means death, always. "My flesh, My blood." Mark well the inevitable strangeness of this statement of Jesus to listening Jews; and for us immediately it is evident that we cannot stay in the realm of the figure. We cannot go any further in that direction, and we must immediately seek the spiritual intention that Jesus had. I am warranted in saying that because of what He said to these very disciples. When they said it was a hard saying, He told them, "It is the spirit that quickeneth; the flesh profiteth nothing; the words that I have spoken unto you are spirit, and are life." The true sustenance of life is flesh. He said that is "meat indeed," that is truly food. His blood is "drink indeed," that is, truly drink. Remembering the words He uttered are spirit, He is dealing with the essential nature of man, the essential hunger of man; with the essential necessity of man as to sustenance is true spiritual life. He has used figures in the realm of the material. He passes from that at once and says the flesh profits nothing, that He had spoken of the spirit; that they had to do with the essential life of the spirit.

Then He used the figure, "My flesh." How may we reverently interpret that word? I do so by going back to the beginning of the Gospel, and looking once more at that marvellous prologue that John wrote. "The Word became flesh." "He that eateth My flesh"; and the spiritual intention must inevitably be that He was referring to the whole fact of His incarnation, as placed at the disposal of humanity; the bread that will meet that hunger and satisfy their need; the eating of His flesh.

Then "His blood," necessarily as shed, necessarily as given up; and consequently as life liberated through death. Again He used a figure that shocked His disciples. They said it was rough, objectionable. But He had taken that figure, "Eat the flesh of the Son of man, and drink His blood." I will dare to put it in another form. He that appropriates for himself My nature, the nature which is here because God is incarnate, and the Word has become flesh, he that appropriates that nature; he that drinks of My blood, is he that appropriates the value coming through the fact that the blood was shed, the value of atonement and redemption. "He that eateth My flesh and drinketh My blood."

Listen to Paul. He was writing to the Galatians. "I have been crucified with Christ; yet I live; and yet no longer I, but Christ liveth in me; and that life which I now live in the flesh I live in faith, the faith which is in the Son of God, Who loved me, and gave Himself up for me." Once more let us take those words of Paul, not attempting to improve upon them, for that cannot be, but let us take them in this sense. I have eaten of the flesh of the Lord Christ. I have become a partaker of His nature. The very life I now live, I live in faith. It is His life in me, dominant, regnant. I have appropriated the wonder and the mystery of the incarnation by faith in Him. Whatever there is in His life of purity, of holiness, of excellence, of beauty is mine.

The apostle was not claiming he was fully realizing it, because when he wrote to the Philippians he said, I have not yet attained, I am not perfect; but one thing I do, I press toward the mark of the prize of the high calling, whatever the attainment. There was the possession of the very nature of Christ. He had eaten of the flesh. He had partaken of the incarnation, and he was hungry no more, and the element of life was there. But he had also appropriated the value of His death, and that means first of all the cessation of all attempt at self-culture. Is not the Church of God losing sight of that today? On every hand today we are called to be Christians on the ground of seeking self-culture; and we are not accepting our relationship to Christ as a gift of grace at the foot of the Cross, the bestowment that comes to us, that can only come through the shedding of the blood of the Son of God.

Yet that is what Paul meant; and in the Philippian letter he also said, "For to me to live is Christ, and to die is gain."

These are figures of speech, so startling that the disciples, many of them said they were hard, rough and uncouth; figures of speech which immediately merge into the infinite realm, upon the wonder of the incarnation by which God can and has put at the disposal of sinning, failing, ruined man a power, not merely a pattern, but a power; and through death, and the shedding of blood has put at the disposal of man burdened, a pardon and a cleansing, as well as a power.

So he that eats of the flesh, and drinks of the blood, he is a partaker of the nature of Christ in incarnation, which includes the Deity as well as the humanity; that is what Peter meant when he said we are made partakers of the Divine nature. He who has reposed his trust in Him, and received that, has eaten of His flesh; and he that reposes his trust in the mystery of Christ's shed blood, has drunk of His blood; and that is meat indeed, and that is drink indeed.

When Paul was writing to the Corinthians he said something in this connection. "And He died for all, that they which live should no longer live unto themselves, but unto Him Who for their sakes died and rose again. Wherefore we henceforth know no man after the flesh." And then the amazing thing, "Even though we have known Christ after the flesh, yet now we know Him so no more." Through the figure we have entered into the fact. Through that which brought Him into the presence of humanity familiarly for a generation, or for only three years perchance in public ministry, through that we have entered into fellowship with Him in the deepest things of His nature. "Wherefore if any man is in Christ, he is a new creation; the old things are passed away; behold, they are become new."

So we go back and end with these words of our Lord spoken on that occasion, resolutely determined to keep them close to this whole chapter, and to interpret the figures by the great statement. "It is the spirit that quickeneth; the flesh profiteth nothing; the words that I have spoken unto you are spirit, and are life." In the realm of our spiritual nature, if we trust Him, believe in Him, yield to Him, we are made partakers of His nature, we eat His flesh, and we appropriate all the mystery of His atonement, symbolized by the shedding of blood; and we drink His blood.

54. Rivers

John vii: 37-39.

THE PARABOLIC illustration upon which our attention is fixed now is that of "rivers." Those of "thirst" and "living water" have already come under review in the story of the Samaritan woman in the fourth chapter. Necessarily however we must bear these in mind as they recur in this passage, for they have distinct bearing upon the present study of "rivers." For the quenching of thirst by living water, the supply is referred to here by our Lord under the figure of rivers.

It will at once be recognized that rivers suggest plentifulness; not a running brook, not even a river, but rivers. Such was the figure which our Lord employed.

Following our regular custom, we ask first, what was the subject our Lord was intending to illustrate when He used the figure? Secondly, what is this figure? How are we to understand it as a figure? Necessarily from those two lines of preliminary thought, we consider the great teaching.

Here we are face to face with something perhaps a little unusual, and yet full of value. In other considerations we have had to enquire what was our Lord intending to illustrate by the use of that particular figure. In this case we have no need to ask that question. We are in no doubt in this case, because this figure of speech was immediately followed in the narrative of John, by exposition. This is stated in verse 39, "This spake He of the Spirit, which they that believed on Him were to receive; for the Spirit was not yet given; because Jesus was not yet glorified."

This is an arresting fact. Here we find our Lord saying, "If any man thirst, let him come unto Me, and drink. He that believeth on Me, as the scripture hath said, out of his belly shall flow rivers of living water." There we have our figure of rivers of living water. Well, what did He mean? "This spake He of the Spirit . . . for the Spirit was not yet given." In the MSS there is no word following "yet." Nothing perhaps can be better than the word that has been supplied by our translators; for the word "given" is for our English understanding. But the text says, "The Spirit was not yet," and evidently the reference was to the Spirit in all His fulness. So the added word helps us. "The Spirit was not yet given"; because Jesus was not yet glorified. That was His subject, in the light of that inspired interpretation of the purpose of the illustration. He was speaking of the Holy Spirit. He was looking forward to a new giving of the Spirit, which undoubtedly at the moment had not been granted, neither was it granted until Pentecost.

Later on in His life He spoke to His disciples of the coming of the Spirit, and spoke of it as the promise of the Father, which said He, He will send unto you. Here He was looking on in His own work, looking on to the ultimate in His own work, the coming of the Spirit in a new way, and in new measure. We cannot read the Old Testament without coming into the presence of the Spirit. We see the Son in the beginning of our Bible, the Word, and the Spirit of God brooding upon the face of the chaos. But His coming to man was spasmodic and occasional. Now there was to be a new sense in which the Spirit was to be given to abide, to remain; as Jesus said later, to be with His own, and in His own.

If we can get back into the mind of the Lord, it is evident from this word of interpretation, He was looking on to that giving of the Spirit; and John has told us why that had not been done, and why that Spirit had not been given in that new sense. Why not? "The Spirit had not yet been given, because Jesus was not yet glorified."

We are halted again. What did He mean by His being glorified? Read again the twelfth chapter of John, and then read the seventeenth, words uttered by our Lord to His disciples, and in the other case words uttered by the Lord to His Father. There we find what is meant by the glorification of Jesus. We may summarize it thus. The glorification of Jesus came when He was lifted on the Cross, out of the earth. When He was lifted out of the earth, above it, He triumphed over it. "Now is the judgment of this world; now shall the prince of this world be cast out. And I, if I be lifted up out of the earth, will draw all men unto Myself." The way of His glorification was the way of His Cross, and that which inevitably followed the Cross, the resurrection. If there was no physical resurrection we are the biggest fools in the universe. If the resurrection is going to be left a subject for doubt, then we are in a perilous state. The glorification was the Cross and the uplifting and the ascension. Then He gave the Spirit.

Here we find Him on this occasion, on the last day of the feast. We are led through that word in interpretation to look through His eyes to what was in front of Him, and the end was the giving of the Spirit; and the way was His Cross, His resurrection, His ascension, His glorifying.

With all that in view, He said, "If any man thirst, let him come unto Me, and drink. He that believeth on Me, as the scripture hath said, out of his belly shall flow rivers of living water. But this spake He of the Spirit." We stay for a few moments with the figure itself, the flowing of the rivers. It is an old story with which every Bible student is familiar. It is important to recognize it was said on the last day. It should be kept in mind that there is a good deal of local colour concerning the story which it is helpful for us to see.

The feast of tabernacles lasted for eight days, seven days and one other, completing the octave. At the time of our Lord's ministry they had superadded to the ritual observed in connection with that feast; and it was a very symbolic and suggestive thing they had done. Every day during that feast there was a procession of priests who carrying some of the golden vessels on their shoulders empty, marched through the streets from the Temple, singing parts of the Great

Hallel, that is, Psalms 113-118. Then they filled those vessels with water, most probably at the running brook of Kedron. The procession then reformed with the vessels filled, and they marched back, still chanting parts of the Great Hallel, and there in the Temple courts in the presence of the assembled worshippers, they poured the water out of the golden vessels.

What did they mean by it? We have rabbinical interpretation. The carrying of the water was symbolical of two things. First the fact that they had been in the wilderness, and God had miraculously supplied them with water over a period of years; and then the fact that when they came into the land, they no longer needed the supernatural supply, because there were springs and rivers everywhere in the land. The feast of tabernacles celebrated the entry into the land, and rejoiced that water had been provided in the wilderness, now no longer necessary. But, said the rabbis, the ritual signified more. It intimated the recognition of promises made to the people of a day that should come when there should be new fertilizing powers sweeping over the nation and the land, and for seven days they repeated this ceremony.

Now on the eighth day there was no procession of priests. The absence, said the rabbis, signified first there was no need for the supernatural supply of water as they had had in the wilderness, but it was also intended to signify that the long hoped for promise of the new dispensation of fruitfulness and rededication had not dawned.

On the last day, the great day, when there was no procession and carrying of the water, Jesus stood and He said, "If any man thirst, let him come to Me, and drink. He that believeth on Me . . . out of his inner life shall flow rivers of living water." This He spoke of the Spirit, and He employed this figure of living waters in that connection. He said, "As the scripture hath said." A great deal has been written about that. Follow all through the Old Testament the figure of rivers. The first occasion is in the second chapter of Genesis, where we are told God planted a garden, and there went forth rivers. That is a figure of speech? No, it is a historical fact, rivers to water the garden.

We go on, all through the literature, and we find that psalmists and prophets are constantly using the figures of rivers illustratively. These rivers proceeded forth, somehow, and in some way from God. We find too that the supreme Old Testament passage concerning the rivers is in Ezekiel chapter 47, that marvellous passage, out of which I take one sentence only. "Everything shall live whithersoever the river cometh." "If any man thirst, let him come unto Me and drink. He that believeth on Me, out of his inner life shall flow the rivers." Everything shall live where those rivers come.

Rivers therefore are always suggestive of life, and in life in two ways, the satisfaction of life in its thirst; and secondly, the fructifying of all life, that it may bring forth a harvest. That cannot be repeated too often. There He stood. John particularly said, He stood. On another occasion He did not stand, but sat. While that does not mean very much to us today, it meant much in an Eastern land. When teaching He always sat, as the teachers all did. But when He was proclaiming as a herald He stood; and on this occasion, as the feast of tabernacles was drawing to its conclusion, and its ritual was ceasing, and all its suggestiveness was passing away, He stood. "If any man thirst, let him come unto Me, and drink."

Who is he that believes on Him? The man that thirsts, and that thirsting soul who comes to Him and drinks, that is the man who believes.

Have you believed in Jesus? I do not care about the creed just now. Do you believe in Him? That is the first question. How are you to know? How am I to know? Ask yourself this; have I come to Him, and taken Him to quench my thirst? Can I say,

> "I came to Jesus, and I drank,
>   Of that life-giving stream,
>   My thirst was quenched, my soul revived,
>   And now I live in Him."

Can you say that? Very well, that is preliminary. He that does that, he that believes on Him, what will the result be? Out of his inner life shall flow the rivers.

The great teaching here is this, that the life-giving Spirit is to proceed to humanity through humanity. He comes from God. He comes because Jesus has been glorified; but if He is to pass on into human life, if He is to come bringing life wherever He comes, this river of the Spirit of God, renewing, regenerating, reviving, uplifting everything, how is He to come? Through you, through me, through human means. He that believes, out of his inner life shall flow the rivers. The great thing, the master thing is just that the life-giving Spirit which this moribund, if not already dead world needs, that life-giving Spirit which is to pass over—to quote Ezekiel—the marshy places and make them bright and beautiful and fruitful, the world will get that through believers in Jesus. "He that believeth on Me, out of his inner life shall flow the rivers."

That necessarily drives us back where we were. Who are they that believe on Him? Those who have come to Him, and have had their own thirst quenched, those who know what it means to have received the gift of the living water, that has become in them a well of water, springing up, laughing up, bubbling up, for ever springing, beautifying, satisfying. Those are the people.

There are two things of supreme importance. No rivers ever flow from the lives of thirsty men and women. I wonder if that ought to be amended, and put thus. The proportion in which the rivers continuously flow is the proportion in which we have ceased to be thirsty.

"Thou, O Christ, art all I want."

Men and women, is that true? What are you thirsty for? Are you thirsty still? As we reminded ourselves in considering the fourth chapter,

"We tried the broken cisterns, Lord,
    And Oh, those waters failed
And as we stooped to drink, they fled,
    And mocked us as they wailed."

That applies to all earthly attempts to satisfy the deep thirst of the human soul.

Have we got beyond that? Let us ask our own souls, Are we satisfied? Because unless we are, no rivers are flowing from our lives. We may be good men and women, doing good things, but the running rivers are not there. The influence we are exerting is not that of the Spirit, because the effluence, the incoming of the Spirit has not been what it ought to be. No rivers run from thirsty souls.

Take the same statement, and turn it round. There is no thirst when the rivers are running. No rivers if we are still thirsty. No thirst? Then the rivers are running.

55. *Light*

John viii: 12.

THIS is the second of the great "I am" claims of our Lord recorded by John. There are eight such found in his Gospel. Three of them are essential. Five of them are illustrative. This is the second such. We have considered the first, "I am the bread of life." This like the first centres upon the Lord Himself. Sometimes He took some parabolic illustration from Nature; but here this is a direct claim, "I am the light of the world."

Necessarily we link this claim with the Person, and with the deepest truth concerning Himself. John opens his Gospel, linking verses 1 and 14, "In the beginning was the Word, and the Word was with God, and the Word was God; and the Word became flesh, and tabernacled among us . . . full of grace and truth." That is the One Who is now speaking, "I am the light of the world."

Still by way of introduction, to go further back, to the book of Exodus, to that wonderful third chapter, in which after forty years in the wilderness Moses was called of God to a very definite position and occupation. Shrinking quite naturally from the tremendous task that was suggested to him, he asked God that question, "Tell me, what is Thy name?" According to the record the answer is in that marvellous passage. The great declaration of God recoiled upon itself, and repeats the affirmation, "I am that I am." That was His name, His memorial name. The centuries passed on, and by that name His people knew Him. Then there came a day when there stood One Who "was made flesh"; and He took the name uttered in the burning bush, and on five occasions He linked it with simple and sublime symbols. "I am the bread of life," and now "I am the light of the world."

Following our usual practice in these studies, we consider first the subject He was illustrating when He said this; secondly the figure that He employed; finally deducing the permanent teaching resulting from the use of the figure, under those circumstances.

What made Jesus say at that point, "I am the light of the world?" Taking it out of its setting, it still stands in the revelation of the New Testament concerning Jesus. Under any circumstance we can imagine Him saying it. It would always have been typically true. But in order to our understanding, it is well to ask ourselves, Why did He say this then? We must see the background in order to understand His claim in itself. In chapter seven we have the account of His presence at the feast of tabernacles, where He made His great claim of ability to quench the thirst of humanity; and His great proclamation that if any should believe on Him, they should become sources of blessing, men and women from whom the rivers of living water should flow. Now immediately following that claim there ensued discussion and division among the people, and among the rulers. It was in the presence of that discussion on the following day that He made use of these words, and it was closely linked with that claim, to that proclamation and discussion.

Note carefully how the eighth chapter opens. The story runs on. There is no break. The Revisers have taken the last verse of the seventh chapter, and have printed it closely connected with the eighth, with a gap between the 52nd and 53rd verses. There should be no gap there at all. If a gap is made, it should be at the end of the first verse of chapter eight. The story really runs on. At the end of the discussion, "They answered and said unto him" (that is Nicodemus) "Art thou also of Galilee?" Mark their contempt. "Search, and see that out of Galilee ariseth no prophet." That ended it for the day publicly. They dispersed. Where did they go? "And they went every man unto his own house; but Jesus went unto the mount of Olives." That is the natural ending of the seventh chapter.

It then begins again, "And early in the morning He came again into the temple." They went home. They had homes to go to. He had none. He went to the mount of Olives. I do not know what He did in the mount of Olives that night. From His habit I think He spent it in communion; but notice that early in the morning He came back into those temple courts, "And all the people came unto Him; and He sat down and taught them." In the twentieth verse we read, "These words spake He in the treasury, as He taught in the temple." That brings the scene back to mind. He had been in the mount of Olives all through the night. They had gone home and gone to rest, the people, but they were back there in the temple precincts in the morning, and He came early to the temple, made His way into the treasury, where He was when He saw the widow casting in the two mites; and He sat down and taught them.

We have no account of what He said. At the feast of tabernacles He had stood and cried. That was the attitude of the herald. Now He took up the position of a teacher. He had come back to carry on among these people His wondrous teaching.

Then follows in the record this little paragraph, the story of the woman. I affirm my conviction that this is a true story, and that it took place here at this time. Probably John did not write that story. Reading the Greek New Testament in Westcott and Hort's text, this is put in at the end of the Gospel. It was so important that it could not be left out altogether. Nestle's text has put it back here, but has put it in within brackets. It might be proven that this little story was put in by Papias, that marvellous extra-illustrator, who later added stories of Jesus, and inserted them. But let that go. He sat down and taught, and I think He was interrupted by the bringing of this woman. We are not dealing with the story now.

At the twelfth verse we read, "Again therefore Jesus spake unto them." It is the resumption of teaching, broken in upon. He had been interrupted by these scribes and this woman. When that was over, and He had dismissed that crowd in a regal way, with august authority, when in the midst of that crowd of accusers and accused had shone a light that was appalling, searching into the deep recesses of the souls of the accusers, and shining into the darkened soul of the woman; then He went on. "Again therefore Jesus spake unto them, saying, I am the light of the world: he that followeth Me shall not walk in the darkness, but shall have the light of life."

This statement is so marvellous from the standpoint of the occasion. The significant word in that statement is "therefore." Why "therefore"? We may read it, and not notice it. We must go back and link it with the darkness that was all round about them, evidenced in the religious rulers and the people concerning God; by the attitude and activity of the accusers of the woman; darkness that was evident in the story of the woman herself. Because of this atmosphere, because of the discussions and the divisions, revealing the darkness in which men were living, therefore He said, "I am the light of the world."

The subject therefore illustrated was that of how the darkness might be banished, and men might see clearly the truth and the way in which to go. "I am the light of the world."

Notice now the figure employed. This is a most fascinating theme. In the old days at school they taught what they called Physics. It had a threefold division, Sound, Light, and Heat. The word here He used for light is common in the New Testament, as common as our word light is; the word *Phos* was common to the people who heard Jesus. Our word light exactly conveys the meaning of that word He used. *Phos* is derived from a word that means to shine, in order to make manifest. *Phao* is the verb.

What is light? Take it and examine it by spectrum analysis, and we discover at once light is a simple thing, and a vastly sublime thing. So the figure He made use of here I do not hesitate to say is very simple, so that every boy who perchance was in the temple courts, or youth near by, seeing the light all about them in the early morning, would understand and see. But examine it. Some say that light consists of seven primary colours, red, orange, yellow, green, blue, indigo, violet. Strictly however there are only three primary colours, red, blue and yellow. All the others result from some combination of red, blue and yellow. I remember the thrill that came to me as a boy with my first box of paints, I discovered one day, quite by accident that if I took a bit of beautiful blue and glorious yellow, I had the most radiant green. And so on. Light is a composite of all these, and they are brought into one, the red and blue and yellow.

But how is it accounted for? There is an interesting subject, how in the last century the great discovery was made about light. To go back earlier than that, the thinkers were under the mastery of Sir Isaac Newton. He had said that light was minute particles projected at great velocity from luminous bodies; that is that light was caused by the projection into the ether by a vast velocity, terrific force of corpuscles or atoms from the sun and stars. Men believed that for a long time. But at the beginning of the nineteenth century they discovered that the true explanation is that light is undulation. That is to say, it is caused by waves, in an all pervading elastic medium, and the colour depends upon the length of rays. Red is the longest. I have been fascinated in the study of this. Light is a wondrous thing.

Then I sought for some definition of light, and I found two. Light has been defined by one of the great masters as "radiant energy." The undulatory waves are there, beating through the ether; but it is radiant, and it is energy. I found something simpler still, and we see the accuracy of this through what lies behind it. Light is "the agent by which objects are rendered visible." Everybody knows that. Light is energy, and its sublimity is discovered. Movement all round the world. Sound, tone is created when the movement is so subtle that sight could not see or grasp it. But it is the same thing. In a picture gallery we see the tone of that picture. We say, we like the tone of that organ. The tone of the picture and the tone of the music. It is the same thing— undulation. The mystery and the marvel of it, but the simplicity of it. I like the last statement, "the agent by which objects are rendered visible." Wherever we see them there is visibility, and always beauty. Visibility, we see it, but colour is beauty in light. The Son of God never uttered a more marvellous word than when He said, in the midst of all the prevailing darkness, "I am the light of the world." What infinite music of eternal vibration, in order to revelation and visibility and beauty was contained in His claim, "I am the light of the world."

We have still got our Bible, and I was glad to get back to it from all these other sayings and readings. I did the old-fashioned thing, and said, Where does light emerge in the Bible, and where does it pass out? It is found right at the beginning, "And God said, Let there be light; and there was light," light became, to translate more literally the Hebrew. That is where it came in.

We go to the other end of the Book, and we look at a city, all bathed in translucent light, and we read this, "There shall be night no more; and they need no light of lamp, neither light of sun; for the Lord God shall give them light; and they shall reign for ever and ever." That is the last place in the Bible where the word is found. We see from the beginning, all through the Literature there are constant allusions to light, and light falling upon human lives.

"Send out Thy light, send out Thy truth that they may lead me." "God is a sun and shield," all the way through light.

"Jesus said therefore, I am the light of the world," the light of the cosmos. That is the word here. Not of the age, but of the cosmos. Immediately we are pulled up. What is meant by the cosmos? That word is used in varied applications. It is used of the whole framework of the universe, the cosmos; and it is sometimes used of man, all men, the sum totality of humanity. It is sometimes used of the way in which man orders his life. The root idea is order, the cosmos is the order. Christ says, "I am the light." "I am the light of," that is, I am the light for, I am the light in the midst of the cosmos. Use the word as you will, the word cosmos; I am the light in the midst of the universe, with all its far flung distances. I am the light in the sum totality of humanity. I am the light revealing the true order, the way in which man should go. Said Jesus, I am the Revealer and the Interpreter of the cosmos.

A little later on He was talking to His disciples, and He said, "I am the way, and the truth, and the life." So He is the light about the Universe. He is the light about humanity. He is the light about the true order of life. Go back to that first definition of radiant energy, the light that is also pure, shining in the darkness, bringing energy, and revealing the true meaning of all things; the light of the cosmos.

Then the value of the claim is revealed in the immediately following declaration; but mark its sublimity. There is no need to dwell upon it. "I am the light of the world. He that followeth Me shall not walk in the darkness, but shall have the light of life."

We conclude this meditation by reminding ourselves of the challenging word that fell from the lips of Jesus on other occasions, when He said to His disciples, "Ye are the light of the world." In that same connection there He said, "Even so let your light shine before men, that they may see your good works, and glorify your Father which is in heaven." What a challenging word. I love it, and do not desire to interpret it, but apply it. "I am the light of the world." "Ye are the light of the world."

One more reference to the incident at the beginning of the chapter. See the light when He lifted Himself up and said to that group of accusing men, He among you that is sinless, let him first cast a stone at her. Down in the darkened secret of their lives the light flashed, and they could not bear it, and they turned and went out from the eldest of them to the youngest. See the light shed upon that woman, into her heart. He knew her. He knew all the circumstances. "Where are thine accusers? Did no man condemn thee?" "No man, Lord." "Neither do I condemn thee." He showed her the possibilities, "Go thy way, no longer continue in sin." "Again therefore Jesus said, I am the light of the world."

56. The Door of the Sheep

John x: 1-9.

It will be remembered that John has recorded eight occasions upon which our Lord employed the Divine name, "I am," in making claims for Himself. Of these three are essential, plain declarations, "Before Abraham was, I am." "I am the resurrection and the life," "I am the way, and the truth, and the life." With these we are not dealing in this present series, which is concerned with the parabolic illustrations.

Of the eight, five were such of the essential claim as it was uttered in the words "I am." This is the third of these, "I am the door"; and it is closely linked to the next study on the good Shepherd.

Yet the phases are so different so that we take them necessarily as separate studies. We consider then this illustration, "I am the door"; following the usual method of enquiring the subject our Lord was intending to illustrate; then considering the figure He employed; deducing from these two things teaching for ourselves.

What was it that our Lord was illustrating? We may take these parables of Jesus, and apply them in ways that are really not appropriate, and so miss the real value of them, unless we know what our Lord was talking about at the time. His friends and His critics were round about Him when He said, "I am the door." Looking carefully at the passage in verse 7 we read this, "Jesus therefore said unto them again, Verily, verily, I say unto you, I am the door of the sheep." Whenever we read "therefore" we ask, Wherefore? What does the *therefore* lean back upon? Go back to the previous verse. "This parable spake Jesus unto them; but they understood not what things they

were which He spake unto them. Jesus therefore said unto them again."
He repeated the parable in a new form, and with a new emphasis,
"I am the door of the sheep." The word "parable" in verse 6 should
not be there, for John never uses the word parable, though we sometimes render it so. That is inadequate. For our understanding, it
would be better if we used the word allegory. That is the word of
John. This allegory spake Jesus to them, and they did not understand. Now we find out why He said again, "I am the door."

But what was the parable? It is the parable of a door; it is the
parable of a way into a fold through the door; the only way into the
fold through the door. So the word "therefore" drives us back to
verse 6, which explains the "therefore." The reason was that those who
heard Him speaking did not understand what He had said, the allegory He had employed of a sheepfold, and a door of entrance.

What then was it all about? Why did He use that parable? It was
a remarkable thing Jesus said. In the background we have the story
of His giving of sight to a man born blind. Everything grew out of
that. It is the only record we have of Jesus dealing with what we
call now congenital disease, a man born blind. We remember the story.
When He had given that man his sight, it aroused a great deal of
interest and attention among the people, and they were very much
puzzled by it. What did they do? Arrested, perplexed, they took this
man to the constituted religious authorities. The Hebrew background
of authority is seen in this story. The Pharisees were those who, as
Jesus said upon another occasion, sat in Moses' seat. They were the
interpreters of the law; but they had become far more than that.
They had become those who claimed full and final authority to interpret
the order of life. The people brought this blind man to them.

Without going into the wonderful story of what happened, I come
to the consummation where I find this statement (ix. 34), "They
answered and said unto him, Thou wast altogether born in sins, and
dost thou teach us? And they cast him out." Be particular when you
read that. Do not imagine they were in some room of the temple
courts, and that they went to the door and put him out. It is far more
than that. They pronounced upon him the word of excommunication.
They put him out of the order in which they themselves officiated.
They resented any interference. As we look back, we see a strange
thing happen. The man born blind, who has received his sight,—and
he is quite certain of that,—who is in controversy with these very
rulers, is approaching a larger understanding of the fact of Jesus
Himself. "Whether He be a sinner, I know not," he said at one point.
Then he went further and said, How has a man who is a sinner done

this thing? They replied, "Dost thou teach us?" and they put him out. They would brook no such interference with their religious, legal, or civic authority. Consequently they put him out. He was cut off by their action from relationship with that whole order of life, in which he had been born, and to which they all belonged.

What happened? Jesus heard that they had excommunicated him, that they had cast him out, and finding him, He said, "Dost thou believe on the Son of God?" And the man answered, "And who is He, Lord, that I may believe on Him?" There is a recognition of superiority expressed in terms of courtesy, "Who is He, Lord, that I may believe?" And Jesus said, "Thou hast both seen Him, and He it is that speaketh with thee." And the man said, "Lord, I believe. And he worshipped Him."

Two scenes. A man excommunicated by the religious authorities. Jesus found him, challenged him on one central point, that of His own personality, and the man did not understand; and yet there was something in the very tones of Jesus, so that the man said, I believe, and he worshipped Him. Excommunicated, put outside, the door shut against him by the religious authority; and Jesus stands in front of him, and opens a door into a new order, receives him to Himself, accepts his worship.

Then Jesus turning to those who were round about Him, Pharisees and others, said, "He that entereth not by the door into the fold of the sheep, but climbeth up some other way, the same is a thief and a robber."

They did not understand Him; therefore He said again, "I am the door of the sheep," and presently, "I am the good Shepherd." The two statements are linked. However, we are dealing with the first. We see something not fanciful, but something very real, though at this distance we may forget the surroundings, the people round. The disciples saw what He was doing. The man had been excommunicated. Then He went to him, He received him. Now He says, What I did was to present Myself to that soul as the Door, entry through which he found himself in a new order, an entirely new economy.

The subject then our Lord was illustrating was the institution of a new order altogether, a new economy, entry into which was through Him, and through Him alone; the fold, and the way into it. This man had been admitted into the fold by that way.

Stay now with the figure itself, an Eastern fold. Jesus said in the first verse "the door into the fold of the sheep." We must be careful to draw the distinction between the fold and the flock. The fold was a walled or palisaded enclosure, always open to the wind. The very word translated fold implies that, the sweeping wind, not a roof, but an enclosing wall. The sheep did not climb the walls. In that country there was only one entry, one door, never two. The door—apparent paradox—was merely an opening in the wall or palisade. It was never a gateway in those Eastern folds, never a door on hinges. It was merely an opening. That is the picture that was in the mind of Christ, familiar to all who heard Him when He said "I am the door of the sheep."

An illustration had much effect upon me many years ago now, and I have quoted it before, but will repeat it. It was my privilege to cross the Atlantic with Sir George Adam Smith. He told me this story. He was travelling in the East one day, and came up to one of those folds, a wall in this case, and there was an opening in the wall. The shepherd was on hand, so Sir George said to him, "Is that a fold for sheep?" "Oh yes," he replied. Sir George then said, "I only see one way in." "Yes," said the man, "there it is, there is the door," pointing to the opening in the wall. Then Sir George said to him, "But there is no door there"; and to his amazement—for it was naturally said, they were not talking of the New Testament, or of Christianity—this shepherd said to him, "Oh I am the door." Sir George said his mind went back to John's record. He said to the shepherd, "What do you mean, by calling yourself the door?" To which the shepherd replied, "The sheep go inside, and I come there and lie down across the threshold, and no sheep can get out except over my body, and no wolf can get in except over me."

That illustration is enough. "I am the door of the sheep." We come to the subject of the shepherd in our next study. But what does all this mean? Keep in mind the surroundings, the blind man excommunicated, and admitted, put outside the ancient order, but brought into close fellowship with Jesus. What did He do that day? His parable illustrates what He did. First we see in that act, perhaps the first of its kind in the ministry of Jesus, His supersedure of a failing religious order. That order had excommunicated the man. What did Jesus do? Christ excommunicated the whole order. He put it outside the realm of authority. That is what He meant when He said, "All that came before Me are thieves and robbers." That verse seems to have troubled some people. He was not referring to the prophets and Moses. He was referring to those who were claiming that final authority that these men claimed, when they excommunicated the man. In that sense in which they had claimed authority they were only thieves and robbers. He claimed to be the door, the Superseder of a failing order.

My mind travels away to that parenthesis in the letter to the

Hebrews, when the writer said "The law made nothing perfect." There the reference was not to the law of God merely, but to the whole economy supposedly based upon the law of God. But it had perfected no thing. All it had done in the case of this man was to put him outside, excommunicate him. Jesus once said, addressing these very rulers, "Woe unto you lawyers! for ye took away the key of knowledge; ye entered not in yourselves, and them that were entering in ye hindered." They supposed they were putting a man outside the pale of religion. They were really preventing him, and yet preparing him for entering into that realm, as it was now to be administered by the Lord Himself.

It is beautiful here to see what He says in the ninth verse, as the result of entering in through the door. "I am the door; by Me if any man enter in, he shall be saved, and shall go in and go out, and shall find pasture." Three things, ponder them. If any man enters through Me into this new order, into this fold, and becomes a member of the flock, he finds salvation. That is the first thing. "He shall go in and go out," the pathway of service. But he shall also find pasture, he shall have sustenance.

How does it all begin? Go back and look at that blind man face to face with Christ. "Dost thou believe on the Son of God?" Some MSS render that "Son of man." Whichever rendering is accepted makes no difference at all; for "the Son of man" was the Lord's favourite description of Himself. If He here called Himself the Son of man it does not devalue the thought. Dost thou believe in Me? Yet the title had been used, whether Son of man or Son of God. And the man said, Who is He, that I may believe? Let us try to put ourselves into the soul of the blind man. For the first time he had been able to see, to look upon the shimmer of the waters of Galilee, had seen his mother's face, and was able to see this Being, and He says, Thou hast seen Him, and I am He. At once the man's soul went over to Him in glad surrender, "Lord, I believe," and he offered Him worship. That is how he went into the fold. That is how every man enters the fold. That is how every human being enters, face to face with Christ Who challenges them. He does not ask us if we believe the Apostles' Creed. He does not ask if we have accepted this view or the other, but, Who am I? Do you believe in Me? Yes, I believe, and believing I worship. So the fold is entered.

The overwhelming revelation is that Christ is the way of entrance to the fold of the Kingdom of God, with all its privileges and all its responsibilities. If other systems professedly having all authority cast men outside, He confronts them and says, Here is the door, here is the way. All this harmonises with what He said to the disciples a little later on. "I am the way, and the truth, and the life; no one cometh unto the Father but by Me." The fold is the place of the Kingship of God found, yielded to, acknowledged; and the way in is Christ. He stands in the gap and says, "I am the door." To go back to Sir George Adam Smith's story, He is the door, and we cannot go out except across His body, and no ravening wolf can reach those sheep except across His body. "I am the door."

57. *The Good Shepherd*

John x: 11-18.

THIS the fourth of the parabolic illustrations used by our Lord in connection with His great claim, "I am," "I am the good Shepherd." We have already considered three; "I am the bread of life," "I am the light of the world," "I am the door." Now that of the good Shepherd is closely linked with that of the door, and by way of introduction we must tarry with that fact. Our Lord had made use of that illustration in that claim, "I am the door of the sheep"; in connection with the same teaching, "I am the good Shepherd."

We ask then, What was He illustrating? Then we will consider the figure itself, in order that from it we may deduce the teaching intended by our Lord, when He used this figure of the good Shepherd.

When the Lord had opened the eyes of the blind man the people brought him to the Pharisees, the religious authorities. The man grew in understanding himself as he talked to them, until they were angry with him; and as John tells us, they cast him out, which meant that they put him out, not of the temple precincts, but they excommunicated him. They put him outside the covenant, and outside the established order over which for the time being they were in authority. Whether their exercise of authority was good or not we are not discussing. We know it was not. When the Lord knew they had cast him out, He found him and there passed between this man and Jesus that little conversation, and He asked, in effect, Do you believe in Me? In that moment Jesus received him to Himself. It was then He said, "I am the door," and by that figure of speech He claimed that He was the way of entry into a new order entirely. That may be put in another way. They had excommunicated the man, and Jesus excommunicated them. He did so on subsequent occasions more definitely and specifically, when He said the Kingdom of God should be taken away from them. By that action He was putting Himself in the place of authority, and He was receiving this man into the entirely new order that He was in the world to set up. Then He said, "I am the door." By that He claimed that He was the way of entry to that new order, that men should enter into it through Him, as this man had done, when he had submitted to Him in belief, and worshipped Him in person.

We now come to the second thing. Under that claim, "I am the good Shepherd," He revealed the nature of the new order. This man had been received into a new order, in which He is the way of entry, and then still in that same realm of ideas, He said, "I am the good Shepherd." Those were the circumstances, and the evident intention of our Lord in the use of these two figures of speech at this point.

We now confine ourselves to the wonderful figure, and ask again What was the figure which He employed? It was a figure of a shepherd with folds and a flock. The fold is an enclosure. The flock is those who are enclosed. It is important to make that distinction. He did not say there should be one fold and one shepherd, but one flock. There may be many folds, just as in that Eastern country. The shepherd in that land may own two or three dozen sheep, and they can be folded in many folds, but it is one flock. The unity was not created by the fold, but by the nature of the sheep, and their relationship to the shepherd.

The shepherd was the one not only able to take charge of the flock. This is an Eastern picture, different from anything we know in this country. The sheep know his voice. That is literally true of Eastern shepherds. If a stranger came along, the sheep would shrink back; they know their shepherd's voice, and follow when he calls. He was in charge of them, and it was his work to lead them out of the fold to pasturage, in order to the sustenance of their life. Of course it was also his work to defend them against wolves, or any enemies. That was the Eastern shepherd.

But when our Lord used this figure, I think there can be no doubt that He was employing the figure in one way. The shepherd was always the symbol of the king. It was Homer who once said, "All kings are shepherds of their people." It was a great idealistic word. As we look down human history we may be inclined to say, amending that statement, All kings should be shepherds. God's kings were always shepherds, and the shepherd was the king. I quote a verse oft quoted. Our Lord was talking to His disciples one day, and said to them, "Fear not, little flock; for it is your Father's good pleasure to give you the Kingdom." I can imagine a purely literary critic coming to that sentence in some booklet published tomorrow, who might indulge in pleasantries. He might say, The writer now broke down in his employment of his figures. He first suggests the flock of sheep, "Fear not little flock." Then forgetting that, he went off to the idea of the family, "It is your Father's good pleasure"; and before he finished, he had forgotten that figure also, and used the figure of a nation, "to give you the Kingdom." We know perfectly well however that though the figures merge they do not mix. Those are the three elements that constitute Kingship ideally in all that Eastern country, and ought to everywhere. The king should be the shepherd of his flock, the father of his family, the one in authority over his nation. When our Lord said quietly, but with august majesty and dignity, "I am the good Shepherd," all those figures, all those implications of the figure of the shepherd and the flock, unquestionably merge in His claim, "I am the good Shepherd."

We come now to the supreme matter. What was the teaching, the thing revealed? What did Jesus claim when He said that? Two things, absolute authority and constant care in and over the new order that He was in the world to establish. God had established the order of the Hebrew people but they had broken down. Need that be argued or even illustrated? Is there anything more ghastly than the failure of the Hebrew people from the beginning to the end? They were always failing, and they never failed more disastrously than when they wanted a king "like the nations." In that act, as God said to Samuel, they had rejected Him from being King. It had gone on through the ages, and the last thing the Hebrew people did to prove their ultimate and appalling catastrophic folly and sin was to crucify the Son of God. So God was superseding the order definitely established; as the writer of the letter to the Hebrews said, the law "made nothing perfect." It broke down and failed, and its failure was manifested in that one incident. When those men in authority put this man out, they revealed their failure. Then Jesus took him in, and admitted him to the new order to which He was the door.

Now He is in authority. I am the King. I am the Father of the family. I am the Shepherd, the good Shepherd of all the flock. We see then a new order emerging in human history, by the act of God. The same Kingdom, the same eternal Throne, but in its administration in earthly affairs, a new dispensation, a new economy. When Jesus said, "I am the good Shepherd," so simple, so beautiful, that all our

hymns express it in the terms of tenderness and love; there is more
in it than that. If there is in the claim the evidences of infinite tenderness, there is the evidence of supreme authority. "I am the good
Shepherd." It marks not only authority, but it does mark care in
every way.

As our Lord went on speaking, He revealed the method of His
authority as the good Shepherd, that great title in which there merge
the ideas of Kingship, of Fatherhood, and Shepherdhood. He shows
how He exercises that authority and that care. In verse eleven He
says, "the good shepherd layeth down his life for the sheep." In verse
fifteen He says, "I lay down My life for the sheep," and again in
verse seventeen, "Therefore doth the Father love Me, because I lay
down My life, that I may take it again." There is a growth of teaching
here. How will He lay down His life? In conflict with the wolf, who
comes to destroy and to harm, to harass, and to kill. In order to overcome that wolf, I will lay down My life; I lay down My life on their
behalf. That is the idea of the first verse. Then presently there is
something else. "I lay down My life that I may take it again." That
is more than dying; that is rising. That is more than going down to
death in the grapple with the wolf, and the wolf kills. But He is
coming through and out and beyond the grapple with the wolf into
the place of victory over him. "I lay down My life, that I may take
it again."

Then follows that august claim, "No one taketh it away from Me,
but I lay it down of Myself. I have authority to lay it down, and I
have power to take it again." Here is the second idea; laying down
His life for the sheep first in conflict with the wolf; laying down
secondly, His life that the sheep may share His life. He takes it again
to bring His sheep into union with Himself; victory over the wolf, and
conflict that issues in victory; and then fellowship with the King
Himself in consequent life. "I lay down My life that I may take it
again."

Thus the two statements are interpreted by what He says in verse
seventeen, "Therefore doth the Father love Me, because I lay down
My life, that I may take it again." "I am the good Shepherd," in complete authority, having the care of the sheep; and My method of
Kingship is first dying to kill the wolf; rising to share My life with the
sheep who have been delivered from the wolf.

Then it was that He glanced on, and took a larger outlook upon
this new order. He said, "Other sheep I have, which are not of this
fold; them also I must bring, and they shall hear My voice, and they
shall become one flock, one Shepherd." Not one fold necessarily,

but one flock. It is interesting to remember how in the next chapter (xi), we have the striking story of Caiaphas, the clever and astute politician. When these enemies of Christ, these men exercising authority in a wrong way, were plotting as to what they should do with Him, Caiaphas rose after their discussion, and introduced his subject by that excellent formula, if one wants to be heard, "Ye know nothing at all." He said this, "It is expedient for you that one man should die for the people, and that the whole nation perish not." Then follows this remarkable little passage of interpretation. "Now this he said not of himself; but being high priest that year, he prophesied that Jesus should die for the nation; and not for the nation only, but that He might gather together into one the children of God that are scattered abroad." "Other sheep I have, which are not of this fold; them also I must bring, and they shall hear My voice; and they shall become one flock, one Shepherd."

Again, what was the deep secret of His authority, the secret of His care, the secret of His laying down of His life for the sheep? "Therefore doth the Father love Me, because I lay down My life, that I may take it again." The deep secret was the Father's love, and the love of the Son in co-operation with the purposes of the Father. So we have the claims of the new order. Jesus the good Shepherd, in authority, caring, acting by laying down His life in conflict with the wolf, acting by laying down His life, by taking it again, that it might be shared by His own; so creating and constituting the new order of the Kingdom of God under His authority.

Go back over the Old Testament, Psalm xxiii, Isaiah xl, Jeremiah xxiii, Ezekiel xxxiv, xxxvii, Zechariah xi, all these are about shepherds, all looking on to the same great Shepherd. Here we stand and hear Him say, I am He, I am the Shepherd fulfilling the idealism of the psalms, realising the ideal of the prophets, all of them; "I am the good Shepherd," I am the Shepherd, the good. That is the form of the statement literally in the Greek. Something may be missed by having changed it. "I am the Shepherd, the good." Presently we come to His statement, "I am the true vine," literally again, "I am the vine, the true." The very form of the sentence suggests comparison with all others, He said "All that came before Me are thieves and robbers," that is, all who claimed absolute authority, as those rulers did when they put the man out. They were thieves and robbers. He said, "I am the Shepherd, the good; and the word good there is beautiful. It is the Greek word *kalos,* which is rendered beautiful, noble, true, as well as good. It was a word that marked the attributes to all perfection; and they all emerge from and merge in Him for evermore. He is the

Shepherd true, noble, beautiful, infinite in wonder. This all ends with the first words, "I am," God manifestly seen and heard, heaven's beloved One. "I am," King, Father, Shepherd true.

58. Death as Sleep

John xi: 11-15, 23-26a.

OUR SUBJECT here is death as sleep; and the story is that of the final sign in the realm of works, wrought by our Lord in His earthly ministry, as recorded by John; that of the raising of Lazarus. In this story we see Him in the presence of death on the physical level, that is, the separation of the spirit and body. Death in the spiritual level is the separation of the soul from God. In that sense, in the day that man ate of the forbidden fruit, he died, for in that day he was separated from God. Man's physical death did not come at once, though that came ultimately.

Twice before in the record of our Lord's ministry we see Him standing in the presence of death. Once it was the child of Jairus, and again it was the son of the widow of Nain. Here death is seen in the case of the brother of Martha and Mary, and on that physical level this is superlative. In the first case the child was dead in the house, and not many hours had passed. In the second case the boy was on his way from the city to burial, but not yet buried. Here we are in the presence of death, of a man who had been dead four days, and buried four days. Therefore this is a superlative case.

So we proceed along the usual lines in these studies, considering first the subject illustrated, the figure of sleep in the presence of death; then simply and quickly take the figure itself, in order that we may deduce the teaching.

What was the fact that our Lord was facing? Jesus said when the news was brought to Him over Jordan, "This sickness is not unto death, but for the glory of God." (verse 4). Again at verse 13, "Jesus had spoken of his death." In those verses there is the common word for death, *thanatos,* which means just what we mean by death. Again at verse 39, "Martha, the sister of him that was dead." At verse 44, "He that was dead came forth." Once more in the 14th verse, "Jesus therefore said unto them plainly, Lazarus is dead," or as it should be, "Lazarus died." The reference is to a fact, an accomplished fact.

In those verses two words, "death," and "dead" occur. In verses 4 and 13 we have the word *thanatos*, the simple word for death. In verses 39 and 44 we have a word associated with the other, in a strengthened form of it, the word *thnesko*, dead. When our Lord used the phrase, "Lazarus is dead," He used yet another and intensive form of the same word, *apothnesko*. It might be rendered, though it is not beautiful, or euphemistic, He has died off; he is simply dead. So by this group of words we are in the presence of death, in the presence of the dead.

What was our Lord doing when He used this figure of speech? First of all we see that He had a clear view of the fact of death. He knew the fact as they saw it. He knew the fact as it was recurring around Him in all the time of His public ministry. He knew the fact as these men saw it, as Martha and Mary saw it in the case of Lazarus; but in His first reference to it He did not use either of these words for death. When the disciples misunderstood Him and thought He really was referring to natural sleep, then John says He said plainly—mark that word—He said distinctly, positively, Oh no, that is not the case of taking rest; he is dead, he has died; he has shared the experience that is covered by the word that men had constantly used; he is dead, he is to be numbered among those who are dead. He saw death as they saw it, and consequently when they did not understand Him, He said the plain thing, He is dead, emphasizing it in the word He used, completely dead, actually dead. The body that has been put in the sepulchre is lifeless; he is dead.

But before we can approach or understand His figure of speech, we have to take the whole story. If He saw the fact of death as they saw it, He knew the fact of death as they did not know it. Here we are in the presence of that outlook of Jesus which is so manifest in all the story of His life; that whereas He saw the near, that which was right under their eyes, He always saw more. He never looked upon life as complete, as it could be viewed at the moment under the circumstances. He saw more. He saw through; and therefore He said, Lazarus is sleeping. They said, He will do well; he will recover. No, He said, he is dead, as you mean death; but I see more than you do. Those are the circumstances, and it was to illustrate that, that He used this figure of speech.

Now take the figure and look at it simply. What is sleep? It is not cessation of being even on the human level. When we go to sleep it does not mean our being has ceased in sleep. What is it therefore?

Unconsciousness of all things around. I am not going into the subject of dreams, those strange experiences that we all have. I am dealing with normal and proper sleep, when we have eaten the sort of supper we ought to eat! We are unconscious of everything. We say sometimes of someone, he was sleeping like a baby. There it is, completely unconscious of surrounding things. That is the figure our Lord used, and therefore we have come rightly and very beautifully to associate the idea of sleep with repose. The words are recurring "Nature's sweet restorer, balmy sleep." That is what those men with Jesus thought when they said, if Lazarus was asleep, he would recover. If a man has been ill, and has really gone to sleep, he will recover, he will be saved; literally that is what they said. The danger is past, for he is sleeping.

Let us notice another thing in passing. This figure that our Lord made use of, was not a new one for death. Sleep as the image of death is common in literature from its dawn. Pagan writers used it as well as those of the Hebrew people. Westcott says the image of sleep for death is very common in all Rabbinic writings. That is the image our Lord took up. Yes, Lazarus was dead. He spoke plainly. One is always thankful He did, for the sake of men who were not grasping the significance of His reference to Lazarus being asleep. He said, he is dead. He died definitely, positively, died off; he is gone, he is lifeless. That is all true.

But Jesus was seeing more than they did. Martha and Mary saw a lifeless corpse, and Martha, dear heart, was blunt in her description of the condition of that corpse as she expected it was by this time. Those disciples who had travelled up, heroically going, as Thomas said, "Let us also go, that we may die with Him"; if they had been able to look into the tomb when the stone was rolled away, they would have seen wrapped in the cerements of the tomb the dead body. That is what they saw, and that is all they saw. But Jesus said, That is not all. As a matter of fact it is not the supreme fact. He is dead, he has lost the consciousness of all the things that are around him, his sisters and friends, and everything else. He is dead; but he is not dead in the full and deep sense of the word. He saw the dead body, but He saw the man; and the man was not in the sepulchre as He saw him. So that He said, So far as this side is concerned, so far as you are concerned, he is dead; but so far as he is concerned, and the things of this side he is unconscious, he knows nothing about them.

We might indulge in many speculations, which are not profitable. I am often asked, Do the loved ones know what we are doing here? I do not think so. Bishop Bickersteth in that remarkable poem, "Yesterday, Today and For Ever," thought there might be circumstances under the government of God, when they are permitted to see and know, but as a rule, so far as we are concerned, they are asleep. They have no consciousness of what is going on here. And are we not really glad that is so, for their sakes? I often am.

What then is the teaching which we have here? First the clear evidence that Christ's outlook on personality was that of its continuity beyond death. Even when as to this world they were asleep, unconscious, and we cannot communicate with them in any way, they were not actually dead, they had not ceased to be. Notice this simple thing. When presently He had told them to roll away the stone, and they had done it, what did He do? He spoke to the man. He spoke to him by the name they had known Him, "Lazarus, come forth." He spoke to the same man, the same personality. That man could not have heard Martha, if she had said, Lazarus, come back. Oh no. That man could not have heard Peter or John, standing there, if they had called into the void, after him. But he heard Jesus, and Jesus addressed him. He did the same with the little girl. He laid His hand on her, and said, "Talitha cumi," little lamb, arise. He spoke to one who could hear Him. Not the father and mother. They could not reach her. She was asleep, so far as they were concerned. She was not asleep so far as He was concerned. And when He approached the bier coming out of the city of Nain, we have exactly the same thing. "Young man, arise," as to one who could hear Him, and one who did hear Him. They all heard Him; and He brought them back from the sleep that was the unconsciousness of the things here and now into consciousness of them, and into the position in which they became conscious of them. Sleep!

But of course the whole thing hinges on that point. I say emphatically, no other voice could have reached that maid, that young man, Lazarus; but His voice could. The fact that His voice could, demonstrates the fact that those addressed were able somewhere, somehow, to hear Him. Lazarus heard, and struggled into an upright position in his grave-clothes, as would be quite possible if, as they certainly did, adopt the Egyptian method of winding him. He could, and did get up, and then Jesus said, "Loose him, and let him go." The little girl, not yet wrapped in her grave-clothes, but lying there, she heard His voice, and she sat up, and opened her eyes. The young man was able to struggle up on his bier, possibly helped from it, and Jesus gave him back to his mother.

So that if we speak of death as sleep we must recognize that the only One Who can wake out of sleep is our Lord Himself, the only

One Who can bring back into consciousness those fallen on sleep. No one else can. We remember that old trite quotation from Gray's Elegy,

> "Can storied urn or animated bust
> Back to its mansion call the fleeting breath?
> Can honour's voice provoke the silent dust,
> Or flattery soothe the dull cold ear of death?"

There is only one answer to Gray, when he thus sings. No, you cannot reach them, but Jesus could, and Jesus did.

Let us go back in this Gospel of John to some things He said on an earlier occasion in His ministry. "As the Father raiseth the dead and quickeneth them, even so the Son also quickeneth whom He will." Again, "Verily, verily, I say unto you, The hour cometh, and now is, when the dead shall hear the voice of the Son of God; and they that hear shall live." And yet once more, "Marvel not at this; for the hour cometh, in which all that are in the tombs shall hear His voice, and shall come forth; they that have done good, unto the resurrection of life; and they that have done ill, unto the resurrection of judgment." Those are the great and astounding facts that He declared in the earlier part of His ministry as recorded in John's fifth chapter. But it is His voice that can call them. It is His voice which they can hear; no other voice.

Seeing that this is so, we realise that they that sleep in Jesus will God bring with Him. Therefore we sorrow not as those that have no hope. For if Christ died and rose again even them that sleep in Jesus will God bring with Him. Some may sing that hymn with new meaning,

> "Sleep on, beloved, sleep, and take thy rest;
> Lay down thy head upon thy Saviour's breast;
> We love thee well; but Jesus loves thee best—
> Goodnight! Goodnight! Goodnight!"

It is said that the early Christians were accustomed to bid their dying friends "Goodnight," so sure were they of their awakening on the resurrection morning. That does not mean that they have ceased to exist. They are existing in a realm where He is in authority, and where His voice can be heard; and being heard they will obey.

Do not forget the solemn words. "The hour cometh, and now is, when the dead shall hear the voice of the Son of God; . . . all that are in the tombs shall hear His voice, and shall come forth; they that have done good, unto the resurrection of life; and they that have done ill, unto the resurrection of judgment." When He spoke to

Martha He said, "I am the resurrection, and the life; he that believeth on Me, though he die, yet shall he live." Lazarus is in the tomb, but "though he die, yet shall he live."

Here is another very familiar word of Scripture which we may often quote correctly but think inaccurately. Jesus did not say, "Yet shall he live again." No, not "again," but "yet shall he live." Jesus said plainly, Lazarus is dead, but he is not dead. He is where My voice can reach him. He is asleep, unconscious of all the things he has been conscious of; but I can find him, I can reach him; and there will come a day when My voice will reach all that are in the tombs. So we say to our loved ones,

"Sleep on, beloved, sleep and take thy rest."

59. *A Grain of Wheat*

John xii: 20-26.

W E FIND ourselves now in the last hours of our Lord's public ministry. As we follow the records, the incident recorded in this paragraph (xii: 20-26) is the last of which we have any record in the public work of Jesus. Preceding this incident there had been His entry to Jerusalem, and His conflict with the rulers. At the end of that conflict there had shone upon Him that gleam of light as the poor widow, passing the treasury, had shown her devotion to the God of her fathers as she cast in all her living. Then it was that the Greeks came. We should note that these were Greeks, not Greek Jews. There is a distinction clearly seen by the reader of the Greek New Testament between Hellenes, and Hellenistes. These were Hellenes,—Greeks.

Immediately after this incident, we have the chapters 13-17, in which we see Jesus alone with His own, the world shut out. At the close of that period with His own, He crossed the brook Kidron, and the end came. This is but to remind us of the atmosphere that necessarily demands careful thought and attention.

We are considering now this parabolic illustration that our Lord used in connection with the coming of the Greeks, taking our usual method, enquiring first, what the subject was He intended to illustrate; then looking carefully at the figure He employed to illustrate His subject; in order that we may consider the teaching that is deduced.

What made Jesus use this illustration? John records that He began by that formula, which shows He intended to draw special attention to what He was going to say, "Verily, verily." When Andrew and Philip came and proffered the request to Him, telling Him what the Greeks were saying, He said, "The hour is come, that the Son of man should be glorified. Verily, verily, I say unto you, Except a grain of wheat fall into the earth and die, it abideth by itself alone, but if it die it beareth much fruit." Patently that was a parabolic illustration, but of what? We start with that question.

We cannot understand this except we notice why the Greeks came. That may be difficult to see, except by general deduction and consideration. I venture therefore to take that general consideration, and make a deduction. These were Greeks, Hellenes. The word marks them as to race and nationality. If they were Greeks, not Hellenistic Jews, they were Greek proselytes to the Jewish faith, because John distinctly tells us they had come up to worship at the feast. We know full well that there were at that time very many who from other nations and other peoples and races and religions, turned towards the Hebrew religion, and became proselytes of the gate, definitely accepting Jewish ritual and the Jewish law, and the Jewish view of God. There is no doubt these Greeks were of that number, and they had come up to worship at the feast.

What made them ask to see Jesus? The first self-evident answer is, He was being talked about. Men everywhere were talking about Him. The thronging crowds, gathering to the feast were all, sooner or later, talking about Him. His fame had gone out everywhere, and the things He had been saying were well-known. Many had received what He had said, and had been obedient, and were enrolled among the number of His disciples, who were more than twelve. After His resurrection, five hundred brethren went up to Galilee to meet Him; and there were multitudes who had been so influenced. Everyone know something about Jesus; and these Greeks, coming up to the feast, would hear about Him.

Now we come to the point where we cannot be definitely dogmatic. It may be their coming was one of curiosity. They had heard about this wonderful Teacher, about the strange supernatural things He had done, of healing all manner of disease, and cleansing the lepers, and all the wonders of His work. They may have thought they would like to look at Him, and to have a conversation with Him. That may all be true; but the whole method of the answer of Jesus makes me believe there was something far more profound in it than that. I see men who had turned from paganism to God, in the Hebrew religion.

That is the first thing. There is no doubt about that. Tired of the hollow, the base, the untrue in the religions in which they had been brought up, all the multiplied religions of the land to which they belonged. These Greeks, for very weariness of heart and soul had gone to the Hebrew religion with its one God, the living God. Here they were, at the feast, keeping the law and observing the ritual, they had come up with the multitudes to worship. I believe they had become not merely disappointed with their pagan religion, but disillusioned in the matter of Judaism. These men seeking after God, seeking after the truth, longing to find it, had turned from idols to the living God. Then they heard about a Teacher, and they felt there was something in what they had heard, something different, something higher, something nobler. They were finding out Judaism was not satisfying the deepest hunger of their souls. So they found their way to the place where Jesus was that day with His disciples all round about Him; and got hold of that delightful man, Philip, who Elvet Lewis long ago said was a man always on the edge of the crowd, never obtrusive, but ready to lead others to his Master. It may be these Greeks were attracted to him because he bore a Greek name. But they proffered their request, and said, Sir, we want to see Jesus. What a world of meaning there was in that. I think they were honest and sincere.

So the human desire lay at the back of what Jesus said. The desire was shared by His disciples. They were a little hesitant about it. They held a splendid committee meeting, splendid because it only consisted of two, that is, Philip and Andrew. They got together. Mark the psychology of this. Philip knew that something was about to happen. He had been with the disciples during these six months in which Jesus had been telling them distinctly that He was going to die. At any rate Philip knew that his Master was occupied with great thinking and great sorrow; and therefore he wondered whether he ought to trouble Him. So he went to Andrew. We are not told of any discussion. It was a good committee meeting, in which they did not waste any time. They both went to Jesus and told Him of the request. I think they were anxious that these Greeks should see Him, men of another religion and nation to see their Lord and Master. They wanted them to hear Him because they were of a wider realm. There is human desire on the part of the enquiring Greeks, and on the part of the disciples. To that Jesus answered, and the figure of speech He used was intended to illuminate, and illustrate what He said in reply to that enquiry and request of the Greeks.

What then made Him say what He said? Notice the first thing He said, "The hour is come, that the Son of man should be glorified."

There we have a full stop. I wish there was not, because we are inclined to stop there. Because of that it has been suggested by some brilliant expositors that Jesus knew the Hebrew people were rejecting Him, and now He saw the Gentile world opening before Him, and therefore He said, the hour is come that the Son of man should be glorified, because the Gentile world was now enquiring, and were coming to Him. I hold that is utterly wrong, and there is no warrant for it. Go back over the Gospel, and notice the repeated references to the "hour." The first reference is when He was talking to His mother Mary at Cana. She had come to Him, hoping that He would work a wonder by which His glory would be revealed, and He said, the hour had not come. What did He mean then? That He would not perform the miracle? No, for immediately He did what she had asked. He told her that His glory would not be seen through the wonder of the miracle He worked, for His hour was not yet come. That hour was referred to again and again, but always as postponed. When the Greeks came and said, We want to see Jesus; He said, "The hour is come that the Son of man should be glorified; verily, verily, I say unto you, Except a grain of wheat fall into the earth and die, it abideth by itself alone." That is the answer. Do not stop with the full stop at the word "glorified" in your thinking. How is the Son of man glorified? How has the hour come? What is the hour? "Verily, verily, I say unto you, Except a grain of wheat fall into the earth and die, it abideth by itself alone." Our Lord was speaking out of His own consciousness. He knew that He was not seen, and could not be seen, as He then stood before His disciples and those Greeks. He meant that they would only see Him in one way. He might have said to Philip and Andrew, You have not seen Me. But they had! They had been with Him for three and a half years. No, He said, You have never seen Me.

Turn on to the fourteenth chapter. He is talking to the group, and Philip is there, and says, "Show us the Father"; and He said, "Have I been so long time with you, and dost thou not know Me, Philip?" He had not known Him, had not seen Him, and none of them had. When He heard the Greeks had asked to see Him, He declared that the hour was come in which the thing would be possible. The hour is come in which the Son of man should be glorified. What is the hour? "Verily, verily, I say unto you, Except a grain of wheat fall into the earth and die, it abideth by itself alone." That is what He was illustrating. We find as we listen to Him, His clear understanding of the only way by which He could be revealed in all the fulness and meaning of Himself, and the only way in which men could ever see Him truly, and know Him. That is what He intended to illustrate.

This incident moves in exactly the same realm as His great soliloquy recorded by Luke alone. In the midst of all the difficulties of His ministry, one day He burst out in these words "I came to cast fire upon the earth; and what do I desire, would that it were already kindled? But I have a baptism to be baptised with; and how am I straitened till it be accomplished!" The same thing. Now let Me tell you what that hour will be, as though Jesus had said, and let Me show you what that hour will be. I will do it by taking a simple illustration; "Except a grain of wheat fall into the earth and die, it abideth by itself alone; but if it die, it beareth much fruit."

Pause now with the figure itself. What is this figure our Lord used? "A corn of wheat" said the Old Version. "A grain of wheat" says the Revised. Either will do to explain the word He made use of. What is a kernel of wheat? One single grain, a seed. Take a seed of wheat, a corn of wheat, a grain of wheat. Jesus said, There are conditions under which any grain of wheat abides alone. But if that grain of wheat is planted, and it dies, and we watch, we shall see first the blade, and then the ear, and then the full corn in the ear. The one lonely grain has been multiplied into full corn in the ear, to borrow His words on another occasion, some an hundred fold, some sixty, some thirty, because that grain of wheat has been dropped into the ground and died.

He is illustrating a tremendous truth concerning Himself. Take hold of the figure in simplicity. Imagine that you hold a grain of wheat in your hand, a little thing, the husk is on it, but inside the husk is the grain, and the scientists can tell you all the things that are in it. But while you look at that grain, you cannot really see it. Oh yes, you say, there it is. Philip and Andrew could see Jesus. There He was. The enquiring Greeks could see Jesus. There He was. The grain of wheat, can I see it? Yes, but I cannot see its meaning. I cannot see its possibilities. I cannot see what really lies potentially within the little grain.

Would I really see it? Very well then; put it in the ground. Then you will have to stand aside. All you can see of it is that it dies. We have to see that. Then presently the blade, the ear, the full corn, 30. 60. 100 fold in the ear. But they were all in the little grain you looked at, that was sown. It is not done. Husk it. Get those grains out, 30. 60. 100; and so the process is running on. Whether it is quite permissible or not, I cannot help remembering something in the Old Testament,

"There shall be an handful of corn in the earth upon the top
    of the mountains;
The fruit thereof shall shake like Lebanon."

The harvest from a grain. We cannot see it, when we see the grain. "We would see Jesus"; and in great wisdom and perfect understanding He saw they could see Him, but they could not see Him. They could only really see Him as He fell and died; that out of that death of His there should spring life, the life that multiplied, life that grew until the harvests should be gathered in. He would be seen in that way, and that way alone.

So we may gather up the general teaching. The Lord applied the principle generally as a philosophy after He had given the illustration, when in the 25th verse He said, "He that loveth his life loseth it." If he love it, hold it and nurse it and care for it, he is losing it. "He that hateth his life in this world," lays it down in self-denial and abnegation, to death, he shall hold it "shall keep it unto the life eternal." That is the great principle contained in His illustration.

He went on and applied it immediately to His disciples. "If any man serve Me, let him follow Me." Where was He going? He was going to the Cross. Where was He going? He was going to resurrection and triumph. Where was He going? The grain of wheat was going to fall into the ground and die. Where was He going? Through that death life should spring, and harvests should result. "If any man serve Me, let him follow Me," and accept that principle. Whether by dying or living, "where I am, there shall also My servant be; if any man serve Me, him will the Father honour."

Then He applied it to Himself. "Now is My soul troubled." The hour is come, "and what shall I say? Father, save Me from this hour?" Shall I ask God to deliver Me from this hour of the death of the grain of wheat? He did not ask that. "Father, glorify Thy name." That was the supreme passion of His heart. Follow through the teaching, and He clearly shows how He was passing through trouble to triumph, through death to life, through suffering to glory. It is Christ seen in glory Who is speaking in life through death, in triumph through trouble that the Christ is seen at all. No, they cannot see Me yet, but they shall see Me; for as the corn of wheat, so I will pass into death, and out of that death will come new life.

So from infinite mystery so profound, all wrapped in the flesh Divine of the Son of man, that men did not see the glory, He came to manifestation through death and through life.

60. The Washing of Feet

John xiii: 1-11.

WE HAVE no parable, nor parabolic illustration in this paragraph; but we have the record of a parabolic action on the part of our Master. Our Lord's application of what He did shows that He intended it to be an illustration in action, and so a parabolic illustration.

It occurs in this wonderful section of John's record in which our Lord is seen at the end of His public ministry alone with His own disciples. All the public teaching was over, and the works wrought in the sight of the multitudes had ceased. He had gathered around Him that first little band whom He had chosen to be with Him, and that He might send forth in His name. Through these chapters (13-17) there was no stranger there. Jesus was alone with His own. There were thirteen men there; our Lord Himself, and twelve others. Very soon the number was reduced. As a matter of fact, this very parabolic action led to the exclusion of Judas.

We give attention then to the action in itself, and proceed first to ask, What was our Lord intending to illustrate in His action on this memorable occasion? Then we will examine the figure revealed in the action, and which He thus employed for teaching His own. Finally we seek to gather for ourselves the teaching that lies within it.

What was the subject He was illustrating? We have a remarkable glimpse here in the beginning, of the mind of the Lord Himself, His consciousness, the matters that were possessing His thought, and hav-ing their influence upon all He said, and all He did. That mind is remarkably revealed in the opening words of the chapter, "Now before the feast of the passover, Jesus knowing." That is repeated in verse 3, "Jesus knowing." We are told of two things, all He did, and all He said on this occasion. Consequently we are approaching an under-standing of what He intended to illustrate, as we recognize His own mind, His own consciousness.

What did He know? First that His hour was come that He should depart out of the world unto the Father. I am not concerned with what follows, although it is important. John here emphasizes the consciousness of Christ at the time. That was the supreme thing, the first thing, that He knew that His hour was come. What hour? That "He should depart out of this world unto the Father." The consciousness of Christ is marvellously revealed to us, and the merging in it of

His knowledge of all that lay before Him, all the terror that was in front of Him, and yet the consciousness of triumph through the terror. He knew His hour was come when the Greeks came. He then said "The hour is come that the Son of man should be glorified." Now the hour was come. The Greeks could only see Him as He went down into death, and came out again in resurrection power, as the grain of wheat falls into the ground and dies. Now, He knew that the hour was come that He should depart out of the world. With all reverence, by way of interpretation, He knew how He was to depart out of the world. He had been telling His disciples for six months over and over again of the method of His going. They, dear souls, had been frightened. Now He knew that the hour had come, and He knew the method of it, He knew the issue of it. Yes, He was departing out of the world, but where was He going? To the Father, and the note of perfect assurance and victory is there. That is one thing He knew.

What was the other thing that John says He knew? I am not concerned with the immediate application of it, but with the general stating. He knew that "the Father had given all things into His hands, and that He came forth from God, and goeth unto God." There was the consciousness that His hour was come, and there was the certain consciousness of His own authority, which He had received from His Father. "All things were delivered into His hands." We look at Him, and as we look we wonder. All things? Just beyond is the Cross, when He was delivered into the hands of sinful men. That is only the surface outlook. All things were delivered into His hands, and He knew that; and He knew that He had come from God, and was going to God. So the lights and glories as of the Urim and Thummim on the breastplate of the priest in the olden days flash through this; the mind of Christ. That is the background. But what else is here? We have the background of the disciples, those who were round about Him, and of all that had been happening amongst them during the previous six months to which we have referred already. Ponder again carefully those last six months, from Cæsarea Philippi, and Peter's confession and the Cross. Do not forget He had never explicitly told them He was going to the Cross till then; but from that moment there was a feeling of estrangement. They could not understand. I am not criticizing them. We should not have understood; and they did not. We find over and over again our Lord told them about His Cross, took them aside to tell them, and to tell them carefully in detail; and in every case we find these two startling facts, that He never told them about His Cross but that He also mentioned His resurrection; and also that in every case, immediately after His emphasizing of His Cross, they were disputing, quarrelling as to who was the greatest. There they were, men thinking about their own preeminence, and their own positions of power; and there is a sense in which that was all permissible, and yet it was entirely self-centered. Who is the greatest? In that Kingdom who shall have the position of power, and two men thought they ought to have it, and got their mother to speak for them. It is a way mothers have sometimes! When they had done this, the ten were angry with them for having done it, and the reason was the ten were angry because they wanted the position themselves. That is not being unkind to them. There is the background. Jesus knew what was in their hearts, and by that symbolic action, that parabolic action, the subject illustrated was first the heart of the Lord Himself, that those men might see Him by a simple act, yet so sublime, that it holds us in its thrall today. Therefore in order that they might understand what was the true responsibility of their discipleship, the subject illustrated in this parabolic action was the heart of the Lord, and the responsibilities consequent upon discipleship to that Lord.

Now the figure itself. What was this that Jesus did? Verse 10, "Jesus saith to Peter, He that is bathed needeth not save to wash his feet, but is clean every whit; and ye are clean, but not all." I am not now concerned with the last part of the verse. "He that is bathed needeth not save to wash his feet." The Authorised Version renders this, "He that is washed needeth not save to wash his feet." The Revised Version has the word "bathed," "He that is bathed." I think the word "bathed" is better, for there are two Greek verbs there, which give us in a flash the picture behind this, and the thing Jesus was using as an illustration. The first of the Greek verbs rendered "washed" in the Authorised, and now rendered "bathed" in the Revised is a verb that means just that, to bathe the whole person, the verb *luuo;* whereas the verb *nipto* is to cleanse the hands or feet, that is, wash, and it is distinct from bathing. Jesus said to Peter, He that is bathed only needs to wash his feet; and in a moment the Eastern habits are revealed. To bathe meant complete cleansing, and the picture behind this is that of a man having been to the baths, and completely bathed, taking his way home through the dust of the highway, contracting dust upon his feet, and when he reaches home he will cleanse his feet from defilement contracted after he has bathed. That is an Eastern figure, and all would be familiar with it as Jesus said, "He that is bathed needeth not save to wash his feet." After the complete cleansing of the bath, that does not need to be repeated; but he does need to be cleansed from any defilement as he walks by the way. That is what our Lord was illustrating. So He said to them, You are all clean. You have all been bathed, but you may have contracted defilement in your walk. The figure of speech was an Eastern one of the bath and the foot washing.

Look at the story once more, and observe what Jesus did. The action must have been very arresting to those men, because it must have been something entirely unusual. To wash the feet of these men sitting round the board was a most unusual procedure. Notice the statement of verse 2, which is open to different meanings, two alternatives "during supper." In verse 4 we are told, knowing these things, He "riseth from supper, and layeth aside His garments." What He did, He did then, "He riseth from supper." The alternative is that during the meal He did this; or at the close He did it, and not at first. It is difficult for the Western mind to see the unusualness of this action. This was not the close of a journey, when they constantly brought water to wash away the dust of the highway. There were constant ceremonial washings of the feet before the meal. Here it was not at the close of a journey, or specifically before a meal. It was either during a meal or at its close. This is important. He suddenly arose, and laying aside His garments, He took a towel and girded Himself, poured water into a basin, and began to wash the disciples' feet. The particular description of that unusual procedure would immediately arrest their special attention. What could it mean that the One Who was practically the Host, suddenly in the midst of the meal, or when it was over, did what men usually did before a meal, or after a journey?

What was He doing? He said to them, Do you know what I have done? They did not understand. Then He explained, and we see to the heart of it. There was the supreme and wonderful revelation of His heart to those men. Two were there, Judas and Jesus, and the heart of Judas was Satan inspired by hatred, as the result of Satanic action, a determination to betray. In the heart of Jesus there was the passion to serve, and to serve in self-emptying action. Watch Him. He riseth, He girdeth Himself, He washeth. What is that? Girding meant far more in the East. The towel was the badge of slavery. It was the slave who was girded about the loins with a towel of homespun or common material. Jesus taking a towel, laying aside His garments, girded Himself, drew it around Him, and took the attitude of a slave, and did the slave's work. Taking a basin, and pouring water, He carried the basin and knelt in the attitude of a slave. Whether Peter was the first, I will not argue; but supposing he was, He knelt down at Peter's feet, and began as a slave would do, to wash the feet of the disciples. When Peter protested, Jesus said, "If I wash thee not, thou hast no part with Me." I love to read his answer, after his protest, "Lord, not my feet only, but also my hands and my head."

Turn over to one of the letters Peter wrote. "Yea, all of you gird yourselves with humility, to serve one another; for God resisteth the proud, but giveth grace to the humble" (I. Pet. v. 5). Yes, Peter came to understand. He came to know that in that hour he saw into the very heart of Jesus. There was the outshining of the grace of God in the marvel of that action. He emptied Himself, He humbled Himself, He bent. He was their Lord and Master. They called Him that. He was their Teacher and their Lord. He said, You are quite right. I am your Teacher, I am your Lord. But what is the Teacher doing now? What is the sovereign Lord of all authority doing now? Behold Him a slave, doing a slave's work to His disciples, and observe the heart of Jesus. So the parabolic action was a revelation of His grace.

It was more. It was the shining of His glory. There is the grace, but there is also the glory. That knotted towel was the badge of slavery; but here is the remarkable fact that the knotted garment was also the insignia of princes; with the very same method of fastening and tying. The difference was in material; for the slave a rough homespun cloth; for princes purple or gold. I think back through the years; and John saw in that girdle not only the badge of slavery, but the girdle of kingship. We do not forget when he was in Patmos, and he had a vision of this Self-same One in all His glory, in that marvellous description he has given, among other things he wrote, "girt about at the breasts with a golden girdle." Yes, he saw that in Patmos, and looking back he saw the sackcloth of the slave transmuted into the glory and purple of sovereignty.

No, said Jesus, you do not understand now, but you will some day. That is what He was showing forth; the transfiguration of service at the lowest to sovereignty at the highest.

Then He applied it in words we have already referred to. "If I then, the Lord and Master, have washed your feet, ye ought also to wash one another's feet." What does it mean? He knew that in the walk of those who were cleansed by the bathing there would be the contraction of defilement; and they would need the washing of the feet. He said, You have seen Me do it; you ought also to be ready to do it for each other. Paul was writing to the Galatian Christians and he said this (vi. 1), "Brethren, even if a man be overtaken in any trespass, ye which are spiritual, restore such an one in a spirit of meekness, lest thou also be tempted." What our Lord was saying to His fellow disciples was, I know the way, all along this pilgrimage cleansed men will contract defilement. When your brother does, your business is not to emphasize the defilement, not to turn to your brother the cold shoulder of pride and indifference. Your business is to attempt to wash his feet, to restore such an one, as Paul says, in the spirit of meekness. As we do that, the grace of our Lord Jesus Christ shines out, and the glory of the triumph of love is manifested in us and through us.

61. The Father's House and Many Mansions

John xiv: 2-6.

THIS parabolic illustration our Lord employed while still in conversation with His own, in those final and intimate hours before He passed to His Cross. Immediately after the parabolic action of the washing of the disciples' feet Judas was excluded. He then referred to His going once more, and told them quite plainly, "Whither I go, ye cannot come." That statement of our Lord—led to discussion. Only four men spoke, and our Lord answered them; Peter, Thomas, Philip, and Jude. In the course of His replies occurs this symbolic illustration.

This is a very familiar passage. I have said these words are parabolic, and they were intended to illustrate; "In My Father's house are many mansions." Following our custom in these studies we consider first the subject He was illustrating, which is of importance; then we look particularly at the figure He employed, in order that we may deduce the teaching from the utterance itself.

The background here is so necessary. We saw that when dealing with the washing of the disciples' feet. Again it is important here. We must bear in mind that strangely perplexing hour for the disciples. Evidence of it comes out in the things they said to Him when He told them He was going. They could not understand "Whither I go, ye cannot come." We are familiar with what happened. Peter said, Where art Thou going? Thomas said, We do not know where Thou art going, how can we know the way? Philip said, "Show us the Father, and it sufficeth us." Jude said, "What is come to pass that Thou wilt manifest Thyself unto us, and not unto the world?" Their perplexity is self-evident.

But observe that all these questions or words spoken by these four representative men, were concerned with spiritual matters. Peter knew that Jesus was going to death. He had been told that again and again for six months. Now they knew perfectly well His enemies were waiting for Him, and that He was going to death. When Peter said, Where are You going? "Whither goest Thou?" he was peering out into the unknown mysterious spaces. Jesus answered him, and in the course of that answer He employed the words we are looking at.

Go on to Thomas. If Peter was trying to visualize a destination, Thomas, not knowing the destination was perplexed about the way. How can we know the way, if we do not know where You are going? Jesus replied to him.

Then Philip, that quiet, unobtrusive soul, who thought great and profound things, and did not talk much about them, blurted out the whole of the agony of humanity, "Show us the Father, and it sufficeth us."

Then Jude, facing the practical present, asked his question. He looked round about the world again, and faced the practical issue of it all. Let us recognize that their immediate earthly trouble was earthly. They were losing Him. After three and a half years in His close company, travelling here and there; watching Him, listening to Him; now He is going; they are going to be left. That was their trouble.

Yet it was quite evident from everything that He had been saying to them, He was going forward with majesty. There was no cringing. He told them He was going to suffer. He told them He was going to die. He told them He was going to resurrection. They never seem to have grasped the fact of the resurrection.

So we look at them, perplexed and fearful. The earth was so real, it was there; their feet were planted on it. They were living in it. They were breathing its surrounding atmosphere, and seeing its hills and its valleys, its lakes and its rivers. While He was there it was so real, and after all was said and done, the beyond was unknown and uncertain. I do not think any of them were Sadducees but Pharisees, prior to their capture by Jesus, and they believed in the Spirit, and the spirit world, and the life beyond. They were not satisfied with a merely moral and ethical code; but they were not clear about the beyond; what did lie beyond, "Whither goest Thou?" They wanted to know the destination, wherever it may be in the far flung spaces of the universe. How are men going to get there? We do not know the destination. We do not know the route. What is the way? said Thomas, and there seems to have been in the mind of Philip, perhaps in the sense of all of them, whatever the destination, whatever the route that led to it, the ultimate was God. He said "Show us the Father, and it sufficeth us."

Then Jude, a little more practical for the moment than the rest, asked how the things they had seen should be manifested to the world.

It was in the midst of His reply to these words of Peter, He said, "Whither I go, thou canst not follow Me now, but thou shalt follow afterwards." Peter then replied, "Lord, why cannot I follow Thee even now? I will lay down my life for Thee." He never said a finer thing, and he meant it. Our Lord replied, "Wilt thou lay down thy life for Me? Verily, verily, I say unto thee, The cock shall not crow, till thou hast denied Me thrice. Let not your heart be troubled; ye believe in God, believe also in Me. In My Father's house are many mansions." That is where He was going. "If it were not so, I would have told you; for I go to prepare a place for you. And if I go and prepare a place for you, I come again, and will receive you unto Myself."

So we come to the figure itself. He was illuminating that whole thinking of theirs. They were in the presence of ineffable sorrow at His departure. They would be here in the world wondering. They would not be able to talk to Him, and to watch His deeds. He will be gone, whither? It was in answer to that wonder that He used this illustration.

What was the figure He employed? "In My Father's house are many mansions." "House," the simple word for a dwelling-place, a place of abode. Do not dismiss it by the use of the word simple. It is far more than simple. It was the word *oikos,* house. They all lived in houses. The dwelling-place is the simple meaning of it. He said in the house of My Father there are many mansions. "Mansions." The word has unfortunate connotations. Some people think the house is a villa residence. Some people have sung about the mansions over yonder. What is this word "mansions"? It is the word *mone,* which means simply an abode. The verb *meno* is a common word in the New Testament; but the word *mone* is not, only occurring here and in one other place, in verse 23; both times from the lips of Jesus. "In My Father's house are many *mansions";* "We will come . . . and make Our *abode* with him." So we have a double idea here, and we see at once that the term "house" is inclusive. I prefer to use for that the word "dwelling-place," and for the word "mansions," "abiding-places." That may not help us very much. Yet I would read it in that way. "In My Father's dwelling place there are many abiding places." The dwelling place is greater than the abiding places. All the abiding places are in the dwelling-place. The great word there is "My Father's house," and the secondary, the subsidiary, is the "abiding place."

What was He talking about? What was He intending to teach when He used this figure of speech? Let us begin on the level of the evident and commonplace. Twice in the course of the ministry of our Lord He made use of that phrase, "My Father's house." The first is in the second chapter of this Gospel. When He was cleansing the Temple, He said "My Father's house." There He was referring to the temple. He said it here, "In My Father's house are many mansions." The first figure is that of the temple itself. He referred to the temple as "the house of God" on other occasions. He called it the house in God in Matthew (xii. 4). He spoke of it as His own house, assuming the place of God. At the terrible end He referred to the temple not as My Father's house, or My house, but "your house is left unto you desolate." His references were all to the temple.

Let us be content to spend time with the simplicities of this. Go back and look at the temple. He was familiar with it, and often went into it. We have accounts of His having been in three parts of the temple. At the feast of tabernacles He was in the treasury. At the feast of dedication He was in Solomon's porch. In the case of the widow, He was over against the treasury, sitting there.

What was the temple like? It has often been described as it existed then. It was in process of building. It was not finished until ten years after the crucifixion of Jesus. There it was, a wonderful building. A quotation from "Jerusalem" by George Adam Smith may help us to see it.

"Herod's temple consisted of a house divided like its predecessor into the Holy of Holies, and the Holy Place; a porch; an immediate forecourt with an altar of burnt offering; a Court of Israel; in front of this a Court of Women; and round the whole of the preceding a Court of the Gentiles."

Again,

"Chambers for officials, and a meeting-place for the Sanhedrim. Against the walls were built side-chambers, about 38 in all." The temple was a house. There were many abiding places in it. I believe that that temple, as a figure of speech and symbol was in the mind of our Lord when He said, "In My Father's house there are many abiding places."

But it is equally certain that He saw the temple in its true significance, and understood its symbolism. Go back to the first words about the construction of that temple, in Exodus. "And let them make Me a sanctuary; that I may dwell among them." He saw it as the house of God. Later, the writer of the letter to the Hebrews, referring to the tabernacle, which was the true pattern after all, said, "All things were made according to the pattern that was shewed thee in the mount." Again, all those things were "copies of the things in the heavens." Once more, "made with hands, like in pattern to the true."

So that temple was patterned after things in the heavens. "In the beginning God created the heavens and the earth." When read next do not think merely of that wonderful stretch of sky some night when the moon is at the full, and the stars are out, a more wonderful sight than in the day; but all the ultimate beauty is seen in the havens. That temple, that tabernacle, and all the account of it is there, is according to the copy of things in the heavens; and it was called the house of God. It had many parts, many sections, many places, all having their value, all having their place. I am not so much concerned with the temple as with the tabernacle of old. It was a copy. "In my Father's house are many mansions." As though He had said, You go up to the temple, and you go into many parts and divisions and rooms. There are many abiding places in the house.

Then of what was He talking to them? What was the meaning of it all? To those men questing after the beyond, and yet earth-bound in their vision and thinking, He was going. They said, When He is gone we have lost Him; and He gave them the universe in a flash, "My Father's house." In that whole universe there are many abiding-places. This earth is one, but it is not the only one. All the symbolism of the tabernacle breaks down in the presence of the vastness of the universe. There are many abiding places, and He was showing them that He was merely leaving one abiding place in the house to go to another. They could not go then, but they should go; and He was going to another abiding place within the house. What for? To prepare a place for them.

What a wonderful expression that is, "To prepare a place for you." Somewhere out in the house of God, that vastness that baffles us, somewhere, that we cannot understand; He is going there to get a place fully furnished for you. How does He do it? By being there. As though He said to them, You will come presently, and when you come you will be at home because you will find Me there, somewhere in the Father's house. He did not tell them the locality. He did not tell them what they wanted to know, some description of locality. He said, It is all in the Father's house. There are many abiding places. He was going to prepare a place for them, and He would come again and receive them.

What wonderful things are written that have their bearing here. Take one or two quotations. Go back to Solomon's time when he had built his temple, and was offering that marvellous prayer. He said, "But will God in very deed dwell on the earth? Behold, heaven and the heaven of heavens cannot contain Thee; how much less this house that I have builded." If we would know the meaning of the phrase "My Father's house," we have it there suggestively, "the heaven" and "the heaven of heavens."

In close connection we turn to the prophet Isaiah. He says this, "For thus saith the high and lofty One that inhabiteth eternity, Whose name is Holy; I dwell in the high and holy place, with him also that is of a contrite spirit; and that trembleth at My word." The house of God, eternity, the whole universe. It is so easy to write, but we cannot grasp it yet, for it transcends us.

Let us take another quotation. Stephen in his great defence said, "Howbeit the Most High dwelleth not in houses made with hands; as saith the prophet;

> The heaven is My Throne.
> And the earth the footstool of My feet;
> What manner of house will ye build Me? saith the Lord;
> Or what is the place of My rest?
> Did not My hand make all these things?"

Later on Paul in that later chapter in the Acts, says, "The God that made the world and all things therein, He, being Lord of heaven and earth, dwelleth not in temples made with hands."

No, that is not God's ultimate dwelling-place. Where is it? Eternity. The Father's house is the whole of the universe, and in that house there are many abiding places. Earth is one. Jesus said, I am going to leave it, but I am not going outside the house of My Father. It has many abiding places, and it is true of you and me, we are in one of the abiding places, but we are in the Father's house. The whole universe is in that house. The loved ones that have gone from us have simply gone into another abiding place. We cannot go yet, but He is there preparing the place; but it is the vastness of the universe.

These men on the earth level, earth-bound, questing after the beyond were shown the beyond is here, for this is part of it. We are in the Father's house. He is there with us. He was going to another abiding place to prepare for us, and if He went, He would come again and receive us, and we will be there together. Oh the wonder of the whole conception.

Thomas said, We do not know where it is. How do we know the way? He said, "I am the way," and that includes the universe, the part of this universe to which He has been; and more than the way, "I am the truth" concerning it. All secrets have their final solution in Me. I am more, I am the life of the Father's house. I think Philip had got nearer when he said, "Show us the Father, and it sufficeth us."

Then mark the marvel of it, "He that hath seen Me hath seen the Father." He has not only seen the Father, but has seen all the Father's house, and has come to understand that within that house are many abiding places. We might indulge in many speculations, not profitable. We are all so very clever and talk about these planets and stars. There was a book written by Mark Twain, not only humorous but philosophic, in which he described in his own curious way a man searching in the universe, for this world. He came across some super-natural being out in the infinitudes of space, and asked him the way to the world, and the being said, Which world, to which he replied, "The world for which Christ died." Oh, said the man, He died for many worlds. I am not sure he was not right. I know that by His Cross He has reconciled all things to Himself in the heavens and on the earth. How far that Cross reaches out into the infinite distances I do not know; but I know they are within the Father's house, and I know that though He is not here as to bodily presence, He is in the Father's house, and He is getting ready for me.

62. The Vine

John xv.

THE allegory of the vine and its application is a complete discourse, occupying the whole of the fifteenth chapter, and the first sixteen verses of the sixteenth chapter. This is one complete discourse of Jesus, recorded by John. Throughout the Gospel His teaching had been of the nature of discussions concerning Himself, with His enemies, or with His friends. That does not mean they are of any less value. Through the background of criticism and opposition we have a revelation of how our Lord dealt with it in the days of His flesh.

The circumstances of this particular discourse are familiar. He was still with His own. After the conversation with them, resulting from the difficulties and enquiries of Peter, Thomas, Philip, and Jude, they do seem to have been hushed into silence. Yet directly afterwards, once more discussion arose, that is after this discourse. In xvi. 17 we have the account of that. "What is that He saith unto us, A little while, and ye behold Me not; and again a little while, and ye shall see Me; and, Because I go unto the Father?" They were puzzled, perplexed. They did not now ask these questions of Him, but they were talking, and He knew they were, and He answered them. Again we find that there fell upon them evidently a very definite silence.

Before the great allegory of the vine there is evidently a gap between the end of the fourteenth chapter and the beginning of the fifteenth, where it is said, He said to the disciples, "Arise, let us go hence." I think there can be no doubt that when He said that, they arose and left the upper room, and it is an interesting though not vital question as to where they went from there. Beyond the great intercessory prayer (xvii) that concludes this section in which He had devoted Himself to His own, we read "When Jesus had spoken these words, He went forth with His disciples over the brook Kidron, where was a garden" (xviii. 1), into Gethsemane.

Where then was this allegory uttered? That question cannot be answered finally. There are varied opinions, but two principal ones. Some believe that He took them from the upper room through the streets and into the temple. Passover was at hand, and at that time the great beautiful gates of the temple were left open all night that pilgrims might pass in and out. If He did take them there, as they passed through that gate they would see with the light of the Passover moon quite likely shining upon it, the national emblem. What was it? The golden vine. It has been suggested that He spoke by the side of those gates, "I am the vine, the true." I do not know personally, I think it is poetically beautiful. Others think He started out of the city altogether, and went down towards Kidron, and somewhere there, under God's sky, He uttered this great allegory. If so, wherever they looked, they could see the vines growing all round there.

When we think of these vines we must not think of the vines in this country, trained up a wall and growing and spreading, or in glass houses. We can see them still by acres in California, small vines, little vines growing in the open; self-contained, everyone of them, but growing. If He went out there, and looked at those vines, and said, "I am the vine, the true," there was so much in what He said would be illustrated as He spoke. They would see here and there in the night, fires burning in which branches cut out during the day, were being destroyed.

He was using the vine as a figure of speech, a parabolic illustration in the form of this matchless allegory. We consider then first the figure of the vine which He employed, that we may deduce the teaching which He intended.

The background is the same as that seen in our last study. His disciples were gathered round Him, perplexed, and fearful of the future without Him. He had made it perfectly evident to them, and they knew it was true, because of the circumstances pointing to it, that they would not have Him with them much longer. He was going away, and Peter was troubled. That was the atmosphere; but He had just made them a remarkable promise. He had said to them, "I will not leave you desolate." I like to translate that literally, "I will not leave you orphans, I come unto you." They had heard Him say that. He was going, and yet He had told them He would not leave them orphans, or desolate, alone, that He would come to them.

Then He showed them how He would come. He would send "Another Comforter." He would send the Holy Spirit, to use the transliteration, the Paraclete, One called to the side of another. We have rendered it in two ways, Comforter and Advocate. He is my Comforter, He disannuls my orphanage; but He is also my Advocate, keeping in mind the things He spoke, keeping me alive to their consciousness, making His presence a real presence. He had told the disciples that.

Now to look at the figure He used, in order to interpret the new relationship with Himself which would be established by the way of the coming of the Comforter, the Advocate, the Paraclete, the Holy Spirit. The vine illustrates the result of that new life into which they were to enter, the new experience they were going to have, of a new relationship with Himself. Such then was the subject illustrated.

Look at the figure of the vine. We cannot go far wrong if we stay in the realm of the material vine that bears grapes. But I think there was more in it than that when Jesus said, "I am the vine, the true." In our versions we read, "I am the true vine." That is not inaccurate, but it fails to carry over something which is there. They are exactly the same words in the Greek, but they are arranged thus. Some Greek scholars may think it is Greek idiom, but I think it is more in this case. He said, "I am the vine, the true." He added to the words, "I am the vine," "the true"; and that suggests there had been things that were false, that were untrue, that had failed; and I have no doubt that was in His mind when He said, "I am the vine, the true."

Our Lord did not create this figure. He borrowed it, and without any hesitation, I say that; He borrowed it from the Old Testament. We find the figure of the vine employed in the book of Psalms. That is the first occurrence (Psalm 80). It is called the psalm of Asaph. It was written in a time when God's people were in trouble as the result of their own disobedience, as so constantly they were in trouble. He says,

"How long wilt Thou be angry against the prayer of Thy people?"
Thou hast fed them with the bread of tears,
And given them tears to drink in large measure.
Thou makest us a strife unto our neighbours."

That is the first part of the psalm,

"Turn us again, O God of hosts;
And cause Thy face to shine, and we shall be saved."

Then the singer broke out into this language,

"Thou broughtest a vine out of Egypt;
Thou didst drive out the nations, and plantedst it.
Thou preparedst room before it,
And it took deep root, and filled the land.
The mountains were covered with the shadow of it,
And the boughs thereof were like cedars of God.
She sent out her branches unto the sea,
And her shoots unto the River.
Why hast Thou broken down her fences,
So that all they which pass by the way do pluck her?
The boar out of the wood doth ravage it,
And the wild beasts of the field feed on it.
Turn again, we beseech Thee, O God of hosts;
Look down from heaven, and behold, and visit this vine."

The psalm closes with this remarkable passage,

"Let Thy hand be upon the man of Thy right hand,
Upon the son of man whom Thou madest strong for Thyself.
So shall we not go back from Thee;
Quicken Thou us, and we will call upon Thy name."

Quite evidently the song was born of the failure of the Hebrew people
at the time; it shows their failure, and cries to God. The vine is
used as the symbol of the nation. That is why they put the golden
vine on the beautiful gate, and it became from that time the symbol of
the nation; but that is where the figure emerges.

Turn to Isaiah, and we are further on in the history of the people.
In the fifth chapter we have the song of the vineyard. There again
we have the vine as the symbol of the nation, which God had created
to bring forth certain fruit, and which was failing.

Again in Jeremiah 2 he speaks of the nation as "a degenerate
vine." In Ezekiel 15, 17, 18 we find three references to the vine as
symbolizing the nation. It was incarnate in the national thought,
emblazoned on the gate of the national temple, the symbol of the

national life. Jesus had said in that temple that the Kingdom of God was taken from them, and should be given to those bringing forth the fruits thereof. Now, while with His own, He said, "I am the vine, the true"; victory as against failure; realisation as against breakdown. "I am the vine, the true." Again, in verse 5. "I am the vine, ye are the branches." Is it possible to conceive of any illustration more perfect in setting forth the relationship between Himself and His disciples that would be established, when He, as to bodily presence was gone; and when He would be there in them, and they in Him by the coming of the Paraclete?

Still staying with the figure itself. He said first, "I am the vine." What did He mean? We often quote that, and the statement in verse 5, "I am the vine, ye are the branches." How do we think of it? We think of the main stem, and the branches growing out of it as a picture of Christ and the believers, He the main stem, and we the branches. But that is not what He said. He said, "I am the vine," and the vine is not only the main stem. It is part of it, in certain senses it may be the principal part of it; but that is not the vine. In the vine we see diversity root, main stem, branches, leaves, tendrils, fruit. I am all that, said Christ, I am the vine. In the recognition of diversity there is a declaration of completeness. The completeness of the vine is created by the fact that Christ is all.

Where then do we come in? Does that shut us out? Of course not. I am everything, said Christ, main stem, branches, everything; and you are the branches; that is, you are parts of Me. You are as closely united to Me in the essentials and entirety of life as those branches are in the vine; and the vine is incomplete without the branches. Our Lord said to these men, Apart from Me, literally, severed from Me, cut off from Me, you can do nothing. And He surely also meant to say, Apart from you, I can do nothing in this world. I must have the branches.

But see the wonder of that. To these men our Lord said, You are going to lose Me, and you are troubled; but I am here, I am with you, I come again. I come with the coming of the Paraclete. I come to you uniting Myself to you so completely that you shall be part of Me, and I part of you; for you abide in Me, and I in you. What a figure it is!

The first teaching is a recognition of the purpose for which the vine exists; fruit, and fruit-bearing. In Ezekiel we find a parable of the vine, in which the prophet tells the men to whom he was talking, who probably were proud of their membership in the national life, that a vine has no value at all except that of bearing fruit. He tells them the wood is no good. They cannot make a clothes-pin out of the wood of the vine. The teaching of Isaiah is in that fifth chapter, in the song of the vineyard that the fruit for which God looked from that nation for the world, not for self-consumption, was two-fold, righteousness and judgment. When Jesus began His ministry, His first recorded words, spoken to John were these, "Thus it becometh us to fulfil all righteousness." At the close, when He was talking, and the Greeks had gathered round about Him, He said, "Now is the judgment of this world." Righteousness and judgment. "I am the vine, the true." Through Me there shall be borne the fruit for which the world waits, and that God expects; righteousness and judgment.

You are the branches, the recognition of the true purpose for which we are members of Christ, sharing His very nature, and His very life, that of fruit-bearing. The figure is that of perfect union. I am the vine, everything; you are the branches, linked with Me. Severed we are useless, only fit for burning; but united, capable of bearing the very fruit that God expects, and for which the world is waiting.

We find the conditions He laid down here. They are two. Take two words; "abide," and "ask." Perhaps one may think that is a curious combination. Every branch in any vine must abide, but what about asking? No, the figure is perfect. Go and look at a vine, whether here or in the East. Get close to it, and listen. You cannot hear anything, but if you could, you would see in every branch movement, a movement of life pressing along, pressing along, towards the grapes. Every branch is not only pressing upward, and growing off the main stem; it is praying; every branch is dependent for sap, life element for maintenance to carry it out, to carry it forward, and press it out into fruit bearing. So Jesus said, If you abide, you can demand, you can ask whatever you are inclined to—a most amazing thing ever said about prayer is that statement. But the condition is that we abide. If we abide there, it is His life in us, our life is for evermore demanding more and more, to press it out to that fruit that God expects, and for which the world is waiting.

There is no need to say a great deal about abiding. Much has been written about it which may confuse some people. What is it to abide? Abiding needs no effort. Effort is made to arrive at a point, not to stay there. Take a homely illustration, a congregation is abiding in Westminster Chapel. They are making no effort to abide; but presently the service being over, they will make an effort to go out of the Chapel. To abide requires no effort. It is being at rest.

Abiding does not mean that we necessarily are always conscious of our position in the upper reaches of our consciousness. A congre-

gation in Westminster Chapel is not saying during the whole hour of
the service, I am in Westminster Chapel. But they know they are
there. Many years ago now a girl who had given herself to Christ, came
to see me one day and she said, "I am going to give it all up, I cannot
be a Christian." I said to her "Why not?" She said "I made up my
mind this week I would never forget Christ, and I got up in the morning, and thought about Him as I dressed, and I had my breakfast and
travelled down to work, and then I got to business, and lunch time
came, and I had never given Him a thought." Dear child! I gave her
this illustration. I said to her, "Do you know Mrs. Morgan?" Yes,
she had seen her. "Well," I said, "she is my wife." I went on, "I am a
busy man, but I don't go about all the time, saying, I am Annie
Morgan's husband. There are hours when I never think of her; but do
you think I ever forget it?" "No," she said, "I don't think you do."
We abide by obedience to the light we have, and walk in the way of
His commandments as we know them; that is abiding.

And asking, dependent, and prayer is not confined to words. It
is the cry and passion of the life to bear fruit. Oh wonderful, wonderful figure, the disannulment of orphanage in union with Jesus Christ.

> "No, never alone, No never alone,
> He promised never to leave me,
> Never to leave me alone."

If we are branches in the vine, that means all the redemptive forces
that the world needs are in Him, and as the result of His coming.
Those resources are all at the world's disposal through those who are
branches in the vine.

63. A Woman in Travail

John xvi: 21, 22.

THIS is our last study. We have considered 34 parables of Jesus,
and 73 parabolic illustrations, 107 in all. How comparatively little
Jesus said; yet in the course of that teaching these 107 illustrations
have been used by Him.

In this last converse with His own, He used four parabolic illustrations; first the parabolic action and interpretation of the washing

of the disciples' feet; then the stupendous illustration of the Father's house and the many abiding places therein; then the allegory of the vine; and now this illustration of a woman in travail. He was now speaking to His own disciples in the presence of the facts that they were facing at the moment, and in view of the change that was to take place, as the result of these facts. In answer to the difficulty raised by the disciples, He used this superlative final illustration. We consider then first the subject He intended to illustrate; then the figure He made use of in order to deduce from that consideration the teaching for ourselves.

The subject illustrated. We must remember the background of the occasion. He was going, and they were sore troubled by reason of that fact; and because they knew He was going as He had told them by the pathway of suffering and death. But their supreme trouble was not so much that of the method of His going, dark as that must have appeared to them; but the fact He was going at all, that He was leaving them. He had been with them for 3 and a half years in very close converse, and He was going from them. Immediately preceding the use of this figure He had given them the allegory of the vine, and His statements in verse 16 was the concluding sentence of that section of the allegory. "A little while, and ye behold Me no more; and again a little while, and ye shall see Me." That has no reference to the second advent. He was not referring to His second advent then. He was referring to the coming of the Holy Spirit, through Whom they would see Him as they had never seen Him before, and would remember all that He had told them. In the course of that conversation He had declared to them He would not leave them orphans, desolate; that He would come to them, when He, the Paraclete should come, Whose office it should be to take of those things of the Christ, and reveal Him to them; and interpret all He had said to them, and make Him, the Christ the consciousness of these men, as they had never known Him before.

If anyone is looking for the experience of the Holy Ghost, they are looking for something the Bible has never promised. The Spirit does not come to make us conscious He is there. He comes to make us conscious that Christ is there. It is the revelation of the Christ that the office of the Spirit is fulfilling. All this He had been teaching them; and He had said this, "Again a little while, and ye shall see Me." It is beautiful to read of the perplexity of these men. Let us try to put ourselves in their places. They said, "What is this that He saith, A little while?" John has recorded this in a good deal of detail. "A little while, and ye behold Me not; and again a little while, and ye shall see Me; and, Because I go to the Father?" What does He mean by the little while? We do not know what He means.

Then Jesus understanding their perplexity, said to them, "Do ye enquire among yourselves concerning this, that I said, A little while, and ye behold Me not, and again a little while, and ye shall see Me?" Then He did not seem to explain it, and yet He did. "A little while?" "Verily, verily, I say unto you, that ye shall weep and lament, but the world shall rejoice; ye shall be sorrowful, but your sorrow shall be turned into joy. A woman when she is in travail hath sorrow, because her hour is come; but when she is delivered of the child, she remembereth no more the anguish, for the joy that a man is born into the world. And ye therefore now have sorrow; but I will see you again, and your joy no one taketh away from you."

This reveals at once what our Lord was doing when He used this remarkably arresting and final figure of speech in the course of His teaching. He was recognising their sorrows. He was moreover declaring that sorrows to them would be inevitable, as He was a Man of sorrows, and they were inevitable to Him. But He was intending to reveal by that illustration the meaning of those sorrows, and the issue of them. There they were, filled with sorrow, and their sorrow would become yet more profound, would become deeper. They would go forth presently, when He was absent from sight, and especially after He had come to them again, and made Himself a reality as they had never known Him before, they would go out by the way of sorrows. He was speaking to them, He was speaking to His Church, He was speaking to us; of the nature of those sorrows. Then He used this figure.

Let us reverently take the figure He employed. It is the figure of motherhood, in its ultimate function. We read here, "A woman when she is in travail." That should be a definite article, not the indefinite, as we describe the difference between articles. "*The* woman." As a matter of fact He made use all through of what we call the generic article, "*The* woman." He is using the figure of motherhood in the ultimate functioning thereof. He is using as a figure the travail of a woman, when she goes down under the whelming floods into darkness and agony, and faces death. There is no profounder figure of sorrow could be employed than that. Do not forget all wars are fought out at last on the heart of womanhood, and the sorrows of the world are consecrated in motherhood.

To me it is a most arresting fact demanding most reverent consideration that the very last time He is recorded to have used an illustration, He adopted this figure. I never read it without feeling somehow He had in mind the Virgin Mother. He was recognizing the fact that His very existence on the earthly plane, in the marvel and economy of the will of God was due to birth-pangs borne by a woman. I think He knew too perfectly well that if Mary, His Mother had passed through that baptism of agony and death, she had come out into the joy and sunlight, when the Man Child was born into the world. So the figure recognises a process of sorrow and anguish, the issue of which is deliverance and life and joy. Do not forget the condition of these men, and what lay before them, and their understanding of it. It was the recognition of process and anguish, into the very deep abysmal depths of the shadow of death; but it was a process the issue of which was deliverance and life and joy. He employed this in His last illustration to His disciples and to His Church.

The reference of course is a wonderful one. One cannot read it without the mind sweeping back over the Bible to the appalling mystery of evil in its genesis in human experience. We remember words spoken there by Jehovah to the woman. "Unto the woman He said, I will greatly multiply thy sorrow and thy conception; in sorrow thou shalt bring forth children." That is the first gleam of evangelical light that shines when sin had entered, when God had whispered shall we dare to say, into the heart of motherhood the secret of the way of ransom and redemption through suffering, through sorrow; but out of the suffering and sorrow children, new life.

It is interesting to see how this figure is employed in the Old Testament more than once. It occurs seven times in the prophecy of Isaiah. (37:3, 49:15. 20.21, 54:1, and 66:7.13.) In every case it is a picture of deliverance and life coming through suffering and pain. We find in Hosea (13:13) he employed the figure in describing an experience through which Ephraim must pass, out of which there should come ransom and redemption. Micah employed it also (4:9.10), and in doing so he described an experience through which Zion should reach deliverance through suffering.

When we come to the New Testament, we find our Lord had employed it already by the use of a word. In Mark 13:8, when He was foretelling earth's convulsions, all the troubles and the sorrows and the convulsions of the earth, He said this, "These things are the beginning of travail." The Authorised Version reads, "the beginning of sorrows." That is not translation, it is attempted interpretation, but it breaks down. He used the very word for child-birth, the beginning of travail. Paul, when writing to the Romans (8:22) said, "We know that the whole creation groaneth and travaileth in pain together until now," "waiting for the manifestation of the sons of God." Travail leading to new life; and so the figure not often employed, is nevertheless found in Old and New Testaments.

In the Apocalypse we find there in the figurative language of the twelfth chapter the picture of a woman bringing forth a man-child through suffering and sorrow.

What does this all mean? Our Lord was showing these men and His whole Church the inevitability of sorrows in His enterprise. I am not referring to personal sorrows peculiar to us; but to the sorrows of Christ Himself, reproduced and carried forward in the Church. Listen to Paul. "To you it hath been granted in the behalf of Christ, not only to believe on Him, but also to suffer in His behalf." Or listen to Paul again, in his self-same letter to the Philippians, when he expressed the deep passion of his own heart, "That I may know Him, and the power of His resurrection, and the fellowship of His sufferings." The inevitability of sorrows for Christ Himself; and it was only by the way of His sorrows that He came to the way of His joy. "Who for the joy that was set before Him endured the Cross, despising shame, and hath sat down at the right hand of the throne of God." He had never realised that joy had it not been by the pathway of sorrow.

What is true of Him is true for the Church. It is only by the sorrows which are the sorrows of fellowship with Him that she can carry out His enterprises. She must have fellowship with the travail, the birth-pangs, the agony through which men and women are born, and new life comes into the world.

To me one of the most fascinating pages in the Acts of the Apostles is found in chapters 13 and 14. Paul was starting out on a missionary journey, and there we have the account of how he came to Antioch in Pisidia. A wonderful work was done there, but persecution arose. He had to flee, and he came to Iconium. There was wonderful work done until enemies came down, and he had to leave Iconium and he went to Lystra. Enemies followed him there again. It was a wonderful time at Lystra. There he probably found Timothy. But his enemies came there also, and nearly caught him. They cast him out and rained stones on him and left him for dead. I can see him lying there for the time being, bruised, bloody and broken, left for dead. Then something happened. What was it? Read for yourselves. He was not dead! Presently he gathered himself up, that broken body. What did he do? Did he try to get away from it all, and go further afield? No, he turned back, and he went back to Lystra, the place where they had stoned him, and then on back to Iconium, and to Antioch in Pisidia from where he had to flee. What did he go back for? He went back to strengthen the Churches, and to show them that what he had been suffering was not against but for the Kingdom of God. He went back to show them, as Luke says "That through many tribulations we must enter into the Kingdom of God," that the sorrows were the very means of bringing life. Paul was sharing in the birth-pangs out of which new life came. That is but an illustration, but these two chapters tell the whole fascinating story, and grip the soul as a revelation of what Jesus was here teaching His disciples.

Yes, we have our sorrows, but "your sorrow shall be turned into joy." He was not promising them compensation for suffering, that they would have suffering now, and must bear it. They will give you such joy presently, that the sorrows will be forgotten. That is not what He said. He said these sorrows shall be transmuted, turned into joy. The woman when she is in travail knows bitterness and sorrow and anguish; but afterwards she forgets the anguish and sorrow because of the child she holds in her arms, the life won out of death. So with you, said Jesus in effect, and so with My Church.

How much do we really know of what it is to suffer in this way? To revert to something which has often been pointed out. We do talk such insufferable nonsense about cross-bearing. Someone has been ill individually, and suffering, and they say it is a great and bitter disappointment. I do not undervalue the suffering, or underestimate the the disappointment. Or someone has lost everything, and they say, We are Christians; we must all bear the cross. That is not the cross. We have never touched the cross so long as our suffering is purely personal. We have only touched the cross when we are in fellowship with Christ, suffering on behalf of others, and suffering that others through our sorrows and our suffering may be brought into life.

O matchless wonder in these simple and yet sublime records of the life and teaching of Jesus, the climax of which is one that shows how all suffering, in fellowship with Him, is of the nature of the pangs of birth, and must issue in the joy of the new life.